A BURNING HUNGER

A BURNING HUNGER

One Family's Struggle
Against Apartheid

LYNDA SCHUSTER

Jonathan Cape
London

Published by Jonathan Cape 2004

2 4 6 8 10 9 7 5 3 1

First published in Great Britain in 2004 by
Jonathan Cape
Random House, 20 Vauxhall Bridge Road,
London SW1V 2SA

Random House Australia (Pty) Limited
20 Alfred Street, Milsons Point, Sydney,
New South Wales 2061, Australia

Random House New Zealand Limited
18 Poland Road, Glenfield,
Auckland 10, New Zealand

Random House South Africa (Pty) Limited
Endulini, 5A Jubilee Road, Parktown 2193, South Africa

The Random House Group Limited Reg. No. 954009
www.randomhouse.co.uk

A CIP catalogue record for this book is available from the British Library

ISBN 0–224–04168–1

Papers used by Random House are natural,
recyclable products made from wood grown in sustainable forests;
the manufacturing processes conform to the environmental
regulations of the country of origin

Typeset by Palimpsest Book Production Limited,
Polmont, Stirlingshire
Printed and bound in Great Britain by
Mackays of Chatham Ltd, Chatham, Kent

for Dennis
because of all his patience

Contents

Illustrations

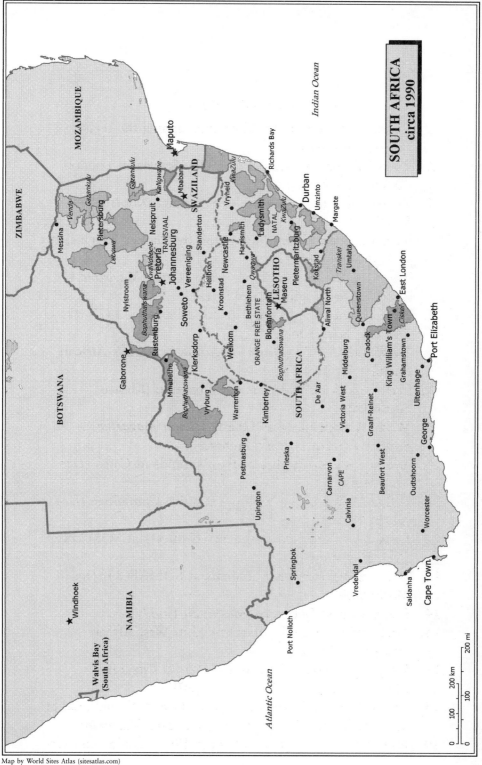

SOUTH AFRICA
circa 1990

Indian Ocean

Atlantic Ocean

MOZAMBIQUE

ZIMBABWE

Maputo

SWAZILAND

Mbabane

Richards Bay

Gazankulu

Kangwane

KwaZulu

Durban

Venda

Vuwani

Vryheid

Umzinto

Lebowa

Pietersburg

NATAL

Margate

Messina

KwaNdebele

Ladysmith

KwaZulu

Nylstroom

Pretoria

TRANSVAAL

Standerton

Harrismith

Kokstad

East London

Nelspruit

Johannesburg

Newcastle

Transkei

Rustenburg

Soweto

Vereeniging

Heilbron

LESOTHO

Pietermaritzburg

Umtata

Bophuthatswana

Klerksdorp

Kroonstad

Bethlehem

Maseru

Qwaqwa

Gaborone

Mmabatho

Welkom

ORANGE FREE STATE

Aliwal North

Queenstown

Cisker

Vryburg

Bloemfontein

King William's Town

Port Elizabeth

Bophuthatswana

Warrenton

Kimberley

Bophuthatswana

SOUTH AFRICA

Middelburg

Cradock

Grahamstown

BOTSWANA

Postmasburg

De Aar

Victoria West

Uitenhage

Priesta

Carnarvon

Graaff-Reinet

George

Upington

CAPE

Beaufort West

Oudtshoorn

Calvinia

Worcester

Windhoek

Springbok

Vredendal

NAMIBIA

Saldanha

Cape Town

Port Nolloth

Walvis Bay
(South Africa)

Map by World Sites Atlas (sitesatlas.com)

200 mi

200 km

100

100

0

0

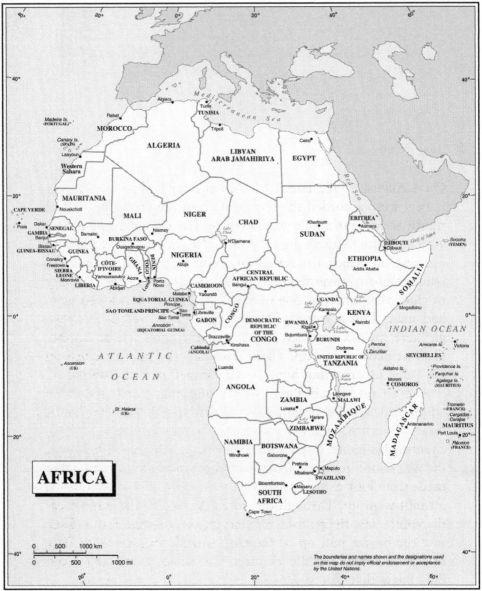

AFRICA

The boundaries and names shown and the designations used on this map do not imply official endorsement or acceptance by the United Nations.

Prologue

On 4 August 1990, Tsietsi Mashinini finally came home.

Few were accorded the welcome given the young man. And rightly so: despite all his years in exile, Tsietsi remained a legend among South Africa's black youth. He led the 1976 Soweto uprising, in which thousands of students rebelled against the white-minority government – and hundreds died. Tsietsi's ability to elude the police, as one of South Africa's most wanted men, had made him a legend. He was spotted dressed as a stylish girl here, a workman there, a priest on the other side of Soweto, the vast black township. Then, just when the police seemed on the verge of capturing him, Tsietsi escaped over the border.

And so on that brilliant winter morning, hundreds of his admirers descended on Jan Smuts International Airport to await Tsietsi's return. They jammed the cavernous arrival hall: chanting his name; singing liberation songs; doing the *toyi-toyi*, the war dance imported from Zimbabwean guerrilla camps that made them look as though they were running in place. Suddenly, a shout went up. Through the doors that led to the cargo area, the youths saw the pallbearers emerge, carrying the coffin. They saw the hearse pull up to the curb outside to receive it. They saw the family huddle around the vehicle, weeping. And they knew that Tsietsi Mashinini had finally come home.

This was not the way it was supposed to have happened. Like so many Africans, Nomkhitha, his mother, believed in the voices of the ancestors. Her long-dead father had appeared to her in a dream to say Tsietsi would return one day to rule South Africa; Nomkhitha had clung to that promise during all the years of her son's exile. But then came the telephone call telling of Tsietsi's sudden and inexplicable death in an obscure West African country. So instead of a triumphal return by a conquering hero, a funeral procession of family and followers bore Tsietsi back to the city of his birth.

It was the end of a story that had, in one way or another, entangled all the Mashininis. For Tsietsi set in motion a series of events that would forever define his family. From the time of the Soweto uprising, the Mashinini name became a magical thing among black South Africans – and a thing of infamy among whites. Many of Tsietsi's twelve siblings and even his parents, heretofore mostly apolitical observers of the country's gross inequities, were inexorably drawn into the fight against apartheid.

His oldest brother rose through the ranks of the outlawed African National Congress' army to command 'freedom fighters', guerrillas who infiltrated South Africa from neighbouring countries and blew up military installations. Another was twice arrested for his political activities, brutally tortured, tried for treason, released – only to go on to help orchestrate the insurrection that rocked the nation from 1984–86 and ultimately brought the white government to its knees. Yet another fled the country when he was only fifteen, was educated by the ANC in Egypt and Tanzania, and became a senior official in the ANC's exiled diplomatic service. Even Nomkhitha, the family matriarch, spent 197 days in solitary confinement in a South African prison.

Yet these are not members of a political elite. Like so many black South Africans, the Mashininis were ordinary people caught in extraordinary circumstances. Their tale is that of perhaps every other family in the townships: impoverished, law-abiding citizens who got sucked into the anti-apartheid struggle by the involvement of a child or sibling – and whose lives changed irrevocably as a result. They became the foot soldiers in the fight for liberation. Mostly unnoticed and often with little publicity, these families made huge sacrifices that, in the end, proved essential in bringing down the white-minority government.

But the Mashininis are unique. Because of its size, the family embraces just about every facet of the anti-apartheid struggle: from the drama of the 1976 Soweto uprising to the township upheavals a decade later; from the desolation of political exile to that of imprisonment; from the exclusionary black-power doctrines of Steve Biko to the all-encompassing non-racialism of Nelson Mandela. Thus, the Mashininis' story is that of black South Africa, in microcosm.

And it is a story that must be told, for apartheid clearly ranks as one of the horrors of our times. Like the Holocaust, its tales are powerful morality plays of the most compelling and universal sort. The Mashininis' saga isn't only about their imprisonment, torture, exile, separation, loss; it is also about the dignity, courage and strength they somehow managed to conjure up – in the face of almost unthinkable adversity – to hold the family together. Theirs is a timeless testimony to the resilience of the human spirit.

I first met the Mashininis in the late 1980s, an American journalist newly arrived to cover the dying days of apartheid. It was a grim time of bannings, detentions and death squads; President P.W. Botha was not about to go without a fight. Desperate to start making contact with black 'comrades' in the townships, I begged a well-connected friend to let me accompany him to Soweto. He finally relented.

So, on a sleepy Sunday morning, my friend took me to meet Mpho Mashinini, the fourth-born son. (There were eleven boys and two girls in the family.) I was immediately drawn to his vibrant, raucous clan with their stories of growing up in Soweto. Home was an airless 'matchbox' house: four tiny rooms inside, a pit latrine and cold-water tap outside. To bathe, the family boiled water on a coal-burning stove. At bedtime, Joseph and Nomkhitha, the parents, had to stack the furniture in one corner of the house, then squeeze the children together on the floor in the living room, the kitchen, wherever they could find space.

Mired in a dreary existence of poverty and political repression, the Mashinini parents cared about only two things: the

Methodist Church and education. Joseph insisted that the children sing in the choir; any time spent in church, he figured, was time spent off the streets and out of trouble. For her part, Nomkhitha became positively fanatical on the subject of schooling. She believed it to be the greatest gift she could give her children – and their only hope for a marginally better future. Even after a full day's work in a clothing factory, then cooking and cleaning and washing at home, Nomkhitha made the children sit with her around the dining-room table to do their lessons; under her tutelage, they knew how to read before beginning school.

Thus, books and grades and God dominated conversation in the Mashinini household, not politics. How did such a home produce guerrilla fighters and revolutionary leaders? To me, it seemed the quintessential story, the story of modern South Africa itself. But Joseph and Nomkhitha refused to talk about the family and its history; with four boys still in exile, they were terrified the government would seek retribution. Besides, the security police – who knew everything that occurred in the Mashinini house – would never have countenanced such a project.

It took apartheid's demise to be able to tell the Mashininis' tale. I returned to Southern Africa several years later, this time as the wife of a diplomat. The decades of civil unrest and economic sanctions had finally succeeded: the white government was no more. Nelson Mandela had been elected president, South Africa transformed into a fully democratic nation, the exiles allowed to come home. The Mashininis were now ready to remember.

One caveat: this book is not intended as a definitive history of the anti-apartheid struggle; that is for a South African to write. Rather, it is one family's rendering of that fight, retold from a great remove of time and distance. I have tried, wherever possible, to corroborate the Mashininis' recollections with newspaper clippings, trial records, other contemporary accounts and documents, and by extensively interviewing their colleagues, friends and relatives. A few characters are not named for reasons of political sensitivity. Other names have been forgotten with the passage of time. Some dialogue has been re-created from memory and thus not given direct quotation. All this I have attempted to weave into a narrative whose shortcomings, whatever they may be, are entirely my own.

CHAPTER ONE

Nomkhitha and Joseph

The story of the Mashinini family begins more than 500 miles south of Johannesburg in the Transkei: the place of Nomkhitha's birth. It is a world apart. Even before the apartheid government went through the charade of erecting a border marker, the boundary between white South Africa – with its paved roads, electric street lights, freshly watered lawns – and this black area was inescapable.

Here the dreamy, desolate landscape stretches for miles. There are few cars and little movement, save the occasional goat balanced on tiptoe to nibble at the thorny bushes. The distant mountains are ragged outcroppings of boulders, lightly smeared with green vegetation and topped with purple-blue shadows. Whitewashed huts dot the undulating hillsides.

For all its poverty of development, though, the Transkei is rich in political tradition. The first white missionaries settled here among the Xhosa people in the 1800s. Their arrival had a profound effect: the Xhosas – who lived in what used to be one of South Africa's largest territorial divisions and numbered more than three million – were among the first blacks to be exposed to Western education. The Transkei became renowned for its missionary schools; the country's first black university, Fort Hare, was established here. That so many black political thinkers and activists – Nelson Mandela among them – subsequently emerged from the region is hardly coincidental.

It was to these dual tendencies – education and politics – that Nomkhitha was born. Her mother, Olive Nonthuthuzlo, came from St Marks, a village dominated by its Anglican church. She was one in a long line of teachers – a not-unremarkable feat for women of that era. Her five sisters and one brother also had teaching certificates. Olive had been a quiet, serious girl with a beautiful singing voice and a penchant for netball; her great passion, though, was reading. Teaching suited her studious nature.

When the time came for Olive to marry, her father, a prosperous sheep farmer who had built St Marks' first sizeable house, wanted an educated man for his daughter. Daniel Boto seemed an ideal match. Of royal blood, Daniel was a praise singer at the chief's court, an interpreter in the local magistrate's court (he spoke several languages), a respected politician, a successful farmer and a poet. This would be the widower's second marriage. Daniel had fifteen children from his first marriage, the oldest of whom was Olive's age.

On her wedding day, Olive left her parents' home for Daniel's village several miles away. Hers was a 'white' wedding, so called because Olive's father could afford to buy a white gown. After the ceremony in St Marks' church and a feast at her father's house, Daniel hoisted Olive – still wearing the prized frock – into a covered wagon drawn by a team of oxen. White flags adorned the lead animal to show that this was a wedding party. Lest anyone miss the message, the bridegroom's best men, astride horses bedecked in beads and white flags, preceded the wagon as a kind of honour guard. They rode at a breakneck speed, now doubling back around the wagon, now racing forward, trilling: 'Li, li, li, li, hallelujah! *Umtshato!* It's a wedding!' Daniel moved the procession steadily forward. His wagon was loaded down with wooden trunks containing bed linen, towels, blankets, crockery and a bedroom set – all gifts provided by Olive's family; a new bride was not supposed to ask her mother-in-law for anything.

The wagon came to rest in Bengu, a speck of a settlement. It sits at the end of a rock-strewn road that snakes for miles through the mountains from the white town of Lady Frere. A forlorn, wind-whipped place, Bengu has sweeping vistas of the land as it rolls gently towards the Great Kei river. Most of its inhabitants lived in shacks. Their floors were cold stone caked with dirt; they cooked on coal stoves that filled the tiny dwellings with acrid smoke; their meagre possessions were usually covered with a thick coating of flies.

Daniel's house, as befitted his position, was Bengu's grandest. Built of brown stone, it boasted three spacious rooms and several outhouses. He also owned a large tract of land. It was a rare thing for an African to own land; most blacks were tenant farmers, paying an annual rent to the government or to a white landlord. But Daniel had inherited part of the property from his father, with the rest bequeathed to him by the chief. He grew maize and wheat; in the orchard were peaches, apples, apricots and pomegranates. Daniel also raised goats, pigs, sheep, horses, cows, geese and shaggy-feathered chickens.

In this house, Olive gave birth to Virginia Nomkhitha – her name means 'attractive' in Xhosa – on 9 May 1935. A son, Mark, followed a couple of years later. The two children would soon become inseparable companions; by the time they started school, their half-siblings had all grown and moved to nearby villages. And so they did everything together: homework, play, household chores. (Neither was required to help in the fields or kraals, where the cattle were kept; hired hands did that work.) Their contrasting personalities complemented one another. Like Olive, Mark had a calm, gentle manner; Nomkhitha, on the other hand, emulated Daniel's exuberance.

Theirs was an unconventional family for the times. Olive had to be away for most of the week; her teaching job in a village near Lady Frere was too distant for her to travel there and back every day. She would leave on Sunday night, riding her horse the fifteen miles to the school, and return on Friday. Much of the child rearing fell to Daniel. He came to favour Nomkhitha and Mark over his other children, but he still brought them up in strict African fashion.

Daniel woke before sunrise every morning to start a fire, then roused Nomkhitha and Mark with a hymn. They joined in the singing; the children knelt while their father prayed. Afterwards, Daniel shooed them outdoors to begin their chores. Bucket in hand, Nomkhitha and Mark had to fetch water from the river that meandered past the village. It was only a ten-minute walk

9

to the riverbank, but the pail, once filled, felt unbearably heavy to a small, sleepy child. And the air could be achingly cold, especially in winter. Upon returning to the house, Nomkhitha and Mark had to sweep their room and dust the chairs. Only then would Daniel give them their breakfast of porridge, bread and tea.

On weekdays, Nomkhitha and Mark walked to school. Unlike many of their classmates, they had shoes, but they went barefoot when it rained to preserve them. After school finished in the early afternoon, Nomkhitha and Mark raced home to more chores. There was water to draw again, and laundry to be carried to the riverbank for washing. The children pounded the clothes on large rocks to get them clean and spread them across the tall grass; while waiting for the laundry to dry in the sun, Nomkhitha and Mark played. It was the best part of the day. They held running races, climbed the huge, overhanging trees, swam if the weather was warm. To dry off, Mark taught Nomkhitha different dance steps. He loved to sing too, although he hadn't inherited Olive's mellifluous voice; but he was a stunning dancer.

The children had to finish their homework by eight o'clock every evening. That was when they and Daniel (and Olive, when she was present) gathered in one room to pray. Then Daniel would read to Mark and Nomkhitha and regale them with stories of his travels or with *intsomi*, traditional Xhosa folktales that usually incorporated some sort of moral lesson.

Sundays were given over to church. Nomkhitha and Mark would jump the stone fence that separated their father's property from the Methodist church next door; both liked attending the services, especially Mark, who was a server. Otherwise, Bengu offered little in the way of diversion. No one had a radio. Mail arrived weekly; newspapers came once a month, delivered by horse-drawn carriage. (The villagers learned of the outbreak of the Second World War only when white sugar suddenly disappeared from the shops and other foodstuffs became scarce.) The most valued entertainment was a visitor. The appearance of a traveller generated much excitement and extreme gestures of hospitality: water would be boiled, tea brewed, precious stores of biscuits brought out. And neighbours would crowd into the hot, dark room where the visitor was staying, eager for news of the outside.

Once a month, Daniel, Olive, Nomkhitha and Mark made the journey to Lady Frere. It was not a grand place: one dusty street filled with small shops and a scattering of churches. Still, it was a town; here you could buy things, catch up on gossip, feel a vitality and movement missing in Bengu. Nomkhitha and her family made a day of it. Dressed in their Sunday finery, they wandered from shop to shop, lingering over a bolt of fine cloth, admiring a stylish hat, exchanging pleasantries with a shop-keeper. (Olive, clearly an educated, Christian woman, was always treated courteously by the white shopkeepers.) When they had seen all that the town had to offer, Olive and Daniel purchased their stores of wheat, sorghum, mealie meal (ground corn) for the month, gathered up the children and began the long ride home.

Impelled by his religion and his position in the community, Daniel believed in sharing his wealth. If a man in the village died, Daniel slaughtered a cow to contribute to the ceremonies; for a child's funeral, he gave a sheep. Every June, when little grew in the southern hemisphere winter and people were in the throes of what was called 'the hungry season', Daniel prepared a feast. He roasted a cow, brewed quantities of sorghum beer, and invited people from miles around. Many of the guests were 'red people', traditional Xhosas whose appellation came from the ochre clay they smeared on their bodies and faces. To Nomkhitha, the women were especially spectacular. They wore shawls folded in a square on their heads, skirts of animal skin, a piece of cloth tied around their breasts, and a sheepskin pouch in which to keep their *inqawe*, a wooden pipe, and tobacco. To complete their maquillage, some scraped out the sticky black ash from the *inqawe* with a twig and applied it to their lips or dotted it on their cheeks.

Although these festivities impressed Nomkhitha as a child, she was most taken with the rites of ancestor worship. African Christianity is overlaid with vestigial tribal rites; chief among them is belief in the ancestors. Daniel taught Nomkhitha to respect her forebears. They are your interlocutors with God, he explained, the link between the living and the Lord. They can intercede on your behalf. If you leave the house, for instance, you must say: I'm going out now, please protect me. If you talk to your ancestors, they will understand. But you must honour them. After hearing your prayers, they expect to be offered a pinch of snuff, a calabash of beer. These were lessons Nomkhitha would take with her into adulthood.

Daniel adhered strictly to the ways of the ancestors. He bought tombstones for deceased relatives and unveiled them with ceremony; if someone were not buried properly, he believed, one's children could be visited by the restless soul. Daniel led his family on annual pilgrimages to the cemetery. It was a dry, solitary spot, littered with saguaros and thorn bushes; from here, Bengu could barely be discerned in the distance. The graves of Nomkhitha's family dated back to the 1800s and were marked with simple stones, painted white, with names chiselled crudely on them. Daniel would pull out the weeds that had sprung up around the headstones. He also tested the stones to be sure they were firmly implanted; cattle liked to rub against them and often loosened or even knocked them down. To communicate with their ancestors, Daniel, Olive and the children would each spit on a small stone and gingerly place it near a headstone. Then they would pray.

These rituals gave definition to Nomkhitha's life. But her identity, her sense of self, came from Daniel's position as a praise singer – *imbongi* – and adviser at the chief's court. Part socio-political commentator, part oral historian, the *imbongi* composed poems about past and present events. Only the most gifted poets became praise singers. Speaking in Xhosa, an extravagant, metaphorical language of clicks and pops, they combined acute political intuition with wit and eloquence. (Many would later trace Tsietsi's oratorical skill when he led the 1976 Soweto uprising to his grandfather.) The *imbongi* commanded respect not only for his talents, but also because of his relationship to the chief. He was among the latter's most trusted counsellors; the praise singer could, if he deemed it necessary, publicly criticize the chief in the poems he recited.

Thus the *imbongi* acted as a kind of social conscience for the community.

Daniel was *imbongi* to Chief Valelo Mhlontlo, who ruled over an area that corresponded roughly to the provincial district of Glen Grey. A chief is born to his position: Mhlontlo was a lesser member of the royal house of the Thembu tribe, the most prominent in the Transkei. (Nelson Mandela's father was a counsellor to the Thembu royal family.) Daniel, as the *imbongi*, preceded the chief in his travels through the Glen Grey region. Tall and handsome, wearing a leopard-skin headdress, English riding boots and britches (of which he was very proud), Daniel cut a striking figure as he galloped on his horse across the countryside, singing the chief's praises and announcing his arrival.

The court was conducted at the Great Place, as the royal residence was called. It stood on a high hill and commanded a stunning view of Bengu's tiny, pastel-coloured huts splayed out below. The chief's house was, of course, the best in the district: a long, low whitewashed dwelling, adorned with a tin roof and a veranda. Those were the living quarters; the cooking was done in a nearby mud-and-wattle hut. A set of yellow, thatch-roofed rondavels, guest huts for visiting counsellors and dignitaries, completed the compound. There was also a small cemetery not far from the main house. Here the chiefs were buried, facing downhill towards their people; their wives occupied plots behind them.

The court sessions were held next to the stone kraal. The chief, wrapped in a wool blanket, sat in front; his dozen or so counsellors, elderly men chosen for their wisdom and integrity, flanked him. In an atmosphere of great solemnity, they heard all manner of cases: marital breakdowns, property disputes, disagreements about dowries. These they weighed and dissected and examined from every angle. The chief and his aides attempted to settle matters themselves so that the disputants would not have to go before the government's magistrate – a costly and often bewildering experience.

The Great Place was also the venue for traditional ceremonies and concerts. Nomkhitha attended many such grand occasions as a child; the chief's compound seemed to her a live thing then, an amorphous moving mass of colour and sound. She particularly admired the dancers: their swathes of pastel-coloured cloth, their intricate necklaces and collars strung with beads; their long, swirling skirts fashioned from cow hides; the knobkerries they brandished with great shouts; their bare feet, adorned with ankle bracelets, that pounded the dusty earth with a frenzied rhythm. The dances evoked ancient Xhosa tales of birth and death, love and war.

Thus Nomkhitha passed her childhood: immersed in her heritage, secure in her privileged status. The racist rules of the white world barely touched her. Later, in adulthood, Nomkhitha would liken the certainties of that time to the architecture of her village. Houses there were always placed in the same manner: first the main hut, then the secondary huts, all in a row. Nomkhitha loved the exactness of it, the reliability. The world was as it should be.

Nomkhitha carried these beliefs with her when, at the age of thirteen, she left Bengu for boarding school. She attended a black, all-girls institution in Mt Arthur, near Lady Frere, which was run by the Methodist Church. Because of the distance from Bengu, Nomkhitha returned only during the December and June holidays. She was not homesick; Olive stuffed an enormous suitcase full of clothes and bedding and mementos that Nomkhitha dragged onto the bus to Mt Arthur. And the family visited her on their monthly outings to Lady Frere.

The Methodists were strict schoolmasters. The girls woke at five o'clock every morning, washed, dressed in their uniforms, ate breakfast, then attended classes until two o'clock in the afternoon; afterwards, they had several hours of homework. Nomkhitha flourished under the regimen. She studied biology, geography, history, arithmetic and English; for sport, she played tennis. Her vivacity and self-assurance attracted a large circle of friends.

For the first couple of years at school, the trajectory of Nomkhitha's life remained unaltered. She decided she would study nursing after finishing at Mt Arthur. There were only two professions open to blacks at that time: teaching and nursing. Although Olive had imbued her with a fierce desire for education, Nomkhitha rejected her mother's career; she was, in fact, alone among her friends in opting to become a nurse. To Nomkhitha, nursing seemed glamorous. The medical studies, smart uniform, the contribution to the community – they all captured her imagination in a way teaching never did. Nomkhitha firmly believed, with the certainty that described her childhood, that she would study nursing and return to Bengu to practise her profession for the rest of her life.

By Nomkhitha's third year at Mt Arthur, however, everything had changed. Daniel was getting too old to farm, his chief means of income; he started selling off cattle to pay for her school fees. That source would soon be depleted. Daniel was not satisfied with Nomkhitha being half-educated, as he put it, so he devised a plan to send her to live with her Aunt Letitia, Olive's sister, in Johannesburg. Letitia had promised to help Nomkhitha get into nursing school and to find a way to support her.

Nomkhitha was thrilled. Her best friend at Mt Arthur came from Johannesburg and had regaled her with tales of *eGoli*, as it was known, the City of Gold. Young people from the countryside dreamed of going to South Africa's biggest city. Nomkhitha was seventeen years old on the night that she and Olive boarded the train for Johannesburg; too excited to sleep, she could only imagine the life that lay before her.

If Nomkhitha's childhood seemed golden, Joseph's, by contrast, was bleak. He grew up feeling the full brunt of the poverty and cruelty inflicted on blacks. As a youth, his father, Hendrik Mashinini, had moved to South Africa from neighbouring Swaziland. A tall, muscular man with a stern countenance, Hendrik worked as a contract labourer, moving from farm to farm as the seasonal employment finished. He and his wife Sara were living in Orange Free State province in 1932 when their fourth and penultimate child, a son, was born. Sara named him

Ramothibe – shepherd – in her native Sotho. And because she was a devout Christian, she also gave him a biblical name, Joseph, in English. (He would use this name with everyone except his immediate family.)

A couple of years later, Hendrik moved his family to a farm near Vereeniging, about twenty-five miles from Johannesburg. Sara's sister lived there with her husband and eight children; she had told Sara that a job was available. Hendrik disliked the vicissitudes of agricultural work, but neither he nor Sara had much education, and being a hired hand was about the best position he could hope to secure. Once again, Hendrik had to build a home for his family. This time, it consisted of a series of squat, stifling rooms made from mud. The doors were wooden boards; big stones held the tin roofs in place. The tiny structures formed a kind of compound: one was for sitting in, one for cooking, one for sleeping. Sara furnished them with odd bits of furniture and old rugs. Outside, Hendrik fashioned a kraal from discarded chicken wire; here he kept hens, doves and rabbits. The latrine was outside too, dug on the edge of what was considered his family's area. Sara used candles or paraffin to light the rooms; she cooked over firewood, which also heated the house. Water came from the taps at the nearby stables. The pipes there often froze in winter and the family sometimes would not have water until ten or eleven o'clock in the morning, when the sun finally thawed the ice.

There were a dozen or so other families living and working on the farm. Hendrik shared with them a patch of land allotted by the farmer; on it, they grazed their meagre herds of cattle. The rest of the vast acreage was given over to the farmer's 400 head of dairy cattle and the maize, or mealies, to feed them. The cows were housed in stone barns. Inside, they had rows of rather crude stalls and a feed box in the centre. A big bin stood in the nearby kraal; here the workers stored the harvested green mealies to ferment during the summer. They dug out the mash and fed it to the cattle in the dead of winter, when the pastures were sparse. No one liked working in the mealie fields: winters turned the earth into a listless, desiccated moonscape; summers engulfed the labourers in brutal heat.

The boss's house provided the farm's one bit of beauty. It was a trim, white structure with a tiled roof and green, sweeping lawns; orchards flanked the grounds. The workers always approached the area cautiously. They were afraid of encountering the farmer, a tall, thin man with a bony nose, pale eyes and gnarly hands. At the sight of him, the labourers abruptly changed their demeanour: they doffed their caps, spoke with diffidence, kept their eyes on the ground. The farmer talked to them in English-accented Sotho. He fancied himself learned in the ways of Africans and was forever explaining a certain custom or habit to his 'boys', as he called them. Yes boss, they would say softly, staring at their shoes and allowing only the smallest twitch at the corners of their mouths – as if he, a white man, had to explain their traditions to them. Their monosyllabic responses were meant to forestall the farmer's temper and the sting of his *sjambok*, a whip made of rhinoceros or hippopotamus hide. The farmer was a stern, uncompromising employer who didn't brook cheekiness in his boys. He had a deep suspicion of outsiders; white, 'do-gooder' types from Johannesburg, he believed, lurked everywhere, trying to incite his workers.

Life on the farm was harsh for the children, too. Joseph and his four siblings had to awaken at four o'clock each morning to milk Hendrik's cows. Then, with little more in their stomachs than the mouthful of steaming milk they managed to filch, the children trudged to school – a journey of one-and-a-half hours each way. The schoolhouse was a small, thatch-roofed mud structure, set amid a clump of trees. It had little in the way of materials. There were no chairs, desks or textbooks; the children sat on the floor and wrote on slates with chalk. One teacher taught all 300 students, who ranged in age from six to twelve years old. (This was a grammar school; after completing school, the children were supposed to work on their respective farms.) Joseph studied geography, history, mathematics, English and Afrikaans. At one o'clock he and his brothers and sisters began the long walk back to the farm.

Afternoons were given over to fetching Hendrik's cattle from the pasture. Joseph and his younger brother Phillip had to finish milking the cows and locking the gates to the kraal before sunset.

Otherwise Hendrik beat them. But Phillip, who was impudent and prone to tantrums, often refused to go; Joseph would have no choice but to set out without him, accompanied only by his dog, Fly, a medium-sized yellow mongrel. Joseph adored the dog. Fly knew all the routines of the farm, even when it was time to bring the cattle back; at the appointed hour, he would bark at Joseph and start off down the trail. Later, when Joseph was older, it would seem to him that he spent half his childhood traversing those huge expanses of fields: trekking to and from school, chasing after cows, helping with the harvest. But he would also mark his love of open grasslands and uncluttered horizons from those days.

The farm provided few amusements. There were no newspapers or radios; a hand-cranked gramophone offered the only entertainment. Joseph spent much of his free time playing with his cousins, fighting with sticks or fashioning toys from abandoned bits of wire. Sometimes the farmer's three small sons came around for a game of football. Joseph liked the boys, who spoke Sotho to him in a friendly manner, but he was terrified of their father and his dreaded *sjambok*.

Joseph's real pleasure came from attending church. This he did unfailingly every Sunday; Sara insisted all the children go to worship. (She also made them say grace before meals and recite prayers at bedtime.) Joseph was raised as a Presbyterian; a minister from Vereeniging came to the farm every three months to conduct services. Lay preachers substituted for him on the other Sundays. They rotated among the various denominations of the workers: one week, the Methodist preacher presided; the next, the Dutch Reformed; then the Catholic; and so on. The service was held in the house of a family who belonged to that week's chosen sect. Joseph loved everything about it: the singing, the praying, the emotionally charged sermons. The Bible, the only reading material available to him on the farm, also fascinated him. And so Joseph eagerly anticipated Sundays – even though he still had to collect Hendrik's cows in the afternoon.

Sara also had secular ambitions for Joseph: she wanted him to be a doctor. But having received virtually no education herself, Sara knew little about matriculation. Besides, she and Hendrik could not afford to pay for his studies. Sara did washing on Mondays and Tuesdays for a neighbouring white family to supplement Hendrik's pitiable salary. She had a little vegetable garden where she grew beans, tomatoes and potatoes; and Hendrik got a bag of mealies with his pay. But they still struggled to feed their family, let alone provide any luxuries. At Christmas, the children each got one pair of shoes, a pair of shorts and a shirt – their entire wardrobe for the year.

As Joseph grew older, he became increasingly restless. He and his best friend Thabiso – the son of another farm hand – met every evening in the barn after bringing in the cows; and in the dim, half-light of dusk, they talked about the future. Both were desperate to escape to Johannesburg. Despite being so close, neither boy had ever been to the city; there were no highways yet, and the train journey took two hours. Still, Joseph and Thabiso knew Johannesburg just had to be wonderful. Some of the young men from neighbouring farms who joined the army during the war had gone to Johannesburg. They would return home on weekends in their smart khaki uniforms and enchant the younger boys with stories of the glittering *eGoli*: the towering buildings, luxurious cars, stylish restaurants. Neither Joseph nor Thabiso had any idea what he would do there. But that was of little import; everything around them seemed dull and of little worth compared with what awaited them in the magical city.

Joseph completed grammar school. In 1946 his dream of escape dissolved: Hendrik died, forcing Joseph, at the age of fourteen, to take on his father's work. Otherwise the Mashininis would be evicted from the farm. (Joseph's older brother, Andrew, had left the farm to work in a mill; Phillip was too young, and his two sisters and mother too weak, to do the work.) It was terrible, enervating labour for a rather scrawny youth: ploughing, planting, harvesting, milking. Joseph began his day at dawn and didn't finish until three o'clock in the afternoon. Because he was the youngest among the full-time hands, Joseph got the worst jobs. He was often yoked into a span of a dozen or more oxen and forced to lead them, barefoot, across the fields. Some of the foremen were kind and spared the whip; but others, perhaps out of frustration or just plain mean-spiritedness, struck the animals and caused them to surge forward – putting all their weight on Joseph. Most days, he could barely make it back to his room to collapse on the bed.

This routine went on for months. Just when Joseph felt he could no longer continue and the family would have to leave the farm, his luck changed. The farmer took a liking to him: he gave him the job of escorting his two youngest sons by bicycle to school in Daleside, a nearby *dorp*, or village. Every morning, Joseph bicycled the six or so miles with the youngest boy sitting in a box behind him; the other boy rode by his side. They went by dirt roads all the way into town. Joseph saw them into the schoolhouse; after propping the older son's small bicycle in the yard, he headed back to the farm to do some light work in the flower or vegetable gardens.

At noon, Joseph returned to Daleside to fetch the children. It was not much of a town: a smattering of squat, brown-brick houses, a post office, a railway station, a garage. Beyond lay Transvaal's endless fields. Dutchmen (as Afrikaners were called by the blacks) owned the handful of shops; they treated their black customers worse than dogs. Forbidden to enter any premises through the front door, blacks were forced to make their purchases through a small window in the back – after every white patron inside had been served. Walking around town was not much better: blacks had to step off the pavement onto the street to let whites pass. Joseph suffered these indignities quietly. He knew little of politics, and so he accepted the affronts, like hard work and poverty, as constants in his life. Still, Joseph liked going to Daleside. The occasional car or train he saw there reminded him of his dreams of the big city.

By the time he was twenty years old, Joseph's life seemed to have hardened into an immutable pattern that often left him despondent. There were few opportunities for him on the farm; he became convinced that if he stayed, he would never escape the hardships Hendrik had known. Joseph wanted a different existence. His older brother Andrew had never returned from his job at a mill in Johannesburg, and so, in 1952, Joseph convinced his mother and remaining siblings to leave the farm to join Andrew. It was a journey into a political maelstrom.

Four years before, the Afrikaner-led National Party had won South Africa's general election (in which only whites were allowed to vote). The party took power promoting white supremacy and black subservience; one of its campaign slogans was *Die kaffir op sy plek* – The nigger in his place. While a random array of racial laws and regulations had been in effect since white settlers arrived in the country about 300 years earlier, the Nationalists codified them in a brutally systematic manner. The new government quickly passed a series of repressive laws: the Population Registration Act, requiring the classification of people by race; the Group Areas Act, designating residential areas by race; the Immorality Amendment Act, making mixed marriages and sexual relations between whites and other races illegal; the Bantu Education Act, relegating blacks to inferior schools and curricula. These laws, among others, became the pillars of apartheid (literally: apartness), the Nationalist ideology that doomed blacks to lives of perpetual subordination.

Race now became the single criterion that determined the destiny of every South African. The Nationalists' myriad enactments gave apartheid its legal foundations; the Dutch Reformed Church provided its religious justification. According to Church doctrine, the Afrikaners were God's chosen people and the blacks a kind of subspecies. Enforcing apartheid was a moral imperative to guarantee the continued purity of Afrikaner society; this message the *dominees*, or pastors, thundered to the faithful every Sunday from their pulpits.

(The Afrikaners' political victory secured their position not only over people of colour, but over the despised white descendants of English settlers as well. Afrikaners comprised a majority of South Africa's whites; whites, in turn, made up about 15 per cent of the nation's total population. Yet up until then the English, as they were called, had always ruled the country.)

The brunt of apartheid fell heaviest on the cities. Here the Nationalists meant to control the burgeoning number of blacks come to seek work, to keep whites from being 'overwhelmed'.

Under apartheid's dizzying rules, a job was essential: with a job, a black person could obtain a pass that would allow him to stay in the city. In this, Joseph was fortunate. He found work almost immediately at Hillbrow Medical School, just north of the city centre, as a cleaner. His siblings were also lucky: Phillip got a job in a garage, while Joseph's sisters, May and Betty, worked as maids.

Joseph washed floors, cleaned windows and polished furniture in the medical school from seven o'clock in the morning until five-thirty in the afternoon. Although it didn't pay well, the job was far less demanding than what Joseph had experienced on the farm. And he ate better. His employers provided porridge, bread and tea for breakfast every morning; at lunch, they served meat. Still, Joseph hated his first months in Johannesburg. He missed the countryside: the tinkling of the cattle bells in the fields, the birdsong that awakened him at first light, the glorious green spaciousness. Joseph felt constricted in his tiny room at the medical school. His one consolation was Fly, whom he had brought to Johannesburg and who stayed with Phillip and his mother in Kliptown, a development to the south-west of the city.

Hillbrow and Kliptown were the only areas of Johannesburg that Joseph knew. He was afraid to venture downtown: so much traffic; so many *tsotsis*, pickpockets who beat you and took your money; so many tall, tall buildings; so many white people speaking English. (Joseph had mostly spoken Sotho with the farmer and knew hardly any English.) The pass system frightened him. Curfew was at 10 p.m.; if your pass said you were allowed to sleep in Hillbrow, you could not be in Berea, for instance, after ten o'clock. The few times Joseph found himself out after curfew, he had to slink along side streets, avoiding the illuminated thoroughfares that were well-patrolled, to get back to his part of town. The police showed little mercy to violators. One thousand blacks were arrested every day for pass law transgressions; that number would ultimately total eighteen million. Joseph's dream of a better life in the city quickly dissolved.

*   *   *

By contrast, things went well for Nomkhitha in the beginning. She lived with her Aunt Letitia and Letitia's daughter in Kliptown; Letitia rented two rooms in a large house from a black preacher. Nomkhitha spent her days filling out applications to different nursing schools. In this, Letitia was very helpful: discussing each question with Nomkhitha, checking the completed form, posting the letters for her. In return, Nomkhitha kept house for Letitia, who was working as a teacher. And when Letitia adopted a small boy, the child of a friend, Nomkhitha helped to care for him.

Nomkhitha relied on her aunt and cousin to instruct her in the ways of the city. Her cousin, who was two years older, had a fashionable wardrobe and liked to give Nomkhitha dresses to wear when they went out. Nomkhitha marvelled at Johannesburg: the smart shops, the beautifully dressed women, the city's frenetic feel. When Letitia took her class on a field trip, she often invited Nomkhitha; the Johannesburg Zoo, with its astonishing array of animals, became Nomkhitha's favourite outing. She felt no desire to make friends with other young women. The ones who visited her cousin seemed rather frivolous; Nomkhitha, by comparison, considered herself a serious person with plans and ambitions. She was content to stay within the orbit of her relatives and their rooms – and wait for her new life to start.

Then the rejections began. Nomkhitha was nervous every time a response from a nursing school arrived and could not bring herself to read it. Instead, she thrust it at Letitia who, after quickly scanning the letter, put her arm around Nomkhitha's shoulders saying, 'I'm sorry, they don't want you.' Years later, Nomkhitha would learn that she had, in fact, been accepted to some of the schools. But her aunt didn't want to lose Nomkhitha's help around the house. So she lied to Nomkhitha. And Nomkhitha, in her dependence on her more worldly relation, never questioned Letitia.

The months passed. Nomkhitha became increasingly frustrated: at this rate, her life would never amount to any more than dusting Letitia's furniture, doing her laundry, washing her dishes, looking after her boy. She didn't know what to do.

Nomkhitha saw no future in going back to Bengu; everything there now seemed so primitive. But determination alone was not getting her an education. About one thing Nomkhitha was very clear: she didn't want to end up a fast woman, a rusker, as they were called. She saw them everywhere, the girls who came to the cities with high hopes, and returned to the village, and great opprobrium, with a baby.

One day, Nomkhitha was outside sweeping the front stoep when a group of young men walked by on their way to the Presbyterian church next door. Joseph was among them. He had joined the church soon after arriving in Johannesburg and his work there had become his passion, the one thing in his life that made him feel like a human being. There were visits to the sick, prayer gatherings for the dead, leadership meetings, Saturday meetings, choir. His activities didn't leave him much time for a social life. Joseph had often noticed Nomkhitha in his comings and goings: a slim young woman with beautiful legs and strong, chiselled features. On that particular morning, bolstered by his friends, he felt bold.

'Hello,' Joseph said, tipping his hat.

Nomkhitha stopped sweeping. A wiry youth with a receding hairline and rounded face was grinning at her; he was so light-skinned that Nomkhitha thought he was coloured, as apartheid nomenclature designated people of mixed race. She wanted nothing to do with such a man and went back to her sweeping.

But Joseph persisted. He made a point of arriving early at church on Sundays in the hope he would find Nomkhitha outside. They never exchanged more than a few pleasantries before Joseph hurried inside for services. Once he saw her at the greengrocer. 'Hello again,' he said, 'may I talk to you?' Nomkhitha gathered up her bags and ran all the way back to her aunt's rooms; I don't want a boyfriend, she repeated to herself, I want school. But one day she relented and spoke at length to Joseph. They began to go on short walks together: Joseph would escort Nomkhitha to the nearby shops and buy her some fruit or sweets. They talked in Xhosa; Nomkhitha didn't know Sotho. Then Joseph would take her home.

After a time, she agreed to spend Sundays with him.

Nomkhitha began to anticipate Joseph's visits eagerly; she liked his neat appearance and disciplined manner. (Even Letitia approved of their liaison because of Joseph's avid church attendance.) Joseph usually dispatched one of his young nephews by bicycle to inform Nomkhitha of their meeting time. At the appointed hour, she and Joseph would stroll slowly along the row of shops, then into the field that lay beyond. There they sat and talked for hours. One afternoon, Joseph spoke of marriage; he hadn't intended to marry so young, but found that Nomkhitha had an irresistible quality about her. Nomkhitha, who had decided she was in love with Joseph, nonetheless wouldn't countenance such a discussion. Not long after, Joseph sent his sister May to visit Nomkhitha on a kind of scouting mission. She reported back to Sara and Joseph's siblings that Nomkhitha was a beautiful woman: this was the one their brother should marry.

Then Nomkhitha discovered she was pregnant. Now she and Joseph had to get married; she would have brought a terrible dishonour to herself and her family otherwise. Besides, Sara insisted on the nuptials as soon as she heard the news. Joseph's brothers travelled to Bengu to meet Nomkhitha's family and arrange *lobola*, the bride price. The Mashininis agreed to pay the equivalent, in cash, of five cows. They also paid for a wedding dress and veil. Olive came north to help Nomkhitha select the household goods she would bring, as tradition demanded, to the marriage. By then, Daniel was too old and sickly to contribute much money; Olive, Nomkhitha and Letitia scoured the city to find an affordable dinner set, cups, cutlery, brooms, sheets, towels. Furniture was out of the question. It saddened Olive that she could not provide her daughter with the same elaborate dowry she had taken to Daniel's village.

Joseph and Nomkhitha's wedding lasted for two days. It was a small affair; Transkei was too far away for many members of Nomkhitha's family or her friends to attend. Thabiso, Joseph's childhood companion from the farm, was his best man. He had stayed behind when Joseph moved to Johannesburg, but made the journey for the most important day of his friend's life. The wedding began with a service at the Presbyterian church.

Throughout the ceremony, Nomkhitha kept repeating to herself, almost as a mantra: I will still go to school, I will still go to school. Afterwards, there was much praying and singing and taking of pictures. In one, Nomkhitha signs the registry while Joseph gazes over her shoulder: he is dapper in a tuxedo and bow tie, a white carnation stuck in his lapel; Nomkhitha has her veil up, as tradition required of pregnant brides. Both look young and hopeful.

Letitia had a reception at her rooming house after the church service. Nomkhitha changed into another dress for the festivities; people sang traditional paeans to the bride and groom, danced in the garden and ate copiously. Olive arranged for two sheep to be slaughtered for the occasion and provided beer as well. The latter was illegal; blacks could drink beer only in licensed establishments. People came from all over Kliptown, many of them uninvited, and the celebration went on all day. Nomkhitha slept at Letitia's house that night; Joseph returned to Sara's. The next day, in a much-diminished re-enactment of Olive's grand, cross-country trek to her husband's home, Joseph loaded Nomkhitha's belongings into a borrowed car and drove the several blocks to Sara's rooms. There they had another party that continued late into the night.

CHAPTER TWO

Joseph, Nomkhitha and the Children

The day after the wedding celebrations, elders from Nomkhitha's and Joseph's family sat down with the newlyweds and, as was their tradition, talked about the couple's responsibilities: From today, you are no longer a boy and girl. Now you are husband and wife; soon you will have a child. You must act accordingly.

It was a difficult transition. Nomkhitha found the living conditions at Sara's uncomfortable. Her mother-in-law rented two rooms in a big brick boarding house; Sara, Joseph, Nomkhitha, Joseph's sister May and her four children all squeezed into the small space. Although always surrounded by people, Nomkhitha felt lonely. She had to stop speaking Xhosa out of respect for her mother-in-law, yet she didn't know Sotho. Nomkhitha, eager to prove herself as a *makoti*, a young bride, devoted much energy to mastering the new language. That accomplishment alleviated her sense of isolation only slightly. Being the dutiful daughter-in-law and wife meant subordinating her culture, her ways, to those of the Mashininis. Nomkhitha had a brief respite when, a few months after the wedding, she gave birth to a son, Mokete. Tradition required that a woman return home the week before the arrival of her first-born, and stay there for the first month of the baby's life. So Nomkhitha got to go back to Letitia's for a glorious, five-week reunion.

Joseph, too, was overwhelmed by the changes. Supporting a wife and child seemed an enormous task; how could he provide a home for them on the pittance he earned? With little confidence, Joseph put his name down for a tiny plot of land offered by the government in the areas reserved for black inhabitants.

The Johannesburg municipality had acquired considerable acreage to the south-west of the city on which to house its proliferating black population. It charged rent for the minute pieces of land carved from these tracts; but tenants owned whatever abode they constructed. The government hoped to engender social stability among the disenfranchised blacks by making them homeowners. Of course, because it retained possession of the land, the government could dismantle the native locations – as they were known – at will and only pay compensation for the dwellings it destroyed.

In this manner, Soweto was created. (The name is an acronym for South-Western Townships.) The place was unspeakably bleak: barren, brown, dusty. Few trees grew there. The streets were narrow and rutted; they flooded when it rained. Hillocks of garbage decomposed by the roadside. It took hours to commute to work in Johannesburg. But with the areas allowed them already crammed, blacks were desperate for any place to live; they flocked to get their names on the government's list for Soweto. Joseph and Nomkhitha rejoiced when, the year after Mokete's birth, they were allocated a plot in the township.

They were among the first families to move to Pitso Street in the Central Western Jabavu section of Soweto. Their neighbourhood consisted of a rubbish-filled field across the road and a smattering of shops. The plot was similarly spartan: the government provided a single cold-water tap and a latrine – both outside. At first, Nomkhitha and Joseph could only afford to erect a zinc shack. In that small space they had to cook, eat, sleep. (They would later build a 'matchbox' house: the ubiquitous, concrete structures that, when seen from afar, made the township look like rows of monochromatic blocks marching to the horizon.) Despite the rudimentary nature of their residence, Nomkhitha and Joseph considered themselves lucky. They had got away from the suffocating closeness of Joseph's family and, unlike many of their friends, they had their own home.

To make more money, Joseph left his job at the medical school for one in a factory manufacturing brushes and brooms. The factory operated on a piece-work system: the more shoe brushes

Joseph turned out, the more he earned. The pressure to produce was tremendous. Foremen were forever shouting at the workers; if someone made a mistake or dawdled, his entire line was penalized. Employees had to punch a time clock to use the toilets. The tea-break lasted exactly fifteen minutes: a bell rang, and the workers rushed to gulp down a cup of the steaming liquid; another bell rang, and workers rushed back to their machines. Joseph hated his job – but kept at it because he had a family to support.

That sentiment became the watchword of Nomkhitha's and Joseph's marriage. In the beginning, Nomkhitha still had hopes of pursuing an education: Okay, I'm married, she would tell herself, but that doesn't mean I can't go to school. I'll find a way somehow. But then the babies started coming: two years after Mokete's birth, Tsietsi was born. Lehlohonolo came two years later. Then Mpho. Then Lebakeng. Then Moeketsi. Then Tshepiso. And so on: a new baby arriving just about every two years. Nomkhitha would give birth to a total of thirteen children – all of them boys, but for a set of twin girls.

At times, she resented the demands of so large a family. But, like many African women of her generation, Nomkhitha felt powerless to prevent her pregnancies. Contraception was viewed very much as a woman's responsibility. Medicines were expensive; Nomkhitha could not afford to buy birth-control pills every month, and she had heard that using them sporadically could make her even more fertile. Nomkhitha dreaded the opprobrium each new pregnancy seemed to bring. Some neighbours made innuendoes about her being an ignorant country girl; others were more forthright and demanded to know why she just didn't get an abortion. But Nomkhitha had seen the injuries, and death, caused by the illegal procedure and feared endangering her health. Years later, she would speak proudly of the courage it took to resist the pressure: 'I never miscarried, never aborted,' she said, 'so I could live and die in peace.'

Nomkhitha and Joseph, by necessity, became consumed with providing for their children. In his endless quest to earn more money, Joseph obtained a driver's licence and went to work at a brewery. His job was to drive salesmen around the Eastern

Transvaal. Joseph left home on Monday morning and returned on Friday, sleeping in a different place every night. He was not allowed to stay in the hotels with his salesman; they were only for whites. Instead, Joseph was relegated to the drivers' rooms: filthy, cramped places filled with all kinds of winged and horned creatures. If the room were not too horrible, Joseph would spend the night there in a sleeping bag. He usually found it unbearable, though, and wound up sleeping in the car. Still, Joseph liked the job. His territory was beautiful, verdant country: here were the open spaces, the cattle, sheep, goats, and the infinite fields of maize that he had left behind. Here he could breathe again.

Joseph stayed at the job for several years, then switched to driving for a construction company – a position that allowed him to work in town, returning home every night. And the salary was better. But he never seemed to have enough money for his ever-expanding family. Joseph often regretted not having continued his education so he could get better-paying jobs. While working at the medical school, he had attended classes three nights a week in the hope of obtaining a junior-high school certificate; his employer offered the study sessions for free. But Joseph was exhausted after a full day's work and by the amount of studying required for the certificate. After two years, he gave up.

While Joseph and Nomkhitha struggled to provide for their family, remarkable political events were happening around them. The African National Congress, the country's oldest black liberation movement, led thousands of people throughout the 1950s in campaigns to defy the apartheid laws. In 1955 it had convened a two-day, outdoor mass-meeting in Kliptown to adopt a set of democratic principles. The ANC solicited suggestions from across South Africa; their request produced an overwhelming response. Members of trade unions, clubs, schools, women's groups, church organizations and cultural associations heeded the call, sending their ideas on everything from brown paper bags to scraps of foolscap. The Freedom Charter, as the final version was called, eloquently proclaimed: '. . . That South Africa belongs to all who live in it, black and white, and that no government can justly claim authority unless it is based on the will of the people . . .'. It was a revolutionary document. The government thought it treasonous: 156 leaders and activists who participated in its adoption were arrested a year later and put on trial.

In the meantime, a group of dissident members was becoming increasingly disillusioned with the ANC. Known as Africanists, they believed that whites had come to dominate the ANC; in their view, white involvement only furthered the black dependency that apartheid created. The Africanists also objected to what they saw as the excessive influence of the outlawed South African Communist Party on the ANC. The proof, they said, could be found in a section of the Freedom Charter demanding that 'the mineral wealth beneath the soil, the banks and monopoly industry shall be transferred to the ownership of the people as a whole'. The Africanists were essentially correct: the two organizations had become inextricably intertwined. To purge themselves of these undesirable elements, the dissidents abandoned the ANC in 1959 and formed their own organization, the Pan Africanist Congress.

Disaster struck soon after. To compete with a similar ANC plan, the PAC called for a day of mass demonstrations the following year on March 21. Blacks were to march in protest against the much-hated passes – an ill-advised public show that was sure to lead to confrontation. Several thousand demonstrators gathered outside the police station in Sharpeville, a small township south of Johannesburg; the crowd was unarmed and generally calm. Suddenly, with no discernible provocation, the police who had been guarding the building opened fire on the protesters. They continued to shoot as the panicked people turned and fled. When it was over, sixty-nine Africans were dead – most of them shot in the back. One hundred and eighty-six people lay wounded.

The massacre provoked outrage and condemnations outside the country. The South African government was unperturbed: it declared a state of emergency, allowing the police to detain thousands of activists without charge or trial. Ten days later, it banned both the ANC and the PAC. The government had effectively ended all means of quasi-legal protest; efforts to defeat apartheid would now take a violent turn.

Nomkhitha followed these events closely. She ran to the shops every evening to buy the newspapers, then pored over the stories. Nomkhitha admired the ANC greatly, but was sceptical: how could these young people ever change things? She tried to engage Joseph in political discussions, much as Daniel had done in their house when she was young. But Joseph wouldn't countenance such talk. He had no reason to believe that things would ever be different; no one he knew owned a shop or a farm. Such aspirations were a waste of time. Joseph's only hope was to earn enough money to educate his children; that was the way, in his opinion, to a better life.

But it was a difficult path. After several years of trying to manage on one salary, Nomkhitha had little choice but to get a job. She found a position as a machinist in a factory that produced women's clothes. The factory was downtown; one of Joseph's relatives worked there and had told her of the job. She sewed side seams in dresses and hems in skirts with about sixty other women. The pay was meagre but much needed; Nomkhitha could barely afford to take time off to give birth to a new baby. She worked until a week before the delivery date, then stayed at home for a month afterwards – less than half the time allowed for maternity leave under South African law. Nomkhitha found it cheaper to hire a babysitter. One of the neighbourhood's old women – aunties, they were called – would accost Nomkhitha on the street during her pregnancy and, jabbing a finger into her burgeoning belly, announce, 'This one is mine. I'm going to look after him.' And when the children were three years old, Nomkhitha could leave them at a nearby crèche.

Joseph and Nomkhitha still barely managed. The family rarely ate meat; Nomkhitha served *pap* (a stiff maize-meal porridge) and cabbage, or *pap* and onions and tomatoes instead. A kindly butcher saved good beef bones for her, which she added to the stew to make it more savoury. There was no money for emergencies: if one of the children became ill, a visit to the local clinic ate up half of Nomkhitha's weekly pay. Joseph used his

Christmas bonus each year to buy the children one set of clothes and one new school uniform. Despite the hardships, Nomkhitha tried not to despair. She had been raised to believe that God never imposed a burden on a person he could not bear; on bad days, Nomkhitha reminded herself that many people in Soweto could not even afford to eat. She took heart from the fact that her children never went to bed hungry.

It was a far cry from the privilege and status she had known as a girl and expected to continue into adulthood. That world had virtually disappeared. Daniel had died soon after Nomkhitha's wedding, and her half-siblings immediately began fighting over the division of his estate. In the meantime, the government passed the Promotion of Bantu Self-Government Act, which established eight, ethnically based Bantustans. Under the law, blacks – who comprised about 73 per cent of the population – were allocated 13 per cent of the country's most underdeveloped land. Although the majority of Africans resided in 'white' areas, they were to become citizens of their own 'tribal homeland'; in this way, blacks could forever be deprived of political rights inside South Africa itself. Transkei was the first to be so transformed. In 1963, the government's Transkei Constitution Act turned it into a semi-autonomous 'homeland'. Daniel's lands were confiscated by the new regime, his stone house knocked down. All was lost.

Reduced to penury, Olive moved to Johannesburg. She searched in vain for a teaching position and was eventually forced to take a job as a domestic with a white family. They knew nothing of the Great Place, the majesty of court, the beauty of an *imbongi's* poetry. Olive's employers could not be bothered to learn her surname, let alone the origins of her quiet dignity and excellent English. To them, she was just another *kaffir* woman come to clean their toilets and change their children's nappies.

Nomkhitha saw her dreams vanish. She had long ago abandoned the idea of becoming a nurse, but still yearned for some sort of profession. Nomkhitha used to pass a secretarial school every day on her way to work. She would stop and stare at the advertisement in the window: the smiling, smartly dressed woman sitting at a large desk, surrounded by office equipment. The tableau looked so respectable, so modern. After allowing herself a few minutes' reverie, she would sigh and continue down the street; they could never afford the tuition fees.

But if Nomkhitha could not achieve her ambitions, she was determined that her children should. She began buying books for the kids with the few pennies she salvaged at the end of every month. Starting with comics to get their attention, she pointed out the pictures and explained the stories. As the children grew, they graduated to more sophisticated books in Sotho and English. It didn't matter that Nomkhitha arose before dawn, worked all day in the factory, returned home to cook supper and wash out nappies – she always read to her children. Her dreams, she decided, would become theirs.

Mokete, Tsietsi, Mpho, Lebakeng and Tshepiso came to be the most politically active of the Mashinini children. Each arrived at his involvement from a different path. For some, it was a studied decision; for others, a hasty act of volition or sheer chance.

Being the first-born, Rocks (as Mokete was called) felt the full weight of his parents' expectations. School was paramount; on this subject, Joseph and Nomkhitha were unrelenting. Joseph beat Rocks when he played truant. Nomkhitha made him – and the other children, as they got older – sit at the dining-room table after supper every night to do their homework. (Rocks developed a passion for the comic books Nomkhitha bought. His favourite was Chunky Charlie: a hero-type who slunk around in a heavy overcoat, laden with various tools that were useful in fighting crimes.) His parents taunted him if he neglected his studies: he would end up like the men who emptied the night-soil buckets left on the streets in the morning, they warned, or as one of the chaps who lugged the fifty-kilogram bags of coal to houses for cooking and heating. Rocks took the admonitions to heart; those people were figures of derision among children in the township.

Joseph and Nomkhitha closely monitored Rocks' progress in school. Any slip in grades during the year prompted a warning to improve; it also put him on a kind of probation, during which it was difficult to extract money from his parents for extracurricular activities. The Mashinini children were expected to finish among the top five students in their class. The family would ridicule anyone who ranked lower throughout the December school holidays; those who succeeded were rewarded with a rand. Joseph always threw a party to celebrate the good grades. He bought sodas, sweets, crisps, peanuts; and he gathered the children around the dining-room table to offer a prayer of thanks. It was the best day of the year. Rocks chafed under this intense parental scrutiny, but ultimately came to see its value. He would be one of the few of his boyhood gang to graduate from high school.

The pressure he felt from his parents turned Rocks into an introverted, measured sort of person. (In that, he took after Joseph. When political violence overwhelmed the township in later years, Nomkhitha often dashed headlong out the door to witness each new confrontation. Joseph, on the other hand, first changed into sports shoes – in case he had to run from the police.) To his younger siblings, Rocks was the serious, bookish big brother. He acted as a kind of surrogate father during Joseph's absence, meting out punishments and inspiring awe; the youngsters knew they had to be quiet around Rocks. His parents also expected him to set an example for the others. That often meant getting blamed for their transgressions: when Tsietsi used to appropriate the meagre spending money given the children – a constant source of squabbles among them – Rocks was censured.

Like all township boys, Rocks was mad about sport. He played football, but not with the same obsessiveness as his younger brothers. He preferred softball, an interest he shared with Tsietsi. Rocks' best positions were first base and shortstop; he and Tsietsi devised makeshift bases and stole the bats from their school. He also trained as a welter-weight boxer. Rocks fought for the Jabulani Boxing Club, where he was considered to have a reasonably good left jab. Nomkhitha hated him boxing; she wanted her children to aspire to something more genteel like tennis. But Rocks dismissed it as an effeminate game. Growing up in the ghetto, you had to assert a masculine image to fend off *tsotsis*, or pickpockets.

Gangs were also a problem. They formed around a particular section of the township: Orlando had its gang, White City its band of youths, and so on. The gangs attacked mostly at night, brandishing knives, hatchets, all manner of crudely fashioned weapons. In an attempt at justice, a teacher at Rocks' school organized a kind of vigilante group to punish the perpetrators. Rocks once identified a boy who had assaulted a rival gang member; he marched him virtually across Soweto to be whipped by the vigilantes. A few weeks later, Rocks encountered the same youth on a train into town. This time, he was surrounded by his cronies; they held Rocks down for four train stops as the boy beat him up, splitting open his forehead.

His family's poverty weighed heavily on Rocks. As a child, he would dream of toys. It was always the same fantasy: Joseph somehow found extra money and bought him all the playthings he coveted. At first, Rocks held his parents responsible for their condition. They had too many children to support; two or three offspring would have been manageable. But Rocks ultimately came to blame apartheid for their impoverished state. He arrived at this conclusion gradually, through the small epiphanies so many black children experienced when they ventured beyond the township.

Rocks' awakening began when Nomkhitha allowed him to go by train into Johannesburg on errands. He was spellbound by the cars he saw there: the speedy, sleek vehicles, driven mostly by whites, that jammed the city's streets. It was a rare thing for a black person to own a car. And all the goods on display in the store windows; Rocks had never imagined such luxuries existed. But he could not afford them. They were for the white customers, who paid with great bundles of notes they produced from their pockets or purses. Rocks, meanwhile, bought only the cheapest items, carefully counting out the coins entrusted to him.

His perception of the disparities between blacks and whites deepened as he got older. Along with several classmates, Rocks participated in a drama festival at an all-white high school in one of Johannesburg's northern suburbs – the first time he had set foot in such an institution. He was astounded by what he saw: the library, auditorium, gymnasium, laboratories, modern classrooms. Rocks' overcrowded, understaffed school had virtually nothing. Everyone knew the government spent far more on white students than on blacks; in fact, it was about twelve times as much. But this most tangible manifestation of apartheid opened Rocks' eyes and angered him.

The more he encountered the white world, the more embittered Rocks became. The sightseers who took the bus tours of Soweto from Johannesburg were a poignant example. Some were foreigners; but many white South Africans also went on the trip, gaping at the township and snapping photographs as though it were a different country. (This would probably be the only time any of them ever ventured into a 'location'.) One stop on the itinerary was in front of Rocks' school. The passengers didn't disembark; that was considered too dangerous. Instead, they threw sweets and coins at the children from open windows – a practice Rocks hated. It made him feel like an animal on display in a zoo.

As an adolescent, Rocks worked during the school holidays at Joseph's construction company. He did odd jobs: filing, making tea, washing cars, delivering messages. Besides the extra money it provided, the work gave him a glimpse of the conditions under which his father worked. Joseph, as the president's driver, was treated respectfully by the company's highest officers. But the other white employees barely hid their contempt for the black workers. With a son's sensitivity, Rocks cringed at the thousand daily little humiliations his father endured.

Of course, Rocks could not talk to his father about what he saw as the injustices of apartheid; Joseph would allow no such discussions under his roof. The 1960s were a time of terrible political repression. After its banning, the ANC had gone underground and, ending a fifty-year-old tradition of non-violence, formed a military wing, Umkhonto we Sizwe (Spear of the Nation). On 16 December 1961, the day Afrikaners celebrated the defeat of thousands of Zulu warriors in the previous century,

Umkhonto exploded a series of home-made bombs around the country. The attacks were timed to avoid injuring people and were aimed at symbolic targets: the Bantu Affairs Commissioner's offices in Johannesburg; a nearby post office; electricity pylons in Port Elizabeth. Umkhonto committed scores of similar acts of sabotage until July 1963, when the police raided its secret headquarters at a farm in Rivonia, near Johannesburg. The officers arrested most of Umkhonto's leaders; eight of them, including Nelson Mandela, were sentenced to life in prison after a highly publicized trial in April the next year.

The raid on Rivonia effectively stilled black political opposition for a decade. What remained of the ANC and Umkhonto were forced to reassemble in exile, far from South Africa's borders. The PAC too had to reorganize outside the country. (Poqo, or 'pure' in Xhosa, a terrorist group with ties to the PAC, had engaged in acts of violence for a brief time; the police destroyed it in 1963 by arresting thousands of its adherents.) An entire generation of black activists was imprisoned, banned or exiled. To deter the resurgence of political movements, the police assumed unbridled powers of arrest and detention and recruited an army of black informers; the government imposed harsh restrictions on the press.

The measures left blacks utterly intimidated. The life imprisonment of the ANC/Umkhonto leaders on Robben Island, off the coast of Cape Town, seemed the end of politics itself. People shunned the discussions that had animated so much of daily life. To speak of such matters was to invite repression. The ANC's protest campaigns of the 1950s, the Freedom Charter, the actions of Umkhonto – all slipped into obscurity, suppressed by parents too frightened to tell their children. Newspapers could not even print Nelson Mandela's photograph. One evening, Rocks asked his father about graffiti he had seen spray-painted on an electrical sub-station on his way home from school. 'Who is Mandela?' asked Rocks. Joseph slapped him across the face and walked out of the room.

If working at his father's construction firm exposed Rocks to the quotidian indignities of apartheid, it also opened his eyes to the future. He decided he would become an engineer. Rocks had wanted to study law, but law required a knowledge of Latin, and his teachers at school discouraged him from attempting the language. Engineering seemed the next best thing: the draughtsmen with their drawing tables and precision instruments appealed to Rocks' sense of order. Nomkhitha was delighted.

When Rocks entered high school, Joseph acquired an old, abandoned trailer from his company and set it in the small yard behind the house. It was a kind of study for Rocks, a refuge from the raucous children who inhabited every corner of his home. He crammed for his matriculation exams there. Rocks also attended study groups at his high school; called 'cross-nighting', these marathon sessions began in the evening and continued until the early hours of the morning. (Rocks' school, Morris Issacson, was one of the few places in Soweto that had electricity.) After supper, Rocks would take a blanket and a thermos filled with coffee and walk back to school. There he and his friends thrashed out the finer points of a subject, filling the blackboard with equations or quotations, until they drooped with exhaustion. They were determined students: one way or another, their lives would be different from their parents'.

Tsietsi, the next-born, was, by contrast with his older brother, a great extrovert. As a youngster, he appeared highly-strung and given to histrionics: when denied something he wanted, Tsietsi cried until he vomited. He would suddenly and inexplicably start to sob, as though he had been hurt. But as Tsietsi grew, he evolved into a charismatic personality who charmed everyone he met.

He was the leader among his siblings. Acknowledged as the cleverest in the family, Tsietsi dominated the dining-room table at night: doing his homework, helping the others, discussing the finer points of a vexing problem. As with Rocks, Nomkhitha imbued him with a love for reading. Tsietsi, in turn, conveyed this passion to the younger children, especially when they had became too numerous to command much of their parents' attention. In this manner, he became something of a mentor to his brothers.

As the second-born, Tsietsi seemed to escape much of the pressure Nomkhitha and Joseph imposed on Rocks. He developed a playful nature and a lively imagination; among his many inventions, he created a clandestine society called The Secret Seven, based on the children's books by Enid Blyton. The Secret Seven included two of his brothers and four friends. Tsietsi found hidden meeting places, to enter which required a secret password. There the seven youths devised stories about engaging in exciting and daring undertakings. At the end of each meeting, Tsietsi brought out a cake or some other special treat that he bought with the two-cent dues collected from the members. Like the books that Tsietsi devoured, the game transported him and the other boys beyond the wretchedness of life in the township; for a brief moment, they could dream childhood dreams.

Like Rocks, Tsietsi was a gifted athlete who excelled at softball, tennis and dancing. But he devoted the most energy to karate. The speed and discipline it required suited Tsietsi's personality perfectly and he liked the fact that the flashy, martial-arts moves made him an exotic figure among the thugs of Soweto. Tsietsi was forever frightening Nomkhitha with sudden karate chops and high-pitched yells. When his siblings begged to learn, Tsietsi taught them turns and kicks, lining them up in the yard for drills. They were thrilled: this was the big brother who deigned to notice them. And they adored him.

To those outside the family, Tsietsi seemed an appealing, if frenetic, youth. He affected what was called an 'American hippy' mode of dress: bell-bottoms, peace symbols, an Afro hairstyle. (Tsietsi habitually stole clothes from Rocks – especially for social engagements with girls, who thought him something of a dandy.) Just as he was a force within his family, Tsietsi exhibited a natural leadership among his peers. He was a whirlwind of activity: president of the Methodist Youth Guild; chairman of a youth burial society; chairman of his school's debating committee and of the Debating Group Association; chairman of a social club; head of a softball club; a freelance writer for the black edition of the *Rand Daily Mail*. Dispatched by Nomkhitha, Rocks spent countless evenings trying to find Tsietsi and bring him home for dinner.

Tsietsi also had a contentious side to his nature. He made and lost friends with equal swiftness – often because of his penchant for provoking people. Tsietsi's siblings knew this aspect of his character well: pushed beyond his tolerance one day, Lehlohonolo (or Cougar, as he was called) threw a stone at Tsietsi's head while he was standing in the kitchen. Tsietsi ducked, and the projectile hit one of the yellow cabinets. The dent that it left became part of family lore.

In the same manner, Tsietsi delighted in testing established limits. One day he decided, against all the regulations, to light up a cigarette in class. It was a free period and the teacher had left the room. Another instructor happened to walk by at that moment; smelling smoke, he entered the class to investigate and found Tsietsi with the forbidden tobacco, surrounded by his friends. The teacher immediately brought them before the school's disciplinary board. Tsietsi was suspended from school for a few days; his companions received lashings with a cane.

Despite his carefree personality, Tsietsi was a brilliant student; Nomkhitha thought he would become a lawyer. A weekly radio programme about famous court cases, *Consider the Verdict*, particularly fascinated him. Tsietsi started out in a chair listening to the show, but in his excitement slowly crept towards the console until, at the climax, he was virtually sitting on top of it. Afterwards, he and Rocks had heated debates in English about the episode's outcome. Sometimes friends from the neighbourhood joined in; the younger Mashininis would listen in awe as Tsietsi, who had a singular command of the language, dominated the arguments.

Tsietsi's love of English and English literature prompted his classmate, Murphy Morobe (who would later become a prominent political leader), to confer upon him the title of 'Shakespeare's friend in Africa'. To Nomkhitha, his oratorical prowess seemed a direct line from his grandfather, the *imbongi*. Tsietsi's talent came to define his adolescent life; he used it to make friends and recruit like-minded youths to his projects. And he employed it to express a nascent hatred of white people – utterances whose virulence surprised his parents.

As head of his debating team at Morris Issacson High, Tsietsi regularly competed against other schools. Debating clubs were immensely popular in the township: students vied fiercely for membership in them, and their debates were always well attended. Khotso Seatlholo, an intense, articulate youth, was in the audience at Naledi High for a contest against Morris Issacson. The topic was 'The Pen is Mightier than the Sword'; Tsietsi argued for the motion. Khotso was spellbound. Unlike the other speakers, who were clutching reams of notes, Tsietsi had only a small index card which he barely consulted. He was bold, eloquent, witty, quick thinking. It seemed impossible that Tsietsi was the product of Bantu education (as it was called under apartheid). He exuded an uncanny confidence; his closing statement brought a standing ovation from the audience.

Afterwards, at a social gathering, Tsietsi sought out Khotso. Khotso felt flattered: Tsietsi was popular, well-known, a prefect at his school. He had a swarm of girls around him. Tsietsi made polite enquiries about Khotso's family and church affiliation; they talked for a while, then Tsietsi left. Khotso gave little import to the encounter.

But Tsietsi returned to see Khotso after school the following week. Again, he asked about Khotso's family, his church, membership in clubs, and so on. Thus began a pattern that continued for several weeks: Tsietsi would appear at Naledi at the end of the school day once a week to talk. He and Khotso would find an empty classroom or, if the weather was fine, sit outside. They covered a range of mostly neutral topics, but occasionally Tsietsi would insert a question about the situation in South Africa. Khotso understood that Tsietsi was trying to tease out his political views. But Tsietsi's approach was so slow and convincing that Khotso, despite his reservations, found himself being drawn to his new friend.

Mpho, the fourth son, shared little of his older brothers' anguish about being a poor township boy. Growing up in the political void of the 1960s, it seemed the normal state of things. His house was like his neighbours' (albeit more cramped), his possessions not dissimilar to theirs. In fact, Mpho felt a great sense of security. Long before he had friends, his gaggle of brothers provided protection and fellowship.

But there were hazards to having so many siblings. At meal-times, Nomkhitha seated the youngest children on the floor of the living room. (The older ones got to eat at the dining-room table with their parents.) She set down a big bowl of *pap* with vegetables or traces of meat and there followed an intense struggle to get at the food. Despite the exertion of sharing from one bowl, Mpho came to think of eating as a highly communal experience. It would take him a long time after leaving home to adjust to using his own plate; having a meal in such a manner seemed so solitary, so lonely.

Eating on the floor required a careful choreography. You had to balance getting enough food to eat with finishing promptly; the first to push away from the bowl got his pick of the after-dinner chores. For Mpho, there was always a kind of tension: resisting the lure of more food allowed him to stand up and claim drying, the easiest of the jobs. Gluttony meant some other brother would assert his right before him. That left the washing-up, an odious task or, even worse, cleaning the floor. The older children were responsible for washing and drying the dishes and setting them on the table for the younger ones to put away. In Soweto, girls traditionally did this type of work; but until 1974, when the twins Lindi and Linda were born, the Mashininis were a family of boys.

As such, they were also obliged to do chores around the house, and to finish them before Nomkhitha returned from work late in the afternoon. The children had to wash the break-fast dishes, clean out the ashes from the morning fire, make the beds, fold their clothes, scrub the tiles and sweep the floor. They were each assigned tasks in different rooms; and they were always grumbling about the injustice of doing a particular chore today when they had done it yesterday. 'Okay, you ate yesterday,' Nomkhitha would retort, 'so should we get someone else to eat for you today?'

Lighting the fire in the afternoon was the bane of Mpho's life. He simply could not work out how to do it *and* play foot-ball after school. Mpho devised three strategies, all of which had serious drawbacks. He could light the fire immediately upon returning home, before heading out to a match. But the fire was sure to burn out in the three hours or so before Nomkhitha's arrival. Or he could dash home at half time, hurriedly kindle a blaze and check the chimney for smoke, then race back to the field across the street to finish the game. The fire rarely caught properly and would be stone cold by the time Nomkhitha entered the house. As a third course of action, Mpho could keep playing until the last possible moment, until he saw Nomkhitha walking tiredly up the street. Then he would sprint home and madly start making the fire.

Football was, unquestionably, the most important thing in Mpho's existence. The rubbish-littered field across from his house regulated the pulse and rhythm of his youth. School, church, household chores – all seemed nothing more than inter-ruptions to the real substance of life: playing football. He could not step outside without seeing that field. It was beckoning, seductive, omnipresent: the stuff of dreams.

In the summer Mpho played barefoot; when he was older and had got a bit of money, he bought *takkies*, or sports shoes. Each neighbourhood had its own team, but would send its best players to participate in area competitions. On Sundays, Mpho and his mates went to the nearby hostels where migrant labourers lived. The workers organized their teams along tribal lines, but were often short of players and paid the township kids to fill in the open positions. Mpho could earn as much as three rand in an afternoon, a princely sum. (He could also take a shower, a unique experience. The hostels had virtually the only showers in the township.) Nomkhitha never knew of Mpho's exploits; he feared she would have been outraged. As it was, she would often march over to the field and, screaming at Mpho, jerk him from a game.

Swimming was Mpho's other great passion. The township had only one public pool, located in White City – a section of Soweto named for its low, white houses made from concrete blocks. Mpho liked to spend the entire day there during the summer holidays, returning home at night ravenously hungry and exhausted from the sun. But swimmers had to pay an entrance fee of two cents and Mpho always struggled to find the money. One method was to 'liberate' it from the gangs that roamed the area. Mpho, his older brother Cougar, and a group of friends often ambushed a squad of Zulu youths who had to pass through Mpho's territory to arrive at the pool. They would thrash the youngsters and appropriate their money. But that didn't ensure a day of swimming: they still had to negotiate the back streets of White City to avoid getting molested themselves by a gang called the Damaras (after a Namibian tribe), bent on relieving Mpho and his companions of their coins.

One day they decided to use Cougar, who had had polio as an infant, as a kind of courier. (The disease attacked his leg and arm, but permanently affected only the latter.) After assaulting the Zulus, Mpho hid the money in the hand of Cougar's disabled arm. Then he pushed Cougar to the front of their group as they approached the Damaras; the gang, seeing that Cougar was disabled, let him pass. At that moment, Cougar accidentally let the precious coins clatter to the ground. There was no swimming for them on that day.

Like his siblings, Mpho was always desperate for money. His one steady source of income came from reselling train tickets. Trains were the main mode of transportation between the township and Johannesburg; taxis and buses hardly ran in the black areas. On Sundays, Mpho's parents sent him to stand in line to buy a six-day ticket for the coming week, the cheapest fare. As a reward, they allowed him to sell the sixth ticket (still valid for another day) back at the station on the following Saturday morning. Mpho charged 30 or 40 cents for the 50-cent ticket, a saving for people who wanted to go into town to shop. He got to keep the money he earned: sometimes he spent it on the admission to see his beloved Orlando Pirates football team play at Orlando Stadium; or he treated himself to an orgy of crisps, fizzy drinks and sweets.

Mpho occasionally went to work in town on the weekends, washing the cars of white people. Nomkhitha didn't like him doing this because it kept him in Johannesburg all day – a forbidding thing for a child. But Mpho had virtually no knowledge of whites; the car-washing forays provided his only contact with them. And so he eagerly looked forward to the treks into town. To him, whites weren't actually people; they were rich other-beings who lived somewhere beyond his range of vision.

Being a Mashinini, Mpho was diligent at attending school. He and the other children arose before dawn; Nomkhitha, who departed at six o'clock, lit the fire and left water warming on the stove so they could wash. Joseph used it first, then the others, according to age. After gulping down a mug of tea Joseph prepared for him, Mpho walked to school. His class consisted of about fifty students and one teacher. The children sat two or three at a desk. The rest of the school was equally over-crowded and operated on a staggered schedule: Mpho's grade spent half the day inside a classroom, the other half sitting under a tree outside. When it rained, the two shifts had to squeeze inside the sultry, suffocating room.

Learning brought little joy to Mpho. The aim of Bantu educa-tion was, in the words of its Nationalist creator, Hendrik Verwoerd, 'to prepare blacks for a status in life as hewers of wood and drawers of water'. Often Mpho's beleaguered teacher seemed to go through the motions of teaching: thirty minutes spent on history; thirty on geography; and so on. Mpho saw these classes as something to be endured. His real education took place at night around the dining table: there his older brothers brought to life the dry, uninspiring stuff of school, stimulating him with their debates and drawing him into their world of books and ideas.

Unlike his older brothers, Lebakeng (or Dee, as he was called) was neither studious nor serious. As the fifth child, Dee saw himself as a kind of nexus between the older siblings and the younger ones. He nonetheless found his closest companionship in a cluster of school friends. He and four of his classmates formed the core of their school choir, where Dee sang first tenor. They dominated their school football team. They designed iden-tical tunics out of old mealie bags and wore them as team uniforms. When they decided to skip their studies to play a match, they did so en masse. (Dee's love of football was such that Nomkhitha's voice alone, wafting across the field and summoning him home, was the only thing that could stop him from playing. Even his sobriquet had football associations: it came from a player for the Moroka Swallows.)

Dee had a bit of the devil in him. His younger siblings saw him as an aggressive, flamboyant type, forever trying to arrange business deals. Dee befriended the children of neighbourhood shopkeepers and wheedled cold drinks and sweets from them. He gambled with fervour; his favourite game was to spin a coin, shouting out to anyone within earshot: Heads or tails? Heads or tails? Dee always managed to have money. Sometimes he appropriated the change his parents left for the children to buy bread and used it to gamble. On other occasions, Dee spent the coins intended for the church collection on *vetkoeke* (fat cakes): greasy, fried confections that could be had at a nearby café. He also rolled dice, but that stopped the day Dee noticed Joseph observing him from the back-yard. For a while, he carried a knife.

His siblings were of two minds about Dee. They often reported him to their parents for stealing the bread money and making them go hungry. Dee would receive a punishment that night, but by the next morning he was always so cheerful that his brothers felt a bit ashamed – until the next infraction. Even Nomkhitha was ambivalent. She knew him to be mischievous and disobedient, and yet he could be so helpful. 'I'm going out now,' he would say, struggling into his football clothes, 'but if you need me, just stand at the door and call.' And when Nomkhitha called him, he indeed came running.

Dee found school boring. He was dogged by the brilliant reputation of his older brothers. Like the others, he did his homework at the dining-room table at night by candlelight. (The house caught on fire three times because of the candles, a not uncommon occurrence in Soweto. Few, if any, homes had electricity. The fire usually started in a bedroom while the family was in another part of the house. Once, all the children's clothes were destroyed.) Dee could not see the point of devoting much energy to his studies. Whites held all the power; blacks had none. When he finished school, he would work for the white man in some prescribed job. That was the way of the world.

Once, Dee and his classmates were taken on a trip to the Voortrekker Monument near Pretoria. A hulking granite structure, the Monument stood as a temple to the struggle between (white) civilization and (black) barbarism. It was constructed so that at noon on December 16, the day that Afrikaners commemorated the defeat of the Zulu warriors, a ray of light shining through the Monument's dome would strike an inscription on a cenotaph. The symbolic tomb honoured Piet Retief, a Boer leader murdered by the Zulus. The purpose of the outing was to make history come alive for the students. But Dee didn't need to gaze upon cold marble friezes to grasp the significance of white domination; under apartheid, he lived it.

A more quotidian lesson could be found in the constant police presence in Soweto. That, for Dee, was a live thing: the police were everywhere, rounding up men whose passes weren't in order. Every day Dee saw long queues of transgressors, miserable and defeated, handcuffed together and sitting on the ground, waiting to be taken to jail. Policemen were the highest figures of authority in the township. It seemed natural that Dee would aspire to enter the profession when he grew up, perhaps as a traffic officer – they got to ride on motorcycles. Then again, maybe he would be a teacher – they dressed better than most of the adults Dee knew.

By the time of Tshepiso's birth – he was the seventh child – Nomkhitha and Joseph were too burdened to lavish much attention on him. He was left mostly to his own devices. At a young age, Tshepiso developed a loathing for school: he despised the overcrowded classroom, the single, harassed teacher, the long list of supplementary reading his parents could not afford. He had to beg his friends to share their books with him. His teacher tormented him on the subject constantly. 'Where is your book?' she would demand in front of the class. Next week, Tshepiso always stammered, I promise I'll buy it next week. But Joseph never had the money until much too late in the school year. The next week Tshepiso would be subjected to the same humiliating interrogation.

Despite his antipathy to school, Tshepiso – as was charac-
teristic of Nomkhitha's children – loved to read. Mpho supplied
him with cast-off books. Tshepiso developed a reputation as the
laziest of the siblings: he would stumble from his bed, search
around the house for a book, then – instead of doing his chores
– crawl back beneath the blankets to read. He spent hours
engrossed in magazines, newspapers, paperbacks, any printed
material he could find. Only Nomkhitha's threats of retribution
would rouse him from his reverie.

His ardour for reading notwithstanding, Tshepiso was, in
other respects, a typical township boy. He excelled at removing
the spokes from abandoned bicycle wheels and, using a wire as
a kind of prod, conducting races through the streets of Soweto.
He collected large pieces of scrap metal to make into sledges
for the sandy hills that dotted the township. He created cata-
pults from smashed bottles, arrows from sticks and bits of wire;
these he employed in competitions among his younger siblings
and friends to shoot down birds.

Tshepiso found it difficult being part of so large a family. He
sucked his thumb until he was seven and was tortured by his
older brothers for it – they smeared his thumb with chili peppers
as a deterrent. In another act of dissuasion, they inflicted small
cuts with a razor blade on the top of the digit. Tshepiso saw
his siblings not only as tormentors, but as the cause of his
poverty. His house felt suffocatingly crammed, especially at night
when everyone was present. Joseph and Nomkhitha slept in one
bedroom, the latest baby between them. The older children
stayed in the dining room: they pushed the table to one side
and pulled out a bed from underneath a sofa. The youngest
ones – Tshepiso included – slept in the other bedroom, packed
into beds, squeezed onto the floor. Tshepiso would dream that
his house had miraculously expanded during the night; on
waking, he peered around the room, hoping to see wide spaces
beyond the bodies of his sleeping brothers.

By Tshepiso's calculations, fewer brothers would have meant
more money for the things he coveted. He yearned to buy a
proper lunch at school. With the coins he received from his
parents, he could only purchase bread and potatoes from the

old grannies who sold food at the schoolyard gates; other kids (whom Tshepiso suspected came from smaller families) bought bits of meat for their sandwiches, cold drinks, ice cream. His school uniform caused him similar misery. The black shorts, white shirt, jersey, socks and black shoes cost more than a domestic worker's monthly wage and the uniform the children received each Christmas had to last for the entire year. Tshepiso washed one of his two shirts every night. He brushed and pressed his single pair of shorts after each use, until they were shiny and threadbare. He stitched the holes that seemed to appear daily in his shoes. Tshepiso longed for shirts and shorts enough to last the entire week, and for a trunkful of shoes.

To have a more prosperous life, his parents told him, you must stay in school. But from a young age, Tshepiso understood the limits of even a good education. White people ruled them. He had seen how at night, Johannesburg, the white man's city, shimmered with light; it seemed to Tshepiso the very essence of hope. Soweto was always in darkness.

Nomkhitha exerted the most influence over the children when they were very young. She was their confidante, the one they played with and cuddled. After work and on Sunday afternoons, Nomkhitha would sit with them on the veranda, talking, telling stories, teasing.

But as the boys grew, Joseph became the figure of authority. They craved his approval; each wanted to be his favourite. This was no easy thing. Joseph held himself apart as a strict disciplinarian – so strict, in fact, that neighbourhood parents used to compel good behaviour in their children by invoking his name. If Joseph found one of his sons being disobedient, he made the child lie down on the bedroom floor; Joseph then took off his belt and gave him a beating. (Behind his back, the boys called him 'The Sheriff'. Rocks thought up the nickname from the Westerns he read).

Misconduct was subject to punishment by the belt. One day, Cougar, Mpho and about a dozen friends were putting small rocks on the rail lines near the house for trains to crush. The boys could have been electrocuted by the line or caused a train to derail. Suddenly, Joseph appeared on the other side of the lines and emitted a low whistle. Cougar and Mpho jumped up, terrified; they knew what the whistle meant. Go home immediately, he commanded them, lie down on the bedroom floor and wait for me to return.

Joseph had an array of belts with which to inflict punishment; some hurt more than others. The most feared was the one the children called Paris, after its manufacturer's name. As painful as the beatings were, the boys preferred to have them administered immediately. Often, Nomkhitha would note a transgression, with a promise to inform Joseph. Then the culprit lived in unbearable anticipation for days.

(Smoking was another major offence; the children avoided smoking in Joseph's presence. Of all the things Mpho would receive in jail after his arrest in 1977, none touched him more than the three packets of cigarettes his father included in his bundle. Mpho had thought Joseph unaware of his addiction.)

Beyond his authoritarianism, Joseph's religiosity had the greatest influence on his children. He had switched to the Methodist Church, Nomkhitha's denomination, because of disputes among the ministers in his Presbyterian parish. Joseph found the Methodist traditions powerful and satisfying. Every Sunday he donned the dark suit jacket, red waistcoat, grey flannel trousers, white shirt, black tie and lapel pin of his men's guild. He sat with the other guild members at the front of church; seated near them were the *manyano*, or women's guild. The married ones wore orange jackets, white collars, white caps, black skirts, black shoes and stockings. The single women's garb was reversed: white jackets with orange collars. The guild members faced the congregants and the rows of hard, wooden pews. Small children, who maintained a murmur of babble throughout the service, played on the worn linoleum floor.

At a raised lectern, the preacher delivered the weekly sermon. He became intensely animated when expounding on a particular biblical passage, gesticulating with both arms and raising his voice to a fevered pitch. Behind him, a simple crucifix hung on the wall; a purple cloth, embroidered with the words 'God is Love', covered the altar. The members of the men's guild listened intently to the sermon. Some held their heads in concentration; others, like Joseph, wiped tears from their cheeks.

When the service ended, the guild members rose from their seats. Pounding leather pillows like small drums and dancing in place, they exhorted the congregation to stand. The worshippers swayed and clapped their hands, their voices lifted in song; those who were moved by the preacher's homily came forward to testify to their faith. The congregants responded with shouts of 'Yes! Yes!' and punctuated the end of each testimony with hauntingly beautiful hymns. The ceremony gladdened Joseph's heart. For two short hours each week, he could forget about the terrors of apartheid: the police, the white bosses, the need to hide one's true feelings, to act submissive. All that seemed to melt away in church. Here Joseph could express himself. He could allow himself to feel all the things denied him in his daily life. Here he felt free.

To ensure that his children found a similar refuge in the church, Joseph made religion a principal feature of their lives. He insisted they attend church services and Sunday school. On Wednesday nights, Joseph took them to interdenominational prayer meetings at private houses in the neighborhood. Saturday nights were given over to gatherings of the Independent Order of True Templars, a teetotalist group. The children's branch, the Band of Hope, presented plays and concerts and held picnics. The older boys joined the Methodist Young Men's Guild. They sang in the church choir. For a brief time, Mpho considered studying for the ministry. They all admired Joseph who, with tears coursing down his face, could enrapture a congregation with his preaching. (Dee believed that Mashinini men cried at the slightest provocation; it was as though they carried an overflowing tank of tears around on their backs.)

Their religious training left a deep impression on all the children. (Even as a freedom fighter years later, Rocks would pray in the guerrilla camps of Angola.) But the very education that their parents championed made the boys turn away from the church; they came to see it as something that blinded Joseph to South Africa's political realities. With few exceptions, the various denominations discouraged resistance to apartheid. Liberation theology, which provided the moral justification for so many rebellions in Latin America, was virtually unknown in South Africa until the 1970s. Instead, the children saw a Church that urged prayer as the path to a better future. In their view, Joseph was waiting for a miracle that would never happen.

The boys also came to believe such passiveness perpetuated a sense of impotence among blacks. Joseph himself felt helpless to protect his children from the arbitrariness of apartheid; the political repression following the Rivonia Trial terrified him. He found security in the daily routine of work, home and church. In a world gone mad, the unvarying procedure provided a feeling of control in his life. It also, in his children's view, bound him: Joseph could not see how things could possibly change. To upset the existing state of affairs was to invite disaster. Better to accept the daily injustices and find the beauty and glory of life elsewhere.

His children had a different sense of their place in the world. By the end of the 1960s, a new ideology began to sprout among university students: called Black Consciousness, it came into being as a rejection of white student leadership. (The youth organizations, with their multiracial membership, were virtually the only groups that actively protested injustices against blacks during the quiescence of the 1960s.) The 'black power' movement in the US greatly influenced the proponents of Black Consciousness, both in ideology and rhetoric. Black Consciousness insisted on the primacy of regaining self-confidence and a sense of independence. 'Black man, you are on your own', became its rallying cry.

The Black Consciousness activists launched education and community action campaigns throughout South Africa, aimed at reviving self-reliance among blacks. Their approach shocked white liberals. The refusal to accept white assistance of any sort and the insistence on creating exclusively black-run organizations seemed a kind of reverse apartheid. The movement's most eloquent and potent proponent was Steve Biko, a medical student at Natal University. (His death in 1977, after being beaten and tortured while in police detention, would cause an international outcry.) With echoes of its counterpart in the US, the concepts of Black Consciousness seized a generation of youngsters who knew little of the ANC.

They saw the ideology's practical application in the ascendance of a black government in neighbouring Mozambique. In 1974, the dictatorship in Portugal collapsed, bringing to a halt the independence wars being waged in its African colonies. In Mozambique, the Portuguese withdrew and the Mozambican Liberation Front (FRELIMO, in Portuguese) took power in 1975. It was a stunning event. Here was an example on South Africa's own doorstep of a black nationalist movement that had succeeded. White colonialists had been expelled, black freedom fighters had assumed control. Victory was possible. On black campuses across the country students devoured FRELIMO propaganda. Graffiti of 'Viva FRELIMO!' suddenly appeared on walls. The takeover also captured the imagination of liberal white youths: the Mozambican flag was raised on the central administration building of the University of the Witwatersrand in Johannesburg, where it fluttered briefly before being pulled down by right-wing students.

Unknown to Nomkhitha or Joseph, their two oldest sons had become involved in politics. It seemed inevitable: the high school Rocks and Tsietsi attended, Morris Issacson, was one of the most politically active in the township. Abraham Tiro, a charismatic Black Consciousness leader taught there for a while; he had a profound influence that continued long after his departure. (Tiro was later killed by a letter bomb in Botswana.) The school's principal, although not outwardly an activist, permitted his pupils to form political organizations. (At other schools, more conservative administrators suppressed anything vaguely resembling opposition to the government.)

The boys' political inclinations were as different as their personalities. Rocks embraced Black Consciousness while in high school. But he became disillusioned with the politics of protest; swayed by the writings of American black militants such as Malcolm X and Stokely Carmichael, Rocks concluded that armed struggle was the only way to liberate South Africa. That view was reinforced after he surreptitiously obtained banned literature on the ANC. (The students who had the forbidden books would pass them to Rocks, covered in brown paper to hide the titles, in the lavatory.) Rocks adhered to his conviction after he received a scholarship in 1974 from Joseph's employer and went to study civil engineering at a technical college in Pietersburg, in the north.

There, having realized his parents' dream of a chance at an education, Rocks decided to join the ANC. He knew the organization had a representative in Swaziland. One day, he and a friend rented a car and drove over the border to Mbabane. They managed to meet with the representative, who directed them to people in Johannesburg. Eventually, Rocks made contact with Indres Naidoo, a third-generation member of the ANC who was among the first Umkhonto recruits. In 1963, Indres had been sentenced to ten years' imprisonment for sabotage; on his release in 1973, he was put under house arrest. Still, Indres organized political classes for Rocks and several other young men. The tutorials met for one hour on Saturday afternoons in Dornfontein, a commercial section of Johannesburg. A black woman who ran a large furniture store and was sympathetic to the ANC allowed them to use a back room. Indres demanded strict punctuality from his pupils. The first lesson examined the Freedom Charter; Indres dissected it, clause by clause. The next lesson analysed the alliance between the ANC and the South African Communist Party. Then Indres discussed the Defiance Campaign. And so on, until he had covered the whole modern history of the ANC.

At the same time, Indres was setting up an underground organization to send recruits abroad for military training. He worked with Joe Gqabi, another early Umkhonto volunteer who had also recently been released from prison. Indres would sit on a bench in a downtown park, eating his lunch; Joe, strolling by, casually joined him. There they discussed potential enlistments to their guerrilla army. (The underground group also had an office on Commissioner Street, in the heart of Johannesburg's business district. Ostensibly an insurance company, the site was considered too unsafe to carry on such sensitive conversations.)

Despite Rocks' repeated request to be sent overseas for military instruction, Indres and Joe decided to keep him in the country. They were eager to build cells that would operate within South Africa and wanted Rocks to be a part of those structures. Indres entrusted him with distributing smuggled ANC and South African Communist Party literature. The illicit material had to be photocopied, then delivered to the appropriate people. It was dangerous but vital work. Virtually unknown in the townships, the ANC could not compete with the Black Consciousness movement without disseminating its own propaganda. Indres thought Rocks perfect for the job. From their first meeting, the youth had impressed Indres with his seriousness and keen intellect. Rocks was forever encouraging his fellow recruits to broaden themselves by reading; he particularly recommended the novels of Hemingway, Zola, Gorky and Sinclair because of their social commentary.

Rocks successfully hid his ANC work from Nomkhitha and Joseph. They believed he was busy studying to become an engineer at school in Pietersburg. If Rocks appeared regularly at the house in Soweto on Saturday afternoons, it was because he liked coming home. Only Tsietsi had an inkling of Rock's political involvement, after Rocks began passing pamphlets from the ANC and South African Communist Party to him.

Tsietsi, meanwhile, had become steeped in Black Consciousness ideology. He was drawn to the clubs that sprang up in Soweto under the patronage of the South African Students' Movement (SASM), a Black Consciousness youth organization. They offered an array of cultural activities to the township youngsters; the emphasis on black pride and self-reliance fitted well with Tsietsi's loathing of whites.

He was an eager participant in a meeting in 1975 to form an SASM branch at Morris Issacson. Flyers inviting students to the assembly were distributed throughout the school and the turnout was enormous. Tsietsi, as always, mesmerized the crowd with his oratory; they subsequently elected him president. His was a small branch. Most students were too frightened to join the organization openly; they knew how severely the security police dealt with Black Consciousness proponents on the university campuses. Still, SASM had strong support within the school. At the branch's monthly meeting, its officers usually presented a programme of cultural interest: a Black Consciousness speaker, a poetry reading, a discussion of African literature. The meeting room was always crammed.

As president, Tsietsi cultivated supporters outside the school like Khotso, the boy he had met after the debate at Naledi High School. At the time, Khotso was vehemently against organizations such as SASM; he thought of them as endless debating forums whose discourses could land you in jail. Khotso wanted only to get hold of a gun and overthrow the government. Tsietsi explained that while armed struggle was an inevitable step in the revolution, a political structure was needed before waging war. Patiently, he began schooling Khotso in the ways of Black Consciousness: whites in this country are defining us, Tsietsi explained, and we must begin to define ourselves. We're not 'non-white', we're black. To assist Khotso in his self-discovery, Tsietsi provided reading material: James Baldwin, Malcolm X, Stokely Carmichael. The banned books opened up new worlds for Khotso. He, like many young black South Africans, was profoundly influenced by the civil rights literature from the US.

Khotso and Tsietsi were constantly arguing. Theirs was an intellectual relationship: Khotso read a book, then debated its merits with Tsietsi. (As friends, they also argued the merits of football clubs and certain girls.) By March 1976, Tsietsi had converted Khotso to the SASM camp. He convinced Khotso to recruit other students to the organization. Tsietsi didn't want them as formal, dues-paying members, but as partisans. He believed they were embarking on a quest for psychological liberation.

In fact, they were rushing towards a future that no one, not even the youths in their most fanciful imaginings, could foretell.

CHAPTER THREE

June 16

On 15 June 1976 Mpho returned home from school and found the garden filled with Tsietsi's friends. They were painting with black and red paint on poster boards, bed sheets, lengths of canvas. 'Away With Afrikaans', the banners proclaimed, 'Away With Bantu Education'. Tsietsi and his companions worked quietly; Mpho could feel a muted excitement and tension. He was desperate to know what they were doing. Mpho approached Tsietsi tentatively, constrained by his position as the younger sibling. 'What am I supposed to do?' he finally asked his brother.

'You must go to school tomorrow as usual,' Tsietsi replied. 'Then we'll come and close it.' Mpho was stunned. He could barely believe what he had heard.

Another boy, busily daubing a piece of cardboard, asked Mpho, 'What time do you have assembly?'

'Eight o'clock.'

'Right,' said the boy, 'before you get into the classrooms, we'll be there. You'll be the first school.'

'But you don't know our principal,' Mpho protested.

'Don't worry, you'll see.'

The boy pushed some paint and a piece of canvas over to Mpho. After considering the various slogans painted by the other youths, Mpho selected 'Afrikaans Is For Boers'. He rolled up the canvas when the paint had dried and hid it under his bed. He intended to carry it to school under his arm the next morning. Nomkhitha would think it was a class project. Two girls from next door, who had been watching over the fence, gestured to Mpho. One of them mouthed: What is going on?

Mpho shook his head. He felt the weight of being admitted to his brother's circle. Besides, he still was not exactly certain what was about to transpire.

After a few hours – and before Nomkhitha arrived home – Tsietsi and his friends finished their work. They hurriedly cleaned up the paint, tidied the garden, collected their posters and departed. Tomorrow, Mpho thought as he headed into the house, will surely be a great adventure.

From the slogans on the banners, Mpho discerned there would be some sort of protest against the use of Afrikaans in black schools. It was an issue that had been smouldering for months. The previous year the Nationalist government decreed that, starting at the junior-high level, half of all subjects would be taught in Afrikaans. (The edict attempted to appease the right wing of the party, which feared the ascendancy of English.) This was an insult beyond tolerance to the black students. They were already crammed into wretched classrooms with too few teachers and virtually no textbooks or other supplies. When they left school they had little hope of securing a job that paid a living wage. Their parents seemed unable – or unwilling – to challenge the authorities to improve the children's lot. And now they were being forced to study in a language most did not know.

In the Mashinini family, Mpho and Dee were directly affected by the decree. At the start of the school year, Dee's teacher began teaching *wiskunde*, mathematics, in Afrikaans. It was as though a cloud descended upon Dee: he found himself trying to master the language and the concepts simultaneously. By the time he understood that *vermenigvuldiging* was multiplication, *snelheid* meant velocity, *tyd* was time and *spoed*, speed – the lesson had finished. Dee felt overcome by hopelessness; at this rate, he would never pass his exams.

Other students were similarly despondent. At Orlando West Junior Secondary, the head prefect, Seth Mazibuko, and fellow pupils sent a petition to the inspector of schools. They requested a meeting to discuss the reinstatement of English as the language of instruction. When he refused – the inspector was not about to be summonsed by mere students – Seth and his lieutenants organized a boycott. Students showed up at school but did not attend classes.

Tsietsi visited Seth during the strike. By now, half a dozen other schools had joined Orlando West. SASM leaders seized on this as an issue that could galvanize township youths. They were eager to broaden the boycott, taking it to all the students in Soweto, even those older ones not directly affected by the government edict. Seth agreed to help.

As a kind of test, Seth addressed a meeting of students that Tsietsi organized at Morris Issacson High School. Seth explained the strike, its inception and goals. Tsietsi delivered a fiery discourse on the importance of supporting the youngsters' Afrikaans boycott. Soon enough, he warned, the senior students would be affected as well. Encouraged by the enthusiastic reception, he, Seth and another SASM activist canvassed other schools in Soweto to assess support for a township-wide boycott. About half the high schools and junior secondaries seemed to be with them; the other half appeared hostile because of fears about the security police.

The SASM leaders called a meeting to discuss the Afrikaans issue on June 13 at a community centre in Soweto. Hundreds of students packed the hall, many of them the contacts Tsietsi and Seth had made in polling the various schools. Six people thought to be police informers were asked to leave. Tsietsi proposed staging a mass demonstration to protest against the imposition of Afrikaans on June 16, the day the students were supposed to sit their exams. A ferocious debate ensued: those opposed to the idea argued that the security police would crush them. People might be arrested, hurt, perhaps even killed.

But the march's opponents were no match for Tsietsi. He was at his most impressive in front of an audience: cajoling, gesticulating, pacing the room, insisting that nothing would happen if the demonstration remained non-violent. Khotso Seatlholo, who arrived at the meeting late, could feel the sentiment in the room turning in his friend's favour. Tsietsi roused the crowd with quotes from great works of literature, his favourite being Tennyson's poem, 'The Charge of the Light Brigade':

When can their glory fade?
O the wild charge they made!
　All the world wonder'd.
Honour the charge they made!
Honour the Light Brigade,
　Noble six hundred!

The proposal was passed unanimously. The students nomi-
nated two delegates from each school to form an Action
Committee, headed by Tsietsi and Seth. They adjourned the
gathering with a decision to work out the actual details at a
meeting on the day before the demonstration. Afterwards, Tsietsi
and a few members of the Action Committee knocked on the
door of Duma Ndlovu, a young journalist who worked on a
black newspaper, *The World*. Duma wrote a column on school
sports; his presence at a match generated much excitement
among the youths, for it meant they would read about their
school in the paper the next day. He knew many of the more
prominent students, including Tsietsi who, in Duma's mind,
stood out from his peers for his assertiveness. Tsietsi wasted
little time with formalities. 'Something big is going to happen
on Wednesday,' he said to Duma. 'Be sure to be in Soweto.'
　'What?'
　'We can't tell you, just be sure to be in Soweto.'
　'Look, I can't get my editor to put me on a story if I can't
tell him what it is.'
　'Tell him it's going to be big. And be there.'
　Over the next two days, the Action Committee delegates
fanned out through the township, visiting the various high
schools and junior secondaries. Their mission was to inform
students of the impending march and rally support. Draw up
placards in secret, Tsietsi's representatives urged the astonished
pupils. Don't tell your parents. During the march, remain disciplined. Follow the instructions of your school leaders. Above
all, do not be afraid.
　Tsietsi convened the final planning meeting in the afternoon
on June 15. He and the other Action Committee members
devised a formula for the march: students from about a dozen

schools would lead the demonstration, picking up youths from other institutions (mostly junior secondaries) along the way. Action Committee members would stay to the right of the marchers, so they could communicate with one another. Each school had a set hour of departure, designed to allow the participants to converge on the Orlando West area from various parts of Soweto at about the same time. There they would link up with students from Orlando West High School and its junior secondary, and continue on to a stadium for a mass rally. Satisfied with the scheme, Tsietsi left his co-conspirators with one last caveat: no violence.

That night Joseph and Nomkhitha prepared for bed as usual. If the house seemed quiet, it was because Tsietsi had yet to return home. Nomkhitha thought about his absence and realized she had not seen much of him lately; he was probably at the high school, 'cross-nighting' with his friends. She would speak to him about it tomorrow after work.

June 16 dawned a bitterly cold winter's day. Tsietsi was already at Morris Issacson when Murphy Morobe, another member of the Action Committee, arrived at the school. He and Tsietsi huddled in a corner of the schoolyard to review last-minute details. Assembly wouldn't start for another thirty minutes, but the undercurrent of excitement among the students was palpable. 'The main thing', Tsietsi whispered to Murphy, 'is not to provoke the police. We have to keep telling everyone to be disciplined, that we're marching to a particular place and then we'll disperse.'

At eight o'clock, as was the custom at Morris Issacson, the deputy principal called the students to order in the yard and led them in morning prayers. Usually he would have enumerated the day's activities, then dismissed the students for class. Instead, as if on cue, the youths held up posters and unfurled banners denouncing the use of Afrikaans. Tsietsi jumped up, exclaiming, 'We are marching!' Someone threw open the gates to the school and Tsietsi led hundreds of youths, most of the student body, out of the yard, shouting '*Amandla*!' (Power!) and thrusting his fist in the air in the black power salute. '*Ngawethu*!' (It is ours!) screamed the excited youngsters in response, a singing, chanting river of humanity that flowed towards Thesele Junior Secondary, about a half a mile down the road.

Mpho, meanwhile, had arrived early at Thesele to stow his banner under his desk where he usually kept his things. He had not brought his textbooks; Tsietsi and his friends said they would close Thesele before classes started. Mpho's fellow students encircled him. They wanted to know what he had under his arm, and where were his books? Mpho, grinning with self-importance, said nothing. He hurried into his classroom, hid the banner and ran back to the schoolyard.

The gates closed at eight o'clock and the students arranged themselves in the yard according to classes. A teacher intoned a prayer. Then the principal, a no-nonsense sort of man, delivered the usual admonishments about arriving late to school and not completing homework. Mpho barely noticed his words; distraught, he was straining to hear any unusual noise or disturbance. The principal seemed about to conclude his remarks and dispatch the students to their classes. Mpho would be caught with no books – a very serious offence, punishable by being sent to the principal's office.

Suddenly, Mpho heard what sounded like faint singing in the distance. The noise became progressively louder. By now, the principal had heard it, too. He went to the gates to investigate, warning the assembled youngsters not to break ranks. Before he could reach them, the gates were thrown open and a wave of students, identifiably from Morris Issacson in their blue-and-gold jackets, surged into the schoolyard.

The orderly assembly dissolved into chaos. The Morris Issacson youths were everywhere, brandishing their placards, yelling at the Thesele students to put down their books, urging them to march to Orlando West. Mpho watched as Tsietsi and his friends followed the principal into his office; the school's siren sounded soon after in an attempt to restore calm. Mpho suddenly found himself organizing a group of his friends to march. After all, had he not helped to make the banners and placards the Morris Issacson students were carrying? And was he not the brother of the student who, at this very moment, was telling the principal – the principal! – that they were shutting down the school? Mpho dashed inside to his classroom and grabbed his banner; racing back to the schoolyard, he unfurled it to the admiring gasps of his friends. Cougar, who also attended Thesele, stood by his side.

Tsietsi emerged from the school and addressed the crowd from a ledge where the principal had stood during assembly. 'Students of Soweto,' Tsietsi shouted, 'we're tired of what is happening. We must take action against the white regime. We're joining the other schools that are on strike. We're closing down schools to show these Boers that we will not accept Afrikaans. We're going to say: away with Afrikaans, away with Bantu education. But we need discipline. We will probably meet the police. But there's to be no stone throwing, no provocation. Please remain disciplined.'

The youngsters roared their approval; they had never heard anything like this articulated publicly. Tsietsi led the mass of pupils out of the schoolyard towards the old Roodepoort road, a large thoroughfare that bisected much of Soweto. As they marched, the youngsters sang a haunting, dirge-like protest song from the 1950s: *Senzeni na? Senzeni na?* What have we done? Oh, what have we done? (What is our crime?) To Murphy Morobe, helping to shepherd the students along, the scene evoked the feeling of exhilaration he had experienced as a child at Christmas.

The marchers had to pass a primary school to arrive at their next destination, Itshepeng Junior Secondary. (Before the march, Tsietsi and the Action Committee members had agreed to exclude the younger children.) Ten-year-old Tshepiso was in the schoolyard, helping to pick up litter, when he heard a deafening noise. A huge group of students from Mpho's and Tsietsi's schools suddenly appeared on the road, singing and waving banners. Tshepiso watched them pass, open-mouthed; he had never seen so many people in his life. A teacher who was supervising them told the youngsters sharply to go inside to class. Tshepiso could not stop thinking about the mass of students all morning, wondering if his brothers were among them.

As the demonstration reached Itshepeng, pupils ran to the windows and rushed out of the doors, drawn by the singing. Dee was amazed at the sudden appearance of hundreds of students, jumping about and carrying signs. He was even more astonished to see Tsietsi at the head of all these youths; Dee had not been privy to the activity in his house during the previous days. He watched as Tsietsi directed the younger pupils to go home and urged the older ones to join the march. Then he saw Mpho, who was carrying a banner. Mpho explained everything to Dee. When Tsietsi ordered the students, after about half an hour, to leave the school grounds, Dee, Mpho and Cougar marched out together.

The numbers of youngsters swelled as the march progressed towards Orlando West. Each time they passed another school, Tsietsi and his lieutenants added those students to the demonstration. Dee began noticing more policemen on the streets. They were only lightly armed and seemed unsure of what to do. Emboldened, the students began to chant in Zulu in a kind of staccato rhythm: *Siyabasaba na? Siyabasaba na?* (Are we afraid of them? Are we are afraid of them?) Dee felt an incredible excitement. For the first time in his life, blacks were protesting on the streets of Soweto. Propelled by the rhythm of their songs, united in their purpose, each seemed a link in an unbreakable chain.

Tsietsi led the marchers through the Dube section of Soweto. The Action Committee members walked along the right-hand side of the road, keeping the students to the left. Although the organizers had mapped out the general direction of the trek from Morris Issacson, Tsietsi determined the exact route as it advanced. He rode up and down the line of demonstrators in a car driven by a journalist. Indicating to his lieutenants the course they must take, he tried to keep to side streets to avoid traffic and the greatest concentration of police. The latter had been taken by surprise and made only feeble attempts to stop the march.

As the demonstrators neared a vocational training centre, they encountered car driven by a white woman. Not knowing of the march, she had tried, as usual, to go to her government job in the township. The terrified woman suddenly found herself engulfed by chanting, singing, jostling youngsters. Tsietsi exhorted them to make way for her. The sea of students parted – and the car sped away to safety.

Tsietsi occasionally stopped alongside the marchers to deliver reports of police movements. As they drew closer to Orlando West, he halted more frequently to address the youths and plead for calm. 'Please be disciplined,' Tsietsi urged them. 'Do not provoke the police. Do not throw stones. If the police confront you, show them the peace sign.' At other times, though, Tsietsi seemed as caught up in the moment as the most excited of the youngsters. Duma Ndlovu, the journalist, came upon him leading a chant. 'Who do you see when you see Tsietsi?' he yelled at the crowd.

'We see a hero when we see Tsietsi!' the students roared.

'Who do you see when you see [Prime Minister John] Vorster?'

'We see a dog when we see Vorster!'

By the time the marchers reached Orlando West Junior Secondary later in the morning, they numbered in the thousands. Seth Mazibuko, the school's head prefect and vice-chairman of the Action Committee, awaited them in the schoolyard on a hill above the road. He and his fellow students had gathered at assembly earlier in the morning; instead of the usual programme, they had sung 'Nkosi Sikelel' iAfrika' (God Bless Africa), the lovely, lilting hymn that was a national anthem throughout the continent. Then they shut the school gates. Seth walked down the hill to confer with Tsietsi on the next move. The Orlando West students were supposed to leave the school to join the demonstration; Tsietsi would then make a speech, pledging solidarity with the students in their boycott and calling on the government to scrap the Afrikaans requirement.

Suddenly, police vans and cars appeared. Having failed in their earlier attempts to quell the march, the security officials now meant to finish with it completely. About fifty policemen, some armed with guns, others with tear gas canisters, faced the students. Many of the men held the leads of German shepherd dogs. The youths continued to sing, wave their placards, flash peace signs at the policemen. The tension was palpable. 'My

God, the police are going to do a Sharpeville on us,' gasped a friend standing next to Murphy Morobe. Tsietsi, Seth and another activist tried to approach the security officers to speak with them. At that moment, the officers let loose one of the snarling Alsatians. The dog tore into the crowd. Terrified, the youngsters picked up stones and threw them at the animal. The police fired tear gas canisters; now the students turned their stones on the security men.

Then the police began shooting.

Screaming youngsters fled in every direction. Some stopped to throw stones at the police who answered with seemingly indiscriminate volleys aimed into the crowd. Murphy heard bullets whizzing by his head. Out of the pandemonium, a youth emerged carrying the lifeless body of twelve-year-old Zolile Hector Pieterson. Zolile's sister ran beside him, her face etched in grief, her hands upraised in horror. Samuel Nzima, a black photographer, captured the tableau on film. The picture would be seen around the world and come to symbolize the brutality of the South African regime.

Fearing that the march was turning into a massacre, Tsietsi clambered on top of an old bulldozer on the roadside and tried to get the youngsters to disperse. People have been shot, he shouted hoarsely. Let us not give the government any more victims. The best thing to do is go home and regroup. The struggle has only just begun.

The youths, outraged by the police actions, responded to Tsietsi's exhortations by exploding in a rampage as they retreated. Using stolen petrol and paraffin, they began setting fire to anything in their path that smacked of government authority. The administrative offices of the West Rand Administration Board (WRAB), post offices, government-owned beer halls and bottle stores – all were attacked. The furious students overturned vehicles from the hated WRAB and set them on fire. Two WRAB employees – a white official and a black policeman – were assaulted and killed.

Amid the chaos, Seth ran to the house of Winnie Mandela, the wife of the jailed ANC leader, Nelson Mandela. She was pulling out of her driveway in her Volkswagen and stopped to open the door for Seth. As they drove off, he looked around for Tsietsi, but in vain. Murphy also lost Tsietsi in the maelstrom. He had tried, unsuccessfully, to get to Baragwanath Hospital in a journalist's car to attend the wounded. Navigating his way back to Orlando West, Murphy saw no sign of his friend – only a township engulfed in flames.

Mpho, further down the line of demonstrators, attempted to run in the direction of home at the first sound of gunfire: jumping fences, dodging the police cars that suddenly were on every corner, ducking at the sound of their bullets. He sought refuge for a while in a house that was crammed with frightened students. The owner kept watch through a crack in a window curtain. When the street seemed clear of danger, Mpho dashed out and resumed hurdling fences through back-yards. He wanted to avoid the main roads, which the police were now patrolling in great numbers.

In Dube, Mpho jogged past an overturned dairy truck lying in the middle of the street; there was milk, cheese and fruit juice all over the road. He stopped long enough to heave a stone through the vehicle's windscreen. Rarely in his sixteen years had Mpho experienced anything so satisfying: the truck clearly came from a white-owned establishment in Johannesburg. This was his chance, finally, to strike back at white power.

Dee, meanwhile, had become immobilized when he heard the shots. In the middle of the stampede he stayed rooted to the ground. Everywhere Dee looked, children were screaming, running, falling down, bleeding. He watched as one boy with a shattered leg tried to flee. Holding his injured limb, the youngster hobbled a few steps, collapsed in the dirt, pulled himself upright, staggered a bit, toppled again. Dee saw all this through a kind of slow-motion haze.

The tear gas pulled him out of his trance. Dee began to run, along with the other panic-stricken children, desperate to escape the choking chemicals. He found himself squeezing into a latrine in someone's back-yard. Six other youngsters were already hiding in the tiny, corrugated-iron hut. Dee crouched in the darkness, listening to the gunfire; he could not get the picture of bleeding bodies being loaded into cars out of his head. His fellow fugitives tried to remain silent as the police swarmed about the area. But the tear gas made them cough; one youth vomited. After about ten minutes, unable to withstand the fear and the stench, the youths burst out of the enclosure.

Two women in a nearby house motioned them indoors. They brought the children a bucket of water to wash the gas from their eyes. And they gave them glasses of milk to clear their throats and settle their stomachs. The students cowered in the house. Dee was terrified; he had no idea what to do. His only thought was to try to get back to his home. He felt he would be safer in his own neighbourhood, on his own turf.

He left the women's house after about an hour and set off towards the Jabavu section of Soweto and home. Like Mpho, he took a long, circuitous route to avoid the police: running and hiding in backyards, avoiding open fields, crossing to areas with large concentrations of houses so he could disappear among them. Dee traversed the township in a state of disbelief. Everywhere he saw municipal offices on fire; shops owned by Chinese merchants – much hated by the blacks – burning; children, giddy with their new-found power, demanding bread, drinks, water from scared storeowners. To Dee's mind, the world had turned upside-down.

Back at Molaetsa Primary, Tshepiso began hearing helicopters hovering overhead. The teacher tried to keep him and his classmates in their seats, but to no avail; the curious children bolted outside. There, in the distance, they saw the burning buildings and vehicles. Tshepiso decided something was terribly wrong. He set off to find his younger brothers, China (as Sechaba was called) and Dichaba, both of whom attended Molaetsa. Dismayed at discovering their rooms empty, Tshepiso raced from class to class; by the time he found them, the helicopters had begun dropping canisters of tear gas nearby. Teachers were screaming, children crying; the yard was in chaos. Tshepiso grabbed his brothers' hands and fled the school.

At first he took the usual route home, but large numbers of youths passed him going in the opposite direction. They were clearly being pursued; Tshepiso could see the fear on their faces. He decided to turn around and follow them. Now Tshepiso was running away from his house, China on one side, Dichaba on the other. He gripped his brothers' hands so tightly he virtually dragged them along the street. The walk to their house usually took about twenty minutes, but on that day they wouldn't arrive for three hours. Each route Tshepiso chose seemed to lead him into crowds of people trying to go the other way, away from the police and guns and tear gas. He kept having to double back, retrace his steps. All Tshepiso wanted was to go home; he and his brothers would be safe there.

As people passed them, some shouted at the three boys to discard their school uniforms. The police were shooting at anyone who even vaguely resembled a student. The afternoon had warmed slightly, so Tshepiso made China and Dichaba stop briefly to shed their jerseys and white shirts and stuff them into their school bags. Then they resumed their race homeward.

When the three youngsters reached their neighbourhood, near Morris Issacson High School, it resembled a war zone. Police cars careened through the streets, shooting at youngsters. Military helicopters were dropping canisters of tear gas. Tshepiso mistook them for explosives; he thought the army was bombing the township. Terrified, he huddled with his brothers behind some boulders on the 'mountain', the sloping field opposite their house. 'Now when I tell you to go,' Tshepiso whispered to them, 'you must make a dash for it.' He waited until the area seemed clear of police, then leaped up and ran across the road, China and Dichaba in tow. Black smoke curled upwards from Morris Issacson.

Dee returned soon after Tshepiso. He felt safer inside the house, but was too excited to remain for long. Dee told Tshepiso he was going to the 'mountain'; from the top, he had a sweeping view down to the end of the road. And the boulders afforded him protection. Dee found several other children already there, sheltering behind the massive rocks. They took turns popping out from behind the boulders, shaking their fists at the policemen on the street, then jumping back to safety. Not everyone was fast enough: Dee helped three boys to extract birdshot from their limbs with a knife and paraffin.

As night fell, Dee grew cold on the 'mountain'. He and his

friends regrouped on a tarred road that ran behind his house. From there, outlined against the sky in the waning half-light, Dee could see the smouldering remains of the Chinese shops. He knew he should return home, but was reluctant to part with the day. He wanted the excitement and the extraordinary feeling of power to continue indefinitely. Dee watched convoys of police vans snaking towards other parts of the township. Finally, shivering and hungry, he bade his fellow combatants farewell and headed for his house.

Nomkhitha was at work in Johannesburg when she heard about the rioting on the radio. She dismissed it as ordinary, criminal-type violence, the kind that plagued the townships. Then suddenly her boss sent the workers home early: Soweto is burning, she said. Nomkhitha hurried to her train. As it pulled into Soweto's Mzimhlope Station, Nomkhitha and the other passengers exclaimed in amazement at the smoking hulks of cars, burned-out bottle stores, scenes of looting. They had never seen anything like it. Nomkhitha rushed home, worried about the children.

Joseph arrived just after Nomkhitha, deeply shaken by the destruction he had seen. Mpho had also returned, and the family gathered in the living room to talk. The children excitedly told their parents of the demonstration, of the police attack, of their response, of Tsietsi's role in the day's events. Nomkhitha and Joseph were astounded. How could youngsters have marched so great a distance? How could they have had the courage to fight the police? How did Tsietsi come to be so involved? 'Why Tsietsi?' Joseph kept murmuring. 'Why Tsietsi?' The march seemed the height of folly to Joseph; surely the family would now feel the full wrath of the authorities.

Nomkhitha too was distressed. She interrogated Dee and Mpho about their involvement, convinced they had deceived her. The two boys insisted they had merely got swept up in the moment; Tsietsi was the leader and organizer. That fact only caused Nomkhitha more anguish. She could not understand why Tsietsi, her favourite, had not confided in her. Nomkhitha wondered what would become of him now. How would he eat and where would he sleep?

The children talked among themselves late into the night, long after their bemused parents had retired to their bedroom. At one point they heard a deep rumble of heavy machinery on the tarred road. The government was deploying 'hippos', armoured personnel carriers which had been designed to withstand the blasts of land mines in war zones such as Namibia and Rhodesia. The noise terrified Tshepiso, who lay motionless among his brothers. He could not stop worrying about Tsietsi. You must not come home, Tshepiso whispered to the darkness. Run away and hide, or you will be caught.

Tsietsi was not coming home; he would not spend another night in his parents' house. Sometime around midnight, he and a fellow student knocked on the door of Drake Koka's home in Soweto's Dube section. Drake, a small, pixie-like man with a round face and goatee, was a major figure in the Black Consciousness movement and a union activist. 'We need your help,' said Tsietsi, who had been on the run since the morning's shootings. 'You have to teach us. You'll be our Godfather, like in the movie.'

By now, the police had killed at least twenty-five children and injured 200 others. Large swathes of Soweto lay in ruins. South Africa, and the Mashinini family, would never be the same.

CHAPTER FOUR

The Children

The rioting in Soweto continued for two more days. Battles raged throughout the township: bands of angry youths set fire to government buildings, throwing stones and bottles at the assembled police. It spread to central Johannesburg when about 300 white students at the University of the Witwatersrand marched from the campus to protest against the indiscriminate killing of schoolchildren in Soweto. Several hundred black workers joined in the demonstration. About a hundred white vigilantes, brandishing knives, metal pipes and clubs, attacked the demonstrators; arriving at the scene, a group of security officers beat the marchers with batons.

Soweto's near-anarchy, and the government's response, stunned South Africans. Not since the massacre at Sharpeville in 1960 had they witnessed anything of this magnitude. Editorials in the English-language press, the voice of the white opposition, blamed the Nationalist government for ignoring an obviously volatile situation. They demanded an immediate accession to the students' demands. Some black newspapers called for an end to apartheid itself.

But the Nationalists – at least publicly – professed to be as shocked as anyone. The Minister of Justice and Police, James Kruger, told members of Parliament that the government did 'not expect anything like this to happen'; agitators, he said, were to blame. To quell the unrest, the government sent 1,500 police into Soweto and effectively sealed off the township. Armed with automatic rifles and other guns, the security men appeared to shoot randomly into the crowds of black youngsters; often, they simply fired from their moving vehicles. The police also shot at people out of the helicopters that dropped tear gas on the township.

Their tactics worked. By the end of the third day, the fighting began to abate. Nearly 200 people had died; thousands of others were wounded. One hundred and thirty-nine buildings and 143 vehicles, many of them belonging to the police, had been demolished or wrecked. But the uprising was hardly finished. Like a forest fire that sputters and dies, only to re-ignite elsewhere, violence erupted in countless other townships across the country.

In Soweto, the police started to raid the Mashininis' home at night, ostensibly looking for Tsietsi. The first raid was terrifying. The police came at about two o'clock in the morning, blocking off the surrounding streets with their 'hippos'. Nomkhitha and Joseph awoke to a deafening pounding on the door; torches shone in every window, illuminating the policemen with their guns drawn. They screamed in Afrikaans to open the door. Joseph let them in and about a dozen security men, black and white, rampaged through the house, shining their lights in the eyes of the sleep-dazed children, pawing through wardrobes, peering under beds and behind the stove, tearing apart furnishings in their search. A white officer demanded to see Tsietsi.

'He isn't here, he never came home,' Nomkhitha stammered, drawing a blanket around her nightgown.

'Where is he staying?'

'We don't know.'

Disgruntled, the policemen stormed out of the house. Joseph, Nomkhitha and the children stood silently around the dining-room table, trying to calm their pounding hearts; the littlest ones shivered from the cold and fear. Nomkhitha put the younger children back into bed. Then she, Joseph and the others began tidying up the chaos the police had left in their wake. They had just finished and were drifting off to sleep when they heard a thunderous noise: torches shone in every window, guns appeared silhouetted against the light, men yelled in Afrikaans that they were going to kick in the door. Joseph raced from his bed to unlock the bolt. And another raid began.

From that time forward, night after night, the police conducted raids on the Mashinini home. Often, they came several times within the span of a few hours. They inflicted a kind of psychological terror upon the family, especially on the youngest members. As the last rays of sunlight disappeared and darkness descended on the township, some of the younger children would start asking Nomkhitha, 'Will the police come tonight? Will the police come tonight?' They took to waking at every noise, running to their parents' bed. At the first hint of the approaching 'hippos', the youngsters roused everyone; the family was usually waiting for the police when they came.

Eventually, Nomkhitha's exhaustion and fury at having her home violated overpowered her fear. 'Get out of my bedroom!' she shrieked at the policemen busy dumping the contents of her dresser on the floor. 'How dare you touch my things!' Once, she began scolding the security men about their weapons. 'I will not answer your questions if you have all these big guns in my house. Get out with these guns, they are frightening my children, they can't sleep at night.' Surprisingly, the policemen complied by putting the larger weapons outside in their cars; the commanding officer explained to Joseph they had to keep their sidearms for their own protection.

On another occasion, Nomkhitha refused to respond to their interrogation until they sat down on chairs. 'It's not my culture!' she shouted at one group. 'Take seats if you want to talk to me. Take seats!' Nomkhitha yelled at the policemen in Xhosa and English; they swore back at her in Afrikaans, muttering about this *kaffir* bitch who gives birth to terrorists. The adversaries made for a striking scene, exchanging insults in mutually unintelligible languages in the dead of night.

Nomkhitha's stridency drove Joseph mad. In contrast to his wife, Joseph was calm, polite, careful not to do anything to upset the intruders. After the police left, Joseph would beseech Nomkhitha not to provoke them; he feared the security officers might do something horrible because of her belligerence. Nomkhitha retorted that he was too passive. But her outbursts frightened the children too. Tshepiso would clamp his hands over his ears to shut out the exchanges between his mother and the policemen, repeating to himself: I wish she would be quiet, I wish she would be quiet.

Even after the security officers withdrew, the Mashinini house remained under constant surveillance. A Volkswagen Beetle was always parked, rather conspicuously, across the street; a second one was stationed up the road. Nonetheless, Tsietsi managed to sneak home every few days. He would furtively approach the back of his family's lot and peer through the leaves that covered the fence. If no policemen were visible, he would give a high-pitched whistle that his siblings recognized. The noise brought them racing to the yard. Tsietsi sent one of them to the front as a lookout, while the others eagerly plied him with questions about his activities. He recounted stories of his escapades and taught the youngsters revolutionary slogans. '*Amandla!*' they chanted, their clenched fists punching the air, 'Black Power!' If he were feeling particularly bold, Tsietsi entered the house to have a bath, change his clothes, eat a meal – all the while singing anti-apartheid songs. Sometimes he stayed for as long as an hour. Then Tsietsi would creep back to the fence, check the area for 'hippos', and disappear into the labyrinth of Soweto's back-yards.

Nomkhitha eagerly awaited Tsietsi's visits; they allowed her to know that he was alive. But she also feared for his safety every minute he spent at home. With all the raids and surveillance, the police were bound to find Tsietsi in the house one day. Nomkhitha could not understand why they kept missing him. She began to suspect they were trailing Tsietsi, hoping he would lead them to fellow student leaders. Or perhaps the black policemen, who often watched the house without their white commanding officer, secretly sympathized with the uprising.

Although the police did not catch Tsietsi, they almost captured Rocks. He had returned to Soweto when his college closed a few days after the uprising began. Rocks slept at home on the first night; after experiencing the police raids, he decided it would be safer to stay with friends. He went back to the house at the end of the week to retrieve his luggage, which he had posted to himself. Rocks was in the bedroom, examining the banned

literature that filled the suitcase and waiting for Tshepiso to bring
him a sandwich from a nearby café, when the police surrounded
the house. Rocks tried to flee through the back door, but to no
avail: policemen, their guns drawn, were everywhere.

Rocks opened the door. The police swarmed into the room;
an officer ordered Rocks to produce his pass book. 'Where is
Tsietsi?' he demanded. 'Where does he sleep?'

'I really don't know, I've just got back from college,' Rocks
answered, speaking rapidly. 'Look, here's my ID, here's my suitcase, you can see where it was sent from. I have no idea where
Tsietsi is.'

The officer ordered his men to search the house; one of them
looked at the labels on the closed suitcase without bothering to
open it. The policemen marched Rocks outside, presumably to
take him away for interrogation. By then, a mass of youths
from the neighbourhood had gathered around the patrol cars.
Perhaps concerned about causing yet another violent incident,
the officer told Rocks to report to a particular room at police
headquarters the next day. As the security men drove away,
Tshepiso appeared with Rocks' food. Unnerved by the encounter,
Rocks told Tshepiso to eat the sandwich; he grabbed his suitcase and left.

For the first weeks after the uprising, Tsietsi and his fellow
activists helped with the burials of the children who had been
killed by the police. This was no easy task. The government
refused to publish a list of the dead; the Action Committee
members had to rely on rumours of which families had been
affected and where they resided. The student leaders were helped
by the Black Parents' Association, a newly formed group of
Soweto professionals. The BPA got undertakers to donate coffins
to the grieving families and the taxi association to provide, at
no cost, 700 taxis for transportation to the funerals. Tsietsi
spent his days traversing Soweto with Winnie Mandela, a
prominent figure in the BPA.

Around this time, the few representatives of the exiled liberation organizations in South Africa attempted to recruit Tsietsi

and other members of the Action Committee. Tsietsi debated with Khotso Seatlholo the merits of the African National Congress and the Pan Africanist Congress, and rejected them both. Tsietsi sensed the groups were trying to steal the students' glory and take credit for the uprising. 'Where have these guys been all these years?' he asked Khotso. Tsietsi was most disturbed by the ANC's Freedom Charter; he could not accept the idea that the country belonged to everyone who lived there. Whites, he believed, tended to impose themselves and their vision on the fight for liberation. It was not for them to tell blacks how to conduct their struggle.

Tsietsi preferred the advice of veterans like Drake Koka, who had remained in the country and assimilated the militancy of the Black Consciousness movement. Besides being a leader in the movement, Drake had the additional allure of having organized an independent black trade union. Tsietsi and some of his colleagues met with Drake late on Wednesday nights in a house in Dube. They christened it 'The House of Exile', after a Jimmy Cliff song: the conspirators anticipated they would soon be in exile because of their activities. Drake discussed political theory and strategy with his young disciples. He bombarded them with basic questions: What are you going to do next? Whom are you going to mobilize? What kind of pamphlets will you produce? Which people will you target?

The youngsters differed from the activists of the 1950s in their restless eagerness. Nelson Mandela's generation had been willing to work, slowly and methodically, towards their goals. By contrast, Tsietsi and his counterparts were impatient to do things that seemed rash and immature; the victories in Mozambique and Angola dazzled the youths, at times clouding their judgement. They often clashed with their mentor. Still, Tsietsi struck Drake as extraordinary, possessing a fearless nature and charisma which, in Drake's view, were the essence of leadership.

The student activists understood they had a unique opportunity. After toiling for years to build a following, a single event had suddenly engaged Soweto's youngsters. Now they had to devise a way to tap that politicization. Drake and other, more experienced, government opponents pressed the students to think beyond the narrow issue of Afrikaans instruction. A sustainable revolt needed to embrace a broad range of grievances; it should also attempt to involve adults.

As a first step, the Action Committee members decided to enlarge their group to include representatives from every secondary and junior secondary institution in Soweto. Tsietsi and his colleagues traversed the township after classes resumed at the end of July, urging students to send delegates from each school to a meeting at Morris Issacson High School on August 2. They also exhorted youngsters to return to classes, which many were still boycotting; school was the only place in which everyone could be organized.

Dozens of students appeared at Morris Issacson on the appointed day, dressed in their respective uniforms. (The school's principal sympathized with the uprising and turned a blind eye to their presence.) Tsietsi presided over the meeting. Two students from each of the township's forty secondary schools were elected as representatives. Tsietsi retained his position of chairman; Murphy Morobe became the vice-chairman, replacing Seth Mazibuko, who had been detained after June 16. During a break in the proceedings, the journalist Duma Ndlovu sought out Tsietsi and a few of his colleagues. 'What do I call you guys now?' he asked. After some discussion, Duma dubbed them the Soweto Students' Representative Council; the group's new title, along with the photograph he took of Tsietsi, arms upraised in triumph, appeared in Duma's story the next day.

When the meeting resumed, Tsietsi launched into a forceful argument for organizing a march into town and a general strike. The two protests had been planned in advance by the old Action Committee at the urging of Drake Koka and others. Tsietsi told the representatives that the students would march to the security police headquarters in Johannesburg on August 4 to demand the release of the detainees. If we take our demonstration into town where there are lots of whites, Tsietsi asserted, the police will be loath to shoot so readily.

Students would involve their parents by convincing them to stay away from work for three days, beginning on August 4.

The strike was intended to show support for the children's demands. The school representatives peppered Tsietsi with questions about the stay-away; with little knowledge of the ANC's protest campaigns of the 1950s, they were incredulous. Tsietsi explained: We don't have guns, but we have economic power. If our parents don't go to work for even a half-day, think of how much white South Africa could lose. If we hurt the capitalists, those capitalists are going to start talking to the government. And the government will have to address our demands.

The representatives agreed to both proposals. They also decided that the Black Parents' Association would present a list of demands about Bantu education, on their behalf, to the government. The meeting adjourned on a buoyant note: everyone was eager to begin the protests again. Mpho, who had been elected as a representative of his school, was preparing to leave the hall when Tsietsi stopped him. 'Are you sure you know what you're doing?' Tsietsi asked softly. Mpho nodded. 'You know, if I had my way, you wouldn't be here,' Tsietsi continued. Mpho nodded again, thrilled at his brother's concern. Tsietsi enquired about Joseph and Nomkhitha and the raids on the house until a group of admirers engulfed him, cutting off the brothers and ending their conversation.

Tsietsi and his colleagues spent the next two days working furiously to organize the protests. Word quickly spread among students of the impending march. But the Soweto Students' Representative Council (or SSRC, as it came to be known) wanted the youngsters to give their parents pamphlets about the stay-away. The activists used various sources to produce the literature, Drake Koka among them. Drake found a young printer in Johannesburg who sympathized with the uprising and convinced him it was his duty to help.

He met the printer at his building at midnight. After paying the watchman a small bribe to gain entry, the two conspirators worked almost until dawn. Drake sent the printer home to the township in a taxi; he did not want the young man to risk being caught in Drake's car with the illegal literature. Drake stuffed the pamphlets into three boxes, which he placed on the back seat of his Volkswagen Beetle. He planned to leave them at an agreed site, to be retrieved and distributed by his young protégés. On the front passenger seat, Drake put a large birthday cake for his daughter's party in the afternoon. Then he started for Soweto.

A policeman stopped him at a roadblock on the outskirts of the township. Drake immediately hopped out of the car and opened the boot, which was empty. 'Ah, you know what to do!' the policeman said in Afrikaans.

'Yes, *baas*,' Drake replied, playing the meek African. 'I want to help as much as possible. Oh, these *tsotsis*, they're doing such terrible things.'

Pleased, the policeman strolled around the Beetle and saw the cake sitting on the front seat. 'Is it someone's birthday then?'

'Yes, *baas*, my little girl. And we would be honoured if you could come around and join us for a cup of tea this afternoon.'

Seeming more pleased, the officer declined. He told Drake he could go – without bothering to examine the contents of the boxes on the back seat. Drake jumped into the car and drove off, sweat pouring down his back.

On the morning of August 4, before daylight, thousands of youngsters descended on Soweto's railway stations. They posted themselves at the entrances, armed with placards that read *Azikhwelwa!* – We won't ride. (The slogan came from the protest campaigns of the 1940s and 1950s; students plucked it from a banned book recounting the history of the anti-apartheid struggle.) Those adults who tried to push their way into the stations were assaulted by the youths, sometimes with stones. Commuters in vehicles fared little better: the students erected roadblocks at the edge of the township, stopping cars that tried to pass and threatening their drivers.

The SSRC's march began later in the morning. The plan was much the same as that of June 16, with older students setting off from their respective schools and gathering others along the way. Tsietsi led the group from Morris Issacson. This time, the demonstrators brandished placards of a different sort: 'Release the Detained Students' they demanded; and 'It Happened In Mozambique, It Can Happen Here'. The change reflected an evolution from protesting against forced Afrikaans instruction to opposing the political system itself. Indeed, the government had relented on the language issue when schools reopened in July, but the uprising had, by now, progressed too far. And, in contrast with June 16, this time thousands of adults who had not gone to work joined the young demonstrators. An estimated 15,000 people converged on a main road leading out of Soweto to march into town; they were a disciplined group, flashing peace signs at policemen who lined the streets and calling out to black security officers to join them.

A barricade of 'hippos' stopped the marchers near the New Canada railway station at the north-eastern edge of the township. Using loudhailers, the police instructed the demonstrators to return home; when they tried to advance, the police began lobbing tear gas into the crowd. The marchers stopped and regrouped. With shouts of 'Peace!' and 'We only want our brothers who are in prison!' they again attempted to continue along the road. Now the police opened up with large quantities of tear gas, chasing the marchers from the area. Incensed, the youngsters retaliated by burning down the houses of black policemen, attacking other buildings and destroying vehicles. Soweto was alight once again.

The violence continued for several days; Tsietsi explained the youths' actions in a lengthy interview in *The World* newspaper. 'The students felt they had had enough,' he said, 'not only of the system of oppression at school, but of the system of this country – the way people are ruled, the way the laws are made by the White minority and all that. Students had had enough of what was being given to them by the White man, our parents and our teachers . . . What the people of today, especially the White people, should realize is that the student of today is not saying the people must be free, but the people will be free. I believe the time is near when people will be free.'

Despite the failure of the marchers to gain entry to Johannesburg, the SSRC leaders were encouraged by the protests, especially the stay-away. They saw the latter as having great potential to damage the government. Tsietsi and his colleagues immediately began planning for another strike later in the month; the more workers they could draw in, the more

84

successful it would be. They found the preparations difficult. For reasons of security, the SSRC leadership led a kind of nocturnal existence, working from late in the afternoon until the early hours of the morning. Tsietsi again went from school to school, trying to keep morale up and resentment against the police simmering. He warned students against intimidating adults this time. The idea, he said, is not to confront them on the morning of August 24 – the date of the next stay-away – but to educate and prepare them.

The brutal methods the police employed to crush their rebellion made some on the SSRC yearn for more radical measures. At a meeting to complete the details of the stay-away, Tsietsi was suddenly called from the room. Khotso Seatlholo took over as chairman; he managed to convince the representatives they ought to attempt another march into town. 'We will always be easy targets for the police in the township,' Khotso warned. 'We are dying in Soweto, but that doesn't affect whites in any way.'

When Tsietsi returned, Khotso informed him they were discarding the idea of a strike in favour of a march. Tsietsi rejected it as a failed strategy. 'Whites seem to value property more than lives,' he said. 'They'll still shoot at us, whether we're in town or in the township. So why waste our lives? We can do something much quieter and more effective: hit them where it hurts, in their wallet.' At that, Tsietsi called for a vote; the representatives agreed to pursue the stay-away. (Tsietsi later issued a statement to the press that condemned 'police action in Soweto by irresponsibly shooting at students on their way to school or black children playing in the location as it has been reported in the newspapers. We see it as an unofficial declaration of war on black students by our "peace-officers".')

Tsietsi's identification as the president of the SSRC, his photograph in the newspapers, his public statements – all seemed to taunt the government and intensify its determination to arrest him. Unable to catch Tsietsi at home, the police tried another tack. They claimed that for his own security, Tsietsi ought to hand himself over to the authorities; a group of disgruntled workers wanted to kill him because of the uprising. When that failed, the police posted a 500 rand reward for information leading to his arrest. Tsietsi Mashinini was now the most hunted man in South Africa.

Suddenly, people who had shunned Joseph and Nomkhitha offered to hide their son. The Mashininis took a dim view of such proposals. The reward was the equivalent of a year's salary for a domestic worker and thus a considerable temptation, especially to poor township residents. The SSRC officers were equally sceptical and decided to limit knowledge of Tsietsi's whereabouts to two people. Barney Makgatle, who was older than most of the activists, became Tsietsi's chauffeur. He had years of driving experience, knew the township's byways, and could spot a roadblock from a long distance. Selby Semela, another SSRC member, took on the role of companion to Tsietsi. A measured, cautious youth, Selby often acted as a balance to Tsietsi's extreme self-confidence. They made for a strange trio: the driver, the comrade and the impassioned leader, traversing the township at odd hours, addressing students at various schools, distributing pamphlets, sleeping in a new safe house each night.

Tsietsi began to lead the police on a chase. With Drake Koka providing an ever-changing array of cars, a mythology arose about Tsietsi's ability to evade capture. People likened him to Nelson Mandela, who was given the apartheid-modified appellation of the Black Pimpernel in the early 1960s for his escapades while being hunted by the government. One such story about Tsietsi had him presiding over a meeting of SSRC members at Morris Issacson High School when it was surrounded by security officers. Acting on information that Tsietsi was inside, they made the youths leave the building one by one. Tsietsi, dressed in girls' dungarees and a beret, sauntered past the policemen; they looked him up and down – and let him pass.

Another tale put him at Baragwanath Hospital in Soweto in the middle of the day. Poppy Buthelezi, a young girl who had been shot by the police on June 16 and was paralysed from the waist down, was hospitalized there. As the weeks passed and the uprising progressed, she heard the parents of other wounded students muttering about how this was all the fault of Tsietsi

Mashinini. One afternoon, a young man bearing a large basket of fruit appeared on the ward. Striding over to Poppy's bed, he handed her the delicacies. 'Tell them you got this from Tsietsi Mashinini', he said, then disappeared down the hallway.

One such story was immortalized on film. Drake had asked a friend's grandson, who was visiting from Germany, if he could rent a car in his name; since the grandson was unknown to the police, the vehicle most likely would not raise suspicion. The young man agreed. Drake rented a small grey car and gave it to Tsietsi and his companions to use. With no real purpose and full of teenage bravado, they drove it directly to the Moroka police station in Soweto, where they remained for a time. As they left the car park, the youths thrust their fists out of the windows in the black power salute – a gesture that was captured on film by a passing photographer, Peter Magubane. Drake would see the picture on display in London after he went into exile. He was astounded by the spectacle: the apartheid regime's 'most wanted' fugitive sitting on the doorstep of the police, virtually daring them to look up from their desks and arrest him.

Nomkhitha feared Tsietsi's luck would not hold. And, if the police did capture him, she believed he would die in detention. The authorities would say he had hanged himself, or jumped from a window, or done any of the other implausible things they gave as explanations for the scores of activists who died while in police custody. Tsietsi scoffed at Nomkhitha when she spoke of her concern. 'I wish I could see my funeral,' he laughed, with all the arrogance of youth. To a black journalist, Tsietsi said: 'I don't say they can't get me. I know they can kill me any time. What they don't know is that they cannot kill the spirit. They will kill me now, but there will be another Tsietsi, a day or even an hour later.'

Despite the brave talk, Tsietsi understood the precariousness of his existence. One night he took Khotso Seatlholo to the weekly meeting at the House of Exile. 'This young fellow is going to be very close to you,' Tsietsi said as he introduced Khotso to Drake. 'I don't know what's going to happen, but in the event of a slip-up or my leaving, please give him the same help you've given me.' Turning to Khotso, he added, 'Any time you do anything as a member of the SSRC, you must consult with Drake.' The formalities thus completed, Tsietsi and Drake launched into a discussion of the night's topic: the failures of the first stay-away. Drake criticized the SSRC for not giving workers advance warning of the strike. They need to be better educated, he insisted, and they need more pamphlets. Tsietsi agreed; he and his associates were already addressing the deficiencies as they prepared for the next stay-away.

But Drake doubted whether Tsietsi would live that long. The police now suspected Drake's involvement with the youth and an officer had told Drake his colleagues would kill Tsietsi when they found him. On the same day, Drake heard that a bullet fired at Tsietsi as he drove through the township had missed his head by millimetres. Drake took the incidents as warnings. Given Tsietsi's penchant for courting danger, Drake decided he had to find a way to get him out of the country.

He considered several plans, only to discard them for one flaw: transportation. The cars Drake could hire had licence plates from Johannesburg or the seaside city of Durban; a group of young black men travelling in a vehicle from those areas, the scenes of much violence, was sure to attract the attention of the police. Drake confided his frustration to a friend, Reverend Legotlo, a clergyman and political activist who had great sympathy for the uprising. Reverend Legotlo offered to drive Tsietsi across the border in his car. Its licence plates from Pretoria, the country's capital and an Afrikaner stronghold, would be less conspicuous.

Drake sent an urgent message to Tsietsi that he needed to see him immediately. Despite Drake's insistence that it had become too dangerous for him to remain, the youth was in no mood to discuss his departure from South Africa. 'I don't want to leave the struggle,' Tsietsi kept repeating. 'What good will I be in exile?'

'You'll continue the struggle outside the country,' Drake suggested gently.

It took Drake several sessions of such exchanges to convince Tsietsi that he would have meaningful work to do in exile.

Tsietsi finally agreed to go, on the condition that Barney and Selby accompany him. As part of his preparations, Tsietsi paid a final visit to Khotso, bringing him a large number of pamphlets; Khotso had been designated as the next SSRC president in the event something happened to Tsietsi. 'I'm going to have to go sooner or later,' Tsietsi told his friend. 'Be very careful after I've gone. Don't be reckless. Don't sleep in the same place twice in a row. Be sure to see Drake at least once a week.' With that, Tsietsi bid Khotso farewell.

Tsietsi also went home to say goodbye to his family. His arrival astonished Nomkhitha; she had just read a story in the newspapers, planted by Drake, that Tsietsi had fled South Africa. Tsietsi was delighted by the ruse. Now the road is clear to go, he explained, but would not tell his parents when he was departing or his destination for fear of further implicating them. Nomkhitha kissed and hugged Tsietsi; she clung to him for an extra second, not wanting to let him go. Yet she knew he would be safer outside the country. Nomkhitha took comfort in the belief that he would soon be back; if the uprising continued apace, South Africa would be liberated in just a year or two. Joseph said he wanted to pray. The family formed a circle, joined hands and bowed their heads as Joseph intoned a prayer for his son's safety. Then Tsietsi left, with a smile and wave of his hand as he vanished into the night.

Drake determined that the youths would leave on August 23 in the evening. On the day of his departure, Tsietsi was interviewed at length by a journalist from Thames Television in London. The reporter and his camera crew were filming a programme on the uprising in the townships and arranged, through Drake, to speak with the student leader. Drake fixed a rendezvous at the Planet Cinema in Fordsburg, an Indian neighbourhood. Tsietsi, Barney and Selby were picked up in front of the cinema and driven to a house in Hyde Park, in the northern suburbs of Johannesburg, for the interview. Tsietsi took an instant liking to the reporter and his colleagues, all of whom had the given name of John; he called them 'The Johns'.

The programme was broadcast in Britain several days later.

Entitled *There Is No Crisis*, it opened with pictures of Soweto in flames. 'Since June the 16th,' the voice-over explained, 'when South African troops and police opened fire on a peaceful schoolchildren's demonstration, the white government has presided over the largest massacre of its black population since South Africa came into existence. Hundreds of blacks have died, thousands have been wounded. Yet the white Prime Minister says there is no crisis.'

'The killing started in Soweto, the huge black township outside Johannesburg,' the narrator continued. 'On June the 16th, Soweto's schoolchildren gathered in protest against the introduction of compulsory teaching in Afrikaans, the main dialect of the ruling white minority. They met dogs, tear gas and bullets. The schoolboy who led the protest was nineteen-year-old Tsietsi Mashinini.'

The film cut to Tsietsi dressed in a knitted cap, open shirt, bell-bottom trousers and *takkies* (sports shoes), sitting in the garden of the house in Hyde Park. He talked about the confrontation between the police and the students. Despite official claims to the contrary, Tsietsi said he knew for a fact that more than 300 people had died by the first weekend of the uprising. He and some friends went to the government mortuary to look for people who were missing and saw bodies with numbers pasted on their foreheads 'packed like potato sacks'. The highest number was 353.

Tsietsi explained the despair that Bantu education caused. 'The black student in South Africa', he said, 'is being fed the type of education that will domesticate him to be a better tool for the white man when he joins the working community. School libraries, school books, they've got nothing to do with civics or anything that is affiliated with politics. We're fed a lot of fiction stories. We don't get much works on democracy, communism.'

The interviewer interjected that Tsietsi was most likely being described up and down the country as a communist. Tsietsi scoffed at such a classification. 'It's just that in South Africa,' he replied, 'if you're not doing what the government expects you to do, then you're a communist, of course.'

Producing an edition of *The World*, the interviewer showed

Tsietsi the headlines: 'Soweto Workers Stay At Home.' (It was the first day of the second stay-away.) 'I'm very, very happy,' Tsietsi said. 'The idea is that we blacks in South Africa don't have arms. The only thing we can hit at the system with is to cripple the economy of the country and make our faint cries reach the ears of the authorities. Because apparently if we demonstrate, they just shoot at us. And if they don't shoot, they detain a whole lot of students. Now we are trying to be as peaceful as possible. Detain the parents at home and the parents are with us and they are prepared to stay at home as long as the students want them to stay at home. With this, we believe the authorities will feel the pinch and some way or the other will have to succumb to our demands.

'The system has done so many things and so much harm to my people,' he continued, 'that the people are no longer interested in having equal rights with the white people of South Africa. They want the tables to be turned so the white man can get a taste of his own medicine and feel what it is like to be oppressed.'

The film cut to a still picture of Tsietsi with his arm raised in a black power salute. 'Now at nineteen,' the voice-over explained, 'Tsietsi Mashinini can expect at best a lifetime in jail if he is caught. As it is, Colonel [J.P.] Visser, head of Soweto CID, has put a 300 pound price on his head. That's about a year's pay for a black domestic worker.'

Returning to the Hyde Park garden, the interviewer asked Tsietsi if the police were liable to shoot him on sight. 'Oh yes, sure,' Tsietsi replied. 'What Colonel Visser has been doing is he went to the Black Parents' Association members and told them that he has official and positive reports that I have a machine gun in my hand. As far as I see it, he has just been trying to create an atmosphere where I can be declared a dangerous element so that when they meet me they don't want to take me to court and be involved in a lot of legal intricacies. They just want to shoot me on sight and get it over with.'

Interviewer: 'Realistically, looking at what you're up against, is not a possibility somewhere in the back of your mind that this might be a futile struggle?'

'I don't think so,' Tsietsi replied. 'Whatever happens, the black people shall achieve what they want. We are aware that is a long struggle, but in the very near future, we will be what we want to be.'

The reporter, John Fielding, accompanied Tsietsi and his colleagues back to the Planet Cinema after finishing the interview, unaware that the young men were poised to flee the country. (The programme, when it was broadcast, would take note of the fact.) He pressed his business card into Tsietsi's hand: call me if you're ever in London, he shouted out the window as the car sped down the deserted street.

Drake and Reverend Legotlo awaited the three youths in the shadows of the cinema. Drake explained the escape plan: the minister would drive them the 650 or so miles to the Botswana frontier, which Tsietsi and his friends would have to cross on foot. The minister, meanwhile, would pass through the border checkpoint legally with his car and wait on the other side to take them to Gaborone, the capital. Reverend Legotlo gave the fugitives church-going clothes to don as a disguise. If the police stopped them along the road, the minister would say they were travelling to a church conference in Botswana.

Drake gave each of the youths 100 rands and wished them Godspeed. 'Don't let me rot in Botswana, Godfather,' Tsietsi whispered in Drake's ear, hugging him.

'I give you my word,' the older man replied.

No one spoke on the journey to the border. Tsietsi and his colleagues were terrified of what might happen when they began their trek on foot; they knew the South African army had orders to shoot anyone trying to cross the frontier. The minister was also grim-faced, checking and re-checking his rearview mirror. As he feared, the group got stopped behind a long line of other vehicles at a police blockade several miles before their destination. Tsietsi and his friends pulled their hats low over their foreheads but remained upright, visible to anyone who cared to look inside the car. Reverend Legotlo hurried outside to the rear of his station wagon and pretended to fix the licence plate.

'Has my bishop already gone through?' he asked the policeman who slowly made his way around the vehicle, glancing in the windows. 'He was on his way to a conference in Botswana.' When the security officer responded that the bishop had indeed passed the checkpoint some time earlier, Reverend Legotlo feigned alarm at being behind schedule – and the policeman waved the car around the barricades.

Reverend Legotlo let the three youths off at a place where they could slip through the border fence. Tsietsi and his colleagues had to navigate a stretch of farmland; by now, the sun had set and the three could barely make out the little huts that littered the landscape. They were afraid of stumbling on an army patrol. In their agitation, they forgot the minister's directions and lost the way. The young men wandered about blindly all night. Exhausted, cold, wet from an intermittent rain, they had despaired of finding the crossing when a South African farmer, a black man, came upon them as the sun was rising. The farmer showed them the path. With a considerable expenditure of spirit, the youths managed to traverse the border and run to a grove of trees in Botswana, where they collapsed.

The second stay-away that Tsietsi and the SSRC planned was a great success. Owners of factories and shops in the Johannesburg area estimated that as many as 80 per cent of their employees failed to report for work; this, with less intimidation by students at railway stations and bus stops. It seemed the SSRC's pamphlets had had an effect. Only a group of Zulus, who lived in an enormous hostel for migrant labourers, remonstrated against the students' dictates. Incited by the police, the workers went on a rampage through parts of Soweto, attacking residents and their houses.

Mpho got swept up in the events. He became very busy after Tsietsi's escape, which he and his family read about in the newspapers. Being Tsietsi's brother gave him a certain cachet. Suddenly, he was surrounded by people who wanted to be his friend. This new-found celebrity caused him much anxiety. Now Mpho felt compelled to perform impeccably, to produce precisely the right answer when asked a question. At times, he resented the attention, suspecting that people sought him out not for his own sake, but because he was Tsietsi's brother. (His younger siblings would share this feeling.)

The uprising of June 16 and the subsequent protests were a kind of crash-course in politics for Mpho, as they were for thousands of other township youths. The youngsters went from ignorance to activism virtually overnight. Years later, Mpho would remember it as a simple, almost idyllic time of political thought. He and his friends did not bother themselves much about doctrines or 'isms', as Mpho called them; in their minds, this was a fight between black and white. South Africa was their land, and they would wage war to the death, if necessary, to regain it. Never again would the arguments seem so explicit, so utterly right.

It was Mpho's job, as an SSRC representative, to translate these sentiments into action. He spent his days visiting the handful of schools under his purview. Class attendance was still sporadic; students dressed in their uniforms every morning and went to school, but not to study. Instead, they waited for instructions from the SSRC leaders. Mpho strove to keep the youngsters engaged. This is only the beginning, he reassured them when the SSRC called for another three-day stay-away on September 13, the start of the revolution. He urged the youngsters to draw their parents into the protest.

With the succession of his friend Khotso Seatlholo as president, Mpho now was actually closer to the inner workings of the SSRC. Khotso entrusted Mpho with pamphlets to distribute in his territory. (In contrast with Tsietsi, who had held himself aloof from his brothers to avoid accusations of nepotism.) Together, Mpho and Khotso went to a famous *sangoma*, a witch doctor, to obtain safeguards against arrest. The *sangoma* made the two friends eat a special meal fortified with meat. He tied small vials filled with dark, evil-looking material – *muti*, or medicine – around their arms with the admonishment they must not eat fried foods, such as chips, that were prepared in shops. Pork was often cooked in the same oil; the *muti* would be rendered ineffective if exposed to pork.

Dee also found himself an object of attention because of Tsietsi's aura. It was particularly true with girls; the Mashinini name seemed to have a magical effect on them. Whereas previously and with much trepidation, Dee had had to initiate relationships, girls now flocked to him. They wanted to talk about politics. And Dee, who never shone in school or in social settings, suddenly could speak with confidence. That he possessed such an ability came as an epiphany to him. Dee felt he had acquired a kind of certitude in being a Mashinini; it surmounted his shyness and allowed him to come into his own.

Dee never returned to his studies after June 16. Instead, he formed a gang with about a dozen young men from the area. Dee, at the age of fifteen, was the youngest; most of the others worked at jobs during the day and gathered at a safe house in the Mofolo section of Soweto at night. The refuge, a small garage attached to a 'matchbox' house, belonged to a woman the youths called Mama. She offered the sanctuary out of sympathy for the uprising, furnishing it with a few cots, blankets and pillows. There the gang cooked their evening meal and discussed the next day's scheme. The young men became a surrogate family for Dee; he visited his parents only during daylight hours when the police presence lessened, staying long enough to bathe and change his clothes.

The gang had no formal ties to the SSRC. Instead, Dee would learn from Mpho what actions the SSRC planned and set off with his group to attend to enforcement. Dee's freelancing caused Mpho much irritation. Once, he arrived at a school to find Dee already informing the students of a particular SSRC strategy. The gang's favourite project was 'educating' the Zulu labourers who had opposed the stay-away. With the authorities inciting the hostel dwellers to violence, the youngsters' hostility shifted to the Zulus; they were seen as substitutes for the police. Almost every night Dee's gang engaged in battles with the workers. The Zulus tied red bandannas around their foreheads, the youngsters donned white ones, and the two groups would go to war on the streets of Soweto with knobkerries, axes and knives.

One night, Dee and his gang got word that the Zulus were planning to attack an area in the western part of the township. The youths decided to launch a preemptive strike. They made bombs out of bottles filled with sand and petrol; the smashing of the glass against the sand when the bottle was thrown created enough friction to ignite the petrol. The gang also armed themselves with stones and other projectiles. They did not want to be drawn into actual physical battle with the strapping, fit labourers; they knew the results could be lethal. Then Dee and his gang made their way to the hostel where the Zulus were holding a meeting. The youths discharged their weapons; the ensuing skirmishes between the two sides continued for a week.

Mpho and his friends also resorted to force to ensure that adults honoured the stay-away. They got into several brawls with the Zulu workers over the issue. One such encounter involved a labourer whose ear lobes had been pierced and weighted in the traditional Zulu fashion so that they hung down like large hoop earrings. Mpho and his colleagues pushed the man's head onto a gate and locked one of his lobes to the post. There they left him, as though in stocks, for passers-by to see.

The youngsters understood they needed adult participation. Without the support of their parents and other workers, the stay-aways would fail; on their own, the students wielded little power over the government. They had to convince adults, especially the migrant labourers, that this was their struggle too. Drake Koka helped to issue a circular after the Zulu disturbances, imploring brother not to attack brother; but the task of including the older generation required a finesse that, at times, seemed beyond the students. Even Nomkhitha and Joseph were reluctant to jeopardize their jobs further by remaining at home. Their resistance appalled Mpho and Dee. You are the parents of Tsietsi Mashinini, the boys chided them. Of all the adults in the township, you are the very ones who shouldn't go to work. In the end, they observed the stay-away, as did many Zulu labourers. And the strike turned out to be the most successful one yet.

Rocks went underground after his encounter with the police at his parents' house. He did not lack for places to stay; horrified by the government's killing of their children, people in the township opened their homes, and meagre larders, to virtually anyone being pursued by the police. Rocks slept on all manner of improvised beds: couches, cots, bedrolls, floors. After only a night or two in one house, he would change to another to ensure his safety.

He resumed working with Indres Naidoo, the leader of his African National Congress cell. The ANC, like the Pan Africanist Congress, was caught unawares by the June 16 uprising and its aftermath. Neither group had enough strength inside the country to offer much support to the students. But Indres' clandestine organization that sent youngsters abroad for military training was suddenly overwhelmed with potential recruits; emboldened by their victories against the authorities, the teenagers wanted nothing more than to learn how to shoot a gun, then return to South Africa to overthrow the government. The trickle of perhaps ten persons a month asking for training turned into a torrent of 100 or more. About 4,000 youths would leave the country by the end of the year. Rocks, with his contacts in the township, helped to recruit many of them.

Desperate for resources, Indres sought out Reinhard Brueckner, a Lutheran minister who was a great supporter of the anti-apartheid struggle. The minister gave him money to create a kind of self-help organization. It hired minivans, or *kombis*, ostensibly to transport youngsters who had been shot by the police to hospital. In fact, the organization was a front for Indres' recruiting efforts. The vehicles ferried enlistees, using secret routes, to neighbouring countries where Umkhonto we Sizwe, the ANC's military wing, had set up offices. Rocks' recruits went to Swaziland. He hid them in various places in the township until Indres determined it was safe to send them across the border.

Rocks also worked as one of the numerous advisers to the SSRC. (Others were Winnie Mandela, the Black Parents' Association and various church leaders.) He counselled a handful of youths within the organization known as the Suicide Squad. The teenagers had made contact with Umkhonto guerrillas in Swaziland and Johannesburg for rudimentary training;

often their instruction consisted of nothing more than a pamphlet that was circulating underground. One such publication, written and illustrated like a comic book to mislead the police, recounted the story of Simon and Jane. These were no ordinary cartoon characters: Simon and Jane had very special friends, who educated them in the art of manufacturing Molotov cocktails.

Paul Langa, the Suicide Squad's leader, was told by his mentors to seek out Rocks. The latter became a kind of scout for the group, identifying potential targets and urging the youths to take their war to the white areas of Johannesburg. Rocks also taught them about explosives. He had acquired his knowledge from a mining engineer and from Joe Gqabi, a Communist and one of the first Umkhonto guerrillas, who had trained for eighteen months in the Chinese city of Nanking. Of course, Rocks' knowledge was purely theoretical. He knew, for instance, that a dynamite fuse should take about six minutes to explode after being lit. Rocks decided to test this one night while instructing the Suicide Squad in a friend's backyard in Soweto; the youths needed to know how much time they would have to escape. With Paul holding the device and his colleagues gathered round, Rocks lit the fuse. He expected it to burn with a proper flame; instead, the device smouldered and smoked like a cigarette. Thinking it defective, Rocks returned to the house to find a torch so he could examine the fuse. He presumed he had several minutes until it detonated.

The next thing he heard was a loud bang. Rocks rushed outside; there he saw Paul, whose thumb and first finger on his right hand had been blown off, bleeding profusely. Rocks bundled him into a car and drove off in search of a doctor. It was long after midnight and he had to wake up a physician who had a clinic in the township. Rocks pointed a gun at the doctor's head while he dressed Paul's wound. 'You do not go to the police about this,' Rocks warned him. 'If you tell anyone, you are a dead man.'

Despite the mishap, the Suicide Squad succeeded in blowing up several targets, including a railway signal box. The saboteurs considered the halting of trains essential to their cause.

Railroad cars conveyed South Africa's workers and goods; paralyse the trains, and you paralyse the economy. Even Rocks tried his hand at such sabotage. He and another member of his ANC cell attempted to derail a freight train near the township of Lenasia. They fixed a hook-like device to the track, but the locomotive easily ran over it, crushing the contraption.

Rocks did most of his underground work in a blue Volkswagen Beetle that he bought with money saved from his stipend while at college. He cut a rather conspicuous figure careering around the township in his brightly coloured car; the police, who had become aware of his clandestine activities, soon identified him as the vehicle's owner. Rocks took to parking the car at one house and sleeping at another. Often, neighbourhood children would rouse him in the middle of the night, saying that the authorities had been around, looking for the driver of the blue Beetle. Rocks decided he would have to jettison the car: one night he parked it at his cousin's house, removed the tyres and put the body on blocks so that the Beetle looked as though it were inoperative.

People were now frightened to let him stay in their homes. The police had arrested several activists who apparently mentioned Rocks' name while being interrogated; a newspaper story reported that the authorities were searching for him. If Rocks were detained, he could have implicated vital figures in the ANC's underground structures. Rocks judged that it was time to leave the country. He had decided long before that he would go abroad for military training after completing his studies; the idea was never far from his thoughts. This seemed an opportune moment to flee.

But just as Rocks was preparing to leave, the government sealed the borders in search of Umkhonto guerrillas. Rocks organized a meeting with Indres to show him the newspaper article that named him as a fugitive and explained his thwarted attempt to escape. 'I'm too hot,' he told Indres. 'You've got to hide me.'

Indres agreed that Rocks was in danger. He knew several people whom he could ask to hide Rocks, people who were not directly involved in the anti-apartheid struggle but whose political or moral beliefs made them supporters of the cause. After some thought, Indres decided to ask Jennifer Hyman, a white journalist. She seemed a perfect choice. Indres and his family had known her for years and he trusted her completely. Sydenham, the all-white suburb in northern Johannesburg where she lived, was perhaps the last place the police would look for a black activist.

Jenny seemed predisposed to help Indres when he approached her with a request to shelter someone important, but she had several stipulations. She would not do anything to jeopardize her job, nor would she do anything illegal. And she was not about to drive anyone to the border. (Jenny had a friend who had gone to prison for helping an activist to escape.) Indres disclosed Rocks' identity to Jenny with a plea not to reveal it to her husband – something she deemed beyond consideration. Clive Emdon, Jenny's husband and a fellow journalist, was entirely sympathetic to Rocks' plight. To work for the opposition press was to challenge the ruling authority; reporters were routinely detained by the police, interrogated, even assaulted. Besides, providing sanctuary for Rocks would give them the opportunity to do more than just chronicle the uprising.

Indres and Jenny decided they would call Rocks by a code-name. She suggested Sipho; her young son and daughter had a storybook entitled *Sipho's Trumpet*. As agreed, Indres delivered Rocks to the small, unremarkable house at 29 Roslin Street in the middle of one night. 'You must be very disciplined,' Indres warned him before opening the car door. 'You mustn't leave the house, you mustn't drink. Jenny is going to give me a full report of your behaviour.' Then he said farewell to Rocks and raced back to the township, where he reported to Joe Gqabi, his fellow Umkhonto leader, that Rocks was now deeply hidden.

Rocks quickly settled into a routine. Clive and Jenny departed for work at their respective newspapers early, dropping Thandi, their daughter, at a crèche; their maid Nelly looked after Joshua, the baby. That left Rocks with the house virtually to himself. Despite the high wall that surrounded the house, Jenny advised him to stay away from the front rooms unless the curtains were drawn. He was not to go into the garden during the day nor answer the telephone. Thus confined indoors, Rocks methodically worked his way through the couple's books. He cooked meals for himself. After Nelly fetched Thandi from the crèche, he spent hours feeding her in the kitchen, playing with her, cradling her.

Jenny came to like him immensely. She had been frightened of bringing a black stranger into her home, concerned that he might feel ill-at-ease with a white family or, worse yet, act obsequiously grateful. Her anxiety proved baseless. Rocks' warmth and charm were immediately appealing, as was his relationship with Thandi; she, quite literally, jumped into his arms whenever he entered the room. Jenny knew little of Rocks' background, but guessed he must come from a large family from the way he cared for her daughter. She also found his intellect impressive. Rocks seemed unlike many activists in the anti-apartheid movement Jenny had known, whose obsession with the cause made them appear one-dimensional. Here was a young man who read widely, who took a keen interest in other societies and other political systems. Late at night, after they had put the children to bed, Clive, Jenny and Rocks would sit in the garden and, under the cover of darkness, discuss politics endlessly.

Jenny's biggest worry was that Rock's presence would be discovered. No one, not even members of their families, knew that Rocks was hiding with them. Jenny tried to dissuade her friends from popping round for tea. As a preemptive measure, she made arrangements to meet the ones most likely to call on her in town. She managed the few unexpected guests by hurriedly concealing Rocks in Thandi's bedroom at the opposite end of the house and confining the intruders to the lounge. As a last resort, Clive devised an emergency escape route for Rocks. He was to scale the ladder that hung on the garden wall (which Clive had put there years earlier for the neighbour's children). Keeping close to the shrubs, Rocks would head to the road, then continue on to the nearby black township of Alexandra. Clive would wait for him at an arranged pickup point when the danger had passed.

Some gatherings at her home, like Thandi's second birthday

party, could not be avoided. Jenny and Clive considered cancelling the celebration, but Thandi had been anticipating it for weeks and would have been inconsolable. And they doubted they could contrive a credible excuse for their respective families. So on the appointed Saturday afternoon, Jenny locked Rocks into the laundry room with a blanket and pillow, a pile of books and a radio that he could play softly. The house filled up with the twenty or so guests: Helen Joseph, a tireless anti-apartheid campaigner; the Naidoo family; uncles; grandparents. As the day was warm, the smallest children took off their clothes and ate their ice cream in their underwear. Jenny could not relax. She had to make certain no one wandered over to the laundry, which would require explaining the locked door. Luckily, the balmy weather kept everyone in the garden; the party passed without mishap, and Jenny saved a piece of birthday cake for Rocks.

Jenny did not worry that Thandi would divulge Rocks' existence. She told her daughter that Rocks was a visitor, a not-unusual occurrence in their household, and made light of his presence. Nelly, the maid, was a bigger concern. One day she asked Rocks why he used the boss's toilet and not hers, the one reserved for (black) servants – the common practice in most white South African homes. 'I'm a journalist from Cape Town and I work for the same organization as Clive,' he replied, reciting the story he and Jenny had invented as his cover. 'When Clive goes to Cape Town, he stays with me.' Nelly seemed unconvinced.

Her suspicions deepened when two white men rang the doorbell one morning, claiming to be electricians come to check the meter. They seemed most interested in Rocks who, despite Jenny's admonitions about staying indoors, was sitting in the garden by the pool. 'Who is that boy?' one man finally asked Nelly.

'Oh, he's my son from Cape Town,' the maid replied. 'He's here to get money from me.'

After the men departed, Nelly said to Rocks: 'I know you aren't who you say you are. Where are your parents? At least I can tell them that you are still alive.' Rocks gave Nelly his address in the township.

The next Sunday, dressed in her best church outfit, Nelly

went to the Central Western Jabavu section of Soweto. She walked up Pitso Street, singing and clapping her hands the way township women are wont to do on the Sabbath when moved by the spirit and coming home from church. Singing and clapping, Nelly made her way to the Mashininis' house where she found Nomkhitha and whispered something in her ear; then, still singing her love of the Lord and clapping her hands to a mighty rhythm, she headed back down the road and returned to the northern suburbs of Johannesburg.

The police raids on the Mashininis' home continued, despite Tsietsi's departure. One night, pushed beyond her tolerance, Nomkhitha snapped from the strain. 'He's gone, he's left, he's not here!' she shrieked, chasing the security men outdoors. 'Now leave my house! Leave my house!'

Nomkhitha's hysteria only intensified ten-year-old Tshepiso's panic. He stumbled through the next day feeling terrified: terrified the police would take his parents away; terrified Joseph and Nomkhitha might get caught in a riot on their way home from work; terrified he and his siblings would be left to fend for themselves. No one explained anything to him. The adults were always huddling, whispering, trying to keep their fears from the children. Nothing that happened after June 16 made sense to him.

As if the police brutality were not sufficient punishment, certain friends and relatives ostracized the Mashininis. Some avoided Nomkhitha, they said, because she was Tsietsi's mother; he was the reason children had died or were in jail. Others stopped talking to all members of the family. A few particularly spiteful types propagated rumours: if you visit the Mashinini house, you will be arrested; if you are seen with a Mashinini, you will be arrested; and so on. (One bit of gossip had it that Nomkhitha was a *sangoma*, a witch doctor.) The revilement took a terrible toll on her and Joseph.

Not everyone treated the couple as pariahs, though. They found much support in their church: there the minister offered prayers for the children who were in detention or had fled and often mentioned the Mashinini family specifically. Members pointedly visited Joseph and Nomkhitha at home to partake of special services for the students. And many congregants spoke of their admiration for Tsietsi. They came forward to tell stories of previous encounters with him. While some were obvious fabrications, meant to aggrandize the narrator by his association with Tsietsi, most seemed true. The anecdotes conveyed a pride in knowing Tsietsi and solidarity with his family.

Despite the pain of having Tsietsi in exile, Joseph and Nomkhitha were glad he had gone. The commanding police officer of the raids on the house used to tell Joseph that Tsietsi would be dead on the day they found him. (The same policeman warned Joseph: 'One day, Mr Mashinini, you will have to account for all that your children have done.') The Mashininis knew that Tsietsi was well; he had telephoned Joseph at work soon after his arrival in Botswana. About a week later, Drake Koka's wife came to the Mashininis' residence to collect some of Tsietsi's clothing. She made frequent trips across the border to sell the African-style shirts and dresses that she designed and thus could move freely and unnoticed between the two countries. Nomkhitha packed a large sack of provisions and a suitcase full of his clothes; Tsietsi, like his friends, had left behind all his possessions. Nomkhitha could be confident that at least he now had basic comforts.

She felt less resolved about the absence of Rocks, Dee and Mpho from the house. Nomkhitha was particularly disturbed by the virtual disappearance of the two younger boys; they came home infrequently to have a wash and a change of clothes. In the interim, Nomkhitha did not know what they ate, where they slept, what they were doing. They were too young to be involved in politics; they needed supervision. But it was useless to mention her concerns to the boys. The police were driving them away; how could they be expected to remain at home amid the constant harassment? To Nomkhitha, it seemed a great irony that the security forces had helped to ensure her sons' participation in the uprising.

Nonetheless, there was a part of Joseph that could not accept his sons' activities. As a father, he felt like saying to them: Stop all this nonsense with politics, you're going to ruin your future, your lives. The few times he attempted to broach the subject, Dee and Mpho retreated into discussions of general events to avoid disclosing their own participation. Rocks' apparent involvement distressed Joseph even more. (He would not learn the full extent of it until many years later.) The scholarship Joseph's company had given Rocks covered every aspect of his engineering studies for four years: transport, tuition, housing, books, incidental expenses. Joseph was ecstatic when Rocks received the grant; he could never have afforded to send his son to college. And now Rocks, along with his brothers, seemed to be jeopardizing it all for politics.

As the uprising progressed into October, the police intensified their raids on schools and arrests of SSRC members. They sealed off whole sections of the township, going from house to house, beating people and carting them off to jail. Horrific stories began to circulate about the savage treatment the police inflicted on detainees. Mpho could only imagine what he would have to endure if arrested: the threats directed at him, the obscenities, the manhandling by Afrikaners who saw their black captives as subhuman, as monkeys at best.

Mpho, like many of his peers, was thus forced to live a nomadic, underground life. He constantly lacked funds for food and to compensate people for providing places to sleep. So it seemed a godsend when a group of older activists began giving small amounts of money to Mpho and his friends. In exchange, they pumped the students for information about the SSRC. Mpho gradually understood that his benefactors were members of the Pan Africanist Congress; they, like their rivals in the African National Congress, were trying to gain a foothold in the uprising.

The philosophies of the PAC interested Mpho. With the students' grievances having progressed from protesting against instruction in Afrikaans to challenging apartheid itself, Mpho realized they needed more sophisticated political allies. He started looking for a movement whose principles most closely resembled the exclusionary radicalism of Black Consciousness: Africa for the Africans; Black Man, You Are On Your On, and so on. The PAC adherents dismissed the ANC as an organization dominated by whites, whose leaders lived the good life in exile. By contrast, the PAC position was simple: this land belongs to the blacks and we want it back. It appealed to the passions of a hot-headed youth such as Mpho; one PAC member convinced him that even Nelson Mandela would join the group if he were free.

The PAC sent a representative from Swaziland to meet Mpho. The man told him he had come to assess the situation in Soweto and to organize an escape route from South Africa for those students who wished to leave. He enlisted Mpho to act as a kind of liaison between the PAC and students in the township. Acknowledging the difficult circumstances under which Mpho was living, the man urged him nonetheless not to flee the country; the organization needed his information.

Dee also suffered from the cruel police measures. One young man in his group disappeared suddenly; soon after, the security forces began harassing Mama, questioning her about Dee and his friends. Dee guessed that the missing gang member had been detained or become an informant. Either way, the police now knew about their safe house. Dee decided he had to leave Soweto. He travelled to Natalspruit, to the east of Johannesburg, to stay with Mark, Nomkhitha's brother, and his wife. Dee knew the place well. He had spent many a school holiday there, with little enjoyment; after Soweto, he found the small township dull and slow. This time was no different. Although the East Rand, as the area was called, had also erupted in violence, Dee could not risk attracting the attention of the police and was forced to stay indoors. He quickly grew bored.

Yearning for his friends and unable to withstand the ennui, Dee returned to Mama's house after a few weeks. He was dismayed to find that his companions had vanished: most were in jail or had fled the country. 'Are you still here?' Mama asked in surprise when she saw Dee. 'All the kids are gone.' Dee felt alone and isolated. The initial, giddy excitement of engaging in what seemed like an imminent revolution had worn off, to be replaced by a realistic vision of what the future held: detention, torture, imprisonment.

An interview that Tsietsi gave in exile came to Dee's attention around this time. In it, Tsietsi spoke of the need for a military-style revolt in South Africa: 'If you could look into the history of the struggle, you could see that all other means have been exhausted. The only thing left is armed struggle against the racist regime.' The idea seized Dee's imagination. He became obsessed with the thought of leaving the country to get military training. Dee pictured himself as an expertly trained soldier, AK-47 slung over his shoulder, returning in triumph to liberate South Africa. Such were the dreams of a fifteen-year-old township boy.

He also saw exile as a chance to study. This was not unprecedented; the brother of one of Dee's gang members had gone to medical school abroad. Perhaps Dee too would choose a profession and pursue it after leaving the country. A career commanded respect and a good salary. On the other hand, becoming a freedom fighter seemed so glamorous. And so it went in Dee's consciousness: one moment he was thinking about military training, the next about schooling, until he felt utterly muddled. Dee attributed his frenzied state to being stranded in Soweto without friends or studies to occupy his mind, only the prospect of imprisonment. Exile, which just six months earlier had been an unthinkable concept, now seemed his salvation.

In his hiding place in the northern suburbs, Rocks read of the myriad police arrests in the newspapers. He got more and more worried: too many people had been detained who knew too much about the ANC underground structures. The incident with the white men claiming to be meter-readers was followed by other, equally suspicious occurrences that led Rocks to believe he was under surveillance. Besides, Jenny and Clive were having marital problems; the tension between them had become unbearable. Rocks got word to Indres that he needed to change houses.

Indres came for him one evening after informing Jenny that Rocks would be leaving. By agreement, she did not know his next destination, but Rocks worked out a plan to contact her if he escaped from South Africa. It was a difficult leave-taking.

Although Jenny was relieved that her house would no longer be the object of police scrutiny, she feared for Rocks' safety. She thought him an exceptional person, one who was destined for leadership – if he survived. Jenny fervently hoped that he would. Thandi, her daughter, clung to Rocks when she said goodbye.

Rocks stayed next in a flat in Yeoville, close to downtown Johannesburg. It belonged to an unmarried couple who kept cats; Rocks soon discovered he had a horrible allergy to the animals. Indres moved him on to a house in Mayfair, to the west. In the meantime, he devised a plan to get Rocks out of the country. Joe Gqabi, the Umkhonto leader, would escort him when he travelled to Swaziland to deliver a message to the ANC.

On the evening of Rocks' departure, Indres drove him to the rendezvous, the home of some friends who lived in the suburbs. It was a tense journey; every other car on the motorway seemed to belong to the police. Despite Indres' nervousness, they arrived at the house without incident. Rocks then had to wait several hours for Joe and the two Indian men who accompanied him in his car. By the time they finished driving the 200 or so miles to the border with Swaziland, it was long past midnight. Rocks and Joe got out of the car some distance from the frontier in order to cross on foot. The Indians, who did not have police records, were going to drive through the border post when it opened at daylight and pick them up on the other side.

Rocks and Joe promptly became lost in the bush. They did not know whether they were in South Africa or Swaziland; the only light in the area came from the border gate, and they could not wander too close for fear of being seen. The two men walked for hours in the direction of what they hoped was Swaziland. Hungry, thirsty, exhausted, Rocks and Joe peered through the waning darkness to try to discern their whereabouts. Only at daybreak did the two realize they had penetrated deep into Swazi territory. Elated, Rocks and Joe approached a nearby settlement, where they paid a villager ten rands to show them the way to the main road. Their Indian friends and the car awaited them there.

A few days later, Jenny received a telephone call at her desk at the *Sunday Express* from someone identifying himself as Sipho. Jubilantly, he launched into a discourse that included one coded sentence: I am free. Jenny thanked him tersely and rang off. Telling her editor she was going out to check on a story, Jenny drove to an address in Braamfontein, just north of downtown, where she asked the security guard at the gate to call Mr Mashinini; she had a message to deliver.

When Joseph emerged from the office building, he saw a white woman sitting in a car. She rolled down the window and said: 'Mr Mashinini, your oldest son has left South Africa and is safe. I got a call from him this morning.' Then she drove away.

Despite the repressive measures the police employed to try to break the uprising, Mpho remained deeply involved in SSRC activities. Khotso Seatlholo, the president, ordered a three-point national campaign for the December holidays: to mourn those who had died, the *shebeens*, or township bars, would close; adults would refrain from buying Christmas presents; students would boycott their end-of-year exams. Mpho spent his days distributing pamphlets that explained the ban on gifts, or Black Christmas, as it was known in local parlance. But the security forces' ceaseless pursuit of students made Mpho's existence increasingly difficult. One of his close friends was arrested; now Mpho, like Dee, no longer felt at ease staying in ostensibly safe houses.

He too tried leaving town. Mpho accompanied Khotso to a meeting in Randfontein, to the west of Johannesburg. The township erupted in violence as a result of the meeting and Mpho had to flee into the surrounding countryside to avoid the police. Unable to return to Randfontein, he and three colleagues had little choice but to start the thirty-mile journey back to Soweto on foot. They felt their way through the night, past sprawling farms and large, snarling dogs that chased them for long distances. At dawn, they came upon an Afrikaner farmer packing crates of eggs into a *kombi*, or minivan; he was about to take his produce to market. Surrounding the farmer, Mpho and his friends drew knives and insisted he give them a ride to Soweto. The terrified man drove them directly to the township, where the boys 'liberated' the contents of the *kombi* and distributed them to passers-by.

Mpho tried staying with relatives in Daleside. He intended to remain there for several weeks, but left after only a few days out of boredom. He tried Mark's house in Natalspruit – with the same result. Mpho gave up and returned to Soweto; like Dee, he found that many of his cohorts had disappeared, gone into exile or to prison. Mpho felt a kind of lassitude. Despite the success of the SSRC's campaigns, there seemed to be little direction to the uprising; the relentless police pursuit denied him any safe haven; he lacked for companionship. Mpho decided it was time to leave South Africa.

He might have gone immediately had he received the letter that Rocks sent him with instructions on how to escape. Instead, Dee intercepted the missive. Dee had been announcing to the family his intention to flee the country for weeks now. At first, his parents paid him little heed: he was not Tsietsi, he did not have a price on his head. Slowly Dee persuaded them that leaving was a good idea because he could continue his studies in exile. This was a half-truth; he also wanted to obtain military training. In reality, all his proposals were the stuff of fantasy. Dee was not being advised by military people, nor by academics; he knew no one in the exile organizations. He simply convinced himself he could accomplish these feats overseas.

Then he read Rocks' letter. Dee was meant to deliver it to Mpho, but when he recognized Rocks' writing on the envelope, he opened it himself. The letter described the route to take across the border to Swaziland and named a person to contact there. The contact would then notify Rocks. Dee was elated. The letter provided him with a plan and the assurance that he would not disappear into a void if he left South Africa. A colleague whom everyone called Tiger organized the transport for Dee and several other activists. The youths decided they would wait until after the New Year, so they could celebrate one last Christmas at home.

Nomkhitha prepared the usual holiday dinner: roast

chicken, rice, potatoes, salad, cake. Everyone, including Mpho and Dee, gathered at the table for the feast; for once, the police had the good grace to leave the family unmolested to enjoy their meal. Out of deference to the SSRC's boycotts no one exchanged gifts. But they prayed together and sang hymns, the brothers, who were part of the choir at church, lustily trying to outdo one another. Nomkhitha felt an ineffable sadness as she gazed around the room: Tsietsi and Rocks were already gone and Dee had informed his parents he would soon be joining them. Nomkhitha wondered when the next time would be when they would celebrate a Christmas together as a whole family.

Dee left on the third night of the new year. He returned home briefly to collect some clothes and to say goodbye to his parents. Despite the balminess of the summer evening, Dee was warmly dressed in jeans, jersey and a jacket. He wanted to be prepared for wherever he might ultimately land in exile. 'We're crossing to Swaziland tonight,' he told Joseph and Nomkhitha when they saw the clothes he was wearing. Joseph gave him a small sum of money. Suddenly Dee felt the full import of what he was about to undertake: leaving family, home and country for an uncertain future. Afraid that he would start to sob, Dee kissed his parents and left.

Tiger had arranged for a driver to meet them and two other youths at Mama's house at nine o'clock. There were few cars on the road as they crossed the eastern part of Transvaal province under a clear, moonlit sky. Now Dee was excited. He clutched Joseph's money in one hand, Rocks' letter in the other. As the hours passed, Dee ate some of the fish-paste sandwiches Nomkhitha had prepared for him. He spoke little to his companions, preferring to stare out of the window at the expanse of stars and to imagine what adventures awaited him.

They neared the border at about two o'clock in the morning. The driver left them at a turn-off to a gravel road. 'Start walking towards the mountain,' the driver said, gesturing towards a rise that was barely discernible in the darkness. 'You'll come across a fence, then another fence, then climb down the mountain.

When you start seeing the scattered huts, you'll know you're with the Swazis.'

The four youths immediately set off into the bush until they came to the mountain where, instead of plunging straight ahead, they improvised a kind of zigzag course across its face. Dee and his companions found it impossible to determine their direction in the dark. They wandered for hours, unsure whether they were making forward progress or doubling back across the mountainside. Like Rocks, at one point Dee became so disoriented he thought they had returned to South Africa. The youths occasionally came on footpaths hewn out of the underbrush, but avoided taking them for fear of encountering anyone or leaving a trail.

Tiger, who was older and more experienced, urged his discouraged colleagues onward. At dawn, they finally spied the first border fence: a few strands of barbed wire, which they easily jumped. Another quarter of a mile brought the youths to the second, equally traversable fence. By now, it was fully light; Dee and his companions were moving through lovely, verdant country. They walked on for about another hour-and-a-half until they saw a few huts, set back from a road; Dee almost cried with relief. The young men approached the settlement cautiously. From a distance, Tiger shouted a salutation in Zulu. After what seemed a lifetime, an old woman wrapped in a traditional blanket ducked out of a hut, looked them over, then brought water and bowls of mealie porridge to the dehydrated, famished youths.

The woman sat on the ground with them, watching as they ate and drank. She did not ask the strangers their identity; from their Western dress, it was clear they were South Africans. After the young men had finished, the woman spoke: You must go on to Mbabane. The authorities there will help you. You are all safe now.

CHAPTER FIVE

Tsietsi

Tsietsi and his two colleagues remained in Gaborone, the Botswanan capital, for about ten days. It was a dusty, sleepy little town. Poised on the edge of the Kalahari Desert, Gaborone appeared almost blinding in its starkness. The place was a scattering of trees, sprawling fields, empty streets. To the boys, who were used to the cacophony and bustle of Johannesburg, Gaborone had a temporary feel, as though it had not quite decided whether to put down roots.

They stayed with a friend of Winnie Mandela. Tsietsi spent much of the time discussing the future with his companions. He had made it clear to Drake Koka in South Africa that they were leaving to obtain military training, not to continue their studies. But under whose auspices? The boys were adamant about not wanting to join either the African National Congress or the Pan Africanist Congress; to them, the organizations were little more than names. The only solution was to try to get training from African countries that were sympathetic to their cause. Mindful that students who were fleeing South Africa faced a similar dilemma, Tsietsi and his colleagues formed the Soweto Students' Representative Council in exile, with Tsietsi as the nominal chairman. Now the Black Consciousness youths would not feel compelled to choose between the ANC or the PAC.

But there was little time to build the organization. Tsietsi and his companions were desperate to leave Botswana to escape the long reach of the South African security forces. (Agents had been known to kidnap refugees in surrounding states and drag them across the border to certain arrest.) Drake knew of their fears; through the offices of a Christian group, he arranged for visas to Holland for the boys. A member of the organization, who travelled frequently to Gaborone, communicated the plan to an official in the Botswanan government. This man, who worked in the office of the president, used government funds to pay for the tickets to Holland and delivered them to Tsietsi. When Drake escaped from South Africa several months later, he would carry a suitcase crammed with 15,000 rands, money donated by the Christian group to repay the Botswanan government.

Unbeknown to Tsietsi and his friends, Drake had obtained student visas for them. The youths believed, as they flew to Lusaka, Zambia, on the first leg of their journey, that they were travelling to Europe to relax for a while; soon they would return to Africa to begin the armed struggle against the Boers. It was the first time Tsietsi or Selby had flown in an aeroplane. When they arrived in Lusaka, the three young men went to the airport bar to celebrate. They were now far enough away from South Africa to stop worrying about being kidnapped. Tsietsi ordered a whisky, Selby and Barney requested beers. They began to get excited as Tsietsi toasted their escape and the start of a new life: they, township boys who could only dream of such things, were going overseas. The one discordant note to their joy was the realization that they had truly left home.

As the celebration progressed, Tsietsi noticed a jumbo jet parked on the tarmac. It was much grander than the plane they were scheduled to take to London, where they would transfer to a flight to Amsterdam. Chaps, Tsietsi said expansively, pointing to the plane, why don't we depart Africa in style? With that, Tsietsi gathered up their tickets and strode to the transit desk in the terminal. He returned a while later, triumphantly brandishing their tickets (now encased in the folder of a different airline) and proclaiming that he had managed to exchange them for the jumbo jet, which was also going to London.

The jet was, indeed, bound for London's Gatwick Airport. But the youths' plane to Amsterdam departed from Heathrow, the destination of their original London flight. They realized their error when, arriving at Gatwick, they found there were no flights to Holland. The immigration official who examined their documents explained to Tsietsi and his companions they could only fly to Amsterdam from Heathrow.

'How far away is Heathrow?' Tsietsi asked.

'A bus ride', the official replied.

'Fine, so put us on a bus.'

The official laughed. The boys did not have visas for Britain; they did not even have proper passports. They were travelling on documents issued by the United Nations office in Gaborone which did not authorize their entry into England. Tsietsi explained that they had visas awaiting them at the airport in Amsterdam. The immigration officer searched the young men's luggage. Finding a pile of newspaper clippings from South Africa, he and another colleague decided the three youths were fugitives. You are being detained for deportation to Zambia, the official told them, and the Zambians are going to send you back to Botswana. The authorities escorted the youths to a holding room, where they would remain until the next flight to Lusaka, in two days' time.

Tsietsi and companions sat on the edge of the beds, numb with despair; they seemed doomed to return to Botswana. Then Tsietsi remembered 'The Johns' from Thames Television. He dug around in his suitcase and produced the business card of John Fielding, the reporter, which the latter had given Tsietsi when he left him at the Planet Cinema; call me if you're ever in London, he had said. Tsietsi dialled the number printed on the card. Almost immediately, the telephone began ringing with people bent on organizing entry into Britain: representatives from the African National Congress, officials from the Home Office, producers from Thames Television. Within a few hours, a television crew and members of the ANC's London office had extricated the youths from the airport.

The ANC representatives were particularly welcoming. They seemed to know all about Tsietsi, Selby and Barney and were at pains to make them feel comfortable. We'll take care of your immigration problems, they said, we'll find you a place to stay, you have nothing to worry about. Despite the reassurances, Selby could not help but feel vulnerable and far from home as they drove through the unfamiliar streets of London. Tsietsi, by contrast, was almost bouncing in excitement as they passed landmarks he had read about in novels: Trafalgar Square, the British Museum, Piccadilly Circus.

The ANC arranged for the youths to live with one of its activists. The woman, a South African exile, resided in a handsome, five-storey house in Hampstead. She gave each of the boys his own room, but they decided to stay together in the same quarters. (For the entire time they remained in London, the three young men would always share a room; it made them feel less lonely.) And she provided them with meals.

After the youths settled in, the ANC held the first of several press conferences for them on 4 October 1976. Tsietsi dominated the interviews: he recounted to the scores of international journalists his escape from South Africa with Selby and Barney; what he believed were attempts by South African agents to kidnap him in Botswana; the horror of the political situation in his country. He and his companions were painstakingly careful – or so they thought – not to associate themselves with the ANC. It was a delicate task. The reporters peppered Tsietsi with questions about the organization; not wishing to offend the people who had organized the press conference, he gave vague replies about his admiration for the ANC leader, Nelson Mandela.

But in South Africa, deliberately or otherwise, Tsietsi's words were taken out of context and reported as though he had given credit to the ANC for the June 16 uprising. The articles angered activists in the townships, especially members of the SSRC. Khotso Seatlholo, who had succeeded Tsietsi as SSRC president, was furious when he read the stories; they were contrary to everything he and Tsietsi had ever discussed. Khotso dashed off a note to Tsietsi in London, reprimanding his friend for betraying their cause and allowing himself to be co-opted by an exile organization. Only when Tsietsi received the letter did he realize how his words had been misinterpreted.

The ANC members did, in fact, try to convert Tsietsi and his companions to their cause. But theirs was a slow, deliberate dance. By now, the British government had granted the exiles permission to remain in the country. Holland, and the possibility to study, were forgotten. In between political discussions, the ANC activists took the youths on shopping sprees to buy clothes and other necessities. They gave them pocket money to explore the city. One afternoon, they brought Tsietsi, Selby and Barney to their offices. The boys found ANC representatives gathered there from all over Europe, including the Soviet Union; they had come to discuss sending Tsietsi and his colleagues on a worldwide speaking tour to explain what happened in Soweto.

Tsietsi exploded. 'You have given up the struggle!' he shouted, pacing the room. 'You are in exile. You have no presence in South Africa. You are absent from the country, you are not accessible to young people. And now you are trying to imply to the world that you supported the uprising!'

Selby was shocked by his friend's outburst. He tried to get him to sit down, but to no avail; Tsietsi was too agitated. In endless, late-night discussions, sequestered in their Hampstead room, the three youths had agreed they would assert their independence of the ANC at every opportunity. But this was extreme. At the very least, Selby believed Tsietsi should have been more respectful of his elders; young people did not speak this way to adults.

Despite Tsietsi's outburst, the ANC representatives persisted in trying to bring the youths into the fold. Their hostess in Hampstead, an ANC stalwart, was particularly tenacious. Tsietsi found her insufferable. One afternoon, after submitting to yet another sermon on the virtues of the ANC, Tsietsi told her, in rather deprecating terms, that the organization was worthless and could go to hell. The woman informed the youths the next day that they would have to leave her home: they clearly did not respect her beloved ANC and she would not countenance their continuous criticism.

Their departure effectively severed the relationship with the ANC. But it did not render them penniless. Tsietsi and his companions had received scholarships and were studying, albeit in a desultory fashion, for their O level exams at a college. The ANC and the Thames Television journalists had arranged the financial help, which continued despite the split with the anti-apartheid organization. The youths used their stipend to pay for a room in a residential hotel. They also embarked on speaking engagements in Britain and Europe for various revolutionary groups that had contacted them when they first arrived in London: Socialists, Maoists, Trotskyites.

During this time, Tsietsi's anti-ANC sentiments became positively rabid. When speaking publicly, he spent half the allotted time attacking the organization, the other half talking about the political situation in South Africa. Tsietsi's obsession became almost pathological. He loathed the ANC's members: to him, they were weak, contemptible people who had been bought out by white communists. Worse yet, they were impeding the genuine struggle back home.

Tsietsi's preoccupation greatly disturbed Selby. He too resented the ANC for attempting to appropriate the June 16 uprising, but the real enemy, to Selby's mind, was the white regime in Pretoria. It seemed a waste to expend so much energy railing against the ANC. Selby had hoped Tsietsi's vitriol would abate with time, but it appeared only to increase in intensity. It was exacerbated, Selby believed, by the youths' sense of being adrift, of lacking direction in their struggle against the Boers. Slowly, almost imperceptibly, Tsietsi's venom began to create a chasm between him and Selby.

In late November, Tsietsi left for a speaking tour of the United States, sponsored by the Socialist Workers' Party. The youths' scholarships had recently been withdrawn; the money from their speaking engagements thus became their sole source of income. That Tsietsi was travelling under the auspices of such a group spawned all manner of sensationalist – and erroneous – stories in South Africa. 'Tsietsi Trained at Vanessa's Red School,' blared one headline in the *Sunday Times*:

> Tsietsi Mashinini, the schoolboy who led the Soweto riots, has been on an intensive training course at the 'Red House' – the 'school for revolutionaries' set up by British actress Vanessa Redgrave. The 'school' is a mansion in Derbyshire belonging to the Workers' Revolutionary Party (WRP),

a fanatical Trotskyist-Marxist group including Vanessa Redgrave and her brother, Corin.

(While not directly succumbing to such 'red-baiting', the US State Department deemed Tsietsi sufficiently politically sensitive to warrant special scrutiny. It sent a cable to its embassy in London, directing the consular section to refer any request from Tsietsi for a visa to the Department's Africa Bureau for an 'advisory opinion'. Consulates usually make such decisions on their own.)

In Boston, Tsietsi participated in a conference against racism that was organized by a group of university students. He electrified the participants with his militancy; people in the US, even veteran activists of the anti-apartheid movement, had never heard such things from a South African black. They were used to the genteel, inclusive philosophies of the ANC. Tsietsi sounded like the most radical of the American black power proponents. He continued to stun audiences in New York, where the American Committee on Africa, an organization with ties to the US civil rights movement, held a press conference for him. 'I'll be in South Africa with a gun in my hand and I think I'm going to enjoy shooting down white South Africans,' he told a reporter for the *New York Times*, when asked about his country's future. He said he could not foresee a South Africa in which whites and blacks 'would live happily ever after' because too much bitterness had been created in the minds of the oppressed black majority.

George Houser, the ACA's executive director, thought Tsietsi difficult to manage. Although well-spoken and colourful, the young South African was somewhat mercurial; George could never be quite certain what he would say in public. For that reason, he decided against sponsoring Tsietsi on a future speaking tour of the US. Tsietsi seemed too unpredictable a personality to submit for scrutiny to the American Congress or State Department – the usual stops for visiting anti-apartheid dignitaries. As it was, in letters to donors, George felt compelled to explain some of the more disturbing statements that appeared in the US press.

After Tsietsi returned from the United States, he and Selby travelled to Botswana. It was their first time back in Africa since escaping from South Africa, a glorious return that felt almost like a homecoming. They met with many of their old SSRC colleagues, now also in exile, to discuss how best to organize scholarships and military training for the hundreds of fellow activists who had fled South Africa. Tsietsi was alarmed to read in the newspapers that Khotso Seatlholo was being pursued by the security forces. He managed to send a message to Khotso in Soweto: Leave now; I don't want you to be arrested.

Khotso had come to the same conclusion. He got Paul Langa, of the Suicide Squad, to escort him to the Botswana border; there, like many of his comrades who preceded him, Khotso became lost and wandered for hours. He was exhausted by the time he crossed the frontier and hitched a lift to Gaborone on the back of a truck. When they arrived, he argued with the driver that the tiny, desolate-looking settlement could not possibly be the capital. Khotso found the house where he was supposed to stay and, after a hot bath and a meal, fell into a drugged sleep. He was roused by someone screaming in his face in Afrikaans: *Word wakker! Word wakker!* (Wake up! Wake up!) Khotso leaped off the bed, convinced he was still in South Africa and about to be arrested – only to find Tsietsi laughing at him.

Theirs was a joyous reunion. A picture of the two appeared in the South African papers, taken by one of the journalists who flocked to Gaborone for an interview. The two activists face each other in identical poses: Tsietsi, tall, slim, dressed in overalls and a striped shirt; Khotso, shorter, baby-faced, a long strand of twisted beads hanging around his neck. They are shaking hands; each youth raises his free arm in a black power salute. But it is Tsietsi, lunging forward, who dominates the photograph. That stance seemed to characterize the changes Khotso observed in his friend. If Tsietsi had gained more confidence since leaving Soweto, he was also less democratic. Now he appeared utterly convinced of the veracity of his ideas, often to the exclusion of his colleagues' views.

Tsietsi's self-assurance was evident in the interviews published in South Africa. 'It is the White man who has the problem, not the Black man', he told the *Mail*. 'Black people . . . need no agitators or communists to know that they are being exploited economically by the apartheid regime, which is responsible for many and various things that put a Black at lamentable physical and mental disadvantage . . . I believe again that all peaceful methods and negotiations with the regime have been exhausted. The only language they will understand will come through the barrel of the gun. I vow I will be back.'

His outspokenness provided ammunition for those bent on discrediting him – something the white regime in Pretoria was keen to encourage. A campaign began, starting with the reports of his Trotskyist ties, that would continue for years. During Tsietsi's stay in Botswana, a newspaper story appeared in South Africa under the headline: 'Is Rebel Mashinini Losing Some Glitter?'

> Does Tsietsi . . . still enjoy the same popularity among Soweto students and those who fled with him as he did during the disturbances? . . . Some of his fellow exiles are critical of his 'head in the clouds attitude'. . . . The impression I gathered from him and other people is that he is a brilliant young man but because of the attention that has been focused on him, he has become a bit arrogant.

Nomkhitha, sitting in Soweto, was perturbed. All those reporters were travelling to Botswana, interviewing Tsietsi – and publishing rubbish. People complained that every time Tsietsi attacked the government, the children who were imprisoned suffered. His words engendered much resentment among her neighbours and acquaintances. Nomkhitha resolved that if the reporters could travel to Gaborone, she could too; and she would tell Tsietsi to hold his tongue.

Accompanied by one of Joseph's cousins, Nomkhitha travelled by train to Zeerust, near the Botswana border. From there, the two women took taxis to Gaborone. They went directly to a hotel, where one of the journalists who had already made the journey told them they would find Tsietsi. He was overjoyed at Nomkhitha's sudden appearance. Tsietsi hugged and kissed his mother like a little boy; she held her son at arm's length to examine him. He looked beautiful to her: healthy, strong, a bit heavier than when he left South Africa.

Tsietsi escorted the two women to the house of an activist lawyer, where they were lodged in great style. The lawyer put his maids, as well as his pantry, at their disposal. Over the next two days, Tsietsi spent hours talking with Nomkhitha. He hungered for news of home and deluged her with questions about Joseph, his brothers and sisters, friends, politics, and so forth. When Nomkhitha explained to Tsietsi that his interviews were making things worse, he seemed deeply concerned and promised to stop.

She asked him about his life. 'I'm trying to drum up money for scholarships,' Tsietsi said. 'The exiled students need scholarships to study. This is the work I'm doing.' It was a refrain Tsietsi often repeated during their conversations: he wanted to help the exiles continue with their education. Oddly, he mentioned nothing of his own intention to seek military training. Instead, Tsietsi talked of wanting to obtain a scholarship for himself because he, too, wished to go back to school. Tsietsi seemed sanguine as he spoke; his demeanour reassured Nomkhitha.

Nomkhitha saved the most sensitive question for the end of her all-too-brief visit. 'Why didn't you tell your father and I that June 16 was going to happen?' she asked, nursing a hurt. (One that, twenty-five years on, she would still hold.)

Tsietsi threw back his head and laughed. 'You wouldn't have allowed me to do it, so I didn't want you to know.' He took her hands in his. 'You must promise me that you'll continue with the struggle. And I promise you that we are coming back and taking over the country.' With that, he kissed her and left. Nomkhitha had no way of knowing that this was the last time she would see him alive.

Despite his promises to Nomkhitha, when Tsietsi returned to London he threw much of his energy into exploring ways of engaging in armed struggle. The embassies of various African nations began contacting Tsietsi and Selby, offering help. As they mulled over the various proposals in their nightly talks, the youths agreed on one thing: they did not want to create yet another exile organization, with offices and staff and letter-heads. Their goal was to find resources to carry on the fight and channel them back into South Africa.

Tsietsi concentrated his efforts on the representatives of the African regimes that seemed most revolutionary: Nigeria, Guinea, Tanzania. The idea was to convince the diplomats that Tsietsi and his comrades were a new group of anti-apartheid opponents, entirely separate from the ineffectual ANC and PAC and their tired tactics. The youths' aim was to overthrow the South African regime militarily. To achieve this, they would need training and money to purchase weapons.

But Tsietsi found himself stymied by the ANC's preeminent position among other nations. He could hardly persuade African governments to support his cause when the ANC was recognized as the vanguard of the anti-apartheid struggle in exile; it was even represented on the Organization of African Unity, the continent's regional political body. This acknowledgment had not come easily. Oliver Tambo, the ANC's president, had spent years toiling in obscurity. He was a virtual one-man revolution after his escape from South Africa in 1960, travelling the world and begging for support. Few countries would receive him, let alone provide aid.

Tsietsi needed to present a credible alternative to attract attention and money. He was helped in his endeavours by the appearance in London of his old mentor, Drake Koka. (Drake had fled South Africa after members of the security forces searched his house one day when he was out. Buried under a dog kennel, they found documents that outlined a plan to send young men abroad for military training.) Drake met Tsietsi, Selby and Barney at their hotel near Marble Arch. He was delighted to see them again, especially Tsietsi; his young protégé looked healthy and well-dressed. They went to the cinema and then to a restaurant for supper to celebrate their reunion. Drake was struck by how Tsietsi had matured in exile; he attributed it to Tsietsi's meetings with diplomats and other dignitaries. Still, Tsietsi seemed unsettled. He complained of not having a proper programme, of feeling adrift as he and his companions tried to hammer out the details of their new group. Drake promised to work with them.

Soon after, Tsietsi and Khotso left for the United States. The purpose of their tour was to educate the American public about the political situation in South Africa and to raise money for the exiled activists in Botswana. Tsietsi's speaking engagements took him to the West Coast; Khotso's, to the East Coast. Khotso quickly tired of the routine: it was too programmed, too deliberate an existence for him. To awaken every morning for three months knowing exactly what he was to do that day made him feel like a circus animal. Khotso would give a talk and then answer seemingly endless, earnest questions; invariably, an enthused group of supporters would want to take their South African celebrity out for a drink afterwards to continue the stimulating discussion. Khotso grew weary of all the conversation. At one point he wanted to quit the tour; it took an expensive, long-distance telephone call from Tsietsi to persuade him to continue.

As much as Khotso detested the experience, Tsietsi thrived. He was in his oratorical element; being in the limelight invigorated him. Tsietsi believed the speaking engagements allowed them to make contacts with dignitaries, black personages, and so forth – people who could ultimately help with their new organization. At times, though, his eloquence proved counterproductive. Some listeners questioned the putative evils of Bantu education: how could so bankrupt and inferior a system produce someone so skilled?

Tsietsi joined Khotso in New York for a lecture at Columbia University. Among the audience they addressed was Tom Karis, a professor of politics. He had just published, along with two colleagues, the second volume of a series documenting the history of African politics in South Africa. Because of his work, the Pretoria government routinely denied Tom visas to enter the country; and so he developed the habit of trying to meet and interview black South Africans who visited New York.

The audience rose in a spontaneous outburst of applause when Tsietsi strode onto the stage. Tom was immediately struck by his poise. Tsietsi began by looking at the microphone and wondering aloud whether he should use it because IBM was its manufacturer. 'I will use it,' he cried, 'to call for IBM to get out of South Africa!' The crowd, which clearly supported economic sanctions against the Pretoria regime, went wild.

Tom had never witnessed such excitement at this sort of meeting. Afterwards, he approached the stage to speak with Tsietsi; Tom watched as the young man was overwhelmed by well-wishers wanting to shake his hand or offer their congratulations. Tsietsi seemed to possess a preternatural magnetism. Finally, Tom introduced himself and asked if they could meet somewhere to talk. Tsietsi was leaving for Washington; perhaps they could have coffee at the station before his departure. Tom arrived at Penn Station at the appointed time. Tsietsi was nowhere to be seen. A few minutes before the Washington train was due to leave, Tom spied Tsietsi. Again, he was surrounded by admirers. Tom could only say a few words to Tsietsi and present him with a copy of his book before the young man was escorted to his train.

Khotso noticed that Tsietsi softened his criticism of the ANC during the tour. Instead, he accused the press of 'putting a wedge between the ANC, PAC and the students. . . . The two liberation movements and the students have a common enemy. The only thing left is for all three to come together and fight the common enemy.' Khotso suspected his attacks were an over-reaction to the earlier stories that had him attributing the uprising to the ANC; the proclamations were an attempt to reestablish his authority. Whatever the reason, Khotso, like Tsietsi's other colleagues, did not think it a good strategy. They would never dislodge the ANC as the premier anti-apartheid organization, and they would gain nothing by antagonizing the group and it adherents. Indeed, the young activists stood to lose their support in the US if Tsietsi persisted in his anti-ANC rhetoric.

For its part, the ANC did not think much of Tsietsi. In a cable to the State Department, a US Embassy official in Gaborone described a meeting with Daniel Tloome, an ANC representative. Asked his opinion of the student leader,

Tloome proceeded to dismiss Tsietsi as a 'young and inexperienced' lad who had taken part in a 'student demonstration' and then fled. He said the US and UK are 'spoiling'
Tsietsi with too much publicity, which makes him think he
is a 'big man'. Tloome also noted with scorn Mashinini's
statement that the 'ANC does not exist'. According to
Tloome, the ANC went underground almost before
Mashinini was born. Mashinini looked around him in South
Africa, saw only a few student groups and naïvely decided
the ANC does not exist.

By the end of their trip, Tsietsi and Khotso were desperate
to return to Africa. Tsietsi flew to Nigeria; Khotso, to
Botswana. Tsietsi and his colleagues had decided to concentrate their efforts on the Nigerians because they seemed the
most earnest among those offering assistance. While Khotso
began trying to organize the thousands of newly arrived South
African exiles in Gaborone, Tsietsi negotiated with two
advisers who were close to General Olusegun Obasanjo, the
Nigerian president. After lengthy discussions, a plan was
agreed in outline. The Nigerian government would provide
offices for the youths in Lagos and money for military
training.

The agreement made headlines in South Africa. 'Mashinini
to Head New Force', reported the *Sunday Times*. The story
continued:

> The Nigerian Government is building up a new 'liberation
> organisation' round a group of about 180 black South
> African student exiles under the leadership of Tsietsi
> Mashinini . . . The Nigerian Government's motivation in
> backing the new group is not clear, but it is apparently
> intended as a 'third force' rivalling South Africa's two estab-
> lished liberation organisations, the powerful African
> National Congress (ANC) and the nearly defunct Pan
> African [sic] Congress (PAC) . . . The establishment of the
> Mashinini group in Nigeria is of questionable importance
> in itself, but it heralds one of the most serious challenges in
> the history of the established liberation organisations – how

they are going to reconcile themselves with South Africa's new black consciousness movement.

Selby was shocked when he heard the news. He and his fellow activists were now going to have a base in Lagos and form a new group – exactly what Selby had thought they all despised. What of their all-night discussions, in which they had deplored what the ANC had become in exile and vowed never to make the same mistake? Selby felt the fissure between him and Tsietsi deepen.

The breaking point came when Selby went on a speaking tour to Canada to raise money for the refugees in Botswana. He collected nearly $10,000, the most he or any of his colleagues had ever raised; Selby was terribly excited. When he returned to London, Selby found that Tsietsi had gone abroad on business. Selby did not know what to do with the cheque; the boys did not even have a bank account. He gave it to Drake to guard until Tsietsi's return. On learning that Drake had taken the funds for safekeeping, Tsietsi was furious; he launched into a screaming tirade. Why would you raise money for the exiles and then give it to Drake? he kept shrieking at Selby.

Selby was stunned: Tsietsi was railing against their beloved Godfather. It seemed to Selby that he had turned into a megalomaniac. The media lionized him so; perhaps Tsietsi had begun to believe everything they said. Selby thought him arrogant even before he went into exile, but now Tsietsi was becoming a monster. Worse yet, he appeared to be coming unhinged. The realization that he would have to break with his friend, after all they had shared, caused Selby much distress.

He quietly went about trying to organize a scholarship through Drake. When a university in California offered him funds to study, Selby told none of his comrades, least of all Tsietsi; Selby was afraid Tsietsi would try to do something to sabotage the trip. Tsietsi was in Nigeria on the day of Selby's departure. Selby did not bid him goodbye; they never communicated again. In the ensuing years, Selby would follow the life of his erstwhile friend from afar. It was like watching a Greek tragedy unfold.

CHAPTER SIX

Mpho and Nomkhitha

By the early months of 1977, nearly 700 activists had died in South Africa in the unrest that followed the June 16 protest. An estimated 4,000 youths had been injured, another 6,000 arrested. Perhaps as many as 4,000 young men and women fled the country to escape the repression that essentially quelled the uprising. Mpho was determined to join their ranks, especially after Dee's departure. Exile no longer seemed a strange thing now that his mother had been to see both Tsietsi and Dee.

Nomkhitha had travelled to Swaziland to be with Dee after her visit to Tsietsi in Gaborone. Dee had been telephoning Joseph at work and Nomkhitha at home, crying into the receiver: I want to come home, there's no schooling here for me, things aren't going well. Worried about her fifteen-year-old son, Nomkhitha filled a bag with clothes and food and got Mpho to organize transport over the border. He arranged for Paul Fakude and Themba Mlangeni, some of his contacts from the Pan Africanist Congress, to accompany her. She met Dee at the George Hotel in Manzini, a hilly, flyspeck of a town. In his mother's presence, the youth seemed more composed; the two talked of how Dee might continue with his education. After spending a few days with her son, Nomkhitha left feeling resolved about his future.

When Nomkhitha, upon returning to Soweto, told Mpho about her discussions with Dee, he too was heartened. One evening, Mpho packed a suitcase and bid farewell to Joseph and Nomkhitha; he told them he would be back in a week or so. Like his brothers before him, Mpho travelled to the border in a *kombi* at the dead of night. As he jumped the fence, Mpho turned around to peer through the darkness in the direction of South Africa. He wanted to picture how it would look when he returned in an invading force of tanks, to wage proper war against the Boers.

The *kombi*'s driver eventually met Mpho on the other side and drove him to a PAC house in Manzini. It was a spacious bungalow with a large garden. About forty South African young-sters – Dee and his friend Tiger among them – lived there, sleeping on foam-rubber mattresses at night, packed into all the rooms. Dee was ecstatic to see Mpho: here was a representa-tive of the life he had left behind, a big brother, a cushion against the older, rougher youths in the house. (The only person younger than Dee was a boy whom everyone called 'Kid'.)

The house was a kind of reception site where people stayed after escaping from South Africa, until the PAC representative could send them to other countries. The representative and his officers did not actually live in the residence; it was too dangerous, too exposed to South African agents and their proxies. They made appearances to welcome newcomers such as Mpho. Afterwards, a PAC official took Mpho to a nearby police station where he declared his presence in Swaziland as an illegal alien, asked for political asylum and was fingerprinted. (This was the usual procedure for South African exiles.)

The refugees ran the house themselves. A PAC official arrived every morning to discuss the assignment of chores. Each youth was expected to tidy his sleeping space and to get his own breakfast; cleaning the rest of the house and cooking dinner were done communally. After the chores were finished, the PAC officer lectured the exiles on the history and politics of the anti-apartheid struggle. Attendance at the two-hour class was mandatory, and everyone in the house participated. Mpho quickly worked out that the discussions were little more than indoctrination sessions, intended to persuade the youngsters of the PAC's primacy over the ANC. Mpho needed no convincing. He had long ago dismissed the ANC as a white-dominated organization; and when his PAC host spoke of how the youths would receive military training to attack the Boers and liberate

Azania (the PAC's name for South Africa), Mpho was positively ecstatic.

For Mpho, leaving Soweto was a kind of liberation in itself. For the first time in his life he experienced the freedom of living in a black-ruled country. He could sleep in the same place, night after night, and not worry about having to flee suddenly. He could befriend the students who attended the elite, all-girls high school next door without fearing the police. He could go to the cinema. He could go for a walk. He could relax.

Still, something nagged at Mpho. For him and his generation of activists, there was only one enemy: the whites. Why then this schism between the PAC and ANC? The more he pestered his hosts for an explanation, the more dissatisfied he became; they only seemed capable of disparaging the ANC. The PAC officials even prevented their charges from trying to make contact with ANC representatives. Mpho and Dee knew that Rocks was in Swaziland with the ANC, but their hosts refused to allow them to look for him. As the days passed, Mpho began to doubt the veracity of everything he had been promised. Despite repeated requests, they were never shown any training camps, and the PAC officials never produced anyone who had actually gone for military instruction.

The PAC leaders decided that Tiger would return with Mpho to Soweto to recruit more youngsters and find a replacement for Mpho. Their hosts arranged for them to travel in a special taxi that plied the Manzini–Johannesburg route. Mpho and Tiger met the driver in the car park of the Manzini library on a dreary, rainy morning; he was a Swazi, and his vehicle bore Swazi licence plates. The driver discussed where he would drop Mpho and Tiger, where he would pick them up, how they should get across the border. He sounded knowledgeable and professional; Mpho felt confident the journey would go well.

They left at 11 a.m. Mpho and Tiger were dropped about half a mile from the border. They easily found the crossing; a woman in a nearby hut pointed them in the direction of the fence. On the South African side, the two youths walked, as agreed, to a general store that stood at a bend in the road, about half a mile from the Oshoek border gate. The place was full of Swazis who had crossed the frontier on foot to shop. Mpho and Tiger waited for what seemed like ages, trying to blend in with the Swazis. They began to get worried: the driver had assured them he would have passed through the border control and be waiting for them by the time they arrived.

They stayed at the shop for two hours. Afraid they looked conspicuous standing around for so long, Mpho and Tiger decided to start walking towards Johannesburg. The schools in the area had just been let out for lunch; they could disappear among the crowds of students. They set off along the road. By now it was raining hard. Several police vans drove by, going in both directions. They trudged through the downpour, peering at every passing vehicle. Then suddenly a police car stopped next to them; two officers jumped out. They grabbed Mpho and Tiger and shoved them into the back seat of the vehicle.

The boys were driven to the police station near the border gate, marched inside and made to sit on benches. One of the officers searched them; finding some pamphlets and Soweto PAC stickers, the man held the contraband up triumphantly for his fellow policemen to see. That set everyone in the station twittering excitedly about the Soweto terrorists they had captured. 'We must make a dash for it back to Swaziland,' Tiger muttered under his breath.

'I can't run that far,' whispered Mpho.

'I've calculated the distance,' Tiger assured him. 'It's not that far. You can do it.'

Mpho looked around. All the policemen seemed preoccupied with congratulating themselves on their catch; one burly Afrikaner had his feet up on a desk, his guns hanging on the wall behind him. Mpho nodded to Tiger.

'I'm going to count to three,' Tiger whispered, 'and we'll run.'

At three, Mpho and Tiger rushed out of the open door. Paralysed by shock, it took the policemen a moment or two to begin their pursuit. Tiger, who ran the 100 metres at school, raced ahead of Mpho towards Swaziland, followed by several security officers. Mpho ran parallel to the border fence, with policemen trailing him. As he entered a wooded area, dodging fallen trees and limbs, he lost sight of Tiger. He hurdled one stump, unaware that a ditch lay beyond it; the noise of his splashing caught the attention of the policemen who were chasing Tiger. Seeing Mpho thrashing about, waist-deep, in the water, they came rushing back and hauled him out. One officer hit Mpho on the head with the butt of his rifle; the others kicked and punched him as they dragged him back to the police station.

Locked into a tiny cell, Mpho fell into a deep sleep on the mat on the floor. He awoke about an hour later. The first thing he did was to untie from his arm the vial of *muti*, the medicine he had got from the witch doctor that was supposed to prevent him from being arrested. He flushed the contents down the lavatory. Then he began improvising the story he would tell the police. Although they clearly thought they had captured someone important, Mpho guessed that they were not really sure of his identity. And he did not have any papers on his body.

Four white policemen entered Mpho's cell later in the evening to begin their interrogation. They punched him, hit him on the back, demanded to know the name of the youth who had escaped. 'What is your name?' one of them shouted.

'Gideon Dlamini,' Mpho replied, giving a common Swati/Zulu name.

'Where do you come from?'

'Swaziland.'

'What are you doing here?'

'I've come to visit family. I jumped the fence, that's the way I always cross. I'm too young to have a passport.'

After several more questions, his interrogators left the cell. Mpho was frightened. He prayed that, being just border police and not the trained torturers of Johannesburg's John Vorster Square, they would soon tire of him. He would continue to play dumb, and they would beat him some more; unable to pin anything on him, they would release him. Or so he hoped. Thinking about all that could befall him in prison made Mpho unbearably tired and he again fell into a deep sleep.

He did not know how long he had been sleeping when the door opened and something was shoved into the cell. In the darkness, Mpho discerned the shape of a man; then he slept again. He awoke around midnight and began pacing the cell. 'So why were you arrested?' he asked the inert form on the floor. Getting no reply, he repeated the question. Again receiving no response, Mpho knelt on the mat and shook the man to wake him. The arm that he touched was cold and rigid. Mpho began screaming and pounding on the cell door. A policeman opened it. 'This person is dead!' Mpho shouted, on the verge of hysteria. 'This person is dead!' he kept shrieking, until the warders dragged the corpse outside.

It took Mpho a long time to get back to sleep. He awoke the following morning to find two plainclothes officers – one white, one black – from Special Branch. Now he was truly terrified. Trained by the Israelis and the Portuguese in interrogation techniques, Special Branch formed the elite corps of the police force. It had an enormous budget, operated clandestinely and carried out investigations with impunity. Special Branch officers concentrated on apprehending enemies of the state; they employed whatever means necessary – solitary confinement, torture – to achieve their ends.

The white officer asked Mpho to identify himself. Mpho began to embroider on the story he had given the previous day: my name is Gideon Dlamini, I'm from Swaziland, I was on my way to visit relatives in Natal province. The white officer seemed sympathetic, which unnerved Mpho. The black officer, an older man, kept repeating that he should tell the truth, tell everything.

The Special Branch men left, to be replaced by uniformed police officers who moved Mpho to a cell next to a Swazi man. Mpho had never seen the other prisoner before. They were treated as though they were fellow terrorists: handcuffed together to walk from the cells to the charge office; guarded by policemen with their guns at the ready; fingerprinted in the charge office, then marched back to their cells. Mpho believed the police might have thought the Swazi man was Tiger. Later in the day, Mpho and the other prisoner were handcuffed together again, shoved into a van and moved to a small police station at Lothair, about eighteen miles deeper into South Africa. 'Why am I here?' Mpho asked the uniformed officers throughout the journey. They only shook their heads. Terrorists were beyond their scope; this was Special Branch business.

At Lothair, a tiny *dorp* consisting of a few shops and a police station, Mpho and the Swazi man were put into separate cells and kept in solitary confinement for three days. Their meals were pushed through the grille of the cell's outer door by other inmates, who obviously had been instructed not to talk to them. Mpho found the food unpalatable: *phuza mandla*, a kind of thin gruel made from powdered maize meal. He refused to touch it.

On the third day, the two Special Branch officers reappeared. They went first to the Swazi's cell, where they spent about an hour firing questions at him and beating him. Mpho was sickened as he listened to the screams, knowing his turn was next. The Special Branch men were no less brutal with him. For two hours, they slapped, punched and pummelled Mpho, occasionally slamming him against the cell wall. Mpho began to bleed from his right ear; one of his eyes swelled almost shut. He kept repeating his story of who he was and what he had been doing near the border. The black officer, who was Swazi by birth, tried to tell the white agent that Mpho was an impostor: his spoken Swati was not nearly as good as his Zulu. Ever the creature of apartheid, the white officer ignored his partner's observation and insisted on doing the questioning himself. Mpho admitted nothing. He was fingerprinted again, and the Special Branch men departed.

He didn't see them again for two weeks. During that time, no one was allowed to speak to him; the common criminals who cleaned his cell were just about the only human contact he had. He was not permitted to telephone his family or a lawyer. Even worse, the Swazi prisoner was released two days after the Special Branch men had visited them. This was a new source of terror for Mpho; now the Special Branch would be concentrating their efforts on his case. His thoughts became almost manic. One moment he was convinced that he, like the Swazi, would be freed; the next, he was certain he would die in jail without anyone knowing. He consoled himself with the thought that Tiger obviously had escaped and had probably notified his parents of his fate. To remain calm and keep from getting depressed, Mpho tried to concentrate on small details of his well-being. He forced himself to eat. When the black policemen were on duty, he washed. (The white officers could not be bothered with such trivial matters.) Still, it was hard not to give way to despair.

When the Special Branch men returned, the white officer strode into the cell and immediately slapped Mpho's face. 'Today you're going to tell me everything, *kaffir*,' he crowed.

'I've already told you everything,' Mpho stammered.

'Rubbish,' said the white officer, kicking him in the stomach.

So the interrogation began, with Mpho denying everything and the Special Branch men brutalizing him. But something had changed; the officers seemed more confident, less floundering, as though they believed they had cracked the case. Indeed, the black agent was positively ebullient. 'Do you know Tsietsi Mashinini?' he hissed, his eyes glinting. 'Do you know a school named Morris Issacson?'

When they produced copies of his birth certificate and the housing permit that listed the members of his family at 924 Pitso Street in Soweto, Mpho knew the game was up. The interrogation lasted for several more hours. After seeing the documents, Mpho found it increasingly difficult to continue the pretence of being an innocent Swazi; he simply stopped responding. That night, as he lay in his cell, Mpho realized he had no hope of escaping imprisonment; the Special Branch officers knew everything. He had lost. (Later Mpho would learn that one of the boys whom he had helped to escape to Swaziland had walked back to the border and given himself up to the South African authorities; he missed his grandmother. The boy divulged much information, including the names of the members of the PAC house, Mpho's involvement, and Mpho's mission for the PAC in Soweto.)

The black agent woke him the next morning. He escorted Mpho to the charge office, where the white officer was waiting. '*Ja*, Mpho, we've got you,' he gloated. 'We've got you.' The officer informed Mpho that he was being arrested under Section 6 of the Terrorism Act: a ninety-day detention order, without trial, that allowed for an indefinite extension. He would not be permitted to see a lawyer or any members of his family.

That afternoon, Mpho was moved to the police headquarters for the Eastern Transvaal at Ermelo. There the officers greeted him with cries of, 'Oh Mpho, we've been waiting for you.'

Nomkhitha and Joseph were already in bed for the night when the police knocked on their door. They thought it was just another raid, but the officer in charge said no, they had come to take Nomkhitha for questioning. Nomkhitha put on a dress and jersey and asked if she could bring a blanket. The police then hurried her outside; Nomkhitha had no time to kiss any of the children goodbye. 'Still praying?' one of the officers enquired snidely as Joseph watched his wife being taken away.

The police put Nomkhitha in an unmarked car. Themba Mlangeni and Paul Fakude, the two men who had accompanied her to Swaziland, were in the back seat. Nomkhitha was not frightened; she had done nothing wrong. She did not believe they would harm her just because she was Tsietsi's mother. The three were driven to a local police station where they sat on benches while their escorts filled out a stack of forms. Then Themba, Paul and Nomkhitha were handcuffed together and led back to the car.

Nomkhitha was surprised when the vehicle drove onto the highway. As she read the names of the towns they passed, she realized they were travelling east, on the same road she had taken to Swaziland. The policemen refused to allow her to ask questions or to talk to her fellow captives. After a while, one of the officers turned to her. 'You've always said you weren't involved, you weren't involved, but look at yourself today in my car. The only thing left for you is to tell the truth.' His words sent a chill through Nomkhitha. The car sped on through the darkness, past illuminated factories belching white smoke into a coal-black sky; past huge mounds of mining waste standing out in relief against the night, like excavated temples of a lost people. I've done nothing, Nomkhitha repeated to herself, I've done nothing.

They stopped at Middelburg, more than sixty miles to the

north-east of Johannesburg. The policemen put Nomkhitha in a filthy cell with female common criminals; the stench from the lavatory was such that she could barely bring herself to use it. An inmate gave Nomkhitha one of her own sheets and a blanket to use on the sleeping mat. The police left Nomkhitha in the cell for the weekend. For nourishment, she was given sickly-looking stew that she found inedible. Her only contact with the authorities was an Afrikaner policeman who came to leer at her. '*Ja*, at last,' he said, 'we've got Tsietsi's mother.'

After two days, the security men drove her, Paul and Themba to their headquarters in Ermelo. Nomkhitha was immediately taken to an interrogation room. 'Did you know that your son is with us?' one of the officers asked.

'Which son?'

'Mpho.'

Nomkhitha now understood she was being detained in connection with Mpho, not because of Tsietsi. She and Joseph knew only vague details about Mpho's arrest; Tiger had called them from Swaziland when he arrived back in Manzini. But until now, they had had no idea where he was being held. 'If Mpho is here, I want to see him,' Nomkhitha told her captors.

One of the policemen left the room. A few minutes later, he opened the door; there stood Mpho. 'What's going on here?' he shrieked, flailing at his jailers. 'What's she done? Why is she here?' Before Nomkhitha could reply, a policeman pinned Mpho to the floor and one of his colleagues kicked shut the door. Nomkhitha could hear her son's shouts echoing in the hallway. She began to cry; she could only imagine what Mpho had endured.

After Nomkhitha was taken away, Joseph drove to his brother Andrew's house in Soweto. He explained to Andrew and his wife what had happened; the next morning, they arrived early at Joseph's home to help with all the children. Joseph went to the nearby police station at Protea to ask about Nomkhitha. The policemen refused to answer his questions and treated him as though he were a child. Humiliated, Joseph asked his bosses at work to make enquiries. Eventually they tracked down

Nomkhitha to a cell in Standerton, near Ermelo. Joseph was shocked when he heard she was so far away; he did not even know where it was.

On the first weekend after learning of her whereabouts, Joseph packed a bag with food and clothing and made the long journey to Standerton. It was a sleepy farming town where Joseph could not find even a toilet he could use. Again, the police refused to speak to Joseph, except to say he could not see his wife. He left the bag for Nomkhitha with them and drove back to Johannesburg, deeply depressed.

Like everyone in the family, Tshepiso did not realize that Nomkhitha was being arrested when the police came; he too thought she would soon return. (Nearly a quarter of a century later, he would not be able to recall the particulars of that night. But the process of trying to remember would prompt him, suddenly, to begin weeping.) Tshepiso only realized what had happened when he passed a poster for that day's newspaper nailed to a tree trunk. It said: 'Security Cops Detain Tsietsi's Mum'. Furious, he tore it down.

He desperately wanted to ask Joseph questions. Why had his mother been arrested? How long would she be away? Would she be all right? But the adults' strategy since the start of the uprising was not to say anything; they were trying to protect the youngsters. The less they knew, the less interesting they would be to the police. Tshepiso understood the futility of attempting to engage Joseph in a conversation about his mother. Joseph would brush him aside; and the other grown-ups – friends and relatives who came to help – were equally evasive.

These visitors divided the cooking, cleaning, washing and ironing among themselves. Because of their help, the house continued to function without Nomkhitha. Occasionally, however, the rotation broke down and it fell to ten-year-old Tshepiso, one of the oldest children still at home, to take charge. Confronted with a gaggle of hungry, crying siblings, Tshepiso would drag a stool over to the stove, climb up and laboriously stir a pot of porridge until it had cooked.

* * *

Mpho's shock at seeing Nomkhitha in police headquarters abated somewhat when security officers assured him that she had been released the next day. Unbeknown to him, she was incarcerated in the women's section of a nearby prison. Mpho found consolation in thinking of Nomkhitha in Soweto. Later, when the authorities eased their restrictions and allowed Mpho to receive food from home, he often found a plate of dumplings included in the package: Nomkhitha's speciality. To him, they confirmed her whereabouts. In fact, the dumplings were made by his Aunt Isabella, cooked in his mother's style.

Mpho was kept in a solitary-confinement cell at a police station in Standerton. The cubicle contained a lavatory and a concrete slab with a foam mat and blanket; for a pillow, Mpho rolled up another blanket. He usually awoke at seven o'clock, when the other prisoners began to stir. At eight his breakfast arrived: mealie *pap* with a greasy meat gravy, which Mpho found unpalatable. The only time he would eat well while in confinement was during interrogations. Then he ate whatever the policemen ordered for lunch. Sometimes Mpho kept the food to savour later in his cell, away from his inquisitors: a pint of milk, packet of chips, good bread.

After breakfast, the guards escorted Mpho, in handcuffs, to the police station, where the Special Branch officers had set up a temporary office. On the first day of his interrogation, an officer handed Mpho a pen and a sheet of paper. Write everything, he commanded, where you were born, where you went to school, the subjects you studied, your friends, girlfriends, your activities in Swaziland, your mission in Soweto. Mpho painstakingly wrote out seven pages of his history; it took him virtually the entire day. The officer read the completed composition, his lips silently forming every word, until he came to the end. He put down the papers and looked up at Mpho. '*Kak,*' he said (Shit). The officer tore up the essay into small pieces and handed Mpho more paper. Write it again, he ordered, even if it takes you all night.

Mpho returned to his cell. Several veteran PAC members in Manzini had lectured the youngsters about how to survive an interrogation. Give the authorities something, they said, otherwise they will kill you; when you provide names, make certain they are people who are deeply underground or safely in exile and cannot testify against you. Following these guidelines, Mpho wrote out exactly what he had recounted the first time. He did not know that his hosts in Swaziland were members of the PAC; he was naïve about such political matters; he had simply decided to return home, which is when he was arrested.

The police tore up Mpho's second version. After the failure of his third, then fourth, composition to satisfy his captors, the security officers decided to ask him questions directly. They also began to beat him. You're talking shit, one of them would roar, hitting him. One policeman became so enraged that he grabbed a pair of handcuffs and swung them with full force at the side of Mpho's head, drawing blood. Occasionally Mpho said things that caught the security officers' attention; they ordered him to write them down. Back in his cell, Mpho had time to think. If they were interested in what he said, it must be incriminating; anything that resembled a signed confession could consign him to jail for life. Mpho refused to write any more.

On some days, the police beat him mercilessly. On others, they left Mpho sitting in an office and ignored him. Once, a security officer who had a farm nearby brought in a large box of fruit and vegetables from his fields. He gave them to Mpho, the only time he tasted fresh produce throughout his incarceration. A few days later, the same policeman made Mpho lie on the floor and walked on him because he was displeased with Mpho's responses to his questions. At weekends, Mpho sat in his cell and thought about Monday and how it would all start again.

Interrogative detention, as conducted by the security police, was a kind of fishing expedition. The aim was to develop background information and intelligence on particular people and organizations. The Special Branch officers who interrogated Mpho were responsible for monitoring cross-border activities and thus interested in his work in Swaziland. They also attempted to determine specific crimes with which a detainee could be charged. Often, after finishing a broad and, quite literally, torturous examination, the officers would present a massive file to the Attorney General and let him decide who should be charged and with what.

Unlike other authoritarian regimes where political prisoners were disposed of unceremoniously, the South African government was bizarrely legalistic. In part, its motivation came from the structures it inherited from the British system and that remained even after the introduction of apartheid. An inquest, for example, was held any time a person died while in prison. But the government's seeming obsessiveness with going through the legal motions also attempted to prove, to the white population and the world in general, that South Africa was still a democracy. Indeed, whites continued to enjoy basic democratic privileges. They had the right of habeas corpus; they could sue a government minister; and so forth. Despite the denial of such rights to the majority of its people, the government hoped its judicial proceedings would keep South Africa from being classified with, say, the Communist Bloc countries, and from being similarly ostracized. The Calvinist Afrikaners justified the rule of apartheid under the rule of law.

One morning, Mpho's captors came for him before dawn. Handcuffing him, they put Mpho into a vehicle and began driving out of town. He repeatedly asked the policemen where they were going, but received no response. When they reached the *veldt*, open, grassy country, the car stopped; the officers pulled Mpho out, handcuffed his arms behind him, attached irons to his legs and slipped a hood over his head. They pushed him back into the vehicle and began a bone-shaking drive over an unpaved road. Mpho was terrified. He thought they were going to kill him.

When the vehicle stopped again, the policemen dragged Mpho out and made him sit on a chair. 'Today *kaffir*, you're going to talk,' one of the officers said to him. 'We're sick and tired of your games. Today you talk or we'll leave your body here and no one will find you.' The policemen pushed a thick stick under Mpho's bent knees; they chained his hands in such a way that they were clasped under the stick. 'We want names, *kaffir*,' the officer continued. 'We want the names of your people in Swaziland, who is being trained, who is doing the training.' With that, the policemen hoisted Mpho up by the ends of the stick and suspended him between two branches of a tree; he swung there, head down, in a kind of tilted foetal position. In the copious lexicon of police torture, this was known as 'the helicopter'. Intended to make its victim feel unspeakably helpless and vulnerable, it slowly stretched muscles and tendons and made blood rush to the head.

Mpho felt the policemen smear a cold, gel-like substance on his fingers, toes, elbows, and the sides of his knees. They were attaching what felt like strings to the areas that were spread with gel. Mpho struggled, trying to kick his way off the tree; suddenly, he was jolted by an indescribable, searing pain that coursed through his body. He began to scream. The pain continued for what seemed like an eternity; Mpho went on screaming long after the electricity had ceased. '*Nou prat*,' said a policeman. 'Now talk. Who was your handler in Swaziland?'

After weeks of interrogation, Mpho knew what they wanted him to say. He shouted out the names of people his inquisitors had mentioned to him: anybody, everybody, to ensure they would not turn on the electricity again. His strategy of not identifying anyone who could be arrested crumbled; he would implicate the entire world to make the pain stop and never return. He was willing to say anything.

The torture session continued for a long time. The policemen applied electric currents to Mpho's body several times when the answers did not come fast enough or failed to please them. At midday, they took Mpho down from the tree, put him in the vehicle, removed the hood and offered him lunch. They were having a *braai*, a barbecue: drinking beers, laughing, smoking, making an outing of their day in the country. Mpho could not eat. When the officers had finished, they hoisted Mpho into the tree and resumed the interrogation. It went on until late in the afternoon; afterwards, they returned him to his cell. 'Write down everything,' one policeman commanded him, and locked the door.

Alone, Mpho gingerly checked his body. The electrical currents had left no marks on his skin. He could not touch anything in his cell; he got shocks from simply brushing up against the wall. Now that the pain had abated, he felt angry and humiliated. He had broken under torture. Mpho could not sleep that night, berating himself for having been weak. Still, he knew that his confession was worthless without his signature. He would regain his dignity, his sense of power, by refusing to put his name to anything.

Mpho informed his captors of his decision the next morning when they fetched him from the cell. 'I said all those things yesterday because I was under duress,' he explained. 'I won't write anything.' Furious, the policemen dragged Mpho to an awaiting car and pushed him inside. 'Today *kaffir*,' an officer warned, 'you're not coming back.'

They drove him to the *veldt*; this time, they did not bother to put a hood over his head. Mpho saw that they were in a graveyard. He also saw a second vehicle, with what looked like a portable generator inside. '*Ag, kaffir*, today we're going to kill you,' said one of the officers as they thrust the stick under his knees, locked him into the foetal position, raised him aloft into the tree, smeared him with gel. 'Put it on high,' someone was shouting, 'put it on high.' Mpho felt the pain again; it would not stop. He vomited. Then everything went black.

When Mpho awoke, he was on the ground being prodded by the policemen. They seemed relieved that he had regained consciousness and that they had not killed him. They would not have to face a disagreeable inquest into yet another death of a black detainee. The officers returned Mpho to the vehicle. He was too weak to remain upright during the ride back to the jail. A doctor visited him in his cell; he did not find any serious injuries from the electric shocks, only weakness from dehydration and lack of food. Mpho was given two eggs, a piece of meat and a glass of milk for dinner that night.

After that, Mpho was left alone for several days. He did not care any more if he went to prison; he had been pushed beyond his tolerance. He would rather die than submit to the electric shocks again. Mpho thought constantly about when his tormentors might return, what they would do, how long it would last. The anticipation of being tortured was a kind of torture in itself.

Thus it was almost a relief when the security officers came back one morning before dawn. They did not go to the trouble of lifting him into a tree, but simply suspended the stick between two chairs. They applied the electric current more carefully: We want answers now, the interrogator told Mpho. We want a signed confession saying you are a part of the PAC underground, that you took people out of the country for military training. Mpho heard himself shouting that he didn't give a damn; they could write what they like.

The Special Branch men returned Mpho to his cell, where he was left in solitary confinement for several weeks. The local, uniformed police were now his warders; blatantly racist, they often withheld Mpho's meals. Mpho languished in isolation. He paced the confines of his cell, logging almost 6,000 steps daily. He read the entire Bible twice. He sang hymns and protest songs to himself. He climbed on the toilet seat to glimpse a bit of sky, a bird, from the window. He waited for the Special Branch officers to come back.

When they finally reappeared, the security men brandished a written statement of all the things Mpho had confessed. They ordered him to sign it; Mpho complied. Such things no longer mattered to him. The statement provided a history of his involvement with the PAC, a description of his recruitment efforts on behalf of the organization, lists of people he had ostensibly helped to leave South Africa, the names of his PAC superiors, and his mission in returning to Soweto. Despite the damning details, Mpho knew that his signature on the document did not necessarily condemn him.

The veterans in Swaziland had explained to Mpho and the other recruits that a confession needed to be signed in the presence of a neutral magistrate; if the oath officer were one of those who had participated in the interrogation, as in Mpho's case, the confession would be subject to debate in a court of law. In one of the more fantastic twists of the country's legalism, few confessions obtained under Section 6 of the Terrorism Act were accepted as evidence. South African law required the state to prove that the statement was made voluntarily; there was a presumption that solitary confinement and detention were, in themselves, coercive. (To say nothing of the Orwellian provision that a detainee could not be released until a satisfactory confession had been made.) Such statements were used more as investigatory tools for the police.

Mpho's existence improved noticeably after he signed the confession. Now he was allowed to receive food and a change of clothing from home. Although his jailers still denied Mpho visits from his family or any other form of communication, he felt more secure; they knew where he was. The warders even summoned a doctor to treat the pain and bleeding in Mpho's ear that he experienced because of the beatings. Mpho bided his time. He knew his file had been sent to the Attorney General's office; he also knew it could take months for the state to charge him with a crime.

Not far away, Nomkhitha was enduring a somewhat different ordeal. The prison bell awoke her every morning at five o'clock. She washed in the tiny bathroom next to her cell and waited for her breakfast of tea and lumpy porridge. Although Joseph regularly brought food for her – hot dogs, fish and chips – the warders took most of it for themselves; Nomkhitha never received more than some bread and a few apples. She was forced to subsist on the prison's indigestible fare: gruel-like boiled mealies, sometimes with fish or fatty meat, for lunch; *samp* (coarse maize) or *pap* for dinner. Her dress size would drop from 44 to 34 during the six months of detention.

The days passed slowly. After breakfast, Nomkhitha cleaned her cell, bathroom and toilet. She washed her clothes. She read the Bible. She climbed onto the desk in her cell to gaze out through the tiny window: in the far, far distance, she could see people walking along a road in the *veldt*. Sometimes one of the older warders talked to her. In the presence of her Afrikaner colleagues, the woman treated Nomkhitha harshly, calling her a communist; she could not be seen being nice to a black prisoner. (The men from Special Branch had told the warders that Nomkhitha was a communist.) But when they were alone, the woman often plied Nomkhitha with questions: Who are you? What have you done? Who is this Tsietsi? Nomkhitha tried to explain to the woman what had happened in Soweto; the warder listened without comment. But a day or two later, she would secretly slip Nomkhitha a chocolate through the bars of her cell.

Once a fortnight, Nomkhitha was taken to Ermelo for interrogation. The Special Branch officers asked most of their questions in Afrikaans; a black policemen translated into English, often mixing it with Zulu. Why did your children leave the country? What was your aim in going to Swaziland? Why did Tsietsi get involved in politics? Did you know that your son Rocks is also highly involved? The interrogations, which lasted for a few hours, were always conducted by the same officers. 'You know, Mrs Mashinini,' one of them said after a few sessions, 'black people are very stupid. It is like taking a nice fat bone and throwing it on the ground. Two dogs come and one gets it. That is what is going to happen to South Africa: Russia is going to take over this country!'

The black interpreter, a kindly old man, often tried to help Nomkhitha by advising her in Zulu how to answer a particular question. Don't say that, he would exhort her; or, Don't answer that. His bosses, who did not speak or understand Zulu, were unaware of this. The black policeman even told Nomkhitha about the boy who walked back to the border: he had mentioned Nomkhitha, among others, as someone he had seen in Manzini among the PAC recruits. That is why she had been arrested. Based on his information, Nomkhitha was able to formulate her defence: she had done what any concerned mother would have. She had gone to Swaziland to check on schooling for her sons; her motivation was maternal, not political. She had given them money to continue their education – something they could not do in Soweto because of the police harassment.

Nomkhitha loved the trips to Ermelo. She got to see the sky, to hear the birds singing, to revel in the flowers and trees along the road; when it rained, she watched the drops fall to the ground with ineffable pleasure. She never saw Mpho after that initial glimpse. But each time Nomkhitha went for interrogation, she acted slightly demented in the hope that her captors would produce him again: jumping up from the chair, rushing to the window, running her hands through her hair. 'Where's

Mpho?' she would demand. 'Why is he arrested?' It never worked; the security officers told her to sit down and relax.

Sometimes her interrogators took her to a room that was clearly designed for the infliction of pain. A large table that looked like a butcher's block stood in the centre; *sjamboks*, the stinging whips made of rhinoceros or hippopotamus hide, and other ominous-seeming instruments that Nomkhitha could not identify, littered the room. The officers sat her down and began their interview. Although they did not threaten her directly, the implication was clear; it frightened Nomkhitha, for she knew they could easily hurt her. But her captors never tortured her physically. The torture was psychological: being in solitary confinement for months; not knowing when she would be released; being away from her children and husband. She worried incessantly about the children. There were six little ones still at home; Nomkhitha was most distraught about the babies, the twins Linda and Lindi, who were only two years old. The worst times were at night, when she pictured the girls snuggled in their bed and ached to hold and cuddle them. On those nights, Nomkhitha cried herself to sleep.

Nomkhitha's incarceration caused Joseph great torment. He was overcome by a sense of helplessness; on some days, he was afraid he would go mad. His family was being torn asunder and he felt powerless to stop it. Tsietsi had fled, followed by Rocks, Mpho, Dee. And now Nomkhitha was gone, too.

Joseph travelled to Standerton almost every Saturday. He stopped first at the police station where Mpho was being held to drop off food and fresh clothing. He tried to talk to the policemen on duty about his son, but they paid him no heed. Then Joseph continued on to the prison where Nomkhitha was and repeated the same steps. On the way back to the highway, he stopped at the police station again to check if the warders had collected Mpho's dirty clothes for him to launder. Joseph always travelled alone or with a friend; he never took any of the children. He knew it would be too upsetting for them. Joseph would tell the little ones on Friday night that he was driving to Standerton the next morning to give things to Mama; the moment he returned, the youngsters ran to him and crowded around, pulling on his jacket and shouting: Did you see her? Did you see her? Their hopefulness made him weep.

That many of his neighbours began staying away again only deepened Joseph's despair. As when Tsietsi was being pursued by the police, rumours were circulating in Soweto: a person could get arrested if he were seen entering the Mashinini house. Friends who had been regular visitors for years suddenly stopped paying calls. Joseph felt hurt, ostracized, lonely. Each evening he made the solitary trek home from the station, with only the police car that followed him everywhere for company.

Even Joseph's bosses at work stopped talking to him in the hallways. Only in the privacy of the firm's cars, when Joseph was driving them to appointments in Johannesburg, did they broach the subject of Nomkhitha and enquire about her well-being. Joseph began to feel like a pariah; no one – neither his fellow workers, nor his bosses, relatives or friends – seemed to understand that Nomkhitha was completely innocent. Even in the most sympathetic of listeners, Joseph detected an underlying suspicion of some sort.

Tshepiso too suffered terribly from the whispers and innuendoes. The entire world seemed to be staring at him when he walked down the street. His friends and their parents did not have to say a word; he could read the opprobrium in their eyes. Tshepiso was suddenly transformed into a self-conscious little boy. He withdrew into himself. Three of his brothers were in exile; another brother and his mother were in jail. The less he thought about these things, the better. The only time he took an interest in his surroundings was when his father and relatives huddled together in the living room, talking in hushed tones about Nomkhitha and Mpho. Then Tshepiso scurried about making tea for the adults, trying to overhear snippets of their conversation, desperate for words that would make his world whole again.

When the Attorney General's office finally concluded its work, Mpho was driven to the police headquarters in Ermelo to hear the charges against him. There he saw Themba and Paul, the men who had been arrested with Nomkhitha; they had also been held in detention. Before Mpho had a chance to speak to them, the three prisoners were escorted inside. Mpho had never seen his interrogators looking so smug. A magistrate read the charges in Afrikaans; a translator repeated them in English. Among other things, the young men were charged with furthering the aims of a banned organization, the PAC; engaging in acts of violence by attempting to undergo military training to topple the state (Mpho only); recruiting and aiding people to leave the country to undergo military training so they could overthrow the state by violent means. The magistrate crisply informed the three they would immediately be transferred to Pretoria; bail would not be considered.

The police took Mpho, Themba and Paul to a nearby court-yard and allowed them to talk. It was the first time Mpho had spoken to someone from home since his arrest. Themba told him that Nomkhitha was still in detention, which shocked and disturbed Mpho. Themba also told him about the boy who had walked back to the border and turned state's evidence. They all agreed that he posed the greatest threat; the three compared notes on their signed confessions to determine if they had a uniform story among them.

That afternoon, Mpho and his fellow prisoners were trans-ported to Pretoria by private car. For Mpho, after almost six months in detention, the journey was utterly pleasurable. They arrived in the capital at rush hour. Mpho saw people waiting in queues to catch buses back to the townships; crowds hurriedly crossing the packed streets; young women sauntering along in miniskirts. Mpho managed to wave at the girls, despite his hand-cuffs. The tableau was a kind of epiphany: ordinary life existed. People got up in the morning, got dressed, went to work, returned home, ate supper, went to bed. They did not worry about having electrodes attached to their toes or being beaten until nearly unconscious – surely a glorious sensation, but so ordinary that no one noticed it.

Themba and Paul were incarcerated in a prison; Mpho, as a minor, was taken to a police station. In contrast with rural, isolated Standerton, the police station in Pretoria seemed almost convivial. Numerous political detainees were being held there; despite his confinement to yet another solitary cell, Mpho could shout to the other prisoners and hear them singing freedom songs. He no longer worried about dying alone. And the food was better, too: the warders now allowed him to receive packages from home. Mpho was most touched by the cigarettes that arrived in one such bundle. He saw them as an acknowledgment by Joseph, to whom he never dared to reveal his habit, that Mpho had achieved manhood.

After a couple of days, Shun Chetty, an attorney whose fees were being paid by the South African Council of Churches, visited Mpho in his cell. Shun informed Mpho that he would be representing him; was there anything he needed? Mpho requested two tracksuits and running shoes. He had been wearing street clothes throughout his detention and was tired of them; he wanted comfortable attire. Mpho also asked for newspapers. To be able to read of current events again was a delight; Mpho felt he had returned to the world.

Shun came back on the following day to begin reviewing Mpho's case. The lawyer was optimistic: Mpho was a first-time offender and the state's witnesses were weak. This, despite the fact that Nomkhitha was going to be called to testify for the government. Shun told Mpho that he intended to get a white barrister to argue for him before the court; whites, said Shun (an Indian), are still the best advocates in this country. Mpho objected strongly. His Black Consciousness sensibilities were offended by the very notion; it's like being a mouse, Mpho said, and asking a cat to represent you against other cats. After a protracted discussion, Mpho agreed that Shun would try to procure the best person, regardless of race. If Mpho did not like him, Shun would find someone else.

An activist attorney involved in several political trials, Shun did not have the time to do the intensive preparation for the trial. He assigned his assistant, Eric Dane, to the case – a young white man whom Shun assured Mpho he could trust. Mpho again had reservations, but Eric seemed so committed to saving him from a long prison sentence that Mpho soon dropped his guard and eagerly came to anticipate the thrice-weekly visits. He was allowed to leave his cell and meet the young man in a consulting room. There the two pored over the charge sheet, Mpho's signed statement and the list of witnesses the state intended to call. Eric repeatedly forced Mpho to focus on each witness. 'What can this guy say about you?' he would say. 'What might he know about you? Think.' The lawyer probed for weaknesses and strengths, trying to determine where they might make the state stumble or where they themselves could falter.

After a few weeks of such instruction, Mpho met the barrister Shun had recommended. Tall, impeccably dressed, Roy Allaway seemed the epitome of the successful counsel. He also seemed ill-at-ease in the presence of a black person. Allaway's first question immediately engendered hostility in Mpho. 'Why do you hate whites?' he asked. In an aside, Eric told Mpho he did not have to answer the question; I'm definitely not going to, Mpho whispered back. Despite the continued artificiality in Allaway's conversation, Mpho decided to give him a chance.

Roy Allaway reviewed the relevant documents; when he told Mpho not to worry about the signed confession, that it had been obtained under torture, Mpho was enormously relieved. Allaway did evince concern about the runaway recruit who was the state's key witness. He worried about the evidence he could introduce at the trial; like the lawyer, Roy questioned Mpho intensively to try to work out what to expect from the boy's testimony. Despite Mpho's initial antipathy, Roy made him feel confident. They had been assigned one of the most hardline Afrikaner judges on the bench, but the prosecutor, in Roy's opinion, was a 'lightweight'. Mpho's signed statement would not be allowed; they would use Nomkhitha's testimony to Mpho's advantage; Roy would get the case dismissed on a technicality. Mpho did not ask Shun for a new barrister.

Mpho slept poorly the night before the trial; he was too anxious to relax. He had dressed in his grey trousers, shirt and jersey long before the warders came for him at five o'clock in the morning. They sat Mpho in a corner of the charge office and told him to wait while they sorted out his papers. There he remained; the warders had neglected to organize transport. A group of angry security officers, who had been waiting for him at the courthouse, finally arrived to escort Mpho to the ornate Palace of Justice, the site of the Supreme Court and some noteworthy treason trials. (Nelson Mandela had been sentenced to life imprisonment there.)

Mpho was led into the courtroom in handcuffs and leg irons. He, Themba and Paul faced the judge's bench; their barrister sat immediately behind them. To Mpho's right were the witness box and the prosecutor's table. The section for the press and the public gallery occupied the back part of the room, behind a rail. Mpho saw Joseph and Cougar, his brother, seated there; he waved to his father excitedly. Joseph waved back. It was the first contact he had had with his son in six months.

After taking on Mpho's case, Shun Chetty had met Joseph to explain the impending trial to him. Joseph was aghast; how could his son, a teenager with no military experience, be charged with trying to overthrow the government? Someone with that intent would surely need a small army at his disposal. When Joseph told his bosses, they were insistent: he must attend his son's trial, no matter how much time he had to take off work. Now, sitting in the public gallery, Joseph prayed that it would go well for his son. Mpho looked to Joseph as though he had lost weight. But at least he was alive.

The morning's proceedings were taken up with formalities. Among others, the state's witnesses would include two security policemen, three students who had been arrested in Soweto, Nomkhitha, the boy who had walked to the border, and an expert on terrorism. After entering pleas of not guilty for the accused, Roy asked that their handcuffs and leg irons be removed and that spectators be allowed to approach them during breaks. The judge granted both requests; at the interval for tea, Joseph and Cougar were able to hug Mpho and talk with him for half an hour. Mpho also chatted with fellow students who had come to observe the trial and several journalists.

At lunchtime, Mpho and the other two accused were escorted to holding cells in the basement. There Mpho met Joe Gqabi, who was one of twelve defendants in a sedition trial taking place in another courtroom. (The June 16 uprising and subsequent arrests of thousands of activists spawned a succession of political trials, the likes of which South Africa had not experienced since the early 1960s.) Joe had returned to Johannesburg after taking Rocks over the border, only to be apprehended on New Year's Eve. He and his co-defendants, known as the ANC 12, were accused of having received military training abroad with the aim of overthrowing the South African government.

Joe told Mpho that he knew Rocks; he also knew of Mpho's imprisonment. By now, Mpho had had six months to think about the circumstances of his arrest. He had become increasingly bitter towards the PAC officers in Swaziland, convinced that his former mentors had betrayed him. Mpho recounted the story to Joe, including what he had learned during the indoctrination sessions in Manzini; all the anger he had suppressed for months erupted. Joe listened patiently. In his quiet, avuncular manner, Joe methodically began to refute, point by point, the PAC claims of primacy in the anti-apartheid struggle and its accusations of white domination within the ANC. His words came as an epiphany to Mpho. It was like going to confession: he unburdened his soul and received solace in return. This, from someone with unimpeachable revolutionary credentials who had tutored Mpho's own brother.

Mpho would spend every lunch break with Joe during his trial. While Mpho ate, Joe continued his discourse: he justified the involvement of white activists, listing the sacrifices many had made. He convinced Mpho of the need, contrary to the Black Consciousness creed of self-sufficiency, to make the struggle an international one. Although he did not immediately rid Mpho of his hatred for whites, Joe provided him with a new perspective; his views made sense to Mpho and appealed to him intellectually. The noonday encounters with Joe Gqabi would prove a watershed in Mpho's life.

The trial began in earnest with the government calling its witnesses to testify. Things did not go well for the prosecution. The *Rand Daily Mail* reported on the dramatic scene that transpired in the courtroom:

Two security policemen yesterday dragged a young State witness screaming from the Supreme Court, Pretoria, after he had given evidence in a Terrorism Act trial. Mr William Tshimong, 20, had minutes before told the court that police had threatened to shoot him if he refused to sign a statement about the accused in the trial. Mr Tshimong told Mr Justice Esselen that five policemen woke him in the night and forced him to make allegations about one of the accused.

'They were completely false and one policeman threatened to shoot me if I did not write what he demanded and sign it afterwards,' Mr Tshimong said. Mr J. Swanepoel, for the State, said he wanted to discredit the witness because of his conflicting evidence.

As Mr Tshimong stepped out of the witness box, he was grabbed by the security policemen who tried to force him out of court before an adjournment had been ordered.

Screaming 'help me, help me please, they will beat me up', the terrified witness was taken from the court and driven away.

Two men who identified themselves as Major N. van Rensburg and Sergeant D. Vermaas of the security police, also argued with defence lawyers who rushed towards them as they held Mr Tshimong.

Police later said he would be charged with perjury.

The other two students, called by the prosecution on the following day, were equally unhelpful to its case. They, too, denied the veracity of their sworn statements, which alleged they were among twenty-three people recruited by the accused for military training. The security police arrested them too and charged them with perjury. The prosecution's other witnesses testified as planned. In the afternoon, when the trial had been adjourned, Mpho and his lawyers reviewed the day's testimony; Mpho returned to his cell convinced that incriminating evidence had yet to be presented. Then he fell into a deep, dreamless sleep. Observing the proceedings that would determine his fate left him feeling utterly exhausted.

* * *

At the start of Mpho's trial, the security officers moved Nomkhitha to a police station in Pretoria. There they informed her that she would be testifying against her son. The policemen did not disclose the questions the prosecutor would ask, but they did promise to release her after she had given testimony.

Although he assumed Nomkhitha had suffered greatly in detention, Joseph was shocked when she entered the courtroom on the third day of the trial. She had lost an enormous amount of weight and looked ill, downcast, nervous. Nomkhitha brightened somewhat when she saw her husband and Cougar in the public gallery, and she was heartened to see that Mpho did not seem damaged by his time in prison. The prosecutor began his questioning by making Nomkhitha recount the story of her journey to Swaziland. She explained that she had been given a lift to Manzini in January by two of the accused; the purpose of the trip was to ascertain the well-being of her son. While in Manzini, Nomkhitha had gone to the PAC headquarters. 'When we went inside the house we saw a number of youths,' she testified. 'One of them was my fifteen-year-old son, to whom I had given money so he could leave the country and further his education.'

The prosecutor asked if the youngsters in the house would be receiving education or army training. Nomkhitha said that a PAC official told her the youths would go to school, while those who were 'big and old' would be sent for military instruction. Pressed by the prosecutor, Nomkhitha recalled that the official conveyed the information to her in the presence of Themba and Paul. Satisfied that he had established the connection between the accused and the possibility that the students they transported would be trained as soldiers to overthrow the South African regime, the prosecutor sat down.

Roy approached the witness box to begin the cross-examination. He asked Nomkhitha to describe her arrest and imprisonment. She explained to the judge that she had spent six and a half months in solitary confinement. A security police sergeant told her that she was being detained because she had given two of her children money to go to Swaziland; for the duration of her confinement, no one informed her she was being held under the Terrorism Act. 'I was kept alone. I was not allowed friends or visitors,' Nomkhitha said tearfully. When she described her fears for the six small children she had left behind in Soweto, Nomkhitha began to weep. The courtroom was silent as Roy offered her a glass of water and a tissue.

When she regained her composure, Roy continued his questioning.

– You went to Swaziland because you were worried about your son?

– Yes.

– He was phoning you daily, asking you to come. Is that correct?

– Yes.

– But the mere fact that you left him behind when you returned to South Africa, didn't bring him back, meant that as a parent you were happy.

– Yes, I was happy. He was safe from being harassed by the police and had a better chance of continuing his education than in Soweto.

Roy returned repeatedly to the idea that Nomkhitha believed Dee would be studying by remaining in Swaziland, not receiving military instruction. By now it was late in the afternoon; the judge informed barrister that he would be adjourning the trial until tomorrow. Roy had intended to dispense with Nomkhitha's cross-examination swiftly and call her as a witness for the defence. But Nomkhitha had so clearly aroused the sympathy of the court by presenting herself as a caring mother that Roy decided simply to continue cross-examining her; he asked that she return on the following day. The judge agreed and ordered the police to remand her for the night. Nomkhitha, looking bewildered, began to sob as the security officers escorted her from the courtroom. 'You promised me I could go home after court,' she wailed at them. 'That was the agreement.'

Appalled, Roy approached the bench. He requested that Nomkhitha be allowed to sleep at home that night and return to continue her testimony the next morning. The prosecutor agreed; Nomkhitha was released to Joseph's waiting embrace.

* * *

In anticipation of Nomkhitha's return, Joseph had allowed the children to stay away from school. Tshepiso spent the day playing football in the field opposite his house but all the time he was looking for approaching cars. It was almost dusk when Tshepiso saw the white *kombi* turn the corner; he began running across the scrubby grass ahead of his siblings and reached the house just as the vehicle came to a stop. Tshepiso raced around the front of the *kombi*, pulled open the door and threw himself into Nomkhitha's arms. She was crying. To Tshepiso, Nomkhitha felt thin and bony, not at all the soft, comforting body that he remembered. Her legs looked like twigs. But none of that mattered; his mother was home.

Nomkhitha returned to the Supreme Court on the following morning to finish being questioned by Roy Allaway. Afterwards, he thanked her: That's exactly what I wanted, he said. You have saved your son. Nomkhitha joined Joseph in the public gallery to watch the rest of the trial.

The prosecutor called the state's star witness, the boy who had walked back to the South African border and given himself up to the authorities. The judge ordered the courtroom to be cleared of spectators and the press; as a minor, the boy's testimony would be given in camera. The prosecutor began to coax what was clearly a well-rehearsed story from the witness: Mpho recruited me at school, the boy explained. He told me about going for military training and returning to South Africa in war planes. He said we would swoop down on Pretoria in supersonic fighter jets. I didn't want to go, but Mpho said it was everyone's duty to do so; this was war. My friends and I were scared of Mpho because he was one of the leaders of our school. So we agreed to go. He took us to Swaziland. We were put in a house and never allowed to go out. They told us we must wait because we would be taken to Tanzania.

– Why did you come back?

– Because my grandmother was dying. And because I decided I didn't want to be a soldier.

Roy listened to the testimony impassively. He had told Mpho he would try to prove that the boy's story had been fabricated by the security police; and he would establish that, contrary to all claims, Mpho was the activist students sought out when they wanted to continue their education overseas. When it was his turn, Roy asked the boy if he had seen a particular martial-arts movie. The witness's eyes lit up; this was clearly one of his great pleasures. He proceeded to describe the film in considerable detail, even volunteering the information that he had seen it in Manzini. At that, the judge sat up abruptly. Young man, he said sternly, I thought you said the gates were locked every night at the PAC house and that you were held a virtual prisoner?

Despite his initial dislike of the barrister, Mpho thought Roy was brilliant in court. He showed the boy to be a liar and an unreliable witness throughout his questioning. Mpho watched the Special Branch agents who were there becoming increasingly irritable; their reaction caused him to feel some optimism. His confidence grew when Roy and Shun told Mpho that, based on the cross-examination, they were thinking of asking for a dismissal. And he was positively elated when the courtroom orderly proffered his own analysis of the trial: 'Ag, you guys are going home.' This was someone who watched proceedings of this nature daily; surely he was a good judge of such matters.

Roy finished cross-examining the boy the next day. The prosecutor made his closing arguments, then yielded to the defence to begin calling its witnesses. Instead, Roy asked the judge to discharge the accused. He said the testimony of the state's star witness was 'reminiscent of Alice in Wonderland', his evidence so inconsistent that it could not be considered reliable. 'The witness has spent six months in solitary confinement and has contradicted himself over and over again,' Roy asserted. The prosecutor agreed, adding that if the court found the evidence unreliable, then he had no case. The judge said he would consider the request and render a judgment on the following day.

That night was the longest Mpho ever experienced. He could not sleep. He played the court proceedings back in his head, over and over, pacing the floor of his cell. The air felt oppressive; he had trouble breathing. He lay down on his mat, then changed to the floor because it might be more comfortable, then gave up and continued pacing. He could hardly keep his excitement in check. After nearly seven months in solitary confinement, he might actually walk out through the courtroom door. How often he had imagined where he would be in Soweto at a particular time of the day. He might be about to return to that life. Mpho no longer thought in terms of months or even weeks; he was counting hours.

His reverie was interrupted by the appearance of the two Special Branch agents who had been attending the trial. One of the officers warned Mpho that if any harm befell the state's witnesses, they – the agents – would come after Mpho. Then, incredibly, the Special Branch man asked Mpho if he would like to work with them after his release; Mpho would be paid for passing information to the police. Stunned, Mpho waited until the officer finished speaking. Turning to the black warder who had accompanied the agents to his cell, Mpho said in Zulu: 'Tell these dogs I never want to see them again.'

Mpho had bathed, dressed and combed his hair several times by the time the sun rose. When he and his two fellow accused reached the holding cells at the Supreme Court, the other prisoners greeted them as victorious heroes; the consensus had it that their acquittal was inevitable. Joe Gqabi asked Mpho to visit his wife in Soweto. The police led the accused into a courtroom packed with journalists and well-wishers; Mpho waved to the large contingent of Mashininis sitting in the public gallery.

Everyone rose to his feet, as was required, when the judge appeared. He immediately launched into a lengthy discourse in Afrikaans, most of which Mpho found unintelligible. Only when he and his co-defendants were made to stand again and suddenly were being hugged and congratulated by the defence team did Mpho understand that it was all over; they had been discharged. A policeman opened the gate of the box where the accused sat, and Mpho rushed into the arms of his family. Then, flanked by his parents and siblings, Mpho left the courthouse and strode outside into the late winter sunshine. He took a deep breath, inhaling the earthy scents of the soon-to-be spring. He was free.

CHAPTER SEVEN

Rocks

Once in Swaziland, Rocks made his way to Manzini, where the representatives of the ANC were not entirely welcoming. He had been instructed months earlier to bring Tsietsi out of South Africa; the Swaziland ANC office planned to give the leader of the June 16 uprising a hero's welcome. But Tsietsi's sudden departure prevented Rocks from fulfilling the mission, thus prompting a rather chilly reception upon his escape.

The ANC officials put Rocks in an abode known, because of the colour of its façade, as the White House. A refuge for the youngsters fleeing South Africa, the building was considered only semi-underground; the Swazi police knew of its existence. The ANC operated other safe houses that were deeply hidden within the local populace, but they were usually reserved for agents working in the country. Stanley Mabizela, the ANC's chief representative, warned Rocks to be wary during his stay in the city: the place was full of spies and informers.

One evening, Rocks walked to the nearby Manzini Arms to telephone Nomkhitha; he wanted to tell her of his safe arrival. The hotel was noisy and crowded. Rocks and two fellow refugees were waiting at the reception desk to place the call when a group of burly Afrikaners entered the lobby. They surrounded the three black men and, drawing pistols, tried to herd them outside to a car. Determined not to be kidnapped and returned to South Africa, Rocks and his friends ran deeper into the hotel, screaming, 'They're trying to take us! They're trying to take us!' Apparently perturbed by the number of witnesses to the intended abduction, the Afrikaners retreated to their car and drove away.

The incident prompted Rocks' ANC superiors to expedite his departure from Swaziland. The journey to obtain military training normally took the refugees northeastward to the Mozambican border town of Namaacha, then to a safe house in Matola, close to the country's capital; from there, they flew to Tanzania. The timing of their travel depended on the availability of space at the next stop. The ANC was overwhelmed by the number of youths spilling from the townships, and the impatient youngsters often had to wait in Swaziland for several weeks. Rocks knew that he was lucky to be leaving after only two weeks. He felt enormously relieved: the more distance he put between himself and the Boers, the better. He was driven to the border one night with some fellow escapees. The road they took was well-paved; in the moonlight, Rocks could make out dreamy, cloud-capped mountains. They passed conically shaped thatched huts that dotted the landscape. They passed small, cement-block houses. They passed huge sugar estates, where the cane grew as tall as a man and twisted and bowed in the wind.

At the frontier, the South Africans jumped the fence. An ANC representative met them on the other side and took them first to the Namaacha police station to declare their presence in the country, then to a shelter. Rocks found Namaacha exceedingly pleasant: high, cool, verdant. The Portuguese, who colonized Mozambique for almost 400 years, used the town as a summer retreat. Rocks understood why when he and his companions descended a few days later to the hot, sultry Indian Ocean coastal plain and the ANC refuge in Matola.

The ANC and its adherents were welcomed in Mozambique after the Portuguese departed in 1975 and were replaced by the black nationalist movement that had fought them for years. As part of its foreign policy, the new government lent support to liberation groups around the world: the Sandinista guerrillas battling the Nicaraguan dictator Anastasio Somoza; the soldiers of Robert Mugabe, who fought the white minority regime in Rhodesia; and so forth. Thus, it was only natural for the

Mozambican government to provide a sanctuary for its brothers from the south in their struggle against the much-hated apartheid regime.

It gave the ANC a number of houses to shelter the youngsters who would be sent abroad. Matola seemed an unlikely locale for such an enterprise: despite its numerous factories, the place felt almost suburban. It had an abundance of trees, and fine houses with lush gardens enclosed by white fences. The ANC compound where Rocks stayed differed little from others in the neighbourhood. It consisted of a large, single-storey main house, with two smaller outhouses and a vast yard. One side was planted with orange and papaya trees and floppy-eared banana plants, the other with vegetables. Scores of young refugees lived there temporarily.

The sanctuary functioned like a military camp. The chief of staff, or commander, lived in the main house, along with his officers and some of the transients. The smaller structures housed newcomers. Youngsters were assigned various chores: cleaning, cooking, gardening. The officers announced the duties at roll-call each morning, in which the youths were required to stand at attention in the yard. At night, Umkhonto we Sizwe soldiers, festooned with grenades and bearing AK-47 assault rifles, took up positions around the perimeter fence. Matola was within easy striking distance from South Africa. In later years, the country's security forces would launch several daring operations against the ANC in Mozambique – including bombing the Matola safe house.

As one of the few literate comrades, Rocks was charged with transcribing radio broadcasts from the BBC and Voice of America as part of his chores. He wrote out summaries of the news programmes each day and read them aloud at the morning political meeting. In this way, Rocks learned of Tsietsi's denunciations of the ANC and his accusations of corruption within the organization. The criticisms caused Rocks great sadness. He could understand Tsietsi's opposition to the ANC because of his militant Black Consciousness creed, but not his vitriol. Tsietsi's proclamations proved a delicate matter for Rocks, not only for their content but because they were levelled by his own brother. Fortunately, few in the house knew of Rocks' true identity; he, like everyone else, used a *nom de guerre*. (He would acquire seventeen such names during his years in exile.) Only those who had been acquainted with Rocks in Soweto were aware of his kinship with Tsietsi.

Despite Rocks' worries, the ANC officers appeared less concerned with Tsietsi's comments than with Rocks' ability to lure his brother into the organization. Almost obsessively, they made Rocks recount the reason he had failed to bring Tsietsi with him to Swaziland. 'What went wrong?' they would ask him. 'Why didn't he go with you?'

'He went underground and escaped to Botswana,' Rocks repeated, exasperated. 'He didn't tell me he was planning to leave.'

'Can you get Tsietsi to join the ANC?'

'I can try.' Rocks was not bothered by this seeming fixation on Tsietsi. He had joined the organization and established his credentials long before Tsietsi had become a national figure. Besides, he felt a strong commitment to the ANC and, like his superiors, was keen to see his brother become a member.

What worried him more was a growing sense of ennui. After completing his daily chores, Rocks spent much of the day sitting around an empty swimming pool filled with rotting frangipani leaves. There were just two commercial flights a week to Tanzania, and the demand for seats was great; the ANC could purchase only a few tickets at a time. Rocks envisioned weeks of boredom stretching before him. So it came as a great relief when he was told he would be flying to Dar es Salaam, the Tanzanian capital, immediately. A rumour that Tsietsi was intending to travel to Tanzania prompted the ANC officers to push Rocks to the head of the queue. This time, they hoped he would succeed in recruiting his brother to their cause. Tsietsi, yet again, determined a sibling's fate.

Rocks was stunned when he landed in Dar es Salaam. He could not believe this was the famous capital of one of Africa's first independent nations; the dilapidation and poverty were shocking. Many of the buildings appeared to be little more than shacks. Few had running water. Raw sewage flowed in the streets. The roads, pockmarked with deep potholes, made those in Soweto seem positively modern by comparison. 'The Boers are right,' thought Rocks, not without irony, 'blacks in South Africa do live better than those in the independent states.'

His perception, however correct, was based on only cursory observation. For security reasons, the ANC restricted Rocks and his fellow exiles to the house where they slept. They were escorted downtown only to pick through second-hand clothing for their wardrobes (most had fled South Africa with no personal effects), obtain typhoid and yellow fever vaccinations, fill out forms for special Tanzanian passports and have their photographs taken. Otherwise, they remained in the house. Rocks received a sponge mat for sleeping on; the sweltering air in the seaside capital obviated the need for a proper bed and bedclothes. People simply pulled out their mats and slept anywhere, even on the roof. The days were taken up with cooking and cleaning duties, similar to those in Matola, and with political lectures. Rocks enjoyed these talks greatly. Many ANC and Umkhonto we Sizwe veterans lived in Dar es Salaam; this was where they established the organization's first exile head-quarters. Rocks found their tales of hardship inspiring. Oliver Tambo, the ANC president, who visited the youths and spoke passionately and with eloquence about liberation, elicited particular admiration.

Tsietsi did not appear in Tanzania. Rocks felt relieved of the task of trying to cajole his brother into the fold and free to move on to his military instruction. Every so often, he and the other youths were told they would definitely be leaving for Angola; nothing happened. Instead, they were woken at three o'clock in the morning and ordered outside to do marching drills. They practised at that hour to avoid being seen by the neighbours; a few old ANC comrades supervised the training. Rocks found the exercises tiresome. He had left South Africa to fight the Boers and could not understand how parading up and down a deserted Tanzanian street would further that aim. He wanted to engage in real combat.

After two months, Rocks thought he would finally realize his dream. He flew westward across the continent with a planeload of other exiles to Luanda, the capital of Angola. Another former Portuguese colony, Angola was a complicated patchwork of Cold War hostilities when Rocks arrived: it had a Marxist central government, aided by thousands of Cuban soldiers who came to the country to help defend it against an invasion by South African soldiers from the south and a United States-supported guerrilla war in the bush. The capital was still a dangerous place; Rocks could hear gunfire on the outskirts of Luanda at night.

He was sent to a transit camp known as Engineering Luanda. The facility housed about 200 cadres, all waiting to be sent to other camps for military training. To pass the time, the youths were made to march in the same fashion Rocks had experienced in Tanzania. The apparent uselessness of this endeavour, along with Luanda's unspeakably hot and moist climate, pushed Rocks beyond his tolerance on one afternoon. 'This is nonsense,' he sputtered at his instructor. 'Go this way, about turn, go that way. I refuse to do it. I came here to learn how to fire a gun.'

'You refuse?'

'Yes, I refuse.'

'Okay, then you can march, by yourself, up and down the camp grounds for an hour.' And so he did, the noonday sun beating down on his head until he could not breathe for the crushing heat. Only his utter determination to become a guerrilla fighter, and his pride, kept him from collapsing.

In Rocks' mind, the Cuban soldiers were among the few worthwhile aspects of the transit camp. They fascinated Rocks, these disciples of the revolutionary luminaries Fidel Castro and Che Guevara. Despite the language barrier – few of the Cubans spoke even a broken English – Rocks and his companions managed to play baseball with them; the Cubans routinely beat the South Africans, who were more accustomed to a kind of softball.

Another of the camp's redeeming qualities was its proximity to town. Rocks and his friends were often allowed to venture into Luanda. They strolled along the Marginal, the promenade lined with palm trees that followed the crescent-shaped bay and looked out onto the South Atlantic Ocean. Soviet-made military vehicles crowded the roads; the city was bedecked with banners bearing revolutionary slogans and similarly political murals painted on walls. Although only two years had passed since liberation, the place was already beginning to decay. Storefronts stood empty, their windows broken and signs peeling in the humid air. Shells of half-constructed buildings, the exposed, unfinished floors for ever frozen in time, littered the city centre. This was how the Portuguese left the country. On the eve of black independence, the white colonialists dismantled their businesses and homes, packed their belongings into crates and sailed away to South Africa, Portugal, Brazil. What they could not take with them, they destroyed. They poured cement down the water pipes of construction projects, sabotaged farm equipment, wrecked factories. If they could not have the country, nobody could.

Rocks practised marching in Luanda for another couple of months until the order came to send him and his cadres to Novo Catengue training camp in the south of the country. His life as a freedom fighter was finally about to begin. Located about 250 miles to the south, the camp was an hour's drive inland from the coastal town of Benguela. It sat alongside the railway that connected Benguela to Huambo, Angola's second largest city, in the interior. The camp was surrounded by mountains covered with scrubby brush, and a stream ran to the south. The Portuguese had built the rudimentary settlement to house railway workers. They left behind a series of long, low buildings, where the Umkhonto we Sizwe recruits slept on air mattresses. The indoor showers were not sufficient to accommodate the camp's 500 or so soldiers; many of them had to wash in buckets. Rocks and the others dug additional latrines and constructed a mess hall with materials the Portuguese had abandoned. A shooting range and several training fields, hacked from the bush, stood about three miles from the camp.

The soldiers were designated as the June 16 Detachment and divided among four companies. Each company had four platoons; a Cuban instructor and an interpreter who translated into English were assigned to every platoon. (The Cubans lived in separate barracks and cooked their own food.) Most of the recruits came from areas around Johannesburg; their urban sophistication and attitudes sometimes created tension with the ANC officers, most of whom had grown up in rural districts and were of an older generation. About twenty or so of the detachment's members were women. They stayed in segregated barracks, but were integrated into the platoons and companies.

Rocks was issued with two Soviet-made uniforms upon arrival. He greatly disliked the heavy brown trousers, shirt, socks, sun hat and boots; they were too hot for the subtropical climate. (He and the other soldiers would eventually receive Cuban uniforms that were lighter in weight and easier to iron.) Rocks eagerly looked forward to the weekends, when he was required to wash his uniforms and allowed to wear the civilian clothes he had selected in Tanzania.

He soon discovered that the bulk of the camp's food also came from the Soviet Union. The menu was insipid: powdered eggs – something Rocks had never seen – hard biscuits from a tin, coarse oats and tea for breakfast, tinned beef or fish and rice for the other meals. Later, the soldiers received tinned vegetables from Italy. They rarely ate fresh produce; the camp's stony soil made cultivating a garden nearly impossible. Only the rare delivery of vegetables from nearby Benguela kept the cadres from becoming ill. After they learned to fire weapons, the soldiers organized hunting expeditions with their AK-47 assault rifles to supplement their diet. The few recruits who had grown up in rural areas had to teach their urban comrades how to track animals. They shot buffalo and other game, and once they killed a python. It took seven men to carry the dead snake back to camp. Rocks relished the meal that evening, a pleasant respite from the monotony of preserved fish.

A bell roused Rocks and his fellow soldiers every morning at five o'clock. The young men gathered with their respective platoons for exercises and a run; they showered, ate breakfast, and stood in formation on the parade ground to hear the day's announcements and a summary of the news. Then they marched off to their lessons. Much time was devoted to the study of history and politics; to be a good guerrilla fighter, the Umkhonto we Sizwe high command believed, one had to understand such matters. Every subject was taught with a Marxist bent. Umkhonto, like the ANC, had become inextricably intertwined with the South African Communist Party by the time Rocks and his fellow dissidents became a part of the organization.

Each Umkhonto unit and training facility thus assumed a Soviet-style structure. To ensure the correctness, as it were, of political thought and education, an elite corps of commissars was formed. The concept of the commissar had its origins in the early days of the Russian Revolution: to guarantee adherence to the Communist Party by the tsarist officers serving in the fledgling Red Army, the Party assigned a political commissar to every unit to serve as a kind of watchdog over the commander. Similarly, the ANC placed commissars in all manner of educational and military groups. In Novo Catengue, there was a commissar for each company, platoon and section to monitor not only the camp's course of study, but its cultural activities as well.

Political instructors conducted the classes. They were trained by Jack Simons, a former professor of African law at the University of Cape Town and a leader of the SACP before the South African government outlawed it and ultimately drove him into exile. Jack was already in his seventies when he was assigned to teach in Novo Catengue and a vegetarian – not the best traits for surviving the Angolan bush. He nonetheless insisted on taking the Umkhonto oath and living as a soldier. Using a Marxist perspective, Jack created a series of lectures that traced South Africa's history. The curriculum he developed, for recruits and instructors alike, was so extensive that Novo Catengue became known in ANC circles as the 'University of the South'.

(The poorer-educated recruits found these courses difficult. For them, the instructors created an array of remedial classes: English, basic mathematics, chemistry, physics. The courses were conducted in a language such as Zulu or Sotho, and in easy English, to aid the students' comprehension.)

Jack Simons sometimes lectured directly to the recruits. Rocks took great pleasure in listening to his passionate discourses: here was a legendary figure from the 1950s and 1960s, one who had rubbed shoulders with Nelson Mandela and others of that era.

In Rocks' mind, they were the founding fathers of what he hoped would be a new country. Jack's systematic approach to his material appealed to Rocks' sense of order; he had not experienced this sort of intellectual exercise since college. Rocks wrote out careful notes of Jack's talks:

> . . . we can distinguish between the emergence of the working class consciousness among our people and the growth of a revolutionary national consciousness. The working people became class-conscious in the period after the First World War as reflected in the rise of the Industrial Commerical Workers' Union. It was at this time that the workers began to form a class in themselves, to become aware of their own special interests as against the interests of the ruling class, but they could not become a class for themselves in the sense of developing a revolutionary image without assistance from outside. That assistance had to come from revolutionaries who were in possession of a revolutionary theory and a revolutionary organization. To provide such theory and organization is our task for the struggle that lies ahead.

At the end of each quarter, Rocks and the other students were tested on their understanding of the political courses. The Cuban officers in Novo Catengue had wanted a way to assess the progress of their protégés in their reports to the Umkhonto hierarchy; Jack devised an examination similar to one used at the University of Zambia, where he taught after going into exile. With a bow to their varying degrees of literacy, the soldiers were given a series of questions about a month before the actual test. They researched the topics in the evenings, after classes had finished, in Novo Catengue's small library. On the appointed day, each examinee went before a panel consisting of the commissar, the instructor and Jack to give an oral presentation on several of the questions. (This was radical departure from the rigid, rote style of education practised in South Africa.) The examinations covered a wide spectrum of material:

> In an attempt to ensure the security and loyalty of its members, the Friendly Society, a secret organization of the British

coal miners, laid down three conditions aimed at protecting their members against police informers; what were these conditions?

Why were the British coal miners forced to create secret societies? Compare this with the conditions in South Africa.

In your opinion, would you say that the Combination Act in Britain is similar to the Suppression of Communism Act and the Suppression of Terrorism Act? Give reasons for your answers.

Who christened the British working class as 'The First Born Sons of Modern Industry' and why? Is the statement true?

What are guilds and how many kinds of guilds are there?

Compare the forced labour system with contract labour in South Africa.

Compare the peonage system with the labour tenant system in South Africa.

What is the first premise of all human existence?

Rocks found the examinations rigorous, but passed them easily. For his scholarship, he was singled out, along with other talented students, for special classes held at night. His superiors thought he showed an analytical flair and gave him an extra hour of political lessons.

The Cuban instructors conducted the military training. There were no textbooks; the Cubans gave lectures that were translated into English by the interpreter. From them, Rocks learned how to shoot Soviet-built firearms: AK-47 assault rifles, Makarov pistols, rocket-propelled grenades. He studied both theory and practice. The camp lacked enough guns for every soldier; while one group listened to lectures, others got to handle the actual weapons on the training fields. They also learned about anti-aircraft and anti-personnel artillery. For a course on tactics, Rocks and his fellow recruits were taken out to the bush and tested on manoeuvres. They studied topography, first aid, unarmed combat. The subject Rocks most enjoyed was military engineering, which explored various aspects of explosives: how to assemble them, how to engage in acts of sabotage and so forth. Having studied civil engineering at school, he liked trying to calculate, for instance, how much explosive he would need to blow up a particular target.

Rocks thought the military training only adequate. It seemed to him too biased towards fighting in rural areas; he believed this was the influence of the Cubans, who had fought much of their revolution in the countryside. The bulk of South Africa's people lived in urban settlements, in townships. What good was it to learn about jungle warfare when what he truly needed to know was how to blow up Johannesburg? The discrepancy ceased to trouble him after a while. Through his political lessons, Rocks began to understand that liberation was not going to happen any time soon; his dream of returning to kill the Boers after six months of training was just youthful fantasy.

Like his fellow recruits, Rocks suffered from bouts of homesickness. He tried not to think about Soweto; such sentimentality, he believed, should be foreign to a freedom fighter's constitution. Rocks forced himself to focus on his existence in the camp. This was why he had abandoned his studies, his future, in South Africa. Still, he despised the soldiers' daily regimen and the physical effort it required: the exercises, the long-distance runs, the hard manual labour. Rocks had not harboured romantic notions about becoming a guerrilla, but the reality of the life he had chosen proved harsh beyond his imagining. The weekends, and their activities, provided some respite. Then he and his companions played football almost ceaselessly; the soldiers organized inter-company competitions that became a great spectator event in the camp. They also engaged the Cubans in games of softball, with the same disastrous results Rocks had experienced in Luanda. And there were cultural groups: drama, dance, choir. (Rocks refused to join the choir; he alone among the Mashinini offspring could not sing.)

Morale in the camp was generally good. But what seemed to be tribalism among the older exiles, the generation of the 1960s, troubled Rocks and many of the newer recruits. They considered themselves the product of the Black Consciousness philosophy, which vigorously opposed such divisions. Indeed, Rocks had never considered himself as a Sotho or Xhosa. But he and his friends believed the appointment of officers was tribally influenced: the camp commander was a Tswana, as was every platoon chief. One of Rocks' comrades wrote a letter to the camp administration to complain about the phenomenon. In response, the commander called all the soldiers together for a special meeting in which the letter was read aloud. Many of the higher-ranking officers, veterans of the ANC's struggles in South Africa before its banning, talked about the organization's intolerance of tribalism. Then they asked for comments from the recruits.

Rocks stood to defend the letter and its writer. 'You say it isn't tribalism, but it certainly looks like tribalism,' he said. 'This should not be accepted. The ANC has always fought against such practices.' There was a murmur of agreement among the soldiers. Many shared Rocks' view, but others voiced their support of the commanding officers. The meeting ended on an amicable note. Although no one was disciplined for the matter, Rocks felt it marked him within Umkhonto thereafter; the Mashinini propensity to defy authority would dog him throughout his career.

Morale in the camp also suffered when, at the end of the six-month training period, the Umkhonto high command began considering extending it. About a dozen or so recruits rebelled at the idea; they were tired of training and wanted to be infiltrated back into South Africa immediately to begin their work as freedom fighters. This was no easy thing. Umkhonto had been mostly quiescent since the bannings and arrests of the early 1960s and its attempt to reorganize in exile. Only recently, with the exodus of students after the June 16 uprising, did it train enough soldiers to launch a series of military operations inside South Africa. The sabotage did little material damage; its symbolism, that of proclaiming Umkhonto's reemergence, was more important. Still, the problems of moving men and machinery across borders persisted for several months. Only in 1979 would the guerrilla group begin to execute daring and effective attacks.

In punishment for their insubordination, the rebellious soldiers were sentenced to several months' detention in the basement of an ANC camp in Quibaxe, to the north. Theirs were among the first expressions of discontent that would afflict the camps in coming years. Diet, living conditions, perquisites accorded officers, the pace of infiltration to South Africa – all combined to create a simmering sense of frustration. The disaffection would culminate in outright mutiny in 1984 among hundreds of soldiers; several were killed or executed when the Umkhonto commanders quashed the rebellion, and many others were imprisoned in Quatro prison camp in the north, a place notorious for its inhumane, and sometimes deadly, treatment.

Rocks' academic prowess spared him such frustration. In early 1978, his superiors picked Rocks, along with about twenty other cadres, to go to Moscow for further study. He was not asked his opinion on the matter; in typical Umkhonto fashion, his commanding officer informed Rocks that he would be leaving the next day for political training in the Soviet Union. This was a much-coveted assignment. Among the recruits, Eastern Europe seemed a glamorous place: the soldiers who returned from visits there appeared healthy, well-fed and in possession of luxuries unknown in the Angolan bush. Everyone wanted to go to Moscow, if only to escape the camp's isolation.

Rocks flew from Luanda on Aeroflot, the Russian airline, with a stop in Cairo to refuel. He arrived in Moscow in the dead of winter. Rocks had never seen snow in such quantity; the snow he experienced in South Africa was never more than a light dusting that barely lasted the day. Nor had he ever felt such cold. He could not breathe in the damp, cottony air. The Soviet authorities quickly whisked Rocks and his companions off to a house, where they were quarantined for one week. Their hosts, who did not allow them outside, explained that the confinement was for the South Africans' benefit: they needed to adjust to the climate. In the meantime, the Soviets subjected the men to medical tests to ensure they were not carrying any diseases from the Angolan bush. And they issued the South Africans, some of whom arrived without so much as a jersey, with long, thick underwear, heavy trousers and coats, and fur hats with ear flaps. Rocks found the winter clothing restrictive and uncomfortable. He preferred to stay indoors; the house was centrally heated – as were all buildings in Moscow – a concept virtually unknown in South Africa that Rocks thought brilliant.

After passing their medicals, Rocks and the other Umkhonto soldiers were sent to study at the Institute for Social Sciences of the Central Committee of the Communist Party of the Soviet Union, otherwise known as the Lenin School. A vast party educational establishment that enrolled only the most promising young Russian cadres and those from foreign communist parties, the elite institution comprised several campuses. Rocks' branch of the school was located near Pushkin, a grim and grey dormitory town about eighteen miles north-east of Moscow. The campus consisted of a rambling, two-storey brick school building with large windows and several multi-storeyed dormitories; a wall with a guarded, wrought-iron gate encircled the grounds.

The students were mostly members of banned or underground communist movements. Youthful fellow travellers from a wide range of countries attended the institution: Zimbabweans, Chileans, Angolans, Palestinians. Many of the ANC's elite took courses there during their exile, including Thabo Mbeki, South Africa's current president. The Novo Catengue youths roomed together. Their lodgings were spacious and seemed utterly luxurious after the privations of Angola: each room had an attached lavatory. Rocks shared his quarters with a young man from Soweto. All the students mingled in a common television room and in the canteen. Rocks found the food a vast improvement from Novo Catengue; he and his comrades were, after all, guests of the Central Committee of the Communist Party. He gorged himself on fruit and vegetables, real – not tinned – meat, and hearty soups.

Rocks studied solely with fellow Umkhonto soldiers. Their classrooms were somewhat rudimentary, furnished only with desks and blackboards. The instructors lectured in English for much of the day; Rocks and the other students were given assignments to complete in the library at night. The curriculum fascinated Rocks: Marxist-Leninist philosophy; socialist economy; capitalist economy; world revolutionary movements;

organizational theory; agitprop techniques. Here, finally, was a chance to devote himself to serious study. Rocks particularly delighted in the school's library, which was stocked with Marxist treatises from all over the world.

As the students were not allowed to wander about Moscow on their own, Rocks' only opportunity to observe, first hand, communism's practical application came on the weekends, when the instructors organized outings for the South Africans. Even then, he knew the view was distorted. The students were accompanied everywhere; the close scrutiny imposed by their escorts and the language barrier made chance encounters with ordinary citizens almost impossible. Rocks saw what his hosts wanted him to see: an endless array of museums and circuses. He began to dream of bear acts, trained dogs, trapeze artists; to his friends, he vowed never to set foot inside a circus again after leaving the Soviet Union. For the entire year of his studies, Rocks would have virtually no contact with any Russians other than those who worked at the school. That intercourse was limited, too; none of the English-speaking instructors ever invited the students to their homes. (Rocks attributed this to racism, a common perception among the African students who studied in the Soviet Union.) Although the school's distance from Moscow prevented clandestine expeditions, Rocks managed to jump the perimeter fence on several occasions and, through pantomime and gesticulation, to purchase vodka at a shop in Pushkin that he smuggled into his room to share with his companions.

Despite communism's intellectual allure, as the months passed Rocks found it increasingly difficult to consider himself an adherent. On the one hand, he, like his comrades, was greatly impressed by many of the accomplishments the Soviets showed them. The apparent success and modernity of the collective farms stood in stark contrast with the miserable, hardscrabble operations of black South Africans. And Soviet military might was undeniable. Rocks and his comrades, as guests of the Central Committee, sat in the reviewing stands at the annual military parade near Lenin's Tomb in Red Square. His perch provided Rocks with a breathtaking view of the spectacle below:

the seemingly endless display of arms, heavy weaponry, tanks, missiles, rockets; the phalanxes of marching soldiers.

Yet for all its outward achievements, Rocks could not dismiss the regime's harshness. He disliked its authoritarianism and was shocked by the almost automaton-like behaviour of the people. Any deviation, anything perceived as even vaguely anti-Soviet, was clearly unacceptable. He knew this was what the South African Communist Party was fighting for; by extension, this was what he, as an Umkhonto soldier, should have wanted. But he had not joined the ANC to replace one authoritarian system with another. Not that Rocks was naïve about such matters; he knew the leaders of his ANC cell in Johannesburg were communists. He, like many of his peers, embraced the ideology in South Africa almost as a reflex because the Boer government so vilified it. The Nationalists' demonizing of communism had as much to do with its appeal as its actual political programme. And the Soviets were among the earliest, and the few, governments willing to help the ANC in its struggle.

But seeing directly how communism worked made Rocks disillusioned. This was potentially dangerous. In the ANC, to openly oppose Marxism-Leninism made one suspect; Rocks and some of his more sceptical comrades fell into disfavour at school by asking questions that were deemed anti-Marxist. By contrast, other students quickly worked out that presenting themselves as devout Marxists was a way to climb up the ANC ladder.

One other aspect of communism disturbed Rocks: religion. Despite choosing to become a freedom fighter, he never jettisoned his Christian upbringing and still held deep religious convictions. He came to believe that embracing communism somehow meant a rejection of his history, his family. This he could not do. Rocks decided he would not join the South African Communist Party. He did not decline membership outright; he simply postponed giving his superiors a definitive answer. Rocks knew he would be returning to an elite position in Angola at the end of his course. He just put his head down and kept his mouth shut.

This was no easy task; Rocks found Russia overwhelmingly bleak and depressing. The snow, soiled by automobile exhausts and air pollution, laid a dull grey blanket over Moscow. Days were absurdly short. Rocks arose each morning to utter blackness; by mid-afternoon, the city was once again enfolded in darkness. He suffered greatly from the cold. He yearned for the hot sun, the dazzling lapis lazuli sky, of southern Africa. Only when the weather warmed and he could lose himself in football games outside against the other foreign students, did Rocks find Russia bearable.

He returned to Novo Catengue at the beginning of 1979 as a political instructor. Rocks had little time to prepare for the job. One day, the Umkhonto high command abruptly plucked the old instructors from the camp and sent them to East Germany for further training. Rocks and the dozen or so others picked from his group as replacements had to begin teaching immediately. Most of them were still learning how to teach. Jack Simons tried to help by giving them special courses. The topics were those Rocks studied as a recruit, only now at a more advanced level: National and Class Struggles in South Africa; An Analysis of the Freedom Charter; A Comparison of ANC Constitutions Since 1919. One of Jack's lectures was on How to Combat Enemy Propaganda:

> The political struggle, no less than the military, requires us to know the enemy. The political leader, instructor, organizer, agitator, must know and explain our policy. This is the first and most important requisite for political mobilization. But he also needs to understand, explain, expose and demolish enemy propaganda. It is used to mystify and brainwash people. We cannot develop political consciousness unless we purge the mind of enemy poison. That is the task of political leaders, external and internal.

As an instructor, Rocks taught a new set of recruits the basic politics of the ANC, the history of South Africa and Marxist-Leninist philosophy. The irony did not escape Rocks that he, who secretly had such doubts about communism, was now charged with imparting its marvels to others. But he had made a kind of Faustian pact with himself before returning to Angola: if he had to sell his soul, as it were, to overthrow the racist regime in Pretoria – then so be it.

Rocks' new position made for an easier life in the camp. He was given more comfortable quarters and was exempted from doing the exhausting physical labour. No longer did he have to excavate trenches, shelters, latrines; nor did he have to engage in the much-hated marching and drilling. But his health was still at risk. The place was infested with flying ants, moths, hornets, lizards, cockroaches, beetles and mosquitoes. Malaria was rampant in Novo Catengue; about half the camp's residents contracted the disease within the first month of Rocks' return. Oddly, none of the Cubans assigned to the camp showed signs of the malady. Rocks, who escaped the epidemic, heard talk that the Cubans viewed it as solely an African disease. To him, such prejudice was in keeping with the general feeling of disdain he sensed from the Cuban officers. They were a different lot from those Rocks had known during his time as a recruit. Fewer in numbers, the Cubans made little effort to hide their feelings about their South African protégés: the Umkhonto soldiers lacked drive; they took too long to be deployed after training; they were not being seriously prepared for combat.

Not long after Rocks' return, the Umkhonto high command received intelligence reports that South African forces were planning an attack somewhere in Angola. All the ANC camps were placed on a twenty-four-hour alert. The officers in Novo Catengue ordered their soldiers to evacuate to shelters in the nearby mountains during the day or to culverts beneath the railway line. Rocks and the others awoke at three o'clock every morning to move out, under the cover of darkness, to the mountainside. They deployed by sectors; Rocks, in addition to being a political instructor, was also the commissar of a motorized platoon. He and the other instructors tried to continue teaching in the bush, but soon abandoned their attempts. The recruits could not concentrate on the lessons. They and their officers remained outside the camp until nightfall, when everyone returned for a meal and to sleep. Only the kitchen staff stayed in Novo Catengue during daylight.

The attack came one cloudy morning at about seven o'clock. Three Mirage jets and two Canberra bombers dived below the mist covering the mountaintops and began dropping bombs on the camp. The officers ordered their men to take cover. From his eyrie, Rocks watched in horrified fascination as the explosives flattened the camp, destroying all the buildings. For good measure, the planes strafed the parade grounds with rocket and machine-gun fire. To Rocks the bombardment was shocking, terrifying, not at all the way he had seen it portrayed in movies.

Novo Catengue's arms and weaponry had been moved to a mountain dugout in anticipation of the attack. Umkhonto soldiers were manning the anti-aircraft guns and opened fire on the planes, hitting a Mirage. But the Cuban officers, who had been charged with operating the heat-seeking, surface-to-air missiles, failed to use them. Although one report calculated that the planes were flying too low for the missiles to be effective, Rocks and others thought their failure was due to cowardice; the Cubans did not even attempt to aim the missiles at the sky. The attack killed three soldiers and wounded eight.

With Novo Catengue totally destroyed, the cadres were forced to stay in the mountains. They ate from field kitchens and slept in the shelters. They spent the next few weeks systematically dismantling every artillery piece and readying them for removal. The camp was to be abandoned; the damage the South African bombers inflicted put it beyond repair. When they had completed their job, Rocks and the other soldiers were evacuated under cover of darkness by Angolan tanks to Lobito, a town on the coast. The trip took about three hours; dragging the heavy guns through the bush to the ocean was a difficult task.

A boat awaited them at the port in Lobito. The soldiers loaded the anti-aircraft guns onto the deck, then went below to rest. By sunrise, the vessel was seaborne, heading northward on the day-long journey to Luanda. The boat's gentle sway lulled Rocks to sleep; he was exhausted after the hurried trek through the bush with his guns and his men. A soldier shook him awake. The officer who was in charge of all Umkhonto camps, a member of the ANC's elite National Executive Committee, wished to see him.

Rocks roused himself and sought out his superior.

– You asked for me, sir?

– Yes, Mashinini. I just wanted to tell you that all this time you've been in the camps, I haven't trusted you. I've had you watched. But after your performance in getting the men and the guns out, I'm beginning to believe in you. That's all.

Rocks returned to his corner, stunned. He did not know how to interpret what he had just heard. He did not know whether the suspicions were the result of Tsietsi's denouncements of the ANC, or his own inclination to question authority. He also did not know that the exchange marked a turning a point in his career as a freedom fighter: from that moment, Rocks would enjoy a rapid rise though the ranks of Umkhonto.

CHAPTER EIGHT

Dee

Dee's stay in the house run by the Pan Africanist Congress in Manzini happened by default. After establishing that they had, indeed, crossed into Swaziland safely, Dee and his friend Tiger got a lift to the city to seek out representatives of the exiled anti-apartheid organizations. Dee intended to follow the instructions in the letter from Rocks that he had intercepted and carried with him over the border. According to the letter, he was supposed to make contact with Stanley Mabizela, a high school principal who, in reality, was an ANC representative. But Dee had no idea how to find the man. He and Tiger wandered aimlessly about until, hungry and exhausted, they happened upon friends from Soweto who had escaped a few months earlier and were living at the PAC house. The two youths readily accepted their offer of a place to stay and a meal.

No one told Dee that members of the PAC ran the residence; he thought it was simply a home for exiles. That it was populated by South Africans, some of whom he already knew, made him feel comfortable. However, it didn't take him long to work out that his patrons were PAC adherents, bent on indoctrinating and recruiting their young charges. During the mandatory history classes he, like Mpho, started questioning the authorities. 'Who organized the anti-apartheid protests of the 1950s?' Dee asked. 'Who were the authors of the Freedom Charter?' The more Dee probed the PAC version of South African history, the greater his disquiet. He did not know much about the ANC, but it seemed to him that his hosts were trying to appropriate for their organization the ANC's triumphs; he began to see them as dishonest. Dee also found their leadership wanting. He was appalled that prostitutes frequented the house and that some of his fellow refugees had contracted venereal diseases.

Despite its eagerness to enlist the thousands of youths who escaped from South Africa after the June 16 uprising, the PAC – as Dee observed – was not very effective. It had not weathered its years in exile well. The organization was riven by factionalism, infighting, indecision; with its poor reputation, the PAC elicited little support from other countries. This was in stark contrast with the ANC, which had developed close relations with Scandinavian, Western and Eastern European nations and received funding from them. Dee and Tiger could not keep quiet about the PAC's obvious shortcomings. As they persisted in voicing their criticisms, their hosts grew increasingly hostile and came to see the youths as troublemakers.

A kind of climax occurred with Mpho's arrest in South Africa. When Tiger returned to Manzini (after barely escaping detention himself), he was wild with anger. 'You sold us out!' Tiger shouted at the house commander, within earshot of the other youngsters. 'This was betrayal, literal betrayal! You sent us to get arrested!' Despite the commander's denial, the confrontation made Dee feel terribly insecure. He wanted to leave the house immediately, but to go where? He could not return to Johannesburg and had no other refuge in Swaziland.

The PAC commander settled the matter for him: he expelled Dee, Tiger and Dee's friend Victor from the house. 'Your accusations of betrayal are jeopardizing our relationship with the other students,' he told the three youths at a meeting. 'We'll no longer feed you, nor give you a place to sleep; you'll not be allowed on the premises. You'll have to leave.'

Dee was relieved: now he would be forced to fend for himself. The youths had heard of a camp that the Swazi government operated for South African refugees, a place deep in the mountains where they could escape the PAC and be sheltered from the Boers. Dee and Victor set out to find it. (Tiger declined to join them; he preferred staying with Swazi friends.) It took several lifts and hours of travelling on desolate roads to arrive at Mawelawela Camp, a former women's prison. Dee almost lost his nerve as he and Victor approached the camp and saw the fortified gates, the barbed wire, the lookout towers.

Inside the camp it was no less forbidding. Scores of refugees slept in what used to be the prison's dining hall, now fitted out with prison bunks and thin mattresses. The latrines were filthy and smelt appalling; most of the camp's inhabitants preferred to use the nearby river. (They also bathed there.) Even the food was prison fare: brown bread and tinned fish, three times a day. A Swazi official assigned Victor and Dee bunks, gave them coarse blankets, and left the youths to their own devices.

They quickly discovered that there was little to do in the camp. A bus occasionally transported the youngsters to a school for refugees in Mbabane, the capital. Dee did not bother to go: the school was not yet fully established and the bus appeared only intermittently. It did not seem like a serious thing. Besides, his goal was to find Rocks, not to stay in the camp. Dee hated the place: the inedible food, the isolation, the violence that often erupted after the policemen, who patrolled the grounds during the day, departed for their homes. Every night, they locked the gates from the outside, leaving the youths to the choking darkness of their mountain hideaway. That was when the terror began. Some of the older, gangster-types would tie hard knots in their blankets and, for no discernible reason, attack a few of their bunkmates; they warned the victims not to complain to the authorities – or they would get it even worse on the next night.

Dee spent most days trying to get a lift to Manzini, in search of Rocks' ANC contact, Stanley Mabizela. His opinion of Swaziland did not improve with time. It seemed a backward sort of place, where men wore tribal skirts and much of the population lived in thatch-roofed huts. Even a city like Manzini, with its smattering of restaurants, handful of banks and solitary cinema, was little more than a town by South African standards. Dee supposed its smallness was to his advantage: eventually he would have to find the ANC representative. He persisted in his search for more than a month. One afternoon, when Dee was beginning to despair of ever leaving Swaziland, the very man he was searching for stopped to give him a lift. Dee could not believe his good fortune.

Stanley too was delighted at the serendipity of their encounter. He drove Dee to his home, where they talked for hours. Stanley spoke at length, and with affection, about Rocks: his intelligence; seriousness; dedication; trustworthiness. Dee was disappointed to learn that his brother had long ago left for Angola. Still, this was the happiest moment Dee had experienced since escaping from Soweto: he had finally arrived among people whom he trusted. Now he could realize his goal of following Rocks into exile.

Dee remained with Stanley for a couple of days, then returned to Mawelawela Camp to collect his belongings. He convinced Victor to accompany him to Manzini to stay at the ANC representative's house. Stanley had explained to Dee that he could not go directly to an Umkhonto camp for military training; he would first have to travel to Mozambique, where his application would be considered. Dee remained in Manzini for several more weeks. There was not much diversion at Stanley's house: his job as the principal of a Swazi high school kept him away during much of the day. Dee read books to pass the time or played with Stanley's children. He found it difficult to think of anything except Mozambique; every evening, when Stanley returned home, Dee pressed him for information about when he would depart.

One morning, before he went to work, Stanley popped his head into Dee's room. 'You're leaving for Mozambique tonight,' he said. Dee packed his few items of clothing in a plastic bag, sat himself in a chair and tried not to stare at the clock. The day was unbearably long. Finally, at around ten o'clock at night, Stanley transported Dee, along with two other carloads of South African students, to the frontier. He followed the same route Rocks had taken. Like his brother, Dee was dropped off before the border gate. The ANC representative wished him well. 'Give my regards to Rocks when you catch up with him,' Stanley said, then drove off into the night.

Guides from the ANC met the youngsters to direct them across the border. As soon as they stepped off the road, they were enveloped in a suffocating darkness. Dee thought of the Mozambican soldiers who, fearing incursions by South African

forces, shot at anything that moved along the fence. He imagined a bullet piercing his heart. He thought of the land mines
planted along the frontier. He thought of how it would feel to
have one of his legs blown off, or perhaps both. He became so
frightened that he began to sweat profusely; he had difficulty
gripping the plastic bag that held his clothing.

Dee did not stop perspiring until he and his companions had
safely crossed the border and were being driven in an ANC car
to the Namaacha safe house. He ate the meal his hosts had
prepared, then went to bed. Dee lay awake for a long time. He
listened to the cacophony of nocturnal insect noises, interrupted
now and then by a burst of machine-gun fire from somewhere
out in the bush. There was no turning back now. He would
have to negotiate two countries, two frontiers, if he wanted to
return to South Africa. That seeming finality filled the teenager
with trepidation. He was heartened when, upon waking in the
morning, his hosts served him freshly baked *pão* for breakfast.
To a boy raised on the hard, tasteless loaves of the townships,
the Portuguese bread with its crisp crust and soft, yeasty interior was a kind of gustatory revelation. Dee took the discovery
as a good omen.

He and his companions travelled to the ANC's house in
Matola, where Rocks had stayed. The cleanliness and strict
organization of the place immediately impressed Dee; they were
in stark contrast with the indiscipline he had decried in the PAC
residence in Manzini. The chief of staff gave him a mattress,
pillow, blanket and his own sleeping space. Dee was delighted
to see that there were girls in the camp (although they slept
apart from the boys). The duty commander assigned Dee to do
indoor cleaning as his first chore; he would graduate to outdoor
work, then to kitchen detail. Dee found all the jobs boring. He
hurried through them in the morning to get to breakfast, which
he thought excellent: fresh fruit, milk, and, of course, the ubiquitous hot *pão*.

Despite the efficiency of the house's military-style structure,
Dee soon began to waver in his desire to be a soldier. He studied
the Umkhonto guerrillas who guarded the grounds every night.
Weighed down with guns and grenades, forced to remain in

their positions until dawn, the freedom fighters and their tasks were not nearly as romantic as Dee had dreamed. He could not imagine having to stand guard night after night. Dee's doubts deepened when he received a letter from Rocks, who had heard, through Umkhonto officials, that his brother was in Matola. 'You must go to school,' Rocks wrote. 'You're too young for military training. You should take advantage of the educational opportunities the ANC can offer. Don't try to follow me, I'm older than you.'

Dee's struggle to decide on his future coincided with having to write his biography for the ANC commanders. Much time was given over to composing these histories. New recruits were required to write painstakingly detailed accounts of their daily lives before going into exile. In this way, the ANC officers hoped to catch spies the South African government might be trying to infiltrate into their organization: any inconsistencies or inexplicable lapses in chronology raised immediate suspicion. The youngsters spent days on their compositions, bent laboriously over pads of paper. Dee's opus numbered several pages. He wrote about his parents; his brothers and sisters; his friends (especially his neighbourhood gang); his schooldays; the football team; the church; the choir; what he'd done on June 16 and afterwards; his escape from South Africa; his time with the PAC, and his stay in the Swazi refugee camp. He also provided the names of friends who were already members of the ANC and could testify to his character.

Dee worked for hours; he was exhausted by the time he presented his history to the commander. The man found Dee dozing in the garden a while later. 'I said,' the commander barked, tearing the document into small bits, 'write your biography!' Dee was crestfallen; he had not kept a copy of the first draft and had no way of ensuring that he would reproduce the same facts in the second version. With a sigh, he pulled out a fresh piece of paper and began to scribble.

After several tries, Dee's biography was accepted. In addition to providing the details of his history, Dee also had to choose what he wanted to do in exile: study or go for military training. He selected schooling: Rocks' letter and the ambivalence he felt about life as an Umkhonto soldier made up his mind. In fact, aged fifteen, he did not really have a choice. The ANC generally tried to discourage the youngest teenagers who streamed out of South Africa after the June 16 uprising from pursuing a military career; Oliver Tambo, the ANC president, thought their inclusion tantamount to using children as cannon fodder. The organization had a responsibility to act as surrogate parents, he believed, and to consider their charges' welfare. Once they completed their studies and were at least eighteen, the youths could then enlist in Umkhonto.

Now Dee had to wait for his turn to travel to Tanzania. He did his chores in the mornings and attended political classes in the afternoons. For the first time, Dee was introduced to the ANC's version of history. The lessons seemed right to him; he felt none of the uneasiness, the dissonance, he had experienced at the PAC house in Manzini. When the political commissar who led the discussions described the PAC as a splinter organization, that too rang true with Dee. Here, finally, was South African history imparted with a certain logic to it.

Dee also attended cultural seminars. The classes were intended to inculcate a sense of pride and counter apartheid's denigration of black customs. They were also meant to alleviate boredom while the youngsters awaited orders to continue to their next destination. Dee studied traditional tribal dances; he also learned the gumboot dance, the leg-slapping routine developed by the black miners in South Africa's gold mines.

On the day that he was finally to leave for Tanzania, Dee travelled for the first time to Maputo. Victor and five other youths who had crossed with Dee from Swaziland accompanied him. Two years after independence, the capital was still a beautiful, colonial city. Perched on bluffs overlooking the Indian Ocean, Maputo had broad avenues lined with flame and jacaranda trees, Mediterranean-style houses with white balconies bedecked with purple or pink bougainvillea and hotels whose *azulejos*, the distinctive blue wall tiles from Portugal, glistened like gems in the sunlight. But the city had also become utterly militarized. Soldiers could be seen on virtually every street corner; several roads had army checkpoints or were barricaded completely. Everywhere he looked, Dee saw posters and murals depicting the bearded, moon-faced likeness of Mozambique's president and former guerrilla leader, Samora Machel. Dee was excited to see black soldiers, a black president, black power. This is freedom, he thought, this is liberation. By the time he arrived at Maputo airport and boarded the plane – his first ever – he was almost giddy.

His mood shifted radically on landing in Dar es Salaam. Dee's reaction to the city's heat, stench and general state of decay mirrored that of Rocks. The further he travelled from South Africa, it seemed to Dee, the worse things got. The kindness of the ANC members, who took Dee and his companions to a flat and gave them lunch, heartened him a little. Some had been in exile for nearly two decades; they were hungry for news from home and pumped the youths for details of the June 16 uprising. Their enthusiasm made Dee feel somewhat abashed. If these people could withstand exile with such grace, he could too.

Dee and Victor were sent to Magadu Camp, about 180 miles inland from Dar es Salaam. The place was exceedingly isolated; about one car passed on the road that ran by the camp every hour. Its closest neighbour was a Tanzanian air force base, located several miles away in the bush. The two boys arrived at night to the strains of liberation songs being sung in Zulu and Xhosa. There were only a few dozen young men in the camp, all awaiting scholarships to study in other countries; they were among the earliest of the 1976 exiles to turn up in Tanzania. Dee and Victor would be the youngest residents. Women stayed in their own camp in the nearby town of Morogoro.

The two new arrivals were introduced to Magadu's denizens at the nightly news session in the meeting hall. The ritual immediately appealed to Dee: one of the residents compiled a summary of the day's news, which was read out and discussed. Dee found it intellectually stimulating in a way similar to his older brothers' debates. The discovery of something so pleasing boded well for his time in the camp, Dee decided. He and Victor stayed until the meeting ended; the commander devised makeshift beds for them in the hall and bade them goodnight.

In the morning, Dee and Victor were assigned to rooms. The sleeping quarters consisted of rows of low buildings whose rooms opened to the outside; inside, they were furnished simply with beds and clothes hooks affixed to the backs of the doors. The lodgings reminded Dee of neat little boxes. The camp's other facilities were equally spare: pit latrines, no dining room, an open fireplace for cooking. But the water taps were plentiful and provided for lengthy, sensual bucket showers. Years later, Dee would speak of those showers with great fondness: every evening at dusk, the youngsters got a large fire roaring in the fireplace to heat, almost to boiling, countless buckets of water. The bathers then went behind the kitchen building and poured the scalding liquid over their bodies. It was a splendid feeling to wash away the day's sweat and dirt. Because the air cooled quickly after sunset in their mountain refuge, the youngsters sat around the fire when they had finished, drinking tea, staring into the flames, talking wistfully of home. The experience was like an infinitely extended stay at summer camp.

At mealtimes, Dee and the others collected their food from the kitchen and sat on hard benches to eat. Dee, whose assessment of a particular place often turned on the quality of meals served, found the camp acceptable. For breakfast he ate eggs, buttered bread, fruit, tea. Lunch consisted of meat, vegetables, rice, mealies; dinner was the same. (He would later grow rather plump on the food and restrict himself to eating only fruit at lunchtime.) The ANC supplied the residents with everything else they needed. The youths were allowed to select a wardrobe from piles of second-hand clothing that arrived every six months: three shirts, two pairs of trousers, one pair of shoes. Most of the clothes came from Scandinavian countries, whose populace were clearly larger than their South African brethren. Dee had to alter all of his selections; these he added to the few pieces he had carried with him from Soweto in the plastic bag. His wardrobe did not amount to much. While this fact would have disturbed him greatly at home, Dee barely noted it in Magadu. The bush, after all, offered little in the way of social life.

In the beginning, Dee relished living so close to nature. The cloying, earthy early-morning smells of the East African bush were unlike anything he had known in the township. As a poor black boy, Dee had never experienced the wonder of viewing South Africa's vast array of wild animals. In Magadu, he saw elephants, baboons, water buffalo, all manner of fabulously feathered birds. One morning Dee opened the door of his room to find a large puff adder sleeping peacefully on the mat outside. He slammed the door shut and started screaming. People came running from all corners of the camp; one old man, who had spent years in exile in the bush, grabbed the poisonous snake and proceeded to skin it whole, like a banana.

Dee also held in high regard the camp's tightly structured organization. He began the day doing his assigned job. The commander appointed each youth to one of Magadu's various committees; Dee worked on logistics. It was considered a plum position, especially for one so new. A truck collected Dee early every morning to transport him to Morogoro, a typical bush town that consisted of a scruffy hotel, a tumbledown bar and a large, open-air market. There Dee helped to purchase provisions for the day and load them onto the truck. Then he rode back to the camp, where he delivered the food to the kitchen.

After completing their duties, the youngsters usually engaged in a political discussion before lunch. Morogoro became a much-dissected topic. It was the site of a conference in 1969 in which the ANC decided to allow non-Africans to become members of the organization in exile – a critical event in the history of the anti-apartheid struggle. The seventy delegates who attended the meeting also adopted a blueprint of how, politically and militarily, the ANC would achieve liberation. Known as the Strategy and Tactics document, it stressed the need to launch a campaign among South Africa's urban working class; the people of the townships would provide the sanctuary that guerrilla fighters in other revolutions usually found in the jungles and mountains.

Dee also studied history under the tutelage of the camp's political commissar. The lessons mostly repeated what he had learned in Mozambique, but he found them fascinating nonetheless. It seemed an amazing thing that he could grow up in South

Africa and be oblivious of the ANC's activities; he took his ignorance as a measure of the government's effectiveness in suppressing such information. The commissar assigned the students books to read, but did not require them to do homework. Their afternoons were free. Dee washed his clothes and otherwise whiled away the time. Sometimes he walked the five or so miles to Morogoro; there was a pleasant park with large shade trees in which Dee liked to sit and watch the bustle, as it were, of the town. He had virtually no money to spend. The ANC provided Dee and the others with a monthly allowance of 100 shillings; with it, he could buy a couple of bottles of beer. Beer-buying day was a special occasion. He would sit in the bar and nurse the drinks for hours, trying to make them last until it was time to walk back to Magadu. On other afternoons, Dee visited the girls' camp.

It was not so much a camp as a kind of hostel, in which the fifteen girls stayed. The living conditions were difficult: every day, they had to build their own fire, cook their own beans, deal with the swarms of ants that infested the house. Some girls became anaemic. They were all homesick; this was not how they lived in the townships. The girls also had to organize their own activities. The older ones, who had escaped from South Africa with their schoolbooks, taught their younger housemates mathematics, English, science. For cultural events, they gathered with the young men in Magadu; the boys reciprocated by calling on them at their hostel. It was during one of these visits that Dee noticed Lindi Zikalala, who had escaped from South Africa with her cousin to Botswana. Barely fourteen years old and politically militant, Lindi had wanted desperately to go to Angola for military training. Instead, because of her age, she was sent to Tanzania. Dee found her quiet, serious nature attractive but could not screw up the courage to approach her. Besides, what hope did he have competing against his older, and more sophisticated, campmates?

Despite all their attempts to pass the time, boredom became a huge problem for Dee and his fellow exiles. On those long afternoons, Dee couldn't help thinking of home, of Nomkhitha and Joseph, his family and friends. He thought of his house on

Pitso Street and the games of football on the field opposite. He thought of his school, his teachers, his church. He thought until he feared his head would burst or he would lose his mind. Dee was not alone in his torment. One of his campmates spent the night, as usual, around the campfire, talking and laughing with Dee and the others; the next morning he refused to put on any clothes and wandered about Magadu stark naked, babbling unintelligibly until an ANC representative came and packed him off to Dar es Salaam.

The novelty of living in the bush ceased to give Dee any pleasure. One afternoon, without saying a word to anyone, he walked to the ANC office in Morogoro. Dee sat down opposite the representative. 'I'm homesick,' he blurted out, 'I'm so homesick, I want to go home. I want to go back to Soweto. No one here has left for school yet. I feel like I'm going to spend the rest of my life in the bush.'

The ANC man, who had clearly heard this kind of outburst before, listened sympathetically. 'Do you know what would happen if you went back to South Africa?' he asked gently.

'No.'

'There's a good chance the security forces would arrest you. They'd regard you as a terrorist who'd been reinfiltrated back into the country to commit acts of violence and would torture you to find out who sent you and your mission. It's unlikely that you'd survive the torture. Even if you did, you'd still be putting your family at risk. The police would go after your family too.'

Seeing that Dee was now properly alarmed, the representative slowly explained to him the process of being sent abroad to study. First the scholarship committee in Dar es Salaam had to determine the level of each student. The committee members did this mostly by reading the biographies the youngsters wrote when they fled South Africa. The members, who had gone into exile a generation earlier, were usually stunned by the students' ignorance of mathematics and science, their appalling grammar and spelling. It was clear to them that the educational system for blacks in South Africa had deteriorated dramatically in the last two decades. These deficiencies made evaluations difficult.

Then there was the problem of finding a place for each student. The committee members had to approach all the embassies in the Tanzanian capital to enquire about schooling for the exiles in their respective nations. Most of the South African students had run away from home without papers or school records, and the Western countries usually required some sort of official proof that a youngster could meet their standards. The Eastern Bloc and African nations were more amenable to accepting the ANC's assessment of its youngsters. So the ANC usually sent university students to places like Bulgaria, Poland, Hungary and East Germany; high school students went to schools in African countries that were paid for by the United Nations. Even then, the committee's work was not finished. Most of the African institutions were located in isolated areas where the urbanized township youths often languished. Indeed, one group was sent to a school in the bush in Sierra Leone – only to have half of the students return to Tanzania on the next flight.

The ANC representative spoke for a long time. 'I promise you,' he said, walking Dee outside, 'the scholarship committee is processing all requests to study. Most of you will be going abroad to proper schools within a few months. In the meantime, don't let yourself be crushed by the bush.'

Dee felt encouraged as he trekked back to camp. He decided to embrace the boredom and not to try to fight it. He began spending more time in Morogoro, passing the time at the ANC office and at the girls' camp (although he still had no luck in finding a girlfriend). One change in his routine helped greatly: he was appointed to the newsgathering committee, and he found the work terribly exciting. Twice daily Dee sat by the camp's short-wave radio, transcribing the BBC World Service's news programmes. He was charged with selecting stories that illustrated some aspect of the South African anti-apartheid struggle. Dee prepared them in a way that was meant to engender discussion; he would then present the stories at the camp's nightly meeting, reading them to the gathered residents as though he were a broadcast journalist.

His participation in so important a ritual made Dee feel more

integrated into the camp, more a part of the ANC. Still, he was
thrilled when, at the end of 1977, a member of the scholarship
committee in Dar es Salaam came to Magadu to inform Dee
and eleven others that they would be going to Cairo to study.
The idea of Egypt seized Dee's imagination; he had been reading
about the Arab–Israeli conflict and now he was about to be
thrust into the midst of the fray. Another group of youngsters,
whom Dee considered less fortunate, would be going to Nigeria.
But his friend Victor was accompanying him, as were several
of the girls from the Morogoro hostel.

The youths were not told of the travel date until the day
before their departure. Dee became frantic when he heard the
news: his only pair of shoes was virtually in tatters. A friend
who owned a pair of *takkies*, sports shoes, and a pair of street
shoes, offered Dee the former. The *takkies* were filthy and smelly,
but at least his toes did not poke out, as they did in his old
pair. Dee washed the shoes and coated them with polish, but
they had not dried by the time he was ready to leave. He climbed
into the truck for the ride to Dar es Salaam clad in wet shoes.
Of all the indignities Dee had to bear in exile, those that offended
his sartorial sensibilities were among the most painful. He would
never forget that, because of the paucity of his wardrobe, he
was forced to wear damp, sticky shoes on so important a
journey.

Dee and his companions received travel documents from the
Tanzanian government at the airport. Dee could barely contain
himself as he boarded the aeroplane: he was finally going to
school. He saw that Lindi Zikalala, from the girls' camp, was
sitting in a nearby row. Dee asked the young woman next to
her to swap seats with him; this would be an excellent chance
to speak to Lindi, perhaps even to impress her. Lindi was amused
by the manoeuvre. She had sensed Dee's interest in her in
Morogoro, but remained somewhat distant from him – and all
boys – for fear of getting pregnant like some of her housemates.
Lindi had come to admire Dee's tenacity and patience; she
decided to let down her guard on the flight and found that, as
they both came from Soweto, she and Dee had a lot in common.

They landed at the chaos that was Cairo's airport. Dee felt

as though he had been catapulted into another world: the pushing, shouting, shoving mass of people offering to carry his luggage, exchange dollars, transport him to his hotel and otherwise attach themselves to his person for various sums of money was overwhelming. Fortunately, an ANC officer was there to meet the youths. On the journey into Cairo, they drove directly into a traffic jam that seemed to have neither beginning nor end. Dee was spellbound by the city and its odours, the swirls of colour, the blaring symphony of car horns. The youths went to the apartment of the chief ANC representative in Egypt for a welcoming party. The official lived with his family in Zamalek, an island in the middle of the Nile. It was a lovely neighbourhood of grand old buildings and stunning river views where many of the diplomats and foreigners resided. There Dee met the staff of the ANC's office in Cairo, ate good food, drank alcohol, listened to music from home. It seemed a propitious start to his new life.

Dee and the other boys stayed, under the auspices of the United Nations Development Programme, in a student hostel in Cairo proper, not far from Zamalek Island. (The girls had separate lodgings.) A four-storey building, the hostel housed about 150 students, most of them Egyptians who came from outside Cairo and needed a place to board. The lower floors were given over to kindergarten- and primary-school-aged children; the high school students lived on the top floors. Dee roomed with other South Africans, but shared the showers and lavatories on his floor with Egyptian students. He found the rooms clean and pleasant and the food delicious. Dee grew to relish Egyptian food: the *shwarma*, or slices of lamb roasted on a large skewer; *falafel*, fried balls of chickpea paste that he ate with salads and pita bread; rice pudding. He also quickly came to like Cairo. The city's frenetic pace appealed to Dee, especially after the torpor of the Tanzanian bush; the skyscrapers, flats and vehicle-clogged roads reminded him of Johannesburg. Best of all were the shops stuffed with inexpensive, American-style clothing.

He began attending St George College, a large, government-run high school located in Heliopolis, a distant suburb. (St

George's students included the sons of the late Egyptian president, Anwar Sadat, and those of the current president, Hosni Mubarak.) About half of Dee's fellow exiles studied with him; the other half went to a different school. A special bus picked up the South Africans at six o'clock in the morning to transport them to St George. The school was structured along military lines: the students assembled in the courtyard every morning, dressed in their uniform of grey trousers, grey blazer, white shirt, tie. They saluted as the Egyptian flag was raised; a band played the national anthem and various military airs. Then the students marched, in formation, to their respective classes. Dee thought the elaborate ritual excessive, especially for the foreign students. (In addition to the South Africans, Ethiopians, Eritreans and Somalis studied at the school.)

From the beginning, Dee had problems at St George. When his schooling stopped after June 16, Dee was about to enter Form One, or the equivalent of junior high school. But Egyptian law required him to enrol in the class that corresponded to his age. With no preparation, Dee was put in the equivalent of Form Four. His curriculum now comprised algebra, biology, chemistry, physics, statistics, trigonometry. Dee was utterly lost. To compound his confusion, despite assurances that lessons would be in English, Dee found that most courses were taught in Arabic.

Over time, he became more proficient in the colloquial Arabic spoken in Egypt. But the course work remained beyond his comprehension. Dee's fellow exiles at St George suffered too, although some had already completed Form Two or Three before leaving South Africa. The boys who attended the other school had an easier time of it: aware of the inferior education the black students received under apartheid and the time they had lost after June 16, the teachers organized special tutoring for them. The girls, who attended an international school, studied in English and could cope with most of their courses. (They struggled more with social and cultural differences. The Egyptians laughed at their short hair and taunted them by shouting 'Are you boys or girls?' And their teachers seemed obsessed with ascertaining that the young women were virgins, constantly grilling Lindi and her companions about their chasteness and lecturing them on the importance of guarding one's maidenhead.)

Dee returned to his hostel every afternoon at four o'clock. He and the others who attended St George spent hours doing homework together, trying to understand the lessons. During the first year, the youths concentrated diligently on their studies: they were on scholarships, a privileged thing among exiles. The ANC and UN officials told them outright that they would be sent back if they failed; they had two chances to pass their matriculation subjects. For a while, Dee and his companions employed private tutors, older South Africans, who came around to the hostel on Saturday mornings and pushed the boys to learn. But their efforts were in vain. Dee passed only two subjects – biology and algebra; he needed four passes to advance to the next form. His schoolmates also did poorly, although the boys at the other institution and the girls all passed their subjects.

Dee was disconsolate. He had waited so long and endured such hardship for the opportunity to study; and now, through a quirk of Egyptian law that required him to be in too advanced a grade, his opportunity was, in effect, half-squandered. He spoke at length with the UN and ANC officials, but they were at a loss to help. Dee could not broach the subject with his teachers or headmaster; they held themselves aloof from the South Africans and were unapproachable. He found his fellow Egyptian students equally distant, something Dee attributed to a latent racism. He had encountered much prejudice in Cairo: often, while walking down the street, Dee would suddenly be drenched in dirty water someone poured on him from the flats above. He thought it an accident the first time it happened. By the fifth incident, he realized it was deliberate. The Afrikaners were clearly not the only racists in the world.

In the midst of his unhappiness, Dee's relationship with Lindi provided him with some comfort. He came to see her as an oasis of calm. Dee admired her serious approach to schoolwork, her quiet way of encouraging him to follow suit, her steadiness. Many of their fellow South African exiles, unused to the regular income their stipends provided, fell prey to Cairo's fast-talking drug dealers and began experimenting with illicit substances, especially LSD; Lindi resisted such temptations. Dee found himself spending virtually every weekend with her.

There were other problems in his life beyond school. Once a week, a hostel employee collected the residents' dirty laundry, washed it and returned it to the students. The South African youths usually found several items missing. As they had been instructed, they wrote a letter to the hostel's management after each incident to complain about the lost clothing. The management claimed to know nothing about it. Dee and his companions soon discovered the whereabouts of their missing clothes: the lavatory. The Egyptian students in the hostel stole the shirts and trousers to dry themselves after washing in the bidet. (They did not use toilet paper.) Dee was outraged: not only did he find the practice revolting, but the Egyptians had appropriated some of his newest outfits. He and his friends confronted the Egyptian students on several occasions, but the latter always denied the thefts. The encounters often ended in fistfights between the two sides.

Pushed beyond their tolerance, the South African students planned an attack against their adversaries. They chopped up old wooden chairs and fashioned them into clubs while the Egyptians were at lunch one afternoon. Dee and his friends lay in wait for the Egyptians to return to their floor. As the unwary students appeared, the South Africans set upon them. Word of the attack spread quickly through the hostel and other residents rushed to join in the fight. The Egyptians were armed with knives, chains, even hair dryers. The pitched battles spread to other floors; several students were wounded and the police and ambulances had to be summoned.

Dee and his fellow South Africans could not stay in the hostel after the brawl. It was too dangerous; the Egyptian students were clearly planning some sort of retaliation. The next morning, Dee and his friends went to school as usual, but instead of returning to the hostel in the afternoon, they went to the home of Zenzile Ngalo, an ANC official in Zamalek. Zenzile worked as a kind of liaison to the UN; after telling him what happened the previous day in the hostel, the South African students announced they would be staying with him until he got them an allowance so they could live on their own. The ANC official lived in a three-bedroom flat with his wife and four children, and the sudden addition of eleven young men made for rather cramped quarters. But the students remained there for the month or so it took the beleaguered official to organize stipends for flats. Despite the discomfort, Dee was not displeased by the turn of events; he had felt too restricted by the hostel's myriad regulations about noise and curfews and longed for a way to escape.

He and the other youths decided to search for flats in Heliopolis, close to their schools, when they received their funds. A modern, middle-class neighbourhood, Heliopolis was filled with high-rise apartments favoured by military officers and their families. The South Africans walked around the teeming streets until they found a 'For Lease' sign in English. They rented three apartments among themselves; with their allowances, the youths had sufficient money to pay the monthly rent and still buy food. Dee's flat was spacious: two bedrooms, a lounge, television room, kitchen, bathroom, balcony. He shared a bedroom with Victor; two others stayed in the second bedroom. Their flat was equipped with beds, sofas, sheets, towels, pots, pans. Dee cooked for himself and washed his own laundry. Life suddenly became pleasant, despite the torment of his schoolwork and the pressure to succeed: now he could dance or have parties or stay awake all night.

Dee still missed his family and home. He wrote letters to Joseph and Nomkhitha, but never received a reply. (Years later he would find out that the security police intercepted everything he sent to South Africa. They made photocopies of the letters, which they passed to his parents after blotting out the address and any references to his whereabouts.) Dee was discouraged by the silence, but did not feel as homesick as he had in Swaziland or Tanzania; Cairo was too bewitching a place. The politics of the region provided endless intellectual diversion. Dee witnessed, from the Egyptian perspective, the signing of the Camp David peace accords between Israel and Egypt. That singular event helped to fuel his fascination with political affairs and the desire, spawned in Magadu Camp while working on the newsgathering committee, to be able to record such moments.

Cairo's abundant nightlife also helped to distract Dee. He and his friends often had parties on the weekends that progressed from flat to flat; the South Africans bought quantities of Egyptian beer, which was cheap and plentiful (and for which Dee developed a great fondness), and invited other African students who were also studying in Cairo. Sometimes Dee took Lindi to the movies, although he did not much like the histrionic Arabic-language films that were the staple of the Egyptian cinema. Or he and Lindi and their friends went to one of Cairo's myriad nightclubs. Dee's favourite was a large boat that sailed slowly up the Nile every Friday night, then returned the following morning. Dee danced, quite literally, until dawn. Occasionally he packed a picnic lunch to eat with his friends among the pyramids and the Sphinx in nearby Giza. On one particularly memorable weekend, Dee, Victor, Lindi and another girl hired a car and driver and travelled to the port city of Alexandria.

Two things marred Dee's otherwise pleasurable existence. The first occurred while he was working in the ANC's offices in Cairo, doing clerical jobs after school to ingratiate himself with the staff. By now, Dee had lost all interest in military training and would do anything to ensure that the ANC allowed him to continue his studies; the best jobs in exile, he could see, required an education. As Dee was filing some papers, he came upon a circular from ANC headquarters in Lusaka entitled, 'Who is Tsietsi Mashinini?' According to the document, Tsietsi was an agent of the US Central Intelligence Agency, a man who had sold out the youth of South Africa, a turncoat who now enjoyed the financial support of the US government. The statement was signed by Alfred Nzo, the ANC's secretary-general. Dee sat down on a nearby chair, astounded. He was devastated by what he had read and did not know what to think. Had his beloved brother betrayed him or the organization that ostensibly cared for him? Dee shuddered to think that the circular had been sent to ANC offices around the world; now he was supposed to make copies of it and pass them to all the South African exiles in Cairo. He decided not to disseminate the document. Dee simply marked the paper for the representative's attention and put it on his desk. He did not speak of the matter to anyone. For the remaining ten years or so of his exile, Dee – like Rocks – would feel haunted by the spectre of Tsietsi, always uncertain of how, as a Mashinini, the ANC perceived him.

The other discordant, and ubiquitous, aspect of his life was school. Acutely aware that he had only one more chance to pass his subjects, Dee grew desperate as the year progressed. It seemed obvious to him that he would not succeed. His five fellow South Africans at St George were equally depressed. Every morning they set out for school, only to lose their nerve at the last moment and seek refuge in a nearby bar. There they sat, nursing beers and chatting desultorily until late in the afternoon, when they walked slowly back to their flats. They roused themselves briefly as the time for the interim tests approached. Then Dee and his companions were a frenzy of activity: revising all night, testing one another, trying to absorb the material they had missed in the lectures. Invariably, they failed. The downhearted youths returned to drinking the days away, occasionally turning up for class to take random notes. Dee slowly began to accept the inevitably of returning to East Africa.

He nonetheless forced himself, in a final burst of vigour, to study for the end-of-term examinations. The UN representative gathered the apprehensive youths together after the tests to announce the results. 'The six boys at St George will be returning to Tanzania,' he proclaimed unceremoniously. 'They didn't pass all their subjects. The other five boys and the girls will be allowed to stay. They passed.' Dee was mortified; he could not look at Lindi across the room. He had failed himself and his family. How could a Mashinini not achieve even the minimum academic requirements? Now he would have to go back to Tanzania, to the bush. Dee felt like crying. He had hated Magadu: the isolation, the boredom, the monotony. It could be years before the ANC might see fit to grant him another scholarship. In the meantime, he would rot.

He was also loath to leave Lindi. The two had become intimate during their time in Cairo; the idea of being forcibly separated was unthinkable. Lindi now seemed ineffably precious to
Dee. One night, before his departure, they decided to draw up
a kind of agreement or contract. It pledged their love, loyalty
and friendship to one another; they promised to continue
communicating and exchanging letters wherever they might be,
and to preserve the relationship until they met again. Neither
knew then that it would be many years before they were
reunited. Dee would carry the document with him for all that
time.

Dee went on a spending spree in the weeks before leaving
Cairo, depleting his cache of Egyptian money to buy the things
he knew he could not find in the bush: soap, deodorant, shaving
supplies, toothpaste, shampoo, cologne, underwear, handker-
chiefs, clothing. He prowled the streets of the city. Dee wanted
to impress everything in his mind, as if those remembrances
could fill the emptiness of the impending bush: the muezzin's
plaintive wail to prayer to the faithful; the cloying spice-smells
of the old *souk*; the hard, satisfying sound his heels made hitting
the concrete pavement; even the cacophony of car horns were
dear to him: they signalled civilization.

All the students who had travelled together from Tanzania
went to the airport to bid farewell to the six youths. Everyone
was stoical. Dee thought he might weep, but he had steeled
himself beforehand to march onto the aeroplane with little
display of emotion. He hung in the window of the jet long after
it left the ground, trying to capture one last glimpse of Cairo's
dust-choked labyrinth of slums. He would miss the place enormously. Returning to Tanzania seemed a return to certain doom.

CHAPTER NINE

Tsietsi

While negotiating the details of his new organization, Tsietsi sent an urgent message to his comrades, Khotso and Barney: Come to Lagos immediately; we have a meeting with General Olusegun Obasanjo, the Nigerian head-of-state. Tsietsi wanted the two young men to take part in the conversation and to brief Obasanjo on their work. The general's evaluation of their fledgling group would determine the scope of Nigeria's support.

The meeting was held in General Obasanjo's office at State House. Obasanjo, who had taken power in a military *coup d'état*, wore his general's uniform. (General Obasanjo would make history a couple of years later by voluntarily relinquishing his office, the country's first general to do so in two decades of almost continuous military rule. He would be democratically elected to the presidency in 1999.) The general demanded to know why Tsietsi and his companions did not join the ANC. Why should I fund a competing or duplicating organization? he asked. Why not simply infiltrate the ANC and take it over?

The bureaucracy is so tight in the ANC that there's no way we could take it over, Tsietsi explained. Besides, we don't agree with their politics or their strategies. The ANC doesn't really intend to fight the Boers. We do. We'll overthrow the racist regime and run the country.

Despite his ostensible desire to have Khotso and Barney participate in the interview, Tsietsi did most of the talking. The meeting, which was supposed to take only fifteen minutes, lasted for one and a half hours. General Obasanjo found the articulate, vigorous young South African a compelling spokesman for his cause. An official photographer captured the tableau in a picture: Tsietsi, adorned in a traditional tunic, cigarette in hand, a look of intensity on his face, leans toward the general to emphasize a point he is making. At the end of the discussion, General Obasanjo directed an official from the Foreign Ministry to give the youths everything they needed. Bank accounts would be opened in Botswana and England for their use. They would report directly to him, General Obasanjo, on their progress. But to obtain military training, the exiles must first transform themselves into a national movement. Only then would the general provide such instruction.

Tsietsi's successful wooing of General Obasanjo was a huge achievement. To have such an important and wealthy patron as Nigeria – which was suddenly flush with funds from oil revenues – meant he could realize his ideal of creating a true army of liberation. Now he would show those flabby, emasculated organizations, the ANC and the PAC, what real revolutionaries could accomplish. This was what he had hoped for, the stuff of his dreams. Tsietsi was almost beside himself with delight.

The next step was for Tsietsi to set up the main office in Lagos. Khotso would be the representative in Gaborone (Botswana) and Barney in London. Khotso began working on transforming the Soweto Students' Representative Council (SSRC) in exile into the national movement that the Nigerian president required. Tsietsi communicated with Khotso often, wanting to know how he was progressing. Meanwhile Tsietsi spent much of his time talking with government officials, holding press conferences, explaining the purpose of his new organization. After a while, Comfort Molokoane, who had been an activist with trade unions in South Africa and had linked up with the SSRC in exile, joined Tsietsi in Lagos. His comrades believed that although Tsietsi excelled in the role of leader, he perhaps needed some help in the day-to-day details of running an organization. This was especially true in a place like Lagos. The overcrowded, slum-ridden city, with its aggressive populace, seemed a waking madness to the more genteel South Africans. Built on a series of islands that were linked by perpetually traffic-jammed bridges, Lagos defied modern practices. Simply placing a telephone call or sending a telex was a major feat. The distinctive, often unintelligible (to an outsider), patois of West African English only made things more complicated. And the relentless rain, heat and humidity were positively enervating.

Tsietsi and Comfort lived in a government guesthouse on Victoria Island, an exclusive area of embassies and beautiful beaches. Although luxurious, especially by the standards of a refugee, the guesthouse felt like a prison to Tsietsi. It had guards, high security walls, little peepholes in the doors. There was no one to talk to save the servants who came and went. Tsietsi and Comfort did not feel much freer outside their lodgings. While the Nigerian government provided an allowance for their expenses, the two young men had to obtain permission from official 'minders' for their activities and travel. It seemed to Tsietsi that their every movement was watched. Despite the restrictions, he and Comfort were in great demand to speak about their organization, flying to various cities in Nigeria and to other West African nations.

After working for several months to establish a kind of head-quarters in Lagos, Tsietsi travelled to Botswana to check on Khotso. He managed to get word to his family of his prox-imity, and Mpho journeyed to Gaborone to see his brother. It was a joyous reunion. Mpho had not seen Tsietsi since his escape from South Africa, but the older Mashinini seemed to be the same irrepressible, self-confident leader, talking of how he would soon return home as victor and Mpho would then have to address him as 'Mr Prime Minister'. Tsietsi plied Mpho with questions about Joseph, Nomkhitha and the other chil-dren. He wanted to know if the police still raided their home, searching for him.

Their discussion of Mpho's imprisonment lent the only discor-dant note to the visit. Tsietsi became agitated after hearing the details of the trial. 'Why did you get a white man to represent you?' he demanded. 'You should have represented yourself.'

Mpho was offended by his brother's seeming arrogance. 'How can you make such judgements?' Mpho retorted. 'You were out of the country. I was in prison. You don't know what it's like.

People organized a good lawyer for me. You wouldn't have done anything differently if you'd been arrested.'

The argument raged for hours. Tsietsi's presumptuousness angered Mpho enormously; it struck him as naïve, ignorant. The activists who left South Africa on the wave of euphoria of 1976 were out of touch with reality. Mpho had experienced the strength and brutality of the apartheid regime; the exiles had not. These differing perceptions would create a chasm between the two groups – those who fled South Africa and those who remained – for all the years of the liberation struggle and beyond, each side claiming moral superiority. Tsietsi and Mpho parted with the matter unresolved.

Khotso, too, found Tsietsi almost unbearably arrogant. Tsietsi provoked stormy, accusatory arguments with him and other comrades, criticizing their performance in some instances and charging them with negligence in others. To Khotso, Tsietsi seemed to be changing. He was consulting less with his fellow activists and instead issuing unilateral orders. Members of the SSRC complained, *sotto voce*, that they felt alienated from Tsietsi. Khotso believed his friend had always had autocratic tendencies; now, isolated in Nigeria (the bulk of the SSRC exiles lived in Botswana) and freed from the restraints of organizational niceties, Tsietsi indulged those propensities. Or perhaps the constant white noise of news stories, intended to discredit him, were simply taking their toll. (TSIETSI TURNS INTO DRUNKARD!; MASHININI INEBRIATED FROM MORNING 'TIL NIGHT!; TSIETSI ABANDONS THE STRUGGLE!) The articles, begun while he was in London, had continued, unabated, in the South African press.

In the ensuing months, Tsietsi divided his time among various West African nations. Just as he had convinced General Obasanjo, Tsietsi now turned his sights on the presidents of Guinea and Liberia. The plan was to coax financial and military support from those nations too. His cadres would receive arms training in the region, then join cells in Botswana for re-infiltration into South Africa. Khotso, using the Nigerian diplomatic pouch – he had become friendly with Lagos' high commissioner in Botswana – sent Tsietsi a stream of progress reports. The liberation of South Africa, Tsietsi believed, would soon begin in earnest.

For diversion, and to escape the tedium of their guesthouse, he and Comfort frequented the clubs that lined Lagos' beach-fronts. It was at one such establishment that Tsietsi encountered Miriam Makeba, the great South African singer who had been in exile for years. Miriam was living in Guinea with her husband, Stokely Carmichael, the militant black American civil rights leader. She performed often throughout West Africa and maintained a network of South African émigrés in the various countries as friends. Tsietsi was thrilled to meet her and Stokely, whose writings he had read and admired while in high school. Miriam was equally charmed by Tsietsi; he became a regular guest at her post-performance parties whenever she appeared in Nigeria.

At a buffet luncheon she hosted for about twenty friends on a particularly sultry afternoon, Miriam introduced Tsietsi to one of her backing singers, Welma Campbell. Welma, a beautiful young woman who also held the title of Miss Liberia, was intrigued. Miriam had presented Tsietsi as a student leader; people gathered around him, posing questions and listening intently to his replies. Tsietsi's self-confidence, his charisma, his faith in the trajectory of his life appealed to Welma. 'I can't rest until I've achieved justice for the black people of South Africa,' Tsietsi explained. 'I feel that the efforts of the previous liberation movements are going in the wrong direction. I can't see any real progress that will lead to something final. All I see is that the efforts of the older generation will be thwarted. We, the youth, are the only hope. We, the youth, have nothing to lose.'

Welma asked Tsietsi several questions about the anti-apartheid struggle and was mesmerized by his responses. She found herself drawn to him. But he did not single her out from among the crowd of admirers at the party. Thus when Tsietsi telephoned her the next day to chat, Welma was surprised and thrilled. He reacted with equal enthusiasm; after ringing off, Tsietsi danced about the room, crowing to Comfort: I've met Miss Liberia! I've met a beauty queen!

*　　*　　*

Welma Campbell seemed an unlikely sort to be the focus of Tsietsi's attention. If Tsietsi's childhood was marked by deprivation, Welma's, by contrast, shone with grace and privilege. She was born into one of the elite families of Liberia, a West African country founded by freed American slaves. Theirs was a strangely stratified society. After declaring independence in 1847 – thus creating Africa's first independent republic – the erstwhile slaves set about re-creating the only life they had known: that of the ante-bellum South. They wore top hats and morning coats, 'introduced' their daughters at debutante balls, danced the Virginia reel and quadrille. They created a government that included a president and vice-president, a Senate and House of Representatives. They named their capital Monrovia, after President James Monroe, who had championed the cause of a 'little America destined to shine gem-like in the darkness of vast Africa'. In a final flourish of authenticity, the Americo-Liberians – as they called themselves, denied full franchise to the members of the indigenous population and turned its sixteen tribes into an underprivileged majority.

Welma's late father, who traced his antecedents to Baltimore, Maryland, was a lawyer and the chief of security to the president; her mother was a congresswoman. Welma grew up in a large house in Sinkor, an exclusive, beachfront section of Monrovia that was dotted with palm trees. She attended private schools, taking her final year of high school in the US, where her mother had also studied. Her childhood consisted of ballet classes with a British instructor and piano lessons and parties. Because of their positions, Welma's parents were frequent guests of the president, her father attired in the requisite top hat and morning coat. Welma herself, as a young girl, was invited on several occasions to the presidential palace to admire its grand ballroom, gilt furniture and splendid view of the Atlantic Ocean.

After finishing high school, Welma enrolled at the University of Liberia. She found the place, like much of Monrovia in the 1970s, a hotbed of activism and discontent. Despite some changes in the political system, the Americo-Liberians, who comprised about 4 per cent of the population, still controlled

60 per cent of Liberia's wealth. The younger generation of indigenous people had little tolerance for the continued inequalities; student organizations, opposition groups and dissidents were increasingly demanding real reforms. Welma became involved in a drama group at the university that had ties to the political opposition. Although she had had little exposure to such matters, Welma came to champion the causes of multi-party democracy and freedom of expression in Liberia. The drama group's evolution into a kind of creative workshop allowed her to experience similarly political art forms from other parts of Africa, too. The group's deputy director, Philemon Hou, was a South African exile who taught the actors anti-apartheid protest songs and the miners' gumboot dance. Philemon piqued her interest in South Africa and the struggle for liberation.

Around this time, Welma came under pressure from her mother to participate in the Miss Liberia beauty contest. Despite Welma's protestations, her mother insisted; a member of their family was organizing the event and Welma's refusal to partake would have been a great embarrassment. Welma, much to her surprise, won. She represented Liberia at the Miss World pageant in London a few months later. It turned out to be yet another lesson in her political education: the Organization of African Unity, the continent's union of states, demanded that the African contestants withdraw from the competition in protest against Miss South Africa's presence. Welma did so, with pride. (Later in the year, she did participate in the Miss Universe contest, held in the Dominican Republic.)

Welma did not take these beauty contests seriously and gladly returned to her activities in the drama workshop at university. She found her interest in her studies waning as she devoted increasingly more time to performing. Through her friendship with Philemon, Welma met an array of actors and activists who inhabited a world that held great attraction for her. Perhaps the most consequential of those meetings occurred when Philemon invited Miriam Makeba to attend the group's awards night. Welma was thrilled to hear the famous singer perform anti-apartheid songs. The members of the workshop had also prepared a programme; Welma did the gumboot dance. Miriam was sufficiently impressed to invite Welma and two others to perform with her at a festival in Nigeria a few months later.

Thus began a relationship with Miriam that took Welma around the world. Whenever she wanted Welma to join her, Miriam sent a telex and an aeroplane ticket to Philemon, who would then take the message to Welma's mother to obtain her permission. Welma would fly to Conakry, the Guinean capital, to rehearse with Miriam for a couple of weeks before the company set off on tour. Welma sang backing vocals for Miriam and danced. She performed in Switzerland, France, Germany, Holland, Belgium, Morocco and Tunisia, as well as at the Africa Games in Algeria, at the first inauguration of President Daniel Arap Moi in Kenya, and at a music festival in Cuba. Welma revelled in the life of the performing artist. She loved being in a new city every night, meeting new people, performing in new venues.

Miriam was protective of her protégé. She insisted that Welma stay in her hotel suite when they travelled. Welma found herself becoming a kind of companion, a daughter, to Miriam. She braided the singer's hair, went shopping with her, helped to apply her make-up before a concert. Welma listened with great empathy to Miriam's incessant talk of South Africa. Her craving for home seemed almost like a narcotic withdrawal in its intensity. Miriam's story, and those of her émigré friends, touched Welma profoundly and made her feel a part of their struggle. South Africa's political narrative was a great morality play; how could anyone remain unaffected? Welma only had reservations about the alcoholism. The exiles all drank to excess, in Welma's estimation, something she attributed to the pain of their expatriate existence.

After her initial meeting with Tsietsi, Welma went home to Liberia. Tsietsi pestered Miriam for Welma's address and wrote her long letters filled with his visions for a democratic South Africa; he also demanded to know when she would next be performing in Nigeria. Welma returned to Lagos on tour with Miriam a few months later. Tsietsi did not leave her side; when Welma was about to depart for Ghana, the tour's next destination, Tsietsi got Miriam to buy an aeroplane ticket for him also.

It was the start of a passionate, all-consuming love affair. Tsietsi devoted himself to Welma, watching her practice sessions, taking every meal with her and the other members of the company, attending each concert. Welma found the attention flattering; she had never experienced anything like it. They spent much of their time talking. Tsietsi taught her words in Sotho, mostly expressions of love. He spoke constantly of his family, especially Nomkhitha, whom he missed terribly. Tsietsi worried about his mother and was prone to bouts of depression, imagining the horrible things that were happening to her because of him. He regaled Welma with stories about his twin sisters, Lindi and Linda, who were only toddlers when he escaped from South Africa and whose nappies he used to change.

Welma thought it extraordinary to encounter a young man who was so sensitive, so human. It was even more unusual that he professed such strong feelings for family life. Tsietsi seemed the antithesis of the Liberian men she had dated, especially one with whom she had recently ended a relationship. Tsietsi restored Welma's belief in herself.

Tsietsi was equally smitten. He told Miriam that he wanted to give Welma a ring and asked that she pay for it. They picked out a lovely band of white gold, adorned with sapphires and diamond chips. Tsietsi presented it to Welma with great ceremony. 'This is an engagement ring', he said, slipping the jewel on her finger. 'I want to marry you. I want you to be my wife.' Welma, who was taken completely by surprise, could not speak. 'Of course, we'll go through a formal engagement,' he added hastily, 'and I'll ask your mother for your hand in marriage properly.' She accepted his offer without hesitation.

Welma returned to Monrovia and told her mother, Emma, that she was engaged to be married. (Her father had died several years earlier.) Emma objected strenuously; she did not want Welma to marry until she had finished university. Welma's desire to do so remained a contentious issue between them when Tsietsi visited Liberia a few months later. Miriam accompanied him; she and other members of the South African exile community, acting as a kind of surrogate family, went with Tsietsi to Emma's house to make the introductions. Emma was not swayed by the ceremonial courtesies. She repeated the objections she had enumerated to Welma. 'So you're worried she won't finish her education?' Tsietsi laughed. 'You needn't be. I don't see why she can't study if we're married. I think it's an eminently sensible thing to do.'

Tsietsi seemed so in control of his life, his arguments so reasonable, that even Welma came to believe in the future he described. He charmed almost everyone in her family with his eloquence and humour. They were particularly impressed by a speech Tsietsi gave at a local theatre, in which he recounted the story of the June 16 uprising and the brutality the apartheid regime inflicted on South Africa's blacks in the aftermath. Eva, Welma's younger sister, thought him a magnificent speaker. She had only read about the events in the newspapers; here was someone who actually participated in them, someone who had made tremendous sacrifices for his cause. To Eva, and scores of others who heard him, Tsietsi appeared a noble figure. Only Emma remained unconvinced.

Despite Emma's obvious disapproval, Tsietsi's visit only deepened his romance with Welma. They swam together every day. They went for long walks, hand-in-hand, through the city. They spent hours talking: about how Tsietsi would liberate South Africa; their plans for the next ten years; their political views. Tsietsi gave Welma tracts by Marx and Trotsky to read and great works of literature. He taught her to play chess. By the time he departed, neither Tsietsi nor Welma could imagine a life apart from one another; Tsietsi had not been so happy since he left South Africa.

Tsietsi returned to Monrovia frequently. This was no easy thing; he and his fellow exiles were frenziedly preparing to launch their new organization, the South African Youth Revolutionary Council (SAYRCO). Tsietsi's comrades knew little of his involvement with Welma. Khotso and most of the other former SSRC members were in far-off Botswana and unaware of Tsietsi's movements. Only Comfort noticed that Tsietsi was now frequently absent from Nigeria. He did not question Tsietsi about the matter, but suspected that it had something to do with his infatuation with the Liberian beauty queen. Comfort

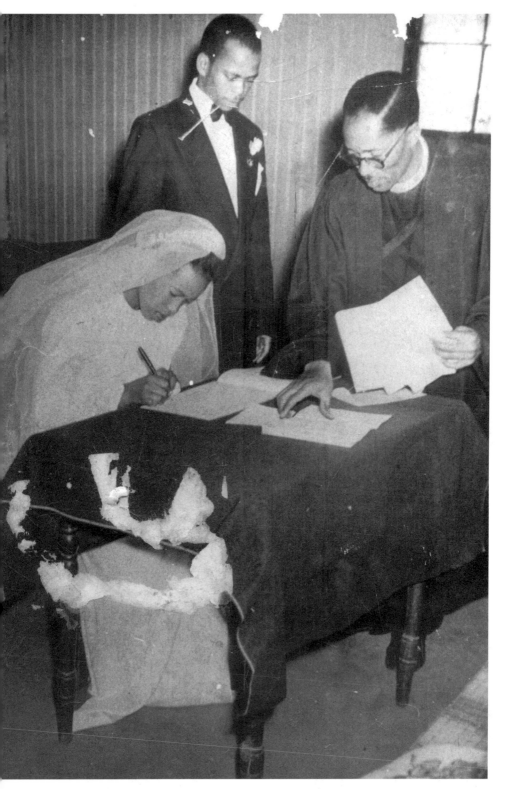

1. Joseph and Nomkhitha Mashinini signing the registry at their wedding on 28 May 1955

2. Tsietsi, Barney Makhatle and Selby Semela in London, January 1977

3. Tsietsi and Khotso Seatlholo, Botswana, January 1977

4. Tsietsi in New York, December 1976

5. Tsietsi on the lecture circuit, 1976

6. Mpho (centre) with Themba Mlangeni (left) and Paul Fakude (right), after they were acquitted on charges under the Terrorism Act on 31 August 1977

7. Nomkhitha discussing Tsietsi's marriage in an interview, August 1979

8. Tsietsi speaking with General Olusegun Obasanjo in Lagos, June 1977

9. Welma Campbell, Miss Liberia 1977

10. Dee with Victor Modise at the Pyramids in Cairo, 1978

11. Dee (far right) and the Executive Committee of the SOMAFCO Students Union, April 1983. Dee was the committee's chairperson

12. Dee with international volunteers at SOMAFCO

13. Dee singing with other students at a SOMAFCO assembly, August 1983

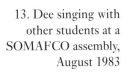

14. Rocks in
East Germany, 1989

15. Tsietsi with an
unidentified friend
in West Africa

16. Joseph and
Nomkhitha, June 1990

17. Joseph, Nomkhitha,
Dichaba (in the striped
shirt), Bandile, Elvis
and Tshepiso, with a
neighbour and Rocks's
son, Sizwe, in Pimville,
Soweto, June 1995

8. Dee with Tsietsi's
daughters, Thembi (above)
and Nomkhitha (below), at
the unveiling of Tsietsi's
tombstone in Soweto on
June 1995

19. Joseph at Tsietsi's grave, October 1997

disapproved of such relationships. One could not be devoted to one's work and to a woman simultaneously; both, in the end, would be compromised. But he held his tongue and said nothing to Tsietsi.

Unmindful of his friend's concern, Tsietsi continued his pursuit of Welma. At each visit, he insisted that Welma stop using birth control pills; she had to have a child. They were, after all, going to get married. Why wait? Welma was so awestruck by Tsietsi, and he so persuasive, that, against her better judgement, she relented. When she discovered that she was pregnant, Tsietsi could barely contain his joy; Welma knew she had taken the right decision. Never, she thought, had a man made a woman feel so loved and wanted. Now Tsietsi and Welma had to get married. Miriam and Philemon went to Emma to ask for Welma's hand. Miriam explained the South African tradition to Emma, that they came as Tsietsi's representatives. Normally they would pay *lobola*, the bride price, but that was not possible in the case of a poor exile. Instead, Miriam brought coconuts as a symbolic offering from one family to another. Emma had no choice but to accede to their request.

Tsietsi and Welma set a wedding date for the beginning of 1979. As Welma was Emma's first child to marry, her mother wanted to make it a spectacular affair. Tsietsi assured his bride-to-be that although none of the other Mashininis would be able to attend, he had informed his family and colleagues of the wedding and everyone was thrilled. Welma floated through the next few months, living from one visit to the next and helping her mother with the preparations.

Welma's first inkling that something might be amiss occurred a few days before the wedding, when she came upon Tsietsi, Miriam and Philemon in the throes of a heated debate. There was a burst of discussion in Zulu and Xhosa, punctuated by Miriam shouting at Tsietsi in English to shut up and listen to reason. 'This is an embarrassment,' she yelled. 'I pressured Emma into agreeing to the wedding, I put myself on the line. Why are you having second thoughts now?'

Welma felt sick. She could not follow the argument in Zulu

or Xhosa, but understood the English snippets well enough. When she tried to interject a question, Tsietsi turned on her. 'You just be quiet, we're talking things out. What's going on in my organization is none of your business.' Welma fled from the room, chastened. She was only twenty years old; she believed she was marrying a future leader of South Africa who concerned himself with delicate political matters. She had to resign herself, as his wife, to being excluded from sensitive issues of the liberation movement. She would have to learn to accept Tsietsi's words without question. This, she told herself, was her role.

In fact, the argument had less to do with the liberation of South Africa than with Tsietsi's singular leadership style. He had informed none of his colleagues, nor his family, of his intention to marry. It was his life; he could do as he pleased. But as the wedding day drew nearer, Tsietsi began to worry about the implications of his decision. Some Nigerian officials and colleagues, who heard of his engagement, tried to dissuade him from making a permanent commitment. How could he fulfil his obligations as both a revolutionary and a husband? By the time Tsietsi revealed his reservations to Miriam and Philemon, it was too late: the preparations for the wedding were too advanced, Emma had invested too much money in the affair. Besides, he loved Welma and the idea of starting a family with her. Tsietsi asked Tshepiso Manyelo, a fellow exile who moved to Lagos to help establish the SAYRCO head office, to be his best man. Tshepiso accepted and flew to Monrovia, where he and Tsietsi had traditional Liberian gowns made for them.

Tsietsi and Welma were married in the big African Methodist Episcopal Church on a main road leading to Monrovia's port. Welma wore a lace dress that had been created for her by a local designer; her uncle escorted her to the altar. Afterwards, the 300 or so guests retired to a nearby beach resort for a formal reception and party. Emma provided an enormous array of food. There was palm butter, the rich, piquant sauce that Liberians use to cook meat and fish; cassava leaf; *jollof* rice, a kind of West African paella; coconut and papaya pies; banana breads.

The wedding cake had three tiers, with maps of South Africa and Liberia, etched in icing, on either side.

Newspapers and broadcast journalists from several countries covered the affair. A film crew from the US news programme *60 Minutes* included the wedding as part of a story it broadcast on the elites of Liberia. The segment showed women in evening or African dress and men in impeccably tailored suits, sipping champagne, smoking cigarettes, laughing. Long tables, adorned with yellow cloths, were arranged on the beach under palms. An ebullient Tsietsi – tall, slim, elegant in his white gown and neatly trimmed goatee – guided Welma around the tables to greet their guests. She was stunning in a closely fitting white cap and long white dress, holding a spray of flowers. Both flashed shy smiles at the camera. A band played in the background.

The congratulatory speeches and toasts continued throughout the night. Miriam performed her signature song, '*Pata Pata*'; Welma also sang. People ate and drank and danced until daylight. It was Monrovia's social event of the year.

Tsietsi's colleagues learned of the wedding for the first time in the newspapers. Khotso, in Botswana preparing for SAYRCO's launch, read about it in the national press. He was furious beyond words: his comrade, his fellow revolutionary, his friend, had not even bothered to tell him. Khotso was almost as perplexed as he was angry. Why would Tsietsi do something like this just as they were realizing their dream? To Khotso's mind, a married revolutionary was something of an oxymoron. Now Tsietsi would have other responsibilities, a wife who would tell him he could not go away anywhere because she needed him at home. Either you were married to the revolution, as Khotso saw it, or to your wife.

Comfort too was astounded when he was informed, not by his friend and colleague, but by officials from the Nigerian government. Several of them called him to ask if Tsietsi had got married. Comfort, who was caught completely unawares, denied it roundly; such a thing could not possibly be true. Surely he would have told his comrades. Then Tshepiso returned to Lagos and confirmed the rumours. He, too, faced hostility from government officials who worked with the South African exiles. One aide to the president told Tshepiso that he had warned Tsietsi not to marry: You go that route, the functionary had said, and you're finished.

Tsietsi, meanwhile, remained blissfully ignorant of his comrades' outrage. He and Welma spent a week at a beach resort for their honeymoon. They had a glorious, relaxing time, swimming, sunning themselves, going for long walks, talking – always talking. Then they flew to Nigeria. Lagos was to be their home: Tsietsi would carry on with his work, and Welma would try to create a life for herself there. After the birth of their baby, she thought she might get a job or work in Tsietsi's organization as a secretary or study. Tsietsi had promised her mother, after all, that she would finish her education.

The couple installed themselves in the government guesthouse in Lagos where Tsietsi lived. After a few days, Tsietsi told Welma she would have to move out and find other accommodation. She was deeply hurt and confused; she suspected it had something to do with the cold reception given her by the South African exiles upon their arrival, but Tsietsi refused to explain. Welma went to stay with her godfather, who was Liberia's ambassador to Nigeria. She passed the time paying calls on Liberian friends and waiting for Tsietsi to organize their new life together. He went to the residence daily; each time, he assured her that everything was all right.

In fact, nothing was right. Tsietsi had returned to a firestorm of criticism from his colleagues. Comfort, in his fury, confronted Tsietsi immediately. 'What have you done?' he asked his friend. 'The Nigerians are all pissed off. This thing has affected us diplomatically.'

Perhaps anticipating an inquisition, Tsietsi became agitated. 'My personal life is no one else's business!' he shouted at Comfort.

'You have no personal life!' Comfort yelled back. 'You're a revolutionary.'

'No one is going to tell me what to do with my balls!' Tsietsi retorted, stomping out of the room.

Not long after, Tsietsi was summoned to the office of a

Nigerian official who worked closely with the South Africans. The man curtly informed Tsietsi that he would have to move out of the government guesthouse; he was no longer welcome. When Tsietsi exploded in anger, the functionary invited him to leave his office; he was no longer welcome there, either. Tsietsi went to the Liberian ambassador's residence and told Welma to pack her suitcases. We're going back to Monrovia, he said grimly. They can call me if they want me.

Tsietsi's marriage remained a source of resentment, especially among the comrades in Botswana. They felt particularly betrayed by the secretive manner in which Tsietsi had acted. Their indignation was exacerbated by the appearance of an article about Tsietsi in a black magazine in South Africa. The story implied that Tsietsi was living an extravagant, luxurious life; that he had married a white woman (citing Welma's surname, Campbell) and thus broken faith with his Black Consciousness beliefs; that he was contemptuous of Khotso's abilities as a leader. The article created a furore among Tsietsi's colleagues: this was arrogance beyond excuse. Some of the cooler-headed exiles questioned the article's veracity; the magazine would, indeed, prove to be funded by the government. But the revelation emerged too late for the meeting that Tsietsi's angry comrades held in Botswana to discuss the matter. The bad publicity, they decided, made for bad diplomacy. They would oust Tsietsi as their commander.

Tsietsi did not attend the launch of the South African Youth Revolutionary Council, which was held a few months later in Lusaka, Zambia. The meeting of the thirty or so former SSRC members lasted for several days. Some of the less well-informed comrades were astonished by Tsietsi's absence and wondered aloud when he would appear. The participants presented papers on the future of the anti-apartheid movement and adopted a constitution, which was dedicated to re-igniting the armed struggle in South Africa. Then they elected officers to the new organization. The youths named Khotso as SAYRCO's president and relegated Tsietsi, in absentia, to the position of representative to Guinea and Liberia. It was a palace coup.

Khotso was surprised at how little regret he felt. He had been secretly relieved when Tsietsi failed to appear at the launch. He was tired of having to justify his friend's indefensible actions.

Tsietsi learned of the vote in Monrovia. He had not gone to Lusaka because he was disgusted by his colleagues' condemnations; he had been chastised enough and did not wish further confrontations. And now his comrades, his friends, had replaced him as president. To hell with all of them, he told Welma. They think they can manage without me, but they'll see how wrong they are. They'll soon be clamouring for me.

CHAPTER TEN

Mpho

For a year after his trial and release from prison, Mpho engaged in little that had to do with politics. His aversion was mostly a reaction to his experiences in jail: he was loath to become involved in anything that carried with it even the vaguest risk of imprisonment and, by extension, torture. But it was also a time of extreme government repression. The relentless police harassment kept political movements and organizations from taking coherent form. On the surface, it seemed like a reversion to the quiescence of the 1960s. There were few opposition groups to tempt him.

To escape the scrutiny of the Soweto security police, Mpho went to stay with relatives in Atteridgeville, a township near Pretoria. He attended parties. He visited friends. He drank beer. He pursued girls. If he caught himself thinking his existence a bit frivolous and devoid of meaning, Mpho quickly dismissed such notions. These were difficult times; he deserved to enjoy himself after the hell he had experienced. He was determined to revel in life's non-political pleasures.

But Mpho seemed incapable of remaining inactive for long. Almost inexorably, he found himself being pulled into a group known as Moral Rearmament. Founded in the 1930s by an American academic, Frank Buchman, MRA began as a Christian organization that linked social issues to personal morality and spirituality. Nations could be transformed, so the thinking went, if each person adhered to four moral standards: absolute honesty, absolute purity, absolute unselfishness, absolute love. MRA ultimately evolved into a social movement, with branches all over the world. Its leaders were generally political conservatives; in Britain, which had the largest membership, most were Tories.

In South Africa, race was the obvious problem to be resolved. In the 1970s, MRA provided one of the few forums where blacks and whites could gather to discuss how to change South African society. The group attracted the likes of Mark Swilling, a brilliant university student from Johannesburg's northern suburbs. His grandmother, who was an ardent supporter, had taken him as a young teenager to several MRA meetings. (Although born Jewish, Mark's grandmother became increasingly drawn to Christianity.) Mark's own association with MRA began after finishing his matriculation exams. As a gift to himself, he took the money he had received for his bar mitzvah and travelled to Europe. His peregrinations included a visit to Caux, Switzerland, where MRA had its headquarters in a castle on Lake Geneva. There Mark met Samuel Pono, a black South African MRA member who was visiting with a group from Cape Town. The two talked at length; it was an awakening for Mark. Young whites, insulated by apartheid's total separation of the races, rarely experienced such encounters.

Mark remained in communication with Sam when he returned to Johannesburg and began studying at the University of the Witwatersrand. He agreed to join MRA; at the time, Mark believed that apartheid was wrong, but could be changed by reinvigorating the morality and spirituality of his fellow citizens. Sam wanted Mark to work as a nexus between blacks and Afrikaners. Black Consciousness, with its credo of utter self-reliance, had provoked great antipathy among whites. But Sam believed there was a new strain of thought within certain segments of Afrikaner society; they wanted to understand why such militancy had taken root. To that end, Sam charged Mark with organizing meetings to link up Soweto activists with Afrikaner intellectuals.

As Mark scoured the township for participants, he became intrigued by the Mashinini family. Tsietsi was a legend in the slums, a larger-than-life figure to whom improbable exploits were still attributed; when he met Mpho, Mark concluded that the younger sibling carried in him some of that charisma, too.

Mark asked Mpho to work for MRA. Mpho found the proposal attractive: in its outline, MRA was not unlike other Christian youth groups that had formed around the country's more radical black clergymen. They were among the few opposition organizations that still functioned. Their Christian nature, and that of MRA, appealed to Mpho's religiosity. Besides, MRA had a lovely house in Bryanston, a suburb to the north, with expansive grounds and a large swimming pool that its members used. So why not join?

Mpho and Mark began travelling throughout the country, giving talks at various universities, black and white. In the beginning, they confined themselves to espousing the essential MRA precept: the need to change people. We have to start getting to know each other, they told their audiences, we're all South Africans. We need to start building a new society, from our universities to our communities to our homes; the future belongs to us young people. If we don't work towards peaceful change, it will be done violently. Sam Pono was delighted; Mpho proved an inspired orator in his brother's mould, who fascinated his white listeners. Rarely, if ever, had the Afrikaner academics encountered blacks other than in menial positions, let alone one so eloquent.

Mpho's experiences with Mark and MRA were a watershed for him, too: they helped to strengthen his conversion to ANC philosophies. This was the first time Mpho had worked closely with white people, something he could never have imagined under the exclusionary doctrines of Black Consciousness and the Pan Africanist Congress. Mpho had gone to prison full of PAC propaganda; under Joe Gqabi's tutelage during his trial, he learned the truth about the ANC's history and principles. Now Mpho realized the ANC had got it right: non-racialism could succeed.

His revelation notwithstanding, Mpho's enthusiasm about MRA soon began to wane. He found himself leading a somewhat schizophrenic existence. During the week, he assumed his MRA role: he had a car available to him with unlimited petrol, a daily allowance for meals, pocket money for incidentals. Mpho traversed the country, mouthing the moderate phrases that made him seem the 'good' black. He reverted to his real life at the weekends when he returned to Soweto. Then Mpho spent his time dodging the heavy police presence in the township, struggling to find transport and money for other expenses, trying to connect with the remnants of the ANC underground. The disparties between the separate worlds were such that no amount of sensible words, in Mpho's opinion, could ever bridge the two.

His ambivalence deepened when he attended an MRA camp in central Zimbabwe. Mpho enjoyed the camping aspect of his trip greatly: he and a handful of South African and Zimbabwean young men lived in tents for a week, sharing a common kitchen and cooking on a *braai*, or barbecue. Their counsellor held daily bible studies and discussions of MRA's four 'absolutes' (honesty, purity, unselfishness, love). The idea was for the campers to return to their homes as 'morally armed' leaders. To Mpho, it seemed a meaningless exercise; he was not morally, but politically, called to be an activist. He argued that this was not the way to achieve liberation. The country could be morally re-armed *after* the end of apartheid; then there would be a need for such beliefs. But not now. Not when they were confronted by a brutal police state. During his stay in Zimbabwe, Mpho came to think of MRA as a kind of glorified tea party: genteel, well-meaning, but irrelevant.

Mark, too, had conflicting feelings about the organization. On the one hand, his affiliation with MRA had pushed him into places he would otherwise not have gone. Mark had never had colleagues, let alone friends, in Soweto until then. He had never experienced the day-to-day pain of black life in South Africa. Most of his white schoolmates from Johannesburg's northern suburbs who went to university became Marxists and radical revolutionaries – but never set foot inside a township. MRA also allowed him a glimpse into the world of the Afrikaner intellectual and its total denial of the country's reality. Yet Mark felt impotent to act on his insights: MRA provided only spiritual guidelines to what clearly required political solutions. How could absolute purity challenge absolute power?

Mpho and Mark, along with a few like-minded colleagues, came to form a kind of radical subgroup within MRA. They ceased to pay much attention to the group's moral standards and instead used its facilities and resources to promote a more activist organization. That body still had to be religious in appearance; the police continued to harass anything that seemed even vaguely political. They created the Student Union for Christian Action, or SUCA, a group ostensibly dedicated to linking up Christian student leaders from the racially segregated universities across the country. Until then, members of black religious student organizations did not speak to their white counterparts, and vice versa. SUCA's supporters would be united by their common faith. But adherents would be required to act on their beliefs, to vigorously oppose what they, as Christians, defined as wrong: oppression, discrimination, unequal educational systems.

SUCA's strategy was to co-opt the leaders of student Christian organizations. Rather than recruiting members, SUCA sought to persuade leaders of student Christian groups to accept its active opposition to racism. Mpho and Mark travelled to universities throughout the country, using MRA as a front. (Among SUCA's founders, the two were the only MRA representatives.) People came to a meeting thinking it an MRA gathering; once inside, Mpho and Mark subjected them to SUCA's broader goals. They enhanced their cover by staying at MRA centres in the various towns they visited. Besides the obvious economic benefits they provided, the MRA lodgings spared Mpho the humiliation of having to arrange separate sleeping quarters.

After a while, senior MRA members became aware of what Mpho and Mark were doing. They arranged a meeting with the two young men to demand an explanation. Mpho, using the group's own terminology, told them this was what he and Mark 'felt called to do'. His words, not surprisingly, failed to mollify the MRA adherents. Mpho and Mark thought themselves secure in their positions; Mark's grandmother was a major contributor to the organization who might reconsider her largesse were the young men expelled. Nonetheless, Sam Pono began distancing himself from the two activists. Mpho and Mark would ultimately leave MRA, although Mpho maintained close ties to Sam.

Now Mpho spent most of his time driving around South Africa with Mark, who was supposed to be finishing his degree at university in Johannesburg. The two worked to create SUCA cells within the leadership of Christian organizations at black and white institutions. They also raised funds to help support the groups and held conferences to disseminate their views. SUCA's exhortation to the student leaders, especially the Afrikaners, was one of action: when you return to your campuses, you must motivate your members to become involved. Your Christian morality demands that you and your followers raise your voices against police brutality, against detentions, against apartheid itself.

This was heresy. It defied the teachings of the Dutch Reformed Church, whose dogma of separate nationhood for all races had, for decades, provided apartheid's divine justification. The Church's doctrines not only relieved Afrikaners of any sense of guilt, but turned the practice of apartheid into a sacred task. Mpho, Mark and their SUCA colleagues were challenging the very underpinnings of Afrikaner society. But they did not stop there. They invited radical black priests, who were beginning to formulate their own version of liberation theology, to address the students. The SUCA recruits, most of whom were white, started engaging in such subversive activities as protesting against the forced removal of blacks from their homes. The students stayed with the victims in their houses to try to fend off the bulldozers and held all-night prayer vigils. For many of the whites, this was the first time they had ventured into a township, let alone protested against a government policy. They found the experience inspiring.

SUCA began to attract the attention of the authorities. In the government's eyes, the organization was corrupting the cream of young Afrikanerdom by exposing them to blacks. This could only lead to cracks in the monolith of Afrikaner unity – a prospect that alarmed security officials perhaps even more than any uprising by the black population. Given the military might of the state, a rebellion would be relatively easy to quash; the erosion of Afrikaner support for apartheid could not be so easily resolved. The police now monitored every

SUCA meeting. Mark took to starting his lectures with a bit of advice for the audience. 'Let's assume there are at least two informers here,' he would tell his listeners. 'If you see someone taking notes, make sure he takes them properly so the powers-that-be hear exactly what it is that we're talking about. Maybe they'll learn something.'

The SUCA leaders took their provocation a step further by planning a trip to newly independent Zimbabwe. The country figured hugely in the psyche of white South Africans, an emblem of their worst fears. Rhodesia, as it was formerly called, had also been ruled by a white minority. For years, the regime fought a war against black nationalists that killed tens of thousands of people; a negotiated settlement to the conflict forced it to hold free elections in 1980 that resulted in the election of a black government. The SUCA activists wanted to demonstrate to their white members that, contrary to South African propaganda, black majority rule did not mean certain catastrophe. The visitors would speak with a broad array of Zimbabweans to hear how liberation had measured up to their hopes and fears.

The planners of the SUCA trip also contemplated meeting with a representative of the ANC, which had an office in the Zimbabwean capital. News of the proposed encounter was reported in the South African press and caused a huge furore. It was bad enough that upstanding Afrikaner youths, leaders of their respective Christian organizations, would come under the sway of the black devils who ruled the country on South Africa's north-eastern border; now they were to mingle with outlawed communists, too. (Hendrik Verwoerd, the grandson of the architect of some of apartheid's most horrifying features and a former prime minister, was to be among the travellers.) This was beyond tolerance. The white students who intended to make the journey suddenly found themselves the objects of harassment: their car tyres slashed, their houses splashed with paint, their telephones besieged by threatening calls. A debate raged among the youths as to whether they should cancel the appointment with the ANC representative. Several whites decided to withdraw from the trip; the remaining youths resolved to pursue the meeting.

A *kombi*-load of ten students made the day-long trek north-ward. They met with ministers of the new Zimbabwean government, business leaders, farmers, politicians, officials from non-governmental organizations. The tension among the South Africans was palpable. They found it difficult to concentrate on the discussions: they were receiving telephone calls in Zimbabwe that threatened all manner of harm if they persisted with the ANC encounter. Mpho and Mark tried to assuage their fears, but to no avail; the white students yielded to the pressure. Mpho went in their stead.

Much to his delight, Mpho discovered that Joe Gqabi was the ANC's representative in Zimbabwe. (After a lengthy trial in Pretoria, Joe had been acquitted and fled South Africa soon after his release.) Theirs was a joyful reunion. He and Mpho met three times; they devoted the first two encounters to discussing the SUCA students and their reluctance to see Joe. The last appointment, which took place in an office in the Zimbabwean Parliament, was more pointed: Joe made plans for Mpho to begin working for the ANC in Johannesburg. Based on the discussions they had had in the holding cells at their trials, Joe said he felt he could trust Mpho. On returning to South Africa, Mpho was to go to Joe's house in Soweto and let someone there know where he could be contacted. In a few months' time, Mpho would receive instructions and funds for his next move: starting a small business, a vegetable stand or corner shop, that would become a rendezvous and refuge for returning Umkhonto soldiers. Avoid political activities that attract the attention of the police in the meantime, Joe warned. I want you to operate in the open. Joe was palpably uneasy throughout the meeting, speaking only in Xhosa and chiding Mpho whenever the latter occasionally slipped into English. After a couple of hours, Mpho stood up to leave. 'Don't come back to Zimbabwe,' Joe said sharply. 'And don't try to contact me.'

Mpho returned to South Africa, exhilarated by his encounter with Joe. He would finally be doing something of value. And he was flattered that a veteran ANC fighter like Joe would entrust him with sensitive work. After a few weeks, when the furore over the SUCA trip had begun to abate, Mpho went to Joe's house in Soweto, only to find that the person he was supposed to meet had fled the country. Mpho now had no way to communicate with Joe; disappointed, he settled back into his job as SUCA's secretary-general.

A couple of months later, Mpho was working alone one afternoon when a well-dressed Afrikaner woman entered the office in downtown Johannesburg. 'Are you Mpho Mashinini?' she enquired.

'Yes.'

'Then you must come with me.'

'Am I being detained?' Mpho asked.

'No,' the woman replied in perfect, unaccented English, 'this is not detention. It's a meeting. Someone at police headquarters wants to see you.'

'Are you arresting me?'

'No, we just want to talk to you. But if you like, I can pick up the telephone and organize an arrest warrant and a lot of policemen.'

'What do you want to talk about?'

'You'll know when we get there.'

Mpho was beginning to panic. 'Will I come back?'

'I promise you'll come back,' the woman said with authority, 'in about two hours.'

'May I telephone a lawyer?'

'Yes, but it's not necessary because you're not being arrested. If it would make you feel better to phone a lawyer,' she continued, 'give him this number and he can ask for me.'

Mpho telephoned an attorney. He was not in his office; Mpho told the secretary that he had to leave for police headquarters at John Vorster Square and repeated the Afrikaner woman's name and number. Mpho was confused: he had never been arrested, if that was what was happening, so politely. He took comfort from the knowledge that at least he would not be swallowed up by the government's vast security network and simply vanish, that he had left his lawyer some leads. He followed the woman downstairs and into an unmarked police car. Mpho sat in the front with the driver; the woman climbed into the back seat. As they drove through the crowded streets of Johannesburg's business district, Mpho watched the people hurrying about and wondered whether this would be the last time for months, or even years, that he would gaze upon such a tableau. He tried to push the thought from his mind.

The woman escorted Mpho through a back entrance to the building and into a lift. As far as Mpho could see, it did not have any buttons to push for specific floors. The door closed, the elevator ascended, the door opened again – all without commands. The woman showed Mpho into a reception area. It looked like the waiting room of a doctor's office: soft chairs, plush carpeting, fish tank. A table at one end was laden with sandwiches and bottles of beer and whisky. The woman told Mpho to wait and disappeared behind a door. Mpho was left alone to wrestle with his thoughts of certain detention. After about an hour, he had so resigned himself to the idea that he decided to take a sandwich. To hell with everything, he thought, this is probably the last decent meal I'll get in months. So he gobbled a ham sandwich, then a cheese sandwich, then another, and another. After that, he attacked the whisky, which he had never tried before. He gulped down a couple of jiggers, felt his throat and chest burn, and sat down again. The burning stopped after a few minutes, and the fear and anxiety about detention returned. He had a few more jiggers.

His escort suddenly reappeared. 'I'm glad you helped yourself to something to eat,' she said. The woman took him down a hallway to the largest of a series of well-appointed offices. There, an elderly, white-haired Afrikaner man greeted him. 'Mr Mashinini,' he said graciously in English, 'please sit down.' The Afrikaner settled himself behind a desk and addressed Mpho in a matter-of-fact tone, as though the two were engaged in a business meeting. 'You know, Mr Mashinini, we see everything, we hear everything, we know everything. And if anyone thinks we, the Afrikaners, are on the way out, they're mistaken. We're here for at least another hundred years.' The man's carefully worded monologue about the might of the South African state went for a long while; then abruptly, and without explanation, he left the room.

The woman re-entered; from behind Mpho, she switched on a tape recorder. The room was suddenly filled with the sound of Mpho's voice, speaking in Xhosa: his conversation with Joe Gqabi in the Zimbabwean Parliament. Mpho began to tremble; now he was certain he would go to prison. Or perhaps even hang. His words, after all, were treasonous. Listening to the tape, Mpho struggled to understand how the South African intelligence services (for he clearly was in their presence) could have obtained such a thing. Did they get Joe? he wondered. Did he betray me? The tape finished, but no one came into the room. By now, Mpho was sweating profusely.

After a seeming eternity, the man returned. He sat down and, with great deliberation, leaned across his desk. 'Look,' he began, 'you probably know by now that we're not the police. We report directly to the Prime Minister. We don't care a whit about your stupid politics. Let the security branch deal with that. We know all about you. You're not dangerous; actually, you're nothing. This business,' he said, with a nod to the tape recorder, 'we can fix in an instant. We just want you out of SUCA, or we'll have to ban it. And SUCA is full of Christian Afrikaner students, so we don't want to do that. We just want you out. Oh yes, and we'll take your passport. So you won't be tempted to take any more white students for meetings abroad.'

The Afrikaner stood to leave. 'We know you're a decent chap and will take our advice. But I wouldn't tell anyone about our little conversation. We don't exist.' With that, he walked out of the room.

Mpho remained in his seat, still expecting policemen to burst through the door and manacle him. Instead, the woman came in and escorted Mpho downstairs. He refused her offer of a lift to his office; he just wanted to get away from her and her boss. Mpho virtually launched himself out the doors of the building and into the throng of rush-hour commuters. Then he began to run, trying to melt into the crowds; he did not stop until he arrived, breathless and soaked in perspiration, at SUCA.

A few days later, several policemen appeared at the door. The officer-in-charge presented Mpho with a letter from the Ministry of Home Affairs, ordering that his passport be cancelled.

(Almost a decade would elapse before Mpho would receive a new document and be allowed to travel abroad again.) Not long after that, Mpho began to feel as if he were being trailed. He thought he saw people following him at night, after attending meetings for SUCA. Mpho had not wanted to stop working for the organization, but the confiscation of his passport made him realize that the warnings at John Vorster Square were not to be taken lightly. Mpho began to extricate himself from SUCA events, especially those that occurred after daylight hours. Even then he felt too frightened to function well; unlike the security police, who were known and predictable, the people who had spoken to him were shadows. Without telling anyone, not even Mark, what had happened, he ceased working for SUCA.

Shortly thereafter, on the evening of 31 July 1981, Joe Gqabi was gunned down in his driveway in the Zimbabwean capital. His assassins were never found.

CHAPTER ELEVEN

Dee

Dee returned from Cairo to a very different place in the East African bush. In his absence, the Tanzanian government had allocated 3,400 acres of an abandoned sisal plantation to the ANC to build a school. The site, known as Mazimbu, was located about twelve miles from the old camp. The ANC had only recently begun constructing the school; when Dee arrived he found one solitary dormitory block, a single-storey, concrete-and-brick structure with a metal roof. The rest of the campus consisted of a smattering of small huts that were used as classrooms and endless expanses of baobab trees, bounded by mountains on three sides.

But the ANC had ambitious plans for the institution, which it named the Solomon Mahlangu Freedom College, in memory of the first Umkhonto guerrilla to be executed by the South African government. SOMAFCO, as it was known, ultimately comprised nursery, primary and secondary schools; nearby, the ANC would build factories and a sprawling farm. The governments of Norway, Sweden and Holland helped to pay for much of the construction. More than 1,000 exiles would study and work in Mazimbu when the facilities were completed.

When Dee returned at the end of 1979, there were about 150 students in the school. Dee recognized many of them from the old camp; they had never left to study overseas. Their presence cheered him somewhat, if only by default: unlike those poor souls, he, at least, had escaped the bush for two years. The youths lived in the dormitory block, which had a large hall and separate wings for the boys and girls. The students slept ten to a room; every morning, the commanders of the rooms roused their charges at six o'clock. The youths showered quickly, then dressed in the school uniform: military-style khaki trousers, a blue long-sleeved shirt, and shapeless Russian-made shoes that everyone called *pão*, because of their resemblance to the puffy Portuguese loaves. Each commander inspected his students to check that their uniforms were clean and pressed. There were weekly competitions to determine which room had the most neatly dressed youths, the best-made beds, the most brightly polished floor.

After inspection, Dee and the others ate breakfast. Then all the students gathered for morning assembly. The youths stood quietly in formation as one of their peers recited a clause from the ANC's Freedom Charter: '. . . Every man and woman shall have the right to vote for and stand as a candidate for all bodies which make laws. All the people shall be entitled to take part in the administration of the country. The rights of the people shall be the same regardless of race, colour or sex . . .' Each student was required to memorize one clause from the document and repeat it before the assembled student body; the honour rotated among the various classes every morning. At first, Dee thought the ceremony was an attempt to indoctrinate the youngsters, akin to, say, the compulsory reading of Marxist tracts. But he found himself deeply moved by the recitation. Here was a great document, a truly South African creation, born of the struggle against apartheid. Dee came to think of the ceremony as analogous to the daily intonation of the Lord's Prayer, another South African tradition.

The camp commander read the day's announcements, led the students in singing *'Nkosi Sikelel' iAfrika'*, then dismissed them to their studies. The paths leading to the classrooms were little more than furrows that turned to rivers of mud in the rainy season and harboured all manner of snakes when dry. The campus itself was still untamed. Elephants and baboons wandered at will; a mad water buffalo charged a hut one day. Despite the makeshift feel, the school was intended as a serious institution. Enough time had passed since the 1976 uprising and the massive exodus of youngsters from South Africa for the

ANC to devise a proper course of study – unlike the haphazard classes that had driven Dee to despair when he first arrived in Tanzania.

The secondary school's curriculum conformed to that of the British system; after passing their examinations in English, mathematics and sciences, the students received a British certificate. The ANC awarded its own certificate for history, literature and something it called 'development studies'. Dee quickly found that history was his favourite subject: not the one-sided version he would have learned under Bantu education, but that which told of his people, his struggle. Now he learned about black South African culture and the heroes of the liberation movement. Dee took particular pleasure in reading about the great chiefs of his country, figures like Shaka, who transformed his Zulu tribesmen into a nation of legendary fighters and subjugated much of the region in the early part of the nineteenth century; and Mantatisi, Queen of the Pedi people and Shaka's contemporary, whose armies conquered large swathes of South Africa.

Dee was inspired by his history teacher, Jackie Selebi, an ANC stalwart (who would become South Africa's ambassador to the United Nations in Geneva and later serve as head of the South African Police Service). Jackie had a brilliant manner of teaching. He held the students in thrall with his stories, making history come alive by comparing, for instance, the likes of Napoleon and Shaka. For Dee and his peers, deprived by apartheid of a narrative of their own, this was magic. But Jackie's talents were an anomaly. The quality of the teaching at SOMAFCO, at least in the early days, was poor; many of the instructors were themselves students, awaiting scholarships to continue their studies abroad. Fewer than one-quarter of the teachers were certified in their profession. In later years, the Dutch government sent instructors to SOMAFCO as part of its aid to the ANC and the level of teaching improved.

As in the ANC's military camps, the youngsters studied Marxist theory and doctrine. Dee felt he would soon know *Das Kapital* as well as he knew the Bible. His classmates who exhibited a flair for these subjects were plucked from the school and sent to institutions in Russia or Cuba for further training. Dee had no interest in going to a communist country and made a point of not excelling in the pertinent classes; he found the study of socialism engaging only as an intellectual exercise. The other courses were easy for Dee, now that he was studying in a language he knew and under a system similar to that in South Africa. He was grateful that the ANC authorities never made him account for his failures in Cairo; they seemed to understand that the Egyptians could not accommodate the shortcomings in the South Africans' education. Still, Dee remained bitter for a long time about his experiences in Cairo. His grasp of the curriculum at SOMAFCO proved he could succeed when placed in the proper class. Had the authorities in Egypt dropped him a grade, Dee believed, he would have done equally well.

Dee had classes until two o'clock in the afternoon, then ate lunch. Afterwards, he and his fellow students were required to do some form of manual labour for a couple of hours. The boarding master sometimes assigned youngsters to the construction site to assist the Tanzanian labourers in building the dormitory blocks. Other youths worked in the fields and with the animals of the school's farm. Still others did landscaping, planting lawns and gardens and generally beautifying the campus; on particularly gruelling days, Dee felt as though he and his friends were creating SOMAFCO, quite literally, with their own hands.

On the afternoons he did not have to work outdoors, Dee took a siesta on his bunk. He wanted to be fresh for the day's most important event: sport. For Dee, this meant football, which commanded his energy and attention in ways his studies never would. That the camp barely had a football pitch when he returned to Tanzania did not deter Dee. He and his friends from Form Three immediately set about constructing a proper one: clearing land, levelling and measuring it, planting grass, nurturing its growth. Dee could always find enthusiastic students willing to devote their spare time to maintaining the field – especially after Dee and his classmates created the camp's football leagues. First they organized the teams. Then they cajoled the Swedish government into donating good sports shoes. And they got the Brazilians to provide uniforms in the colours of South African teams; Dee's were the yellow-and-black of the Kaiser Chiefs, which had a fanatical following among those who lived in Soweto.

The game consumed much of the youths' free time: planning, talking tactics, training, anticipating, playing, analysing afterwards. This was a good thing. The long afternoons, empty and endless, were deadly for the exiles; they had caused Dee great despair in the old camp. Football gave the refugees a sense of purpose, a focus to their lives. Other sports, for those who wanted a broader scope of activities, provided the same distraction. There were karate classes, jogging groups, boxing clubs (for the exiles who came from the Cape region, which had a great boxing tradition; Nelson Mandela, in his youth, trained as a heavyweight).

Dee remained on the playing field until the very last moment, then dashed back to the dormitory with barely enough time to shower and eat supper. The students had a mandatory two-hour study period after their evening meal supervised by the boarding master. This deprived Dee of any excuse not to complete his homework; it was also when he could work on longer projects. Afterwards, Dee and the others gathered for the evening assembly. There the news team presented a synopsis of the day's political events: seated at a table in front of their peers, the two readers punctuated their narration with recorded snippets of sound as though it were an actual radio broadcast. The students heard stories from the Voice of America, Radio South Africa, the English service of Radio Moscow. If the reports from Radio Moscow sometimes seemed to dominate the presentations, Dee paid little heed; for him and his friends whose opinions he valued most, the BBC provided the definitive word on any issue. Discussions that ensued among the students after the presentation often became heated, and the meeting would last far into the night. Dee enjoyed the assemblies for these debates; he also liked the opportunity to socialize with girls. The time after assembly and before bed was prime for negotiating trysts.

The weekends took on an almost ritualized sameness. Dee and his friends appropriated the school's kitchen which, for a long time, was nothing more than a fireplace. There they prepared *vetkoeke*, fat cakes, the greasy, fried confections that Dee used to buy on Sunday mornings with the money Joseph gave him for the church collection box. All week long, Dee anticipated the preparation of the delicacies, so redolent of home and his early youth. Then there was laundry to do; the campus' trees and shrubs were suddenly bedecked on Saturday mornings in all manner of clothing. By noon, however, the place was empty, evacuated. Everyone had walked to the nearby town of Morogoro: it was a business day.

The students went to Morogoro to sell clothes. In addition to their Russian-made school uniforms and sports gear, the youths selected other garments from among the mountains of donations that came to the ANC from various countries. A few times during the year, Dee and the others were allowed pick out two pairs of trousers, two shirts, two jackets and underwear. They then sold the items to the locals and made what was considered a sizeable sum of money. The practice was strictly forbidden by camp rules, but the youths justified it by their need for funds. They found the ANC's monthly stipend wholly inadequate; it barely paid for a bottle or two of beer. Dee and his comrades pleaded, petitioned, cajoled and generally complained to the camp authorities to raise their allowance – to no avail. Thus the need for a moneymaking enterprise. Dee could sell a shirt for about five times his entire monthly stipend; jeans fetched twenty times that amount. (A good, stylish pair of jeans could also entice some girls into bed.) 'The world dresses us,' Dee told his friends as he carefully sorted through the heaps of clothing, 'and we dress the Tanzanians.' Dee usually kept a few pieces for himself, but also had something of a cushion in the stockpile he had brought from Egypt. He and the others who had been to Cairo were known as the camp's best-dressed students for a long time after their return.

Dee frequently encountered his fellow students on the streets of Morogoro, each trying to hide the bag of goods he was carrying – and straining to catch a glimpse of what the competition was offering. After completing his transactions, Dee began his rounds of the town's bars; no one, it was said, returned from Morogoro sober on a Saturday. He went to the discos after particularly lucrative deals. Dee drank and danced for hours, long into the night; when he had exhausted his money, he sought out the other bleary-eyed youths to begin the long walk back to SOMAFCO.

On Sunday mornings, Dee ironed his now-clean laundry and generally tried to recover from the previous night's revelry. His recuperation was vital; on Sundays, the students held their football matches. This was fierce, merciless sport. At one point, the school had almost a dozen teams; the best among them competed against other schools and colleges. Their prowess was such that they even played the Tanzanian national team. The games were among the camp's most important events; virtually everyone turned out to sit on the ground or under the tin roof that served as a grandstand and cheer for their favourite teams. Even the local Tanzanians became fans and would hike from the surrounding settlements to watch the matches.

His dedication to football notwithstanding, Dee missed Cairo. Things had improved greatly in Tanzania, what with a proper, functioning school to attend and various activities to occupy his attention. But this existence was not life. Life was what he had experienced in Cairo, that which replicated most closely his circumstances in Johannesburg. In the years of his exile, Dee had come to understand this need in him. Almost daily he silently thanked Rocks for dissuading him from becoming a guerrilla; he realized how unfit he was for that life. Dee sometimes wondered if his youth made him ill-prepared for the rigours of exile. He had seen other youngsters, his contemporaries, snap from the isolation; some simply walked off into the bush, where the frantic ANC officials would find them, wandering aimlessly. Then again, he had seen the same thing happen to adults. People were so lonely in the camp. The ANC discouraged the students from reading the South African newspapers and magazines that sometimes appeared for fear of exacerbating their homesickness. But everyone listened to Radio South Africa, with its familiar accents and descriptions of the place; one could go mad hearing such things. Dee became obsessed with the idea of being in contact with Joseph and

Nomkhitha, of somehow getting a letter to them and receiving a reply. One night in his bunk, he became panic stricken while thinking about his brothers: he could no longer conjure up Mpho's face. He had gone into exile without photographs of his family and now his memory of them was fading.

Lindi offered a kind of refuge for Dee. He wrote to her constantly for the year or so that she remained in Cairo. Here was someone from home who understood his loneliness; with her, he did not have to maintain the façade of unstinting belief in the inevitability – and imminence – of South Africa's liberation. Indeed, most days he felt as though his exile would never end. These were heretical thoughts best kept to himself; she was the only person he could tell. The two were reunited briefly when Lindi spent a few weeks in Mazimbu after finishing her matriculation exams in Egypt. Although Dee felt his attraction had grown during their separation, he was wary of becoming too attached to her; Lindi was preparing to leave for Cuba, where she would study to be a medical technician. They would write to one another frequently over the next few years, exchanging photographs and descriptions of their dreams for the future.

In the meantime, Dee sought solace in other love affairs. At the end of his first year at SOMAFCO, five young women became pregnant; one of them was Dee's girlfriend. (This, despite the ANC providing free contraceptives to the students.) Dee was twenty years old; the girl, eighteen. The ANC authorities, appalled by the number of pregnancies, decided to make an example of those involved. They punished the young men by expelling them from school for a year and putting them to work in a nearby carpentry workshop. The Vuyisile Mini Carpentry Factory, as it was known, produced the frames, doors and furniture for the new dormitory blocks that were under construction. Dee and the other youths were removed from the dormitory and given quarters with the factory workers, most of whom were Tanzanian labourers or former Umkhonto fighters.

The suspension destroyed Dee. He lost an entire year of schooling; as factory employees were not allowed to fraternize with students, he also lost a year of sport and friendship. Instead, he was forced to spend his day in overalls and boots, performing mind-numbing tasks. Dee felt the punishment grossly unfair. Several other young women at the school had previously fallen pregnant; it was his bad luck that the ANC chose to use this instance as a warning to others. Not that Dee found fault with the standards set by Oliver Tambo, the ANC's president. He knew the president was a deeply religious man who lent a certain morality to the organization. But Dee decided that Tambo's zeal to eradicate anything that might interfere with educating the exiled youths was somewhat excessive; sex and football, after all, were the students' only diversions in the bush.

Dee did little during the year he was suspended from school. His girlfriend eventually gave birth to a son and moved to Sweden, where she would live for many years. Dee worked his shift; in his spare time, he drank heavily. After several beers, he often found himself questioning his very decision to go into exile. He had left to become a freedom fighter, to liberate his people from the white racists. Once he jettisoned that goal, he set out to obtain an education. Only now he could not even go to school. Dee regretted his impetuousness in leaving South Africa. There, the police brutality notwithstanding, he could at least have had more control over his life. He did not want to learn a trade and work in a factory for the rest of his life; he wanted a profession. Nomkhitha had burned too much of her ambition into his consciousness for him to accept anything less. The only thing that kept Dee from utter despondency was the calendar: every day he marked off brought him that much closer to returning to school.

When the year finished, Dee felt as though he had been let out of prison. (Although in more candid moments, he would profess a grudging pride in now being able to create things with his hands.) He returned to SOMAFCO determined to succeed in his studies and enjoy his student existence. To that end, Dee decided to run for the position of chairman of the six-member Student Council. He did not campaign strenuously; he had been active in student politics previously and had made a name for himself. Besides, as the Form Four candidate, he was a kind of *éminence grise* among the students. (The Form Fives were too busy trying to pass their matriculation exams to care about such matters.) Dee won easily.

He immediately set about organizing activities he thought appealing, dances being foremost among them. Dee selected a Saturday afternoon for the first one. He assigned students to a catering committee to oversee the baking, the making of fruit salads, and the brewing of potent beverages. To create a club-like atmosphere, Dee arranged for the hall to be illuminated with special strobe lights. He tested and re-tested the sound system for acoustic quality; he borrowed cassettes from students who were known to have particularly good music collections. The youths, dressed in their finery, turned out in large numbers. They danced frenetically through the night and did not want to leave when the lights were turned off. The next day, they could talk of nothing else. The dances became much-anticipated events in the camp; Dee and his fellow council members noticed that students stopped disappearing to Morogoro on the Saturdays that the gatherings were held.

Dee also helped to organize trips to the beach at Dar es Salaam. This was not an innovation; the ANC officials occasionally packed the students into old, camouflage-coloured Mercedes Benz trucks (a donation to the organization) and drove them to the coast. Dee and the other council members decided to try something that was more intimate and less of a mass outing. They divided the youths into small groups; each group travelled by bus to the seaside on alternating weekends. With fewer students to feed, those responsible for catering could provide better food. The beach excursions were considered an important form of enter-tainment. They got the exiles out of the camp, however briefly, and out from under the control of ANC officials. An entire, care-free day stretched deliciously before the students, in which they were at liberty to do as they pleased. They dumped their clothes, shoes and towels together under a clump of palms, where their possessions would be safe from the gangs of local youths roaming the beach. Then the South Africans ran, shouting and laughing, into the crystalline-green Indian Ocean. The water intimidated Dee at first. He watched admiringly as the youths from the Cape, who had spent their lives in close proximity to the sea, plunged headlong into the waves. It was lovely to see them swim, and Dee slowly took courage from their fearlessness. Afterwards, the exhausted students lay splayed across the sand, like so much jetsam left to dry in the late afternoon sun.

Besides the dances, which were more for socializing than anything else, Dee and his council planned cultural evenings. These became elaborate, drawn-out affairs that often lasted far into the night. Members of the school's various units, or clubs – music, opera, traditional dance – created special works for the events. The units functioned as serious, artistic companies, each with its own distinctive uniform: the Zulu dance unit wore traditional Zulu dress; the Xhosa unit, Xhosa dress; and so forth. The choir was particularly popular for its repertoire of freedom and church songs. Students spent long hours in rehearsals; like sport, these endeavours consumed considerable portions of time that would otherwise be given over to loneliness. And their performances were well-attended: here was something evocative of home that gladdened the heart.

Dee greatly enjoyed his year-long stint as chairman. He and his council members were popular among the students, partly because the leaders they succeeded had been widely disliked. Their predecessors were serious-minded exiles from South Africa's student movements who attempted to impose their views on SOMAFCO. But the constituents did not want to be led in such a manner; like Dee, they were a group of frustrated youths who, for the most part, regretted leaving their country. (Or at least they pined for it every day.) Dee understood how they felt and focused on trying to keep them engaged. He enjoyed trying to raise the students' spirits, and discovered that he had a flair for public relations. He had found his vocation.

The year he spent as Student Council president transformed Dee. He no longer felt himself the scared, lonely boy who hiked to the ANC office in Morogoro so many years earlier to demand that he be sent home. Now he was a young man with decisions to make about his future: where, and what, he would study after matriculating. For the first time since leaving South Africa, Dee felt he had regained a degree of control over his life. He would not only survive exile, but prosper as well. Perhaps his sense of resolution came with the opportunities the ANC, having had time to organize, could now offer the exiles. Perhaps he had simply grown up. As if to underscore the transitions, Dee realized one day that Tsietsi had ceased to be a matter of concern. The ANC authorities seemed to have lost interest in the young leader; they stopped pestering Dee about being his brother. And they no longer invoked Tsietsi's name at celebrations honouring the June 16 uprising. Dee resented the omission, but there was little he could do. Time was passing; people were forgetting.

CHAPTER TWELVE

Tsietsi

On their return to Monrovia, Tsietsi and Welma took up residence in her mother's home. It was a majestic house in the city's
exclusive Sinkor section with six bedrooms, a wide veranda,
and high security walls topped with shards of broken bottles.
The young newlyweds had their own bedroom and a small den,
but generally lived as one family with Emma, Welma's mother.
The place was constantly filled with Emma's relatives from
upcountry, come to the capital to visit.

One night, not long after they moved in, Tsietsi and Welma
were watching television in the den with one of Welma's young
cousins. Welma told the boy to go to bed; his head was drooping.
He refused and continued watching the programme. Thirty
minutes later, he was stretched out on the sofa, snoring. 'No,
don't wake him,' Tsietsi admonished Welma when she tried to
rouse the boy. 'Pick him up and carry him.'

'You carry him,' she retorted, 'I'm six months pregnant.'

Tsietsi fixed her with a stare. 'Okay, if you don't do it, you'll
see.' He gathered the sleeping child in his arms and, after
depositing him in his bed, returned to the bedroom he and
Welma shared. Tsietsi locked the door. Turning to Welma, he
suddenly began to hit her.

'What are you doing?' Welma shrieked, trying to shield her
face. 'What are you doing?' Emma, alarmed by her daughter's
screams, tried to enter the bedroom. Finding the door locked,
she began pounding on the outside and demanding that Tsietsi
allow her entry.

When Tsietsi finally opened the door, Emma was astounded

to see her pregnant daughter cowering on the floor. Welma was in a state of shock; no one had ever hit her before. 'What did she do to you?' Emma demanded of Tsietsi, thinking her daughter must have committed some unspeakable act to warrant this behaviour.

'She doesn't want to listen,' Tsietsi said, looking down at Welma. Then he burst into tears and was kneeling beside his wife, apologizing profusely and vowing never to hit her again. Through his sobs, Tsietsi begged Emma's forgiveness: it was the lack of privacy, he explained, the tension of living with so many other people; it would never happen again. Emma did not know what to think. Here was someone who had harmed her daughter, her pregnant daughter; she could not conceive of allowing him to remain in her home. Yet banishing him might sow greater discord between Tsietsi and Welma.

Tsietsi's departure for Guinea soon after the incident saved Emma from having to resolve her dilemma. He was invited by the country's president, Sekou Toure, to train with his army. Miriam Makeba had introduced Tsietsi to the president, a long-reigning dictator of unspeakable ruthlessness who took a liking to the young firebrand. For the next several months, Tsietsi and Welma commuted between Monrovia and Conakry, the Guinean capital built on a peninsula that jutted into the Atlantic. As it was easier for Welma to travel, she often made the journey to spend a long weekend with her husband. Tsietsi lived on a military base, which Welma was forbidden to visit; so he would take leave to stay with her at Miriam Makeba's house. Miriam and her husband Stokely Carmichael had lived in Guinea as guests of the president for over a decade. Her home was in an affluent part of town near the sea; a jagged outcropping of rocks projecting into the water served as a dramatic backdrop. There were other lovely villas in the neighbourhood, occupied mostly by foreigners or prominent government officials. But the rest of Conakry was barely more than a village: foul, dilapidated shacks and crumbling French colonial buildings. A ban on virtually all private enterprise had destroyed the economy, crippling the country's development.

Still, there were a couple of hotels and a few restaurants. Tsietsi and Welma would go out for a meal or take long walks, hand-in-hand, along the beach. Occasionally they went to see a French film in the city's one cinema. (Tsietsi had acquired some knowledge of French, which Welma already spoke.) The visits evoked the earlier, happier days of their courtship. Welma found the time they spent together blissful; she could almost forget the incident at her mother's house. Tsietsi was enthusiastic about being in a programme that would prepare him for the life of a revolutionary and spoke, as always, of his dreams of liberating South Africa. But he still missed his home and family terribly. It seemed to Welma that the years in exile had done little to lessen the ache; if anything, the pain had only deepened with time. Tsietsi talked incessantly about Nomkhitha and Joseph, especially Nomkhitha, reminiscing about the things they had done together and studying the pictures of his parents he carried with him.

Tsietsi's burgeoning friendship with Stokely Carmichael provided some diversion. By then, Miriam had separated from the black American activist, who maintained a house a short distance from hers. Tsietsi met Stokely often when he was in Conakry. The two would sit outside under a coconut palm, endlessly discussing the liberation of the African people. Stokely had, by this time, become completely integrated into African society: he wore the traditional Guinean robe and had taken the name Kwame (for Kwame Nkrumah, the founding father of modern Ghana) Toure (for his Guinean benefactor). He was fixated by what he perceived as the universal relegation of Africans to second- or third-class status. Why should extortion be called 'black' mail? he demanded of Tsietsi. Why is it a 'black' list? 'Black' sheep? Tsietsi greatly enjoyed the repartee and had much respect for his friend's oratorical skills, even if he did not always agree with the arguments.

The impending birth of his child also heartened Tsietsi. He could barely contain his excitement as the due date drew near. He made Welma promise to contact him at the first sign of contractions. Welma unexpectedly went into labour two weeks early; she sent a cable to Conakry informing Tsietsi of the birth of a daughter. He arrived in Monrovia a few days later. His was pure joy at seeing the infant. Tsietsi barely allowed Welma to touch their child; he wanted to do everything himself. He taught Welma how to use a single pin to secure the nappy, South African style. He warmed his daughter's bottles, gave her baths, tied her onto his back with a blanket and walked the hallways of the house until she fell asleep. Tsietsi was happier than he had thought possible: he had, in a small way, regained his family. Welma told Tsietsi she wanted to christen the infant Nomkhitha. She knew that it would please him.

In Soweto, Joseph and Nomkhitha had learned of Tsietsi's marriage from that article in the magazine. The implications that her new daughter-in-law was white (because of her surname) and that Tsietsi was now living an extravagant lifestyle puzzled Nomkhitha; none of this corresponded with how she remembered her son. She was greatly troubled by the story. It seemed a bad omen to her, a message of some sort whose true meaning she should strive to understand. Nomkhitha began having trouble sleeping at night: she would wake with a start and remain sleepless for hours in her bed, fearing that Rocks and Tsietsi and Dee were dead and that she would never know how they died. At those times, she prayed for her sons. She prayed that one day they would all be together again.

Then she and Joseph received a letter from Tsietsi in Liberia, informing them of his marriage and the birth of Nomkhitha's namesake. He made no mention of the magazine's insinuations. The letter thrilled Joseph: now, at least, he had confirmation that Tsietsi was alive. His son was getting on with his life, starting a family. But the letter did not give Nomkhitha peace. His marriage seemed a frivolous thing; he had not left South Africa to pursue romance. In Nomkhitha's estimation, Tsietsi's decision to get married and have a child was too hasty. Why had he rushed these matters? He was still so young. The knowledge that she had no choice but to accept the facts of Tsietsi's life only heightened her distress; she had already spent too many years resigning herself to her children's fate.

The publicity surrounding Tsietsi engendered a new wave of gossip and innuendo from acquaintances. In an interview with

Drum (a black South African magazine), Nomkhitha expressed her exasperation at, yet again, being ostracized. The interviewer wrote that:

> What really gives her sleepless nights is the way some mothers point fingers at her and murmur curses because they think Tsietsi was responsible for the death, arrest or self-exile of their children.
>
> 'I feel as any mother would. As a mother who has three children who have left the country, I know how some of those who accuse me feel, although it is unfair. I never had anything to do with the student movement. I never even knew that Tsietsi was involved. As far as I was concerned, he was just like the boy next door,' she said.
>
> 'The other thing is that people are quick to jump to conclusions. When it appeared in the newspapers that Tsietsi was marrying Welma Campbell, many concluded that she was a white girl. They talked behind my back that Tsietsi was travelling in luxury all over the world and living in the lap of luxury, while their children suffered,' she said.
>
> 'I wish people could remember that I am not in any way responsible for any of Tsietsi's actions. He does not consult me with whatever he does. I wish they would please leave me alone,' she pleaded.

At least the police had, over time, begun to pay less attention to the family. Now the security men only appeared at the house on June 16 every year. The officer in charge always carried a very large dossier; after seating himself on a chair in the lounge, he opened the file and began to question Nomkhitha. 'Now let me see,' he said, thumbing through the mountain of papers, 'Tsietsi has not come back yet? Do you know where Rocks is? Or Dee?' It did not take Nomkhitha long to answer the officer's questions; sometimes he tried to prolong the process by asking her opinion of the government. The policeman posed the same questions to Joseph. Then he closed the file and departed, promising to return the following year.

* * *

When Tsietsi finished his course in Guinea and returned to Monrovia, he, Welma and the baby moved into their own home. Welma's family owned an apartment building on Benson Street in the city centre; Emma arranged for them to live in one of the units, rent-free. It was spacious and airy, with a living room, dining area, kitchen and bedroom. The apartment looked out on the two-storey, pastel-painted structures of the business district, their display windows covered by thick metal shutters at night and on the weekends. A few high-rise buildings, mostly government ministries, poked over the horizon. Sometimes at dawn, Tsietsi and Welma were awakened by a muezzin's call to early prayers from a nearby mosque. Welma thought they could be happy in the apartment. It felt like home, especially with the presence of little Nomkhitha; and they had their privacy now.

One evening, Tsietsi was playing chess with a friend in the living room. He called out to Welma, who was cooking in the kitchen, to bring him another beer. 'I'm too busy,' she replied. Afterwards, when his friend had left, Tsietsi confronted Welma in the kitchen.

'Why did you embarrass me like that?' he demanded. 'Why didn't you get the beer for me?'

'What's the big deal? You always get your own beer.'

'Here's the big deal,' Tsietsi said, slapping Welma across the face.

Horrified, Welma immediately left for her mother's house with Kiki, as they called the baby. Tsietsi followed her there, pleading contrition and promising never to hit her again. Because she wanted to believe him, Welma agreed to return to the apartment. Thus began a nightmarish pattern in their marriage. There would be long periods of harmony, during which Welma could convince herself that Tsietsi's violent rages were anomalous occurrences. Then, with no obvious provocation, and always after a bout of drinking, Tsietsi would suddenly strike her. Welma left the apartment after each incident; the second time she went to a friend's house. It took Tsietsi a while to find her, but he eventually appeared at the door sobbing, apologetic, vowing never to raise a hand to her. The next time

Tsietsi struck her, Welma took a taxi to her sister's house at Firestone Rubber Plantation, about twenty miles north of town; she intended to hide indefinitely. Tsietsi found her in the end and convinced Welma, with much cajoling, to come home.

Welma was mortified by the turn her marriage had taken. That Tsietsi was, at once, the witty, sensitive man with whom she had fallen in love only compounded her predicament. She felt terribly confused. She was too embarrassed to confide in anyone and devised intricate explanations for her friends and family each time she ran away from home. Her mother confronted her after neighbours in the apartment building reported that they were hearing fights; Welma dismissed the stories as gossip. Only when she sent Kiki to live with her mother, so the child would not witness her father's violent outbursts, did Welma confess the truth about her husband.

Tsietsi's rages caused Welma serious problems at work. Welma had answered an advertisement from the Liberian Broadcasting Corporation for a job as a continuity announcer, someone who would greet viewers when the station went on the air and read the list of the evening's programmes. Although Welma had never worked in broadcasting, she thought her theatre training could compensate for a lack of experience. She took a voice test and wrote a mock script at her interview. A week later, a producer at the network telephoned to say they wanted to hire her.

Welma enjoyed the job immensely and was soon promoted to newsreader. She worked from 5.30 in the afternoon, when the station began broadcasting, until its close at midnight. Tsietsi at first professed to be delighted at her luck in obtaining the position. He sometimes accompanied her to the studio in Paynesville, about fifteen miles from Monrovia, and spent part of the evening there. He stopped the practice after a while. That was when Welma noticed a change in his attitude towards her job. 'And what have you been doing all night?' he now greeted her when she returned home after the station went off the air. It was much worse if he had been drinking. Please God, Welma would pray as she ascended the stairs to the apartment, let me find him sober. When he was not, and he hit her, Welma sometimes could not go to work until the swelling on her face went down.

Tsietsi begrudged Welma the camaraderie she found at work. 'Here I don't have my friends, my mother, my family,' he told her by way of explaining his outbursts. 'You're off having fun, while I'm all alone.' Welma felt great sympathy for him. Tsietsi had done little since returning from Guinea. He mostly spent his days waiting, as though expecting his erstwhile comrades from the South African Youth Revolutionary Council to contact him. Anything he undertook seemed to be provisional, stopgap, a way to kill time until the call came from his organization. Tsietsi had still thought himself a leader when he left Nigeria in a fit of pique; as time passed and no one begged him to reconsider his decision, he realized that the SAYRCO leadership position had slipped from him. After that, Tsietsi put all his energy and drive into obtaining military training and, through President Toure in Guinea, organizing a similar course for fellow exiles – but to what end? He was no longer wanted. He had become irrelevant.

Khotso Seatlholo, the president of SAYRCO, visited Tsietsi in Monrovia. Khotso needed to know when he could begin sending recruits to Guinea for training. Tsietsi seemed withdrawn and isolated; he had not remained informed on developments within SAYRCO. This was in stark contrast with the activist of June 16, who had somehow managed, amid the tear gas and police bullets, to keep abreast of everyone's activities. Tsietsi has lost his spark, his enthusiasm; to Khotso, he appeared defeated by his domestic situation. Over a beer, Khotso told his old friend of his hurt at not being informed of Tsietsi's intention to marry. Tsietsi shrugged his shoulders. 'I'm sorry,' he said, putting an end to the conversation.

Tsietsi hoped that he might find meaningful work after the *coup d'état* that occurred in Liberia in April 1980. The event was not unexpected. President Tolbert had done little to address the continued inequalities between the Americo-Liberians, who still controlled much of Liberia's wealth, and the majority indigenous population. Hundreds of students and unemployed youths had gone on a rampage in the previous year to protest against an increase in rice prices; scores were killed. Tolbert arrested dozens of dissidents on charges of treason or sedition. The political tension in the country rose to an unbearable pitch. Liberia smouldered on the brink of civil war until an unknown master sergeant, Samuel Doe, and sixteen cohorts jumped the fence of the Executive Mansion late one night, disembowelled Tolbert in his bed and declared themselves the nation's new rulers.

Welma, Tsietsi, Kiki and Welma's sister Eva were staying at Emma's home when the coup took place. Emma, a member of the House of Representatives, had gone to visit her constituents in the town of Marshall. A group of soldiers suddenly appeared in front of the house in a small truck. Tsietsi went outside to speak with them; when he asked how the revolution was faring, one of the soldiers threatened to drag everyone out of the house and shoot them. Somehow, Tsietsi managed to dissuade the mutineers from committing murder. Instead they took a radio from the house, then roared off in their truck. Tsietsi recounted the story to the terrified women. 'I'm not a Liberian, I'm South African, I'm used to death,' he said to Eva. 'The soldiers were shocked at someone standing up to them.'

As a member of the Liberia's elite, Welma was ambivalent about the coup. She had spent much of her adult life working with liberation movements; indeed, as a university student she had fought for multi-party democracy and freedom of expression in Liberia. If Tolbert had only enacted a handful of reforms, such as allowing the formation of other political parties, he might have prevented the coup. Everyone save the president himself seemed to know it was coming. But few people had expected lower-ranking officers to overthrow the government. Welma was somewhat dubious about the efficacy of the new rulers; she hoped they would incorporate the leaders of the opposition political parties into the regime.

Then the killings began. After summary trials, thirteen former government ministers, dressed only in their underpants, were lashed to telephone poles on a stretch of beach behind the Executive Mansion. A row of soldiers with rifles faced them.

At the invitation of the new government, members of the international press were present to record the event. The drunken state of the executioners slowed the process considerably; it took a long time and many volleys for some of the prisoners to die. The scenes, broadcast around the world, were shocking.

Everything changed in the country. The overthrow of the old guard, ostensibly to 'liberate' the majority indigenous population and make Liberia a democracy, turned out to be a sham. Samuel Doe, the new president, simply replaced one governing minority group (the Americo-Liberians) with another (members of his own tribe, the Krahn). Only now the new rulers were among the least educated and most inexperienced people in the nation. Political opponents were arrested, certain newspapers banned, journalists detained. Welma escaped the purges of Americo-Liberians from important posts because of her popularity; but she quickly learned to be circumspect in her job. She and her colleagues received rather pointed queries from Doe's office if news about the president happened to be read as the third or fourth story of the night, not the first. And certain issues were to be avoided all together. Welma once featured a well-known poet and writer on an arts programme that she produced. For his performance, the man had himself tied to a pole and recited a poem he had composed about how coup-mongers tied people to poles and shot them without proper trials. During the broadcast, the producers received a call from the Executive Mansion: the programme must be stopped immediately. The producers had no choice but to comply.

Tsietsi also became deeply disillusioned. Tolbert, for all his deficiencies, had at least taken an interest in the anti-apartheid struggle. He granted scholarships to South African students; refused entry to the country of anyone possessing a South African passport; helped to lead the campaign at the United Nations to impose sanctions against the South African regime. But Doe, who was barely literate, had little knowledge of the South African liberation movement and no interest in supporting it. Despite this, Tsietsi was willing to give him a chance. 'Let's wait and see what happens,' he told Welma. 'Sometimes you have to pay a price for revolution.' But the accretion of stories of lawlessness and corruption became too overwhelming for Tsietsi to ignore. Over the years, he had constructed a fantasy of how a popular takeover would transform a nation; what he saw in Liberia discouraged and depressed him greatly. Doe's ignorance appalled Tsietsi so he decided that, after liberating South Africa, he would become a teacher.

His disgust at the president's lack of education prompted Tsietsi to volunteer to teach at a night school for adults. Such institutions were popular in Monrovia then; across the city, one could find day labourers, who had barely ever set foot in a classroom, poring over the alphabet every night. Tsietsi worked at a school that was within walking distance from the apartment. There, from 7 p.m. until 11 p.m., he taught high school mathematics and science to adults who had never received their diplomas. Tsietsi was excited about being involved in a project to help people. He received a salary that, along with the allowance and medical assistance he got from the United Nations High Commission for Refugees, supplemented Welma's earnings; at least now Tsietsi felt he was making a contribution to his family's existence.

But Welma could see that the job was not sufficient for him. It did nothing to satisfy Tsietsi's crushing desire to work for South Africa's liberation. His rages against Welma continued unabated. Tsietsi seemed to possess two personalities. There was the Tsietsi who had charmed Welma with his wit and intelligence during their courtship and could still hold her in his thrall. That Tsietsi escorted her to parties on the weekends and danced all night, went on outings to the beach for a swim or a picnic. He still drew a crowd at the formal affairs they attended. He and Welma were frequent guests at receptions given by the American ambassador, William Swing. The ambassador had heard Tsietsi give a speech years earlier in the US and had been greatly impressed by the young man's passion. Tsietsi never lost an opportunity at the US cocktail parties to speak out, with eloquence and force, against the South African regime and America's continued support for it.

Then there was the other Tsietsi. His erratic behaviour shocked his friend, Comfort Molokoane, who had lived with him in Nigeria and came to Monrovia for a visit. One afternoon, Tsietsi suddenly exploded over a minor misunderstanding with Welma: screaming, throwing things, threatening her. Comfort had to leave the apartment. The scene inside was too painful to witness. To Comfort, Tsietsi seemed the fallen hero, defeated by his circumstances and frustrated by his dependence on Welma. And Welma, in Comfort's view, no longer looked at Tsietsi as the great revolutionary, but as a husband from whom she had certain expectations.

One day Tsietsi took umbrage at Welma's mode of greeting friends, men included, with a hug and a kiss on the cheek. He dissolved into a violent rage, accusing her of having other lovers. Welma was stunned; this sort of salutation was part of her culture. Now she felt compelled to withdraw from people. No longer could she maintain an open, carefree personality; in Tsietsi's presence, Welma had to be distant and measured with her friends. She began to feel imprisoned by her marriage.

Welma sought out Philemon Hou, who had been the deputy director of her drama group at university, for help. Philemon was perhaps closest to Tsietsi among the few South Africans living in Monrovia. Tsietsi respected his opinion, both as a fellow exile and as an elder. Philemon and his wife, Georgia, came to the apartment to have a chat with Tsietsi. Philemon would brook no nonsense from the young man and warned him that he would call the police if Tsietsi hit Welma again. Tsietsi listened intently to Philemon's words and agreed not to strike his wife.

The next time he erupted in anger, which happened a few days after the visit, Tsietsi put his hand into his pocket. 'Okay, I'm not going to touch you because I promised Philemon and Georgia I wouldn't,' he said. 'But I can still do a lot without touching you.' With that, Tsietsi laid a pistol on the dining-room table. He had been given the gun during his military training in Guinea. 'Now, tell me,' he said, picking up the loaded weapon and aiming it at Welma, 'are the rumours from South Africa true? Are you a CIA plant? Are you?'

Horrified, Welma ran to the bedroom, threw some clothes

into a suitcase and left for her mother's house. She would never return to the apartment. Tsietsi appeared at Emma's the next day, reciting the usual litany of apologies. Welma refused to talk to him. He returned the following afternoon, pleading for Welma to come home. She again declined to speak with him. After a week of such supplications, Welma noticed that Tsietsi had lost a considerable amount of weight; he probably was not eating. He looked frightful. She allowed Emma to give him some food. When Tsietsi began presenting himself at the house every day thereafter at meal times, Welma felt compelled to permit him to stay. But they did not live as husband and wife. Welma was pregnant with their second child and had been hospitalized several times for bleeding. Fearing she would lose the baby, her doctor ordered Welma to remain in bed. She ultimately gave birth to a healthy girl, whom Tsietsi named Nomathemba, or Hope. The baby's entrance into the world, however, did not bring about a reconciliation between her parents. Philemon, aware of Welma's fears about Tsietsi, convinced him that, according to African tradition, he should not share the bed of a woman who had recently given birth. Tsietsi accepted his friend's advice.

His mental health seemed to deteriorate further. Now Tsietsi cringed at the colour red: whenever he saw a red object, he told Welma that it reminded him of blood and made him sick. Welma thought his behaviour neurotic; she attributed it and his rages to his drinking. She believed he needed treatment of some sort. Welma had a cousin who, in an effort to cure his alcoholism, had sought the help of a traditional African herbalist. Her cousin had not taken a drink in the five years since his cure. Very reluctantly, Tsietsi agreed to visit the herbalist.

The woman worked from her house, behind the enormous, open-air Waterside Market. Emma, Welma and her cousin accompanied Tsietsi; the herbalist seated them on little chairs in her backyard. She handed Tsietsi a glass. 'I'm going to put a little alcohol in this potion,' she explained. 'After you swallow it, you will never want to drink again.' Tsietsi obediently downed the concoction in her presence. Then he and the others took their leave and returned to Emma's car. A short way down the road, Tsietsi leaned out the window and vomited up the potion.

After that, he and Welma resorted to a spiritual healer. Mother Doe (no relation to the president) was a much sought-after preacher, whose church lay across the Mesurado River on Bushrod Island. An ordinary woman who had had a vision, a kind of revelation, several years earlier, she claimed to be able to heal people through her prayers. Welma, having been raised in a devout home, thought Mother Doe might indeed possess such powers. Tsietsi was sceptical. He always spoke of how the white South African settlers had given blacks the Bible and taken away their land; he refused to submit to an institution that he believed had subjugated people all over Africa. Thus, despite his religious upbringing, Tsietsi would go to church only for a wedding or a christening. But he never objected to Emma taking his children to worship on Sundays.

Tsietsi, Welma and Emma visited Mother Doe at her house for a couple of prayer sessions. They also attended her church. Surrounded by people praying and uttering exclamations, with a choir singing vigorously in the background, Mother Doe placed her hands on Tsietsi's head and pleaded with God to bring about a healing. Tsietsi stood silently, looking rather uncomfortable. Welma thought his faith not sufficiently strong; whatever the reason, the healer did not cause him to abandon alcohol.

Welma suggested Tsietsi consult a psychiatrist. Tsietsi objected; he did not need that kind of help. After much prodding, he relented and began seeing a Ghanaian doctor who had trained in Britain. Tsietsi went to a therapy session once a week; he also took medication the doctor prescribed. The drug subdued him, making him quieter and more withdrawn. But there were no more violent episodes with Welma. After a few months, however, she noticed that Tsietsi had suddenly become garrulous again and was acting in an odd way. 'Have you taken your medicine?' Welma asked him one day.

Tsietsi became defensive. 'I'm not taking that stuff any more,' he said belligerently. 'I'm just not.'

Now Tsietsi's emotional state seemed to worsen daily. One

afternoon, Welma's cousin burst into Emma's house to report that she had seen Tsietsi walking aimlessly down the centre of Tubman Boulevard, one of the busiest roads in the city. Emma raced off in her car to find him. He proffered no explanation for his behaviour. A few days later, Welma left Thembi, the baby, in the living room with Tsietsi while she was working in another part of the house. She returned an hour later to find that both her daughter and Tsietsi had disappeared. Unbeknown to Welma, Tsietsi had buttoned Thembi inside the front of his shirt, South African style, and walked out of the house. He cut a strange figure: a man with a baby stuffed into his clothes, sauntering down the road; several people came to Emma's house to tell Welma what they had seen. By now, she was frantic. When Tsietsi returned a couple of hours later, he silently handed Thembi to Welma and left the house again.

Later that week, Tsietsi suddenly appeared in the living room where Welma was playing with the baby. He stood at the threshold, mute. Welma tried to engage him in conversation, but Tsietsi stayed in the doorway, staring at her in silence, his eyes unblinking. His gaze terrified her. It seemed menacing in a way she had never experienced before. Tsietsi maintained his pose for several minutes, then walked into his bedroom and closed the door. With that, Welma rushed into her bedroom. She had already decided: she would not live her life in fear. She quickly packed a few bags with essentials for the children, grabbed Kiki and Thembi, and slipped out the back to summon a taxi.

Welma gave the driver the address of her sister Cornelia's house in Gardnersville, about three miles away. It was a small, government-built dwelling; Cornelia had to squeeze Welma and the children in, alongside her own family. Welma did not mind. She had to satisfy the overpowering urge to hide somewhere unknown to Tsietsi, to get to a safe place and sever all contact with him. Cornelia called Emma to inform her of Welma's whereabouts. In his unbalanced state of mind, Tsietsi never found out where Welma was.

Emma, a strong-willed congresswoman of considerable stature, visited the office of the United Nations High

Commission for Refugees to say that Tsietsi was in trouble. He needs more help, she told them; perhaps you should consider sending him abroad for better psychiatric care. Several days later, Emma telephoned Welma to tell her that Tsietsi had been sent to the UNHCR's office in Senegal for analysis. Welma, with her daughters, immediately moved back to Emma's house.

As soon as she had settled in, Welma asked her mother to help her prevent Tsietsi from returning to Liberia. Welma was afraid that the UNHCR officials in Senegal would simply dismiss Tsietsi's problem and allow him to come back to Monrovia without proper treatment. It was a difficult decision, for it meant depriving her daughters of their beloved father. But Welma felt they would be better off growing up without his mercurial rages. As for her, she was finished with Tsietsi. And so Welma wrote letters, which Emma delivered on her behalf, to the Bureau of Immigration at the Justice Ministry, the Foreign Ministry, the Directorate of Police. In them, she explained that Tsietsi Mashinini, a South African exile and her husband, had threatened her on several occasions and needed psychiatric treatment that could not be got in Liberia. His return to the country could endanger her life; if this could be prevented, it would be most appreciated.

As Emma called on the various ministries to deliver the petitions, she had a little chat with the officials in charge. Although Welma never enquired about what measures were taken, she understood that Tsietsi's name was put on a list at the airport and all other ports-of-entry that prevented him from coming into the country. Years later, she would learn that he had tried to return to Liberia – only to be refused and bundled off to an awaiting international flight.

CHAPTER THIRTEEN

Rocks

After Rocks' evacuation from the destroyed Novo Catengue camp, he and his fellow officers were sent to a guerrilla base in northern Angola. The new camp, built on an old coffee estate on a high plateau, was cool and often shrouded in mist. Initially appointed chief instructor of recruits, Rocks was quickly promoted to staff commissar, then made a camp commissar. (The equivalent of second-in-command of political thought and education.) Despite having attained a respected status within the Umkhonto organization, Rocks felt restless in the camp. He often clashed with his counterpart who commanded the military operations; the officer was too regimented, too inflexible, for Rocks' liking. Rocks found himself questioning his perpetual distaste for authority. He wondered whether the intellectual combativeness that Nomkhitha instilled in her children had made them into intractable anarchists.

One day, about a year after Rocks' arrival, the camp commander summoned him to his office. Rocks was in the midst of organizing the celebrations for Women's Day. 'Do you see that truck?' the officer asked Rocks, indicating a vehicle that was parked outside.

'Yes, sir.'

'That truck is going to transport you out of here. Pack your bags. You're going back to the capital for more training.'

The officer did not divulge the meaning of the new orders. Bewildered, Rocks did as commanded. His instructors in Luanda were equally secretive, although one did intimate that Rocks would be leaving Angola upon completion of his studies. That bit of information cheered Rocks immeasurably. His courses gave him few clues as to his next job: combat training; creating clandestine cells; working with mass organizations. After several weeks of such instruction, an officer presented Rocks with a false Zambian passport – the ANC had an entire department devoted to such undertakings – and put him on an aeroplane to Mozambique.

In Maputo, Rocks learned that he would be joining what were known as the operations structures of Umkhonto. Specifically, he would work in Internal Reconstruction, the unit of Umkhonto's political wing that organized cells within South Africa. This was a relatively new endeavour, born of a trip that ANC and Umkhonto leaders took to Vietnam in 1978. They went to consult with General Vo Nguyen Giap, the celebrated conqueror of the French and American armies, on how best to conduct guerrilla warfare. The general stressed the importance of mapping out a comprehensive, long-term programme; to succeed, they needed a clearly defined political, as well as military, strategy. Adopting such an approach would require Umkhonto to strengthen its underground networks and build mass-based organizations within South Africa.

The Umkhonto leaders accordingly embarked on a plan to bolster their political operations. They singled out a group of promising young cadres in Angola, Rocks among them, for the programme. Rocks was charged with creating a proliferation of cells in South Africa. He was also to re-establish the ANC as the leading anti-apartheid organization in the consciousness of government opponents. In workshops, Rocks studied such subjects as how to make contact with potential recruits and how to identify sympathetic activists. His lecturers were Umkhonto luminaries, members of the regional command that bore the unlikely name of Senior Organ. Here were veteran guerrilla fighters; Rocks regarded them, and their discourses, with awe.

Rocks studied and slept in a large, Umkhonto safe house. (Mozambique was too close, and the South African Defence Forces too powerful, to risk operating actual guerrilla camps.) The house sat in a lovely old section of the city, a bluff that overlooked the Indian Ocean and the port. The neighbourhood was comprised of Portuguese colonial-style houses with pitched roofs; Rocks loved living there. Being so close to the border, the instructors could provide their protégés with the latest South African newspapers. Rocks read voraciously: politics, sport, community events, the women's section – anything that could give him a sense of home. He felt like a man led to a cool stream after a long drought. Finally he was at South Africa's doorstep: having endured years of isolation in the Angolan bush, of training for combat that never came, of preparing to fight an enemy thousands of miles away – now he had his chance. Fighting the Boers was no longer an abstract thing. He and his comrades spent hours analysing the current political situation in South Africa and planning how they would execute their missions. For Rocks, it was the culmination of what had seemed like an eternity of waiting.

In the meantime, he greatly enjoyed being in a city again. He and his comrades often went out in the evenings to see a film or eat a meal in a restaurant. During Portuguese rule, Lourenço Marques, as it was then called, had been a favourite holiday spot for South Africans, with its glistening beaches and elegant hotels. It was also a city of unbridled nightclubs and other interracial entertainments where white South African males, constrained by the excessive strictness of their Calvinistic society, engaged in activities otherwise forbidden to them at home. The revolution put an end to much of those pursuits, but Maputo remained a lively place. It gave Rocks the opportunity to celebrate having left the Angolan bush behind.

(The Mozambicans were somewhat contemptuous of their guests and their desire for an urban exile. Some of the former Mozambican guerrillas had spent countless years in the countryside fighting the Portuguese; being poorer and less urbane than their ANC counterparts, they felt they more readily accepted such privation. Privately, the Mozambicans complained that the South Africans were only interested in armed propaganda, not armed struggle.)

When Rocks had completed his courses, his Umkhonto officers dispatched him to Swaziland, which was to be his base of operations. One night he was driven from Maputo to the border town of Namaacha, where he had first entered Mozambique. Only now he was headed in the opposite direction: not fleeing South Africa, but moving towards it. The thought filled him with joy. Rocks met up with Umkhonto guides who would help him cross the border and avoid the patrols that guarded both sides of the frontier. The place was particularly dangerous: a triangular piece of South Africa jutted into the border at Namaacha, and Pretoria's defence forces maintained a communications outpost on a nearby hill. To reach Swaziland, Rocks had to traverse two sets of fences and a generous stretch of no-man's land in between. It was a nerve-fraying exercise; he half-expected the area to be awash suddenly in searchlights and to hear gunfire. But he made it to the Swazi side without incident. After resting a bit to recover his calm, Rocks walked to a rendezvous point to wait for his ride to Manzini.

There he joined the Umkhonto structure known as Transvaal Urban Political Machinery. As the name suggested, Rocks would concentrate his work on the eastern cities of Transvaal province; fellow Umkhonto officers in Swaziland were responsible for rural regions and military activities in that part of Transvaal and in Natal province. Guerrillas who operated from other border states divided up the remainder of South Africa among themselves. Rocks held the title of secretary, the equivalent of deputy chief. His duties included organizing political cells within South Africa, infiltrating existing organizations to convince them to follow ANC doctrine, distributing leaflets. Rocks had several people under his command; he supervised their training of recruits who would be sent into South Africa to create cells. The members of those cells, in a kind of revolutionary mitosis, created additional cells. And so on.

Despite Umkhonto's ostensible commitment to strengthening its political operations, Rocks quickly discovered that he had constantly to compete with his military comrades for funding – usually to his disadvantage. The officers in the Military Machinery unit were responsible for organizing attacks on targets in South Africa; they deserved the bulk of the money allocated to the Swaziland office, they argued, because their work was more tangible. Indeed, Umkhonto's operations were increasingly palpable within South Africa. The guerrillas launched rockets against police stations in the townships, sabotaged several power plants and railway lines and, in an especially spectacular move, bombed four installations belonging to SASOL (the South African Coal, Oil and Gas Corporation); fires raged at one oil storage tank for almost a week. Rocks' activities, by contrast, were more abstract. It was harder to measure the effect of a workers' strike on the country than, say, that of a damaged electrical sub-station. Rocks thought his superiors' predilection for daring pursuits short-sighted; from his training in Moscow, he had come to believe that only by cultivating political opposition within South Africa would the ANC defeat the Boers. Umkhonto fighters alone could not win the war.

Rocks' former life in Angola now seemed distant. He had exchanged the isolation of the guerrilla camps for the immediacy, and perilousness, of an underground existence. Swaziland's smallness and economic dependence on South Africa made it virtually subservient to Pretoria's wishes; Swazi police hunted down ANC members and allowed their Boer counterparts to operate within the country. Rocks had to be in continuous motion to stay alive. He worked from several safe houses in Manzini and Mbabane, the nation's capital. He learned the local language, Swati, sufficiently to pass for a native and devised several covers, among them an insurance salesman and a Swazi policeman. He also had numerous aliases; Vusi Kumalo, a common name, was the one he used most frequently. (To this day, many of Rocks' Swazi acquaintances believe his name was Vusi.) Rocks nurtured a network of reliable Swazis with whom he could take refuge at a moment's notice. In public, he had to be vigilant at all times, checking behind him to determine if he were being shadowed, varying his movements, dodging and ducking to escape suspected surveillance. Rocks avoided such places as restaurants and bars. He did allow himself to go to the cinema, however, because he could enter and exit the auditorium under cover of darkness; Rocks missed the beginning and end of most films that played in Swaziland in the 1980s.

It was a life of almost unbearable tension. Rocks felt he could never let down his guard, never relax. He and his comrades began drinking heavily to escape the sensation of being constantly in danger. For the first time in his life, Rocks suffered from migraine headaches and neckaches; the pain, at times, was incapacitating. A Swazi friend, who was a polygamist and kept a wife upcountry, north of Manzini in a remote area, occasionally invited Rocks to slip away to his rural home for a few days. But the retreat offered only momentary respite.

The rigours of his underground existence began a slow, alcohol-induced disintegration for Rocks. He had never imagined his life like this; but neither could he fathom living his parents' life: resigned, acquiescent, defeated. He had no choice. This was a sacrifice he had to make. His commitment precluded escaping the cruelties of his job; he could not go to his superiors and say: I'm tired of this, I'm taking off. Where would he go? He lacked proper documents, he had jumped the border fence. And he lacked money. Exile had seemed an easy thing when he was certain of an imminent and victorious return home. That he now understood how long liberation would take only exacerbated the feeling of being entrapped by his own beliefs. Rocks resolved simply to try to survive.

That resolution was greatly eased by Rocks' encounter with Sebenzile Motse, a bright Swazi university student. The two met at the house of a mutual acquaintance in Mbabane. Sebenzile, who was studying sociology and statistics, got into a heated debate with Rocks about Marxism-Leninism. (She did not know he was a member of Umkhonto; his friend had introduced him as Vusi.) Rocks found himself immediately attracted to the articulate, thoughtful young woman. The two began to date, as it were; Rocks' aversion to public places limited them somewhat. They developed an intellectually combative relationship, marked by long hours of philosophical exchanges, that Rocks enjoyed immensely.

Slowly Rocks felt Sebenzile out on the subject of apartheid and the ANC. She was sympathetic not only to the organization, but to Umkhonto as well; she did not flinch when Rocks finally revealed his true identity and the nature of his existence.

Indeed, Sebenzile began to help Rocks in his operations. She introduced him to numerous Swazis who favoured the South African cause, thereby expanding his pool of contacts to be used in an emergency. She helped Rocks to rent safe houses from people she knew. She even travelled to South Africa as an Umkhonto courier on occasion. Rocks was overjoyed at having found a woman in whom he could trust and confide.

Sebenzile's family formed the one discordant note in their relationship. Sebenzile did not reveal the extent of Rocks' revolutionary activities to them, only that he was a South African exile and vaguely involved with the ANC. That bit of information alone was enough for her relatives to oppose the affair. Sebenzile's high-caste family, rabid in its anti-ANC sentiments, generally reflected the country's conservatism and immoderate respect for tradition. An absolute monarch ruled the nation, along with a hierarchy of chiefs; he had suspended the constitution years earlier, banned independent political parties, muffled the press. Despite the king having been made an honorary member of the ANC at its founding in 1912, the organization was seen as a threat to Swaziland's practices. Sebenzile's family tried to dissuade her from continuing the relationship with Rocks, but to no avail; her defiance created much animosity between Sebenzile and her kin.

The continuous stream of couriers that Rocks sent to South Africa allowed him to establish contact with his family. For years, Joseph and Nomkhitha had had little information about their oldest son. Twice they received telephone calls in the dead of night from men who refused to identify themselves: I have been with Rocks recently and he is well, each said hastily, then disconnected the call. A young man in the township once told them that Rocks was an Umkhonto commissar in the Angolan camps. Nomkhitha and Joseph did not know how to react to this revelation; they did not know if it were an important post and if they should be proud of their son's achievement. They were just thankful to be informed of Rocks' existence.

Thus Joseph was delighted when he received a message from Rocks telling of his presence in Swaziland and giving instructions on how to find him there. Joseph travelled to Manzini by himself. In comparison with South African cities, it seemed a small town to him: a scattering of tiny shops, a couple of hotels, one police station, several churches. That night, Joseph was picked up at a designated point by an unknown driver and taken to a house. He found the place unoccupied; Rocks arrived a few hours later. The two were overjoyed at being reunited. It had been more than six years since Joseph had seen his son. He appeared healthy, if somewhat skittish; he also appeared to have become more reserved, almost secretive, in the intervening years. Rocks dispensed with Joseph's queries about his work in a perfunctory manner, then plied his father with questions about the family and home.

They spoke for most of the night. Joseph told him that Nomkhitha had given birth to another son (their last child), Bandile. She had spent years trying to find a job after being released from detention; the owners of the garment factory where Nomkhitha had worked told her they would not employ communists. People refused to hire her when they heard her surname. She had finally found a job with their church, helping to feed pensioners. Joseph recounted the details of Tsietsi's wedding and how it had become a celebrated story in the press. He described the diminished police presence around the house. And he talked of the anguish of having Rocks, Tsietsi and Dee in exile. 'I think about you boys all the time,' Joseph said. 'I wonder where you are, what kind of lives you're leading, whether you're safe, whether you're even alive.' He paused to give Rocks a chance to respond, but Rocks simply nodded at him. 'I could go mad worrying,' Joseph continued. 'We sometimes say special prayers at church for all the children in exile, but we're too scared to do it openly. The security police are everywhere. I've had prayer meetings at the house where we mention your name and Tsietsi and Dee. They give me a lot of comfort.'

Joseph looked around the barely illuminated room. 'You know this isn't what I wanted for you,' he said. 'You were always so serious about your education. I would prefer that you study, that you become an engineer.' He shrugged his shoulders. 'I suppose I have no choice but to accept what you're doing.'

Rocks did not know what to say. Joseph continued, in Rocks' view, to be blinded by his religious beliefs to South Africa's political realities. It angered Rocks, but also hurt him; he desperately wanted Joseph's approval. Rocks was amazed at how little his feelings for his father had changed. Despite attaining the lofty title of commissar, despite running a string of underground guerrilla operations, despite being armed at that very moment with a pistol jammed into his waistband – he still feared Joseph. Rocks longed to light a cigarette, but could not bring himself to do so in front of his father. Instead, he asked about the political situation in South Africa.

Joseph, who had always remained aloof from such matters, could speak only vaguely. He thought there had been an increase in anti-government activity of late, especially among community-based organizations and trade unions. Students who had been sentenced to prison after the 1976 uprising were returning to the townships, their political ardour undiminished. People had become bolder. The news, however imprecise, gratified Rocks; this was exactly what the ANC and Umkhonto were trying to foment. The grey-green light of dawn began to filter in through the drawn curtains. With great reluctance, Rocks told Joseph he had to go, hugged him and slipped from the house. He felt terribly homesick taking leave of his father; listening to stories of the family and Soweto made him realize how much of his previous life he had missed. After Rocks' departure, Joseph bowed his head and prayed for his son's safety.

Rocks' yearning for his family only deepened with an event that occurred not long after Joseph's visit: Sebenzile gave birth to a son. Rocks could not be with her at the clinic during the labour for fear of being arrested. But he and a friend fetched her when she was released with the baby to go home; Rocks remained in the car and sent his companion to accompany her outside. Rocks was overcome by emotion as he lifted the blanket to look at his son for the first time. He and Sebenzile named the baby Sizwe, or nation, a traditional Swati name. (Rocks had wanted to call him Fidel, after the Cuban dictator, but Sebenzile disabused him of the notion; it would have raised too many eyebrows in so conservative a place.) For all his happiness, Rocks felt a certain sadness, too: the celebration of a new Mashinini seemed incomplete without his family.

As the months passed, Swaziland became an even more dangerous place to work. Pressured by their South African counterparts, the Swazi police assiduously pursued suspected ANC/Umkhonto cadres. Rocks was stopped one night at a road-block on the crowded highway to Mbabane. He could have escaped into the nearby bush, but felt confident of his ability to persuade his interrogators to free him; Rocks had previously talked his way out of similar situations.

'Where are you from?' one of the policemen demanded.

'South Africa. I'm here visiting friends.'

'Show me your passport.'

'I'm sorry, but I've left it back at my hotel in Manzini.'

'Where are you going?'

'To Mbabane, to meet my friends.' Rocks tried to appear calm in answering the officer's questions, all the while watching, out of the corner of his eye, another policeman slowly circle the car.

'Open the boot,' the other officer commanded. Rocks tried to protest, saying that he was already late for his dinner engagement, but the policeman insisted. With a sigh, Rocks opened the boot of his car. The security men rooted through the sundry items, triumphantly exclaiming when they came upon a pile of ANC pamphlets. They immediately arrested Rocks. He was tried and sentenced to twenty days' imprisonment for being in the country illegally, then deported to Maputo. Umkhonto soldiers promptly escorted Rocks back to Swaziland to resume his work.

Pretoria's security forces too became more brazen; Rocks narrowly escaped being kidnapped and taken to South Africa one night. He, along with a colleague, was supposed to meet some contacts from the townships in a safe house in Manzini. Rocks agreed to pick up the colleague at a bar familiar to both, then drive to the meeting. On the appointed evening, the man did not appear until two hours after the scheduled time; he also brought along a woman who was unknown to Rocks. Her presence, and the uncharacteristic tardiness of his colleague, raised suspicions in Rocks. He decided not to go on to the rendezvous with the township contacts. The colleague and the woman went by themselves; along the way, the man was seized and transported back to South Africa.

Not long after that incident, South African forces raided a house down the street from where Rocks was staying. The house resembled the one where Rocks slept; in the morning, the owners came to warn Rocks that the security men had come looking for him but had been given the wrong address. Such invasions increased in frequency thereafter, with South African agents breaking into houses in the dead of night, grabbing suspected ANC or Umkhonto comrades and spiriting them over the border. More than 100 of Rocks' colleagues were deported. Rocks found himself becoming almost unhinged by the strain of living under such conditions.

A kind of climax occurred when an assassination squad that worked under the purview of Umkhonto's military and political units (they had recently been combined) killed one of Swaziland's leading security officers. The Swazi government immediately branded Rocks and others as ANC terrorists who were wanted by the authorities. It broadcast pictures of them on television and published their photographs in the newspapers. (The squad, in fact, consisted of only a handful of people assigned specifically to carry out such murders.) Rocks found it virtually impossible to carry on his underground work. It thus came as a relief to learn that he and several other comrades had been selected to go to Moscow for intelligence training. Although Rocks would miss Sebenzile and Sizwe greatly, he would at least have a respite from worrying about being kidnapped or killed – that is, until he were smuggled back into Swaziland after completing his course.

For his second sojourn in the Soviet Union, Rocks lived in Moscow proper. The KGB provided a flat for him and nine other comrades that was within walking distance of Red Square and the Kremlin. The four-bedroom apartment occupied an entire floor; the South Africans lived and studied there. Rocks thought highly of the course. The KGB instructors were well-trained and seemingly cosmopolitan, a stark contrast with the ideological automatons Rocks had encountered at the Communist Party school during his previous time in Russia. Rocks learned about intelligence collection and processing; which chemicals were best for invisible writing; how to use tape recorders so tiny they seemed designed for elves. The students practised on equipment and weapons from both the East and the West. Rocks handled an M-16, the assault rifle of US forces, for the first time; he came to think of the gun as inferior to the Soviet AK-47.

Rocks' studies dispelled any notions he might have acquired from the spy novels he read as a youngster. He had particular contempt for the James Bond stories. Rocks found the real thing far more interesting. He enjoyed, too, the sense that he and his fellow students were, in a way, pioneers. Umkhonto had done little intelligence work previously; Rocks and the others were among the first soldiers to study such subjects. Their courses were meant to prepare them to recruit agents within the South African security forces, to turn the tables, as it were, on the Boers and counter the successes they had experienced in infiltrating Umkhonto and the ANC.

The KGB instructors, an affable lot, sometimes stayed after classes to drink vodka with their students and chat. The South Africans were free to roam the city when their teachers left, but rarely did; they were constrained by the amount of homework they had to complete for the next day. At the weekends, the students were ostensibly at liberty to do as they pleased. But their hosts often dragged Rocks and the others, once again, to an endless array of circuses, ballets, theatre presentations. Rocks found the experience more tolerable this time. The course lasted for only six months; Sebenzile and his son awaited his return to Swaziland. Rocks knew, based on his previous stay, how to get through the days and weeks. But he still could not relax. He jumped at every loud noise, spent much time looking over his shoulder in public, suffered agonizing migraines. Only drink seemed to bring him any sort of peace.

CHAPTER FOURTEEN

Mpho

After his terrifying experience with the intelligence services, Mpho decided to confine himself to political work. A black youth protesting against the government's policies aroused less interest, surprisingly, than one who associated with Christian white students. Mpho simply could not stay away from anti-apartheid activities, especially now. The years of quiescence that had followed the 1976 uprising and the government repression were giving way to a new vitality in the townships in the early 1980s; hundreds of community-based groups, targetting a wide range of local economic and social grievances, were allowed to proliferate – as long as they did not directly threaten white rule.

The most visible among them in Soweto was COSAS, the Congress of South African Students. The organization's leaders, who saw themselves as the successors to the 1976 student movement, mobilized thousands of youths around such issues as improving the quality of teaching and extending the school age-limit. Unlike their predecessors, the new student leaders sought to include larger segments of the community; and so they also supported a disparate array of workers' and rate-payers' protests. Everyone, it seemed, had a movement to join, with one exception: those young adults who did not study and were unemployed. The COSAS activists attempted to correct the deficiency by calling for the creation of an organization that would embrace this group.

They singled out Mpho, who had never returned to school and was now twenty-two years old, along with his friends Tsheko Tsehlana and Oupa Monareng, to form the new movement. He and his comrades caught the attention of the COSAS leaders at the clandestine political study groups they attended. Older activists conducted the underground work-shops; many of them had completed prison sentences from their involvement in the 1976 uprising and had known Tsietsi. The participants met daily; the idea of creating a political home, as it were, for unemployed, non-students emerged from their discussions. The concept captured Mpho's imagination. He spent long hours debating with his friends the form the new organization would take; they, and their mentors, ultimately decided to found a youth congress.

The congress would adhere to the Freedom Charter and the political aims of the ANC. Mpho had long before become a confirmed believer in the Freedom Charter. He could mark the trajectory of his political evolution from Black Consciousness to the Pan Africanist Congress, to disillusionment with the PAC while in exile, to embracing the ANC's non-racial ideals during his talks with Joe Gqabi in prison, to working with whites. The Freedom Charter was the answer to his epiphany that not all whites were the same. The system was wrong, not the people. Now Mpho and the others saw themselves as repeating history, as resurrecting the ANC's Youth League of the early 1950s that had included such legendary figures as Nelson Mandela and Walter Sisulu. They had grand plans to establish youth congresses in townships across the country, culminating in the creation of a national organization. They would take up the struggle for young people where the imprisoned ANC leaders were forced to desist.

The launch of the Soweto Youth Congress, or SOYCO, as it would be called, took months to prepare. Mpho and the others began by trying to meet with every youth group in Soweto: karate clubs, church choirs, football teams (usually under a tree on Sunday morning before a match), dance clubs (which were run by the municipality and not terribly popular until after 1976, when they became one of the few activities open to young-sters after the schools were closed; some superb dancers were ultimately recruited as activists). Mpho alone spoke to fifty or sixty such groups. He talked about how he and his comrades were going to form a political youth organization that would address issues pertinent to young adults: the gap in education caused by the boycotts of the 1970s; unemployment; the difficulties in acquiring a trade; and so forth. They intended to form branches in the various neighbourhoods of the township, from which they would create the larger Soweto Youth Congress. Most of the listeners did not seem to realize that the group would be affiliated with the ANC, and Mpho obviously could not tell them. Still, several pastors abruptly escorted him from church meetings for dealing with 'earthly and secular' matters.

Mpho and his friends often consulted with Winnie Mandela in the tiny *dorp* of Brandfort, about 250 miles from Soweto in the Orange Free State, to which she had been banished in 1977 for her political activities. The black township was a dreary and isolated place: her small, 'matchbox' house lacked indoor plumbing and heating; most of her neighbours spoke only Sotho, which she did not understand; she was forbidden to meet with more than one person; the police had her under constant surveillance. It was a difficult, lonely exile. Winnie nonetheless managed to start a crèche, a clinic and a sewing group for the community. By the time Mpho visited her in the early 1980s, she had become something of a local celebrity. Winnie could always get the butcher or grocer to open for business, even if Mpho arrived after midnight. By then, too, she was increasingly defying her banning orders. Mpho always found her house abuzz with visitors: black businessmen, ministers, activists from the province's largest city, Bloemfontein.

The visits to Winnie usually lasted for three or four days. One did not simply sit down with Mama, as everyone called her, and discuss an issue. The strategy sessions ranged over hours and into the night, interrupted often by the arrival of other visitors or the need to attend to other business. Mpho and his comrades reported to Winnie on the work they were doing in anticipation of SOYCO's launch, the groups they had contacted, the branches they would establish. She, in turn, gave them funds to help pay for their travels and to print pamphlets. She organized meetings for them with people who could provide more money or aid them in other ways. Mpho valued her assistance immensely. She was still the Winnie Mandela who had caught the world's imagination with her strength and courage; the extreme militancy and erratic behaviour that in later years would alienate many of her supporters, including her husband, had yet to manifest itself.

Mpho came into his own during the heady days of preparation. He did not emerge as a leader in the mould of, say, Tsietsi; rather, his genius lay in his ability to traverse several worlds. After years of trying to find his political bearings, Mpho could move with equal ease among white liberals, Afrikaner Christians, ANC adherents, stiff-necked supporters of Black Consciousness. People of wildly different creeds trusted him – no mean feat in a place as polarized as South Africa. It was a talent that would serve him well in the coming months.

Given his aptitude, Mpho's friends were little surprised when he managed, under somewhat bizarre circumstances, to obtain an office for the SOYCO activists. The office was provided by an Afrikaner professor at Stellenbosch University, whom Mpho had met during his association with the Christian youth group. The man believed a kind of silent majority of blacks and whites existed that would change South Africa without bloodshed; these people simply had to be brought together and educated. The professor held conferences and congresses so the putative peacemakers could find one another. To appear credible to the non-governmental organizations that funded his projects, the professor needed to have blacks in his enterprise; and so he asked Mpho to work for him. Mpho and his friends, Oupa and Tsheko, consented to do so part-time. The youths saw the arrangement as a fair exchange: the professor used them to gain legitimacy with his benefactors; they used him for their struggle.

The professor rented an office for Mpho and his comrades in a high-rise building in central Johannesburg. Their job was to write an analysis of the country's political situation. The youths accomplished their task with ease: seven newspapers were delivered to the office daily, from which Mpho or one of the others would write a report. They posted the discourse weekly to the professor in Cape Town. Sometimes he sent them pamphlets, uplifting little anecdotes and personal testimonies with religious overtones about how blacks and whites had 'found' one another, to distribute around town. Otherwise, Mpho and his friends were left alone. They quickly turned the office into a planning centre for the SOYCO launch. Activists filled the place day and night, mapping out strategies and arguing about what should be included in the organization's constitution. (This was written by Popo Molefe, a contemporary of Tsietsi, who had been detained for seven months in 1976.) Away in Cape Town, the professor remained oblivious to the youths' activities. Mpho and his friends had only indirect contact with the man: once a month, they presented themselves at another of the professor's offices in suburban Park Town, where a beautiful, vapid secretary gave them their salaries and took their telephone bills to pay.

Mpho and his friends often clashed with their mentors, whom they referred to as the senior comrades, the young men and women who had begun to return to the townships after serving jail sentences for their participation in the 1976 uprising. In creating SOYCO, the senior comrades sought to build an organization that would not be banned. They had been sobered by their prison experiences; their goal was to do everything legally to ensure SOYCO's longevity – and thus its efficacy. The older comrades also feared that making SOYCO too radical would frighten adults away and prevent them from joining the organization. These were the lessons they had learned from 1976. Mpho took a dim view of such caution. He felt it was tantamount to asking permission to carry on the struggle; compromise, in his mind, meant fighting on the government's terms. The country had gone beyond the 1960s, when people needed to be educated politely about politics. Now was the time to incite the black population.

Among their more militant moves, the younger activists decorated the SOYCO t-shirts in the black, green and gold of the ANC. T-shirts, and the mottoes they employed, would become a potent tool of the myriad organizations that were springing up around the country; youngsters came to consider them powerful political statements. Using the ANC colours, Mpho and his friends created shirts with the slogan 'Soweto Youth Congress' on the front and 'Freedom in Our Lifetime' on the back. The older comrades thought the design utterly foolhardy. The authorities would see a display of such colours as promoting a banned organization, thereby making SOYCO itself subject to prohibition. After much heated debate, Mpho and his friends decided to refrain from distributing the shirts at SOYCO's launch, where the security police were certain to be present; they would dispense the clothing and membership cards, which also bore the illicit colours, at the more discreet branch meetings.

SOYCO's inaugural assembly was held at a social hall in the Dube section of Soweto on a Saturday afternoon. The activists chose the day and hour to allow the maximum number of people to attend. They took great pains to publicize the event, distributing handbills in various neighbourhoods, publishing advertisements in black newspapers and putting up posters around the township. Mpho and his colleagues expected the security police to ban the gathering at any moment. Still, the appointed time came with no objection from the authorities; people crowded into the hall, filling the dozens of rows of folding chairs and spilling into the aisles and out the door.

After the opening prayer, Popo Molefe, who was acting as the master of ceremonies, explained the reason for the gathering. We are here to launch the Soweto Youth Congress, he intoned over the speaker system. After the bannings in 1977, there was a lull in political activity. We need to revive ourselves and this is the answer. The launch of the Soweto Youth Congress today is an historical moment. The last time this happened was when our great leaders launched the ANC Youth League, and that was to respond to the oppression of that time. It has become tougher for us, but it is happening now. We need to support the comrades who took the initiative to create this organization.

With that, Popo invited a series of speakers to address the audience. They were mostly old-timers, contemporaries of Nelson Mandela who had been involved in the ANC's Youth League and the Treason Trial of the 1950s. The idea was to link SOYCO directly with the ANC, without saying it overtly. The audience clearly understood the intention. They interrupted the orators with constant shouts of '*Amandla!*' (Power!) and

'*Ngawethu!*' (It is ours!). Women ululated. Despite the obvious presence of police informers, there was electricity in the air, a feeling of energy being released; it seemed to Mpho a kind of catharsis after years of being forced to suppress any sort of political expression.

The SOYCO constitution was read aloud in its entirety; someone from the audience proposed that it be adopted. Then Popo called for the election of officers. This was merely a formality; the names had already been decided in the hours of discussion prior to the launch and circulated among the branches. Still, the proceedings were a jubilant affair. An elections official was proposed and confirmed; he, in turn, requested nominees for the various positions. When he announced the post of coordinator, someone shouted out Mpho's name. The elections official asked for a second; in response, the audience began singing, '*Mpho wethu, siyo mlandela!*' (Our Mpho, we will follow him!) Mpho was surrounded by a group of singing, clapping, dancing youths, who hoisted him onto their shoulders and carried him around the hall before depositing him on the stage. Mpho's friends were all elected to the executive in a similarly celebratory manner.

The meeting lasted throughout the afternoon and into the early evening. As the singing SOYCO members streamed out of the hall, they were met by police slinging tear gas at them; people dispersed hurriedly. Mpho and the other officers had to melt into the night through the back streets of the township. Racing through yards and jumping fences, Mpho felt as though he had just signed a ticket to detention. The hall had been crawling with informers; an hour after the meeting's end, the police at Protea station would surely have all the details. Oddly, Mpho did not dread the life he would now have to lead. He almost welcomed the risks after what had seemed an eternity of political dormancy; he felt energized. This time, he was entering the fray with more maturity. Mpho and his friends had discussed how their lives would change after SOYCO's launch and agreed on certain strategies: they would sleep in the same place for only two nights consecutively; they would not organize appointments more than twenty-four hours in advance (to make their movements harder to detect); they would stop seeing the people they routinely visited. For Mpho, that meant curbing a relationship he had recently begun with Hloyi Sekgothudi, a highly political and committed activist whose petite stature belied her steely nature. The interruption bothered him, but Hloyi, who was likewise involved in the burgeoning community-based organizations, understood. They still managed to arrange some intimate moments.

Mpho and the other SOYCO officers became intensely busy after SOYCO's launch. The group's task was to mobilize the residents of the township. At its weekly meeting, the president would inform members of the latest national political developments and workshops or campaigns that had been organized to address the issues. The meetings were not without risk. One activist who attended the early-evening sessions always departed before eight o'clock, which he called 'police time'. Like clockwork, at 7.50 the young man stood and made his way to the door, even if it meant interrupting a speaker or the completion of a vote. 'Can't you wait a minute?' the exasperated chairperson once asked him.

'No,' the youth answered over his shoulder, 'this is police time.' In fact, the SOYCO officers posted lookouts to signal the approach of security officers. But their warning system sometimes failed; the door was suddenly kicked in and the room flooded with police – usually at a few minutes past eight.

Mpho, as SOYCO coordinator, helped the branches to organize a variety of campaigns and programmes: stay-aways to protest against the detention of activists, which had continued unabated; workshops to teach the history of the ANC and tell the story of the 1976 uprising; football matches, whose advertisements always included political messages; music festivals. The intervals at such events provided the SOYCO officers with an opportunity to make speeches. They had one driving purpose in everything they said or published: to revive a consciousness of the ANC. This obviously required careful choreography. When, for instance, the SOYCO officers wanted to advertise a strike, they often printed two sets of pamphlets. The first spoke only of the impending action, giving the date and time; the second, which would be distributed with great discretion, read, 'Heed the ANC's call to stay away . . .' Mpho found the afternoon rush hour during the week the best time to dispense such literature, because he could blend into the crowd. Weekends, when few security police worked, also proved opportune.

SOYCO enjoyed considerable success. At the apex of its existence, the organization had almost a dozen branches in Soweto, with hundreds of card-carrying members. Its popularity was such that activists in other cities sought out the SOYCO executive to help to create similar youth congresses. Mpho and his comrades assisted in establishing branches in Alexandra township, to the north of Johannesburg, Port Elizabeth and East London in Cape province, and Pietersburg, in the northern part of the country. The leaders in the various locales embraced all the SOYCO trappings: the constitution, the pamphlets, the t-shirts and membership cards emblazoned in the ANC's colours. Mpho and his fellow officers simply changed the names on the paraphernalia they printed in Johannesburg. They travelled to the various cities, mostly at night to avoid the police, to deliver the things and organize the branches. Mpho stayed in each place for about a week, the time it took to prepare for the launch and for the event itself. He or another officer usually returned to advise the branch when its members embarked on a particular campaign.

Mpho had not felt such exhilaration since that morning on 16 June 1976, when Tsietsi and his followers marched into his schoolyard. But in the half dozen or so intervening years, Mpho, and the movement, had matured. He no longer limited his vision to a single issue, such as Afrikaans instruction. He and his fellow activists saw themselves as revolutionaries; now they wanted nothing less than freedom. Despite their radicalism, they were a more measured group than their 1976 predecessors. Mpho and the others had goals and strategies; after every anti-government campaign, they analysed what course to take next. They studied the events of 1976 to avoid its shortcomings. The comrades, many of whom had participated in the uprising, concluded that they erred in not organizing the entire country and in alienating workers and other adults. They resolved not to repeat those mistakes.

Their views were also tempered by encounters with veterans of Robben Island, the prison located on a desolate, forbidding bit of land in the South Atlantic Ocean off the coast of Cape Town. Nelson Mandela, and the others who had been given life sentences at the Rivonia Trial of the 1960s, were jailed there. Mpho found the older ex-prisoners a great source of inspiration and information. It was a pleasurable experience to hear them speak of the ANC's campaigns of the 1950s and 1960s; to talk with someone who knew Nelson Mandela, knew his philosophies and his ways, was itself an education. Mpho and his friends spent hours listening to the tales: they were young and impressionable and practically dizzy with everything that their elders had to impart. For the first time in his life as an activist, Mpho felt a connection with all those who had preceded him. Once, in the Eastern Cape, an old charwoman who worked in the white suburbs and had participated in the earlier ANC boycotts, urged the young people to continue their fight: 'Do it! Do it now, or you'll never do it again!' Everywhere he travelled, Mpho learned about how the previous generation had been involved in the anti-apartheid struggle – stories the government had sought to silence. The histories gave Mpho courage.

In contrast with 1976, Mpho did not feel isolated; the activism he promoted was not limited to Soweto. Disenfranchised people across the country were joining all manner of civic organizations. Mpho began to sense a kind of inexorable momentum: nothing could stop change in South Africa now; too many people were involved. The country seemed to be hurtling towards some sort of monumental confrontation. Years later, it would become clear that the government hastened its own downfall by packing the protagonists of the 1976 uprising off to prison on Robben Island, where they received the revolutionary education of a lifetime. The place had become a kind of finishing school, where the older comrades educated the next generation of convicted activists in the ways of the ANC. The prisoners surreptitiously conducted a wide range of courses in history, politics and economics and held heated debates on the subjects. In this way, many of the youngsters who went to prison after the 1976 uprising as committed Black Consciousness supporters were converted to the ANC credo of non-racialism. The students entered jail as youngsters – and departed as ANC leaders, ready to carry on in the name of their mentors.

What they did marked a decisive moment in the struggle against apartheid. The young leaders, along with a group of veterans, merged the organizations that had proliferated throughout the country, harnessing their energy and giving them a common direction. In August 1983 they formed a coalition of more than 500 community, church, youth, professional, workers' and sports organizations, known as the United Democratic Front. The alliance comprised the most expansive grouping of anti-government opponents in three decades. The leaders initially established the front to fight a proposed change to the constitution that would create three segregated chambers of Parliament: one for whites, one for Indians and one for 'coloureds', people of mixed race. Although the new laws now gave Indians and coloureds the right to elect their own national representatives, the white government could overrule their parliaments. The ostensible reforms excluded blacks; they would be allowed to vote only for local township councils.

Critics saw the moves as creating an aura of reform. They were a sop to concerned whites, a gesture to international condemnation of apartheid. In that respect, they succeeded: white South Africans overwhelmingly approved the measures in a referendum in November 1983. And the British and US governments voiced their support. Anti-apartheid activists condemned the tri-cameral system as an attempt to further divide South Africans of colour, thereby ensuring the continuation of white domination. The black township councils, lacking any funds and utterly beholden to the whims of the white government, were little more than shells. The UDF leaders embarked on a campaign to discredit the reforms. Their aim was to discourage blacks, coloureds and Indians from voting for representatives to their respective bodies in elections that were to be held during the coming year. They organized rallies, meetings, workshops and informational sessions throughout the country. In the process, the activists raised the political awareness of blacks as never before; 'conscientizing', they called it.

Once again, Mpho found himself clashing with the older comrades over a perceived reluctance to trumpet their ANC affiliation. SOYCO became an important UDF member in Soweto, the country's largest township; as SOYCO leaders, Mpho and several of his friends felt the UDF should openly adopt the Freedom Charter. The UDF would be the ANC in everything but name. The senior UDF activists demurred; as a coalition, it strove to attract as broad a spectrum of anti-government activists as possible. Some dissidents, such as those who still subscribed to the Black Consciousness movement, did not embrace the ANC's policies. (The UDF would become far bolder in promoting the ANC in later years.) Despite the differences within the alliance, the UDF proved successful in its immediate task of boycotting the elections: few Indians, coloureds or blacks voted.

And then the townships exploded. The eruption began in an area known as the Vaal Triangle, south of Johannesburg, as a protest against rent increases by the local town councils. The councillors had taken office despite the insignificant voter turnout; township residents saw them as little more than corrupt lackeys of the white government. They had no legitimacy to impose such hardships on the impoverished residents, who had already endured several similar increases. The councillors' use of deadly police force to try to quell the protests quickly escalated into virtual war: mobs attacked and killed several councillors, incinerating their lavish homes, setting fire to municipal buildings and shops, burning cars. The police killed dozens of blacks in response – which further inflamed the aggrieved people. Over the coming months, the violence would spread to all corners of the country. Township dwellers in obscure places, who had barely taken note of the students' uprising in 1976, went on murderous rampages against the authorities. The difference this time was the UDF. Under its guidance, blacks throughout South Africa had become a highly politicized group that spanned a wide philosophical and generational spectrum.

Now the focus of the UDF shifted from the tri-cameral parliament to local grievances. It adopted the issues that its affiliates, the community-based organizations, had championed. People protested against anything they associated with the government: poor education, high rents and rates, low wages, the presence of the security forces in the townships. They held marches, strikes and rallies almost daily throughout the country. The revolt was reinforced by a call from Oliver Tambo, the ANC president in Zambia, to make the townships 'ungovernable'. The anti-government demonstrations often turned violent, with the security forces firing into the crowds; the subsequent funerals of the martyred comrades themselves became political events, begetting more violence and more death.

Mpho saw the chaos as an opportune moment in which to reinvigorate a campaign demanding the release of Nelson Mandela. A Free Mandela Committee had been established in 1980 and joined the UDF after the latter's creation. When Mpho and a few of his SOYCO comrades attended a meeting as observers, they derided what they considered its timidity. 'You are armchair revolutionaries,' Mpho told its leaders. 'All you do is put out occasional statements to the press.' Mpho and his friends envisioned the campaign as something monumental. Their idea was to declare publicly the banned leader's name, to bring it back into people's consciousness, to make it a household word again. They wanted to call streets, areas, institutions after him. They wanted to hold meetings to prepare for his release. They wanted, in essence, to unban him by popular acclaim.

Leaders of the committee, and the UDF itself, were not enthusiastic; the plan was sure to get them banned or arrested. It would also scare off some of the more measured organizations within the UDF coalition. Mpho and his friends, once again, found themselves marked as firebrands. For Mpho, the argument about intensifying the campaign became a metaphor for all the disagreements he had with the UDF leadership. He wanted militancy, regardless of the consequences; they wanted moderation (by revolutionary standards) and longevity. Mpho and the others resolved the problem by starting their own

movement. The Release Mandela Campaign embodied everything that Mpho and his comrades demanded of the government. The eradication of apartheid meant the freeing of their
leaders from prison, unbanning their organizations, negotiating
with the ANC. The issues that other campaigns focused on,
those of rent, education, wages, employment, were obviously
important. But for Mpho, the ultimate question the government
had to address was when blacks would be allowed to vote. The
response could come only with Nelson Mandela's release.

Perhaps influenced by the wariness of their elders, Mpho and
his comrades took great care to keep the campaign legal. They
opened an office in Braamfontein, north of the city centre. The
activists resisted the desire to put the ANC leader's image on
their t-shirts or a quote from one of his speeches – both prohibited because he was a banned person – and instead designed
what Mpho considered the dullest shirt in history: the words
'Release Mandela Campaign' printed over a green background.
Their pamphlets were equally non-inflammatory. We want to
see Nelson Mandela walking the streets of Soweto hand-in-hand
with his wife, one such publication demanded. The posters
announcing a Release Mandela Campaign meeting were also
unremarkable, adorned only with the date, time, venue. Mpho
and his friends got veteran ANC activists to speak at UDF rallies
about the protests of the 1950s and 1960s; the orators used
carefully chosen code words to convey their message to the
audience.

This was the work Mpho and the others were seen to be
doing. But in the half-light before dawn, when the newspapers
were delivered to the downtown corners of Eloff and Commissioner streets, someone from the campaign would stuff the
editions of the *Sowetan*, the black daily, with ANC propaganda.
The activists pasted up posters bearing Mandela's face in the
middle of the night, next to those announcing a Release Mandela
meeting. They clandestinely distributed pamphlets from the
ANC that called on people to support the campaign. Winnie
Mandela professed delight at their activities. Mpho became
obsessed with the campaign; he felt he could not rest until it
achieved its goal.

Despite their attempts to avoid arrest, the activists still ran foul of the security police. Mpho was apprehended in Krugersdorp, north-west of Johannesburg, for distributing Release Mandela literature. He was badly beaten before being released; his face swelled horribly from the attack and he lost a molar on his lower jaw. He was arrested briefly in the Bantustans of Ciskei and Venda for similar pursuits. Mpho greatly feared the police in the rural areas and tribal 'homelands'. They were a terrible lot: far from the centre of power and criticism, lacking in sophistication, the security officers in those places felt few constraints. One of the Ciskei officers became so enraged during an interrogation that he hit Mpho with a table.

Still, it seemed to Mpho that the security forces had changed their tactics somewhat in the years since 1976. They still employed brute force in confronting mass protesters. But the police in urban areas, with obvious direction from the government, appeared to be more concerned about the country's image abroad; they did not want their practices to attract international scrutiny – and condemnation. Now they seemed to employ more covert tactics. Mpho was acutely aware of attempts by the security forces to infiltrate organizations such as SOYCO and the Release Mandela Campaign, apparently to gather information that could be used in court cases against detained activists. He and his comrades were constantly trying to detect spies, with varying degrees of success. One girl told them that after every Wednesday-night meeting of SOYCO, the police intercepted her three blocks away and interrogated her as to the organization's intentions.

The security forces often tried to recruit the activists' girl-friends as informers. They pursued Hloyi tenaciously once they understood that she was close to Mpho. One black policeman proposed having an affair and courted her with flowers and fruit. Others were more direct, offering money for information about Mpho and SOYCO. One night, while Mpho was visiting Hloyi at her home, a group of security officers appeared. Mpho thought they had come to arrest him, particularly when they escorted him outside; in fact, they were trying to distract Mpho so they could talk to Hloyi. A few policemen remained indoors, trying to cajole her into becoming an informer and sticking money into her jacket pocket. Hloyi found it easy to resist their entreaties; she was a hardened activist with an acid tongue that she used freely against policemen and other representatives of authority. (The security forces' hidden work was generally not so comic. The full extent of their concealed activities would later come to light, including the existence of police 'counter-insurgency units', or death squads, which were involved in assassination, arson, bombing and kidnapping.)

The violence in the townships, and the ruthless government response, continued unabated throughout the first half of 1985. In March, the police opened fire on mourners at a funeral gathering in Langa in the Eastern Cape, killing twenty people and wounding twenty-seven others – the worst massacre in South Africa since Sharpeville in 1960. (And committed, ironically, on the 25th anniversary of those shootings.) The country was in a state of civil war. By now, Mpho was living underground; he could not attend SOYCO or UDF meetings for fear of encountering the security forces that were virtually occupying the townships. Rumour had it that the police were trying to piece together a court case against the SOYCO founders. Mpho found it increasing difficult to keep abreast of those who had been arrested, fled the country, disappeared. Most nights he slept in Johannesburg. Once in the white city, as he called it, Mpho felt relatively safe; the police usually did not come looking for blacks there. Mpho often stayed with Mark Swilling, his friend from his Moral Rearmament days, in Mayfair, to the city's west.

As the months progressed, Mpho knew the unrest could not continue for much longer without provoking a drastic government reaction. Activists talked of an impending mass detention. Determined not to be caught, Mpho became even more cautious: he began staying indoors during the day, going outside only after nightfall. Thus he was at home in Soweto, watching television on the little black-and-white set that Joseph and Nomkhitha had rented, when the government declared a state of emergency in mid-July. P.W. Botha, the country's president, announced the details of the declaration, wagging a finger in his peculiarly obdurate manner to underscore his speech; Mpho felt as though the president were pointing directly at him. (The emergency was not nearly as draconian as anticipated. Although it allowed for the unrestricted detention and interrogation of suspects, the measure applied to only thirty-six of South Africa's 300 magisterial districts; the government did not wish to appear too heavy-handed.)

The government's declaration effectively paralysed the opposition groups. It stripped the leaders of the ability to meet and organize anti-government activities. It also deprived them of most means of communication; with the newspapers now severely restricted in what they could report, no one knew what was happening. Mpho panicked. He had no idea what had become of his friends or of other activists, if they had gone underground or been arrested. He feared the government would decimate the leadership of the anti-apartheid movement in the same way it did after the Rivonia trial in the 1960s, thus imposing a similar quiescence for years. There was one difference, however, between now and then: the degree of popular participation. Everyone was involved now. Theirs had become a mass movement; protests of some sort would persist even if the leadership were jailed. Mpho took comfort from the idea that alternative structures, unions and the like, would continue the struggle.

Over the next several days, Mpho furtively tried to make contact with other activists. He found only one of his friends, Tsheko Tsehlana, who turned up in Mayfair at the appointed time for the weekly meeting. The two young men decided to return to the township. They were hearing stories of the arrests of comrades who had travelled by bus to the Eastern Cape to attend the funeral of a beloved UDF organizer, Matthew Goniwe. (His charred and mutilated body, along with those of three colleagues, had been found not far from his abandoned car on a road near Port Elizabeth; a police death squad would later be shown to be responsible.) Mpho was desperate to find out if Hloyi had been one of those arrested on the bus. But the heavy police presence in Soweto forced him to remain indoors.

Mpho slipped back to Mark's house in Mayfair after a few

days. The police seemed to be arresting every activist in the township, pulling people out of their homes at all hours of the day and night. Mpho did not know who was left on the outside; he had no way of contacting anyone. One night, while walking in Braamfontein, Mpho and Tsheko passed Frank Chikane on the street. The UDF leader, a clergyman, was dressed in workmen's clothes, a hat pulled low over his brow; he looked like a common labourer or thug. Mpho had gone halfway down the block when he realized whom he had just seen. At that moment, Frank called Mpho's name softly and hurried off into the dark. Mpho followed him at a distance for a mile or so to a house in Hillbrow. Tsheko trailed Mpho. Once inside the building, Frank informed them of the latest arrests. Everyone has gone underground, he warned the young men, use caution when you move about town.

Unable to do anything for fear of being apprehended, Mpho decided to leave Soweto for a while. He arranged to travel with a friend to Bloemfontein in the Orange Free State. The night before his journey, Mpho returned home to pack a bag. It was close to midnight when he let himself in the door; everyone in the house was asleep. He had sent word to his parents that he would be returning home to gather some clothes before leaving Soweto. Nomkhitha had left food for him on the stove. While he was eating, Mpho suddenly heard a sickeningly familiar pounding on the windows and doors. He calmly walked into his parents' bedroom and woke up Joseph. 'They're here,' Mpho said.

'What do you mean, they're here?' Joseph demanded grumpily.

'The police.'

By now, his siblings were awake, sleepy and scared by the commotion. Joseph opened the front door, and the living room was filled with plainclothes men, brandishing guns and torches. *Daar is hy*, one of them said in Afrikaans, there he is. The policeman pointed at Mpho. 'Pack some clothes,' he ordered. 'You're coming with us.' The officer told the others to search the house. Mpho accompanied them as they examined the rooms, confident they would not discover anything incriminating. He had often reminded his family not to keep any anti-government material, not even a pamphlet, in the house. As Mpho expected, the police found nothing – until they spied his teenaged brother China, who was wearing a UDF t-shirt as pyjamas. The officers decided to arrest him, too.

As always, the process terrified Mpho: the guns, the armoured vehicles standing outside the house, the gloating policemen hurling taunts at him. The officer pushed Mpho and China onto the floor of a van, whose seats were filled with other people. China was shaking with fear. Mpho tried to reassure his brother that the police had no reason to hold him; he would soon be released. His efforts to soothe his brother were thwarted by a fellow detainee, who kept whispering in Sotho: Where are they taking us? Where are they taking us?

CHAPTER FIFTEEN

Tshepiso

Over the next several months, the government used the powers it assumed under the state of emergency to detain, by its own count, almost 8,000 people. (Groups that monitored such things estimated that the numbers were actually far greater.) Many prominent leaders of the United Democratic Front were among those arrested; they were to be tried for treason. The government seemed bent on incapacitating the UDF organizations by removing the leadership, much as it had done to the ANC in the 1960s. The strategy fitted with the Nationalists' view that 'agitators', who were part of a 'revolutionary alliance' comprised of the ANC, the South African Communist Party and trade unions, were causing the unrest in the townships. Render the principal culprits ineffective, so the thinking went, and peace would return to black areas.

Perhaps blinded by their belief in apartheid's ultimate ascendancy, the Nationalist authorities could fathom neither the depth nor the tenacity of the uprising. This was a revolt that had seized the imagination of all manner of blacks – and liberal whites – in a way that no previous protest, including that of 1976, ever did. Other activists rose up to take the places of their jailed leaders. They broadened the consumer boycotts and student strikes and the demonstrations against local councillors in an attempt to end the policies of apartheid. Youths continued to go on rampages, despite the presence of massive numbers of police and even army patrols in the townships. Three or four activists died every day in the violence. Still more arose to replace the fallen comrades.

* * *

Tshepiso counted among those millions of young blacks swept up in the political events. He was, by now, almost eighteen years old and studying for his matriculation examinations. His position as the seventh of the thirteen Mashinini children poised him between his politically active older siblings and the somewhat indifferent younger ones. Tshepiso did not outwardly possess the disposition of an activist. He was bookish and applied himself with great seriousness to his studies; he always ranked among the top five in his class of seventy or so students. (Joseph, who took much pride in his accomplishments, kept all of his reports.) Tshepiso's determination to go to university accounted for his dedication to learning. For as long as he could remember, he had held to the belief that one needed an education to succeed in life; his teachers, as well as Nomkhitha, drummed the credo into him. Tshepiso did not know what profession he would pursue, only that he wanted a university education and the security of a good job.

His religiosity also seemed to preclude political activism. After attending a course, studying the Bible and passing an examination, Tshepiso was confirmed, much to Joseph's joy, as a fully-fledged member of their Methodist church. After that, he began singing with the choir as a tenor. On Sunday mornings, he would get up early, bathe, dress in his best clothes and walk across the field opposite his house, gown in one hand, hymnal in the other. When he arrived at the church, Tshepiso would don his gown, then walk slowly through the sanctuary to the front to take his place among the choir members. There they led the rest of the congregation in singing hymns. Those few hours were transcendent, blotting out, however temporarily, the hardships of his life in the township. On one memorable Sunday, none of the other tenors appeared, and Tshepiso had to bellow out their part on his own. The accomplishment made him feel exceptionally proud.

But as the country descended into turmoil, Tshepiso found it increasingly difficult to accept the anti-political stance of his pastor. His discomfort reached a climax when the minister invited an entire police squad to attend a service. Tshepiso entered the church to find one side of the sanctuary filled with security men. He was offended by their presence, these fellow blacks who, at the bidding of their government bosses, had tortured and killed people in the townships. Tshepiso took his seat among the choir in a state of agitation. By the time the sermon began, he had decided what he must do: in the middle of the clergyman's fiery oratory, Tshepiso rose with great deliberation and walked out the church door, never to return.

Through Mpho, Tshepiso also became involved with Moral Rearmament, the Christian organization that linked social issues to personal morality and spirituality. He attended three of the organization's youth camps: two in the Karoo, the vast, desert-like plateau that extends across the south-central part of Cape province; and one near Stellenbosch, inland from Cape Town. Tshepiso, who had rarely left Soweto, revelled in the experience: the rigours of living in the bush, climbing mountains, meeting 'coloured' and white youths. Upon awakening each morning in the camp, Tshepiso was required to have what was called 'quiet time'. The Moral Rearmament adherents believed that if you could clear your mind of unclean, impure thoughts, God would tell you what He wanted you to do that day. Every camper had a little note pad and pen by his bedside and was supposed to copy down these thoughts before arising. It was an appealing discipline to Tshepiso; he believed it a good thing to take time to reflect on the universe and how to spend the day. But he was somewhat sceptical that it was God's voice, and not his own, dominating his ruminations. His uncertainty about the exercise only increased at the sessions where everyone read his ostensible communications aloud: it seemed to him that most people attributed to divine revelation things they were otherwise too inhibited to say.

Tshepiso thought the group's moral standards – absolute honesty, purity, unselfishness and love – admirable. No one, he believed, could practise them fully; they were simply goals to try to achieve. But he disliked the majority of the group's members as individuals. Tshepiso found them too conservative, too fixated on private morality, too apt to dismiss the country's urgent problems. They avoided anything that was directly and overtly political. Tshepiso could not talk with the others about the horrific things that had happened to him in Soweto. They acted as though they were living in a different world, that these incidents did not occur just down the road. The members' seeming aversion to reality notwithstanding, Tshepiso was content to remain engaged with the organization as long as he got the occasional trip to the countryside.

Thus, his interest was piqued when Kim Beazley and David Mills from the Australian branch of Moral Rearmament came to South Africa, speaking of a special course. The training session, which was held annually in Australia, was intended to teach leadership skills to an elite group of young adherents. Tshepiso was shown a leaflet on the course and urged to apply. He found the proposal attractive: not only would it allow him to escape the oppression of South Africa, but it marked him as a potential leader. Tshepiso was flattered. The leaflet's description did not espouse the more unpalatable of the organization's tenets; and so Tshepiso applied for the course.

In the meantime, he felt himself drawn inexorably to politics. Since 1976 and the involvement of his brothers in that uprising, Tshepiso had been conscious of the terrible inequities in his country. He grew up believing that when things changed, Rocks, Tsietsi and Dee would return home; he therefore had a duty to try to hasten those transformations. Besides, he thought the UDF a brilliant vehicle that managed to bring together disparate opponents of the government and harness their energy into a formidable force. The UDF's pull was irresistible. Everywhere he looked, Tshepiso saw UDF posters and pamphlets and people wearing the organization's distinctive orange-yellow t-shirts with the red-and-black lettering: UDF Unites, Apartheid Divides. Mpho, before he was arrested, provided Tshepiso's introduction into anti-government activities. Tshepiso accompanied him to meetings of various UDF groups; once again, an older Mashinini was leading a younger sibling into politics.

Tshepiso found the student and youth movements particularly appealing. He became close friends with youths who led branches of the Congress of South African Students in their respective institutions. Their t-shirt, in his opinion, was inspirational. It consisted of a white background with two black faces in the shape of South Africa, punctuated by the group's motto: Each One Teach One. Tshepiso thought it the most powerful slogan he had ever heard. It succinctly captured the essence of the students' contention that what little educational opportunity had existed in the townships now was destroyed; how could they attend class when so many schools were being raided by the security forces? The only way to learn was through other means. Tshepiso wore the garment with pride, albeit some trepidation. One could be arrested and tortured for displaying certain shirts, which was why wearing them figured so prominently in the consciousness of the young comrades. When they attended political funerals, they no longer came clad in sombre, dignified clothes; they wore the t-shirt of the fallen comrade or their particular organization. It made the youths feel daring and defiant.

Under the tutelage of his friends, Tshepiso began holding informal COSAS meetings at his school, Mafori-Mphahlele, one of the township's most conservative and apolitical. He did not create an official COSAS branch; he simply invited other interested students to come together after classes finished for the day to discuss various issues. Tshepiso and his comrades supported campaigns to abolish the prefect system, to put an end to corporal punishment and to improve the quality of education. The group grew rapidly. At COSAS rallies, Tshepiso would often see a massive, solid block of green, the colour of his school's tunic, among the swirl of hues that were the uniforms of other institutions.

Tshepiso became deeply involved in the Soweto Youth Congress. Mpho's role in the organization was one reason for him to join the group, but the beauty of SOYCO's membership card motivated Tshepiso equally. The rectangularly shaped document had the SOYCO logo printed on the outside; unfolded, it spelled out the organization's aims and name of the holder's branch. Tshepiso delighted in the fact that the card fitted perfectly in his wallet. It was almost worth becoming a member simply to possess such a thing. SOYCO's activities and campaigns also proved compelling: the group held seminars to analyse the country's political situation, it arranged funerals for fallen comrades, and it formed street committees as alternatives to the discredited local councils.

The street committees had their origins in a scheme designed by Nelson Mandela in the 1950s known as the Mandela, or M-, Plan. The idea was to create a contingency structure that would allow the ANC to continue to operate even if it were banned. Under the M-Plan, the township was divided into cells, consisting of approximately ten houses on a street; a steward, who would personally know every family in his domain, headed up each cell. Several streets constituted a zone, which had its chief steward. The chief steward, in turn, reported to the secretariat of the local ANC branch. In this way, the organization could always mobilize its members, even if it were outlawed from making statements in the press or calling public meetings. The ANC only implemented the plan piecemeal, but it was never forgotten and acquired a kind of mythical aura as its details were passed from one generation to the next. In adapting the programme as a way to organize the townships after they had become 'ungovernable', the UDF activists felt they were linking their struggle with the ANC's past attempts at resistance.

Tshepiso had various duties as a member of a street committee, from helping to organize demonstrations against local councillors to thinking up ways to improve the area. He spent one afternoon digging the garden of a pensioner who lived alone and planting it with vegetables. His idea was to encourage her, and her inquisitive neighbours who observed the process over the communal fence with loudly voiced commentaries, to be self-sufficient and fully use what little space they had. To keep the peace, he and the other activists convened a 'people's court', to which residents could bring complaints about transgressors. The accused, if he could be found, was forced to appear before the tribunal and put through a trial of sorts by the youths; a guilty verdict meant the imposition of a range of punishments including, as meted out by some street committees, whipping with a rubber baton.

Because of his involvement, Tshepiso developed close relationships with many of Mpho's activist friends. They spent hours discussing politics with him. Tshepiso felt honoured that these young men, who held important positions in their organizations, paid him any heed; yet he could not rid himself of doubts about their motives. Were they including him in their inner circle because of his individual worth – or because of his surname? Years had passed since 1976; yet another generation of Mashininis struggled with the implications of Tsietsi's legacy.

Tshepiso was devoting so much of his existence to political activities that he began to fear he would fail his matriculation examinations. Panicking, he tried to set aside time each day to study. He found the majority of his subjects – English, Afrikaans, Sotho, biology – relatively easy to master; mathematics and physics were another matter. That the teacher who taught the courses vanished at the beginning of Tshepiso's last term only exacerbated his difficulties. Tshepiso did not know whether the instructor resigned or was arrested or went underground; he never learned of the man's fate. But without proper instruction, Tshepiso understood that he could not succeed. Anticipating his failure did little to assuage his disappointment when he received the expected results; he desperately wanted to go to university.

Thus, when Tshepiso resumed his studies at the start of the new school year, he replaced mathematics and physics with business and history – courses he could readily teach himself were the instructor to disappear later. Even in those classes with teachers, the lessons were not particularly illuminating. Tshepiso's school, like all institutions in the townships, suffered from a paucity of books and pedagogical materials; Tshepiso often had to share one text with nine other youngsters. Worse still, the security forces that now patrolled the townships in an attempt to restore calm launched frequent raids on schools. Tshepiso experienced several such disruptions: policemen and military troops would deploy throughout his building, sitting in the rooms with their guns and Alsatian dogs. The invasions terrified the youngsters, who cowered in corners and were unable to continue with their studies. Once, Tshepiso remained defiantly in his seat at the front of the room when a solider appeared in the doorway; he thought the other students would follow his lead. Then Tshepiso glanced behind him, only to see all the desks empty and his fellow pupils squeezed against a far wall in fear. This is it, Tshepiso thought, this chap is going to fuck with me. Instead of shooting Tshepiso, the soldier launched into a lecture in English about the perils of becoming involved in politics. Then he departed.

(During a similar raid at Morris Issacson High School up the road from the Mashininis' home, Tshepiso saw scores of screaming youths run from the building. His curiosity was aroused as they raced through the field opposite his house. He and some friends crossed the road and climbed up the 'mountain', the boulder formation where he had played as a child, to get a better view. At that moment an armoured personnel carrier, a Casspir, happened by; the soldiers inside saw Tshepiso and the others and eased the cumbersome vehicle onto the open stretch of land to chase them. The youths ran in the opposite direction. The soldiers began shooting at them with large rubber bullets; one grazed Tshepiso's head as he ran, hit a rock in front of him and bounced onto the ground. Tshepiso bent down to grab it. The bullet was stingingly hot; he dropped it immediately, only to pick it up again and continue sprinting. Tshepiso wanted the small missile: he had heard them described but had never seen one for himself. Later he would learn that a boy, hit by the same type of bullet, died instantly on that day.)

Tshepiso decided he would have to seek out alternative sources of instruction if he were going to pass his examinations this time. He began attending a Saturday school in Bosmont, a 'coloured' township near Soweto, that was funded by the German government. There Tshepiso took courses intended to help students master their matriculation curriculum. He and some like-minded friends in the neighbourhood organized an after-hours study session; much as Tshepiso's older brothers had done, they wandered over to Morris Issacson after supper, appropriated an empty room and spent the night quizzing each other. Tshepiso also took in the occasional seminar on a specific examination subject, given by students at the University of the Witwatersrand in Johannesburg as a way of helping township youths.

At times Tshepiso found it difficult to maintain his tenacity of purpose. Activists initiated sporadic boycotts of schools in Soweto; Tshepiso came under great pressure from many of his fellow comrades, whose slogan of 'liberation now, education later' seemed to question his commitment to the uprising. Tshepiso often felt torn between two life-long dreams. The headiness of the uprising, the excitement of participating in perhaps the most serious challenge ever to the racist government, sometimes proved overpowering. Tshepiso had been too young in 1976 to be any more than a bystander in that revolt; now it was his turn.

He became a promoter of consumer boycotts. Tshepiso traversed the township, distributing pamphlets at shops, taxi ranks and railway stations that urged people to boycott white-owned businesses. The UDF hoped that strangling such enterprises, which depended overwhelmingly on black buyers, would put pressure on the central government to meet its demands. Similar campaigns had been launched in townships throughout the country; the refusal by blacks to patronise white stores in Port Elizabeth, for instance, would cause more than 300 businesses to go bankrupt. Some activists enforced the boycott with what Tshepiso considered excessive zeal. The comrades would search the bundles of township residents returning from town; those found to have made purchases were punished by having their boxes of soap powder poured into the street. Others were made to drink the bottles of cooking oil they had bought. Tshepiso abhorred such tactics; he believed people should be convinced of the boycott's importance by means of persuasion.

To Tshepiso, the funerals for those killed by the security forces revealed the uprising's most noble tendencies. All manner of people came together to make arrangements for the night vigils, organize transport, choreograph the various participants. The ceremonies took on an almost ritualized sameness: the thousands, sometimes tens of thousands, of mourners who filled the sports stadiums; the fiery oratory of the speakers; the angry chants and political slogans the listeners shouted in response; the ineffably sweet melodies of freedom songs the mourners sang, borne heavenward on the wind. (And the sickeningly inevitable clash between the security forces and the participants as they departed the proceedings that resulted in more deaths and more funerals.) Here was strength, determination and unity among his people, as Tshepiso had never experienced. He had no illusions that such displays of 'ungovernability' alone would force the regime to recognize their demands. Nor would black consumer boycotts bring the government to its knees. But Tshepiso sensed that each action chipped away at the structure that was apartheid. Taken together, along with the revolt's other campaigns throughout the country and the work of the ANC in exile, they would eventually succeed.

The increasing inclination of other countries to impose economic sanctions on South Africa – which the conservative administrations in the UK and US would resist until the late 1980s – also encouraged Tshepiso. After decades of seeming indifference, the world was finally taking note of apartheid's horrors. Tshepiso and his friends considered the sanctions matter a serious thing, if only because the Nationalist government opposed it so vehemently. Tshepiso awoke one morning to find anti-sanctions graffiti sprayed on walls around Soweto. Everyone knew it could not be township graffiti; the comrades did not possess spray paint. They did their lettering by hand. This was clearly the work of the Nationalists, whose spokesmen insisted that sanctions would hurt blacks more than the government. Tshepiso found the argument amusing; blacks could hardly suffer more than they already did.

As the uprising turned into a mass-based movement, Tshepiso was amazed to observe residents in the township who remained aloof. They appeared content to continue with their lives as always, arising every morning to be abused by their employers at work, endure an unspeakable journey home in a jammed minibus or train, be denied their rights as full citizens. People all around them, who had never participated in a single political act, were getting swept up in the excitement of the moment. Perhaps those who refused to take part were still too frightened of the terrible consequences of opposing apartheid; perhaps they had simply become inured to their pain.

Tshepiso counted his father among this group. For that reason, he kept his political activities from Joseph. When

Tshepiso returned home late from a rally, he would jump the garden fence – the gate was locked at night – and softly knock on the window of the room where the children slept. One of his siblings eventually admitted him to the house. One night, just as he had hopped over the fence, the front door flew open unbidden. There stood Joseph, practically shaking with rage. 'Where have you been?' he demanded.

'At a meeting,' Tshepiso replied meekly.

'What kind of meeting?'

'A student meeting.'

'What kind of student meeting?'

Tshepiso did not answer. His silence further enraged his father. 'So now you are getting involved in student politics?' Joseph shouted. 'You know where all this will lead! Do you want to end up in jail or in exile? I forbid you to get involved. I will not lose another son to politics!' With that, Joseph turned on his heel and stomped off to his bedroom. Tshepiso sank into a chair in the darkened lounge. He understood his father's fears, given everything that the family had endured. But Tshepiso would not renounce his political activities. It was one thing for Joseph, a middle-aged man with a family to support, to refrain from participating; he could not expect his children to follow suit.

At the other end of the spectrum, in Tshepiso's view, were those people who threw in their lot with the activists but did not fully comprehend what was happening; Tshepiso thought of them as politically unsound. He and his friends spent countless afternoons reading about the history of the anti-apartheid struggle, dissecting past tactics, discussing current strategies. But the dilettantes, as Tshepiso saw them, were just angry and bored and did not know how to focus their energy. They called themselves activists when they were clueless as to the word's true meaning. To be a comrade was not an overnight achievement; one had to be politically disciplined, inducted into the struggle, in possession of a mission. Tshepiso tolerated them because they had at least made a conscious decision to become involved. But they were an embarrassment at times, bringing shame to the image of the comrade within the black community. These youths used the uprising as an excuse to dispense with the ordinary details of life: school, studies, parental authority. In Tshepiso's opinion, they alienated the township's more conservative element, the very people the UDF sought to include.

'Necklacing' represented the worst of the excesses committed in the name of the uprising. This was a particularly gruesome form of mob justice, reserved for those thought to be government collaborators, informers and black policemen. The executioners would force a car tyre over the head and around the arms of the suspect, drench it in petrol, then set it alight. Immobilized, the victim burned to death. Tshepiso found the practice disgusting and horrifying; he could not fathom making anyone, not even those who cooperated with the regime, suffer in such a manner. The practice left everyone vulnerable. Tshepiso feared that anyone bearing a grudge could accuse him, however falsely, of misconduct, and that he would be set alight without a chance to prove his innocence. Not that black councillors and their kind did not deserve to die. Tshepiso believed Umkhonto assassins should shoot them; this was war, after all.

The government's state-of-emergency declaration unwittingly did more to encourage enlistment in the UDF, in Tshepiso's view, than any of the organization's recruiting campaigns. Because the authorities cast such a wide and indiscriminate net, they inadvertently 'conscientized' a range of people who had little previous connection with the revolt. Some of Tshepiso's school friends, apolitical youths who would never dream of becoming activists, were detained and beaten by the security forces. The young men joined the rebellion after their release; why suffer at the hands of the police for nothing?

Tshepiso was staying at his cousin's house in the Pimville section of Soweto when he heard that Mpho had been arrested. The police who took Mpho away had a list of people they were seeking that included Tshepiso's name; the information terrified Tshepiso. He had heard the stories about people being whipped in detention, given electric shocks, made to stand on one leg for hours. He saw the scars on friends who came out of prison. Mpho had told him of his own experiences of torture, and

Tshepiso admired him greatly for having survived the ordeal. He did not think he had the inner strength required to emerge intact from jail. Determined to avoid arrest, Tshepiso began a kind of underground existence.

He remained at his cousin's house in Pimville. Every few days, Tshepiso surreptitiously made his way to school at mid-morning, crawled through a hole in the fence and summoned one of his friends. 'Have the police been here looking for me?' he asked anxiously. Receiving a negative reply, Tshepiso nonetheless assumed an air of heightened alert. 'I can't stay,' he whispered, anxiously scanning the horizon. 'I've got to get out of here, got to keep moving.' Then he navigated a circuitous route to his home, crept inside for a change of clothing and melted back into the township. Despite his fear, Tshepiso relished the adventure of living a hidden life; being pursued by the police made him feel like an important fugitive.

When it became clear after several days that the security forces were not actively seeking him, Tshepiso began to relax. He was obviously not significant enough to warrant serious pursuit – a realization that was, at once, reassuring and slightly disappointing. In the meantime, the school year was progressing. Tshepiso now had to attempt to study for his examinations in the midst of complete chaos: the state of emergency had banned COSAS, the student organization, outright; students had stopped attending classes in protest; all teaching was disrupted. Tshepiso had only his supplemental courses to prepare him for the tests. At one such place of instruction, Tshepiso encountered a group of wealthy whites that were offering their homes as retreats to township students. A young couple, Helen and Tony Duigan, invited Tshepiso to live with them; he would have a place where he could study in peace. Faced with having to decide between education and activism, Tshepiso chose the former: this time, he would avail himself of every opportunity to matriculate successfully.

Tshepiso went to stay with the Duigan family near Bryanston, north of Johannesburg. Tony worked for the South African Broadcasting Corporation; Helen was a schoolteacher. They lived on about ten acres of what was known as a small-holding, a kind of suburban farm. The bucolic setting included a stream, one cow, several dogs. Although the couple were members of Moral Rearmament, they did not provide Tshepiso with shelter as part of an organized programme; they simply wanted to do something to help Soweto's youngsters. Tshepiso, who immediately liked the couple, thought them relatively enlightened. (For instance, they made one of their three young children share a bedroom with him.)

He quickly settled into a routine, rising each morning with the children, eating breakfast, then immersing himself in his books. He was given a small wooden cabin on the edge of the property in which to study; he stayed there until the children, Francois, Leon and Murray, came home from school. They played together for a while, chasing one another across the garden or kicking a football. Then Tshepiso returned to his studies until supper. In the evening, he relaxed with the family. Although he was not required to do so, Tshepiso milked the cow every day. He, the township boy who had never possessed anything more feral than a dog, found the process exhilarating.

Tshepiso remained with the family for about two months. Nomkhitha and Joseph, delighted that their son was studying in a safe place, visited him a couple of times. He dismissed the occasional feeling of guilt at having left his comrades and the township to pursue something utterly personal; this was something he simply had to do. The question of whether to sit for his examinations was more troublesome. He would be breaking the boycott, and betraying his fellow activists, by taking the tests. Yet Tshepiso believed that had COSAS not been banned, its leaders would have ordered students to return to their classes and continue with their courses. After much deliberation, Tshepiso did take his matriculation examinations, which his hosts helped to organize; he was afraid the opportunity would elude him if he did not seize it now. Besides, he could better serve the struggle against apartheid as an educated man.

Around this time Tshepiso received word that he had been selected for the Moral Rearmament leadership-training course. Sam Pono, the black MRA member who had befriended Mpho during his involvement with the group, thought Tshepiso a brilliant and gifted student. The organization would pay for him to go to Australia. Tshepiso could not believe his good fortune. Here was a chance to leave South Africa, to see another part of the world, in a manner he would never have imagined. He told his parents he was going.

He immediately set about organizing the proper documents. Obtaining a passport was relatively simple: Tshepiso filled in the necessary forms at the Department of Home Affairs. Then he applied for a visa from the Australian government. Tshepiso had to provide a medical certificate stating that he was in good health – easily done – and a declaration from the police confirming that he was not a criminal. Procuring the latter filled him with dread; what if he were still wanted by the authorities? With great trepidation, Tshepiso went to a police station in Pretoria, close to the Australian Embassy. He told the duty officer what he needed and was sent to a room at the back of the building. There he gave a policeman his particulars, then sat down to wait. From here, Tshepiso thought, I'm going straight to a cell. When he was sent to another room for finger-printing, Tshepiso could not stop his hand from shaking. 'What's the matter with you?' the officer demanded, forcing Tshepiso's finger on the ink pad, then onto paper. 'Relax!' Tshepiso waited for what seemed like an eternity. When a policeman finally handed him his certificate, Tshepiso bolted out of the station and sprinted to the Australian Embassy to present his documents.

On the day of his departure, Tshepiso's home was crowded with chattering friends and relatives, many of whom had travelled long distances to bid him goodbye. Tshepiso found it difficult to succumb to the excitement. He was convinced that somewhere along the way, the police would stop him. Tshepiso nervously presented his ticket and luggage to the agent at the airline counter at Jan Smuts Airport and received his boarding pass in return. He hugged everyone in the long line of well-wishers who had accompanied the family to the airport. Nomkhitha held him an extra second or two before he joined the queue at passport control; yet another son was leaving her. Unlike the others, however, she felt sanguine about his journey.

Tshepiso grew increasingly agitated as he waited to show his documents to the immigration authorities. This is where all the excitement is going to end, he thought, presenting his passport to an official when it was his turn. The officer studied the passport, looked up at Tshepiso, studied the passport again, then peered closely at Tshepiso. Tshepiso felt rivulets of sweat beginning to course down his back. Any moment now, the officer would pick up a telephone, whisper into the receiver – and the place would be swarming with police. The officer stamped the passport and handed it back to Tshepiso. 'Have a nice trip!' he said.

Tshepiso stumbled into the departure hall and slumped into a chair. An announcer asked the passengers travelling to Perth and Sydney on the South African Airways flight to board the plane. Tshepiso was shown to his seat. He buckled the safety belt and waited for someone to tell him to leave the aircraft, he was being arrested. Throughout the closing of the doors, the announcements, the safety demonstrations, Tshepiso gripped the armrests of his chair; he could not relax. As the aeroplane began taxiing to the runway, Tshepiso cocked his ear for the pilot's voice over the intercom informing passengers that the flight was being recalled to the gate. The plane hesitated for a moment, then with a shudder gathered speed, roared down the runway and left the ground. They were airborne. Tshepiso was free.

CHAPTER SIXTEEN

Dee

Dee, sitting in the ANC camp in Tanzania, listened elatedly to radio accounts of the uprising in the townships. After all the years of quiescence that followed the 1976 revolt, this was an astonishing thing. He could not have imagined that so many political leaders and organizations would emerge to challenge the South African government. That the world was finally paying attention to the apartheid regime and imposing sanctions against it also heartened Dee. Still, he had few illusions about being able to go home any time soon; the reports of killings and wholesale detentions testified to the state's undiminished might.

At times Dee worried about his family in Soweto. He generally tried not to think about them; the nearly ten years in exile had taught him the perils of those types of emotional excursions. But hearing the horrifying descriptions of deaths by 'necklacing', Dee feared for his brothers' safety. He hoped, and sometimes prayed, that they were not involved in such matters. He listened to every foreign radio broadcast he could to glean information. The new arrivals to the camp were another good source of news: fresh from the townships, many having narrowly escaped capture by the security forces, the young men and women provided recent details of the revolt. Dee listened closely to the briefings they gave at assembly. The speakers, so full of politics and revolution, amused him. You're in exile now, he wanted to say to them. Forget all your bravado about overthrowing the state; tomorrow you're going to be cleaning latrines.

His fascination with the uprising notwithstanding, Dee was

also consumed with studying for his matriculation examinations. The impending tests made him terribly nervous; after his failure in Cairo and the year-long suspension from school in Mazimbu, he could not endure another disappointment. He was anxious to get on with his life. At the appointed time, Dee travelled to Dar es Salaam, the capital, to sit for the week-long examinations with Tanzanian high school pupils. After each test, Dee hovered around the little knots of chattering students, eavesdropping on their post-mortem of the questions; he discerned that he had not done as well as the Tanzanians. Dee knew he could not compete with them. He took comfort in the fact that he had even come this far. Merely passing his subjects – English, mathematics, biology, agricultural and two ANC-mandated topics, development studies and history – would be victory enough.

When Dee learned that he had indeed passed, his triumph quickly dissolved into an anxiety of another sort: what would he do now? Dee knew that he wanted to study radio broadcasting. It was a revelation that had come to him gradually over the years, listening to the BBC and VOA and developing an interest in politics. But the ANC was always struggling to find places for their students to continue their education abroad. Aware that he would have to go where the ANC could send him, Dee fervently hoped for any place other than the Soviet Union. Dee was friendly with one young woman who had gone to Russia to learn photojournalism; during her five years there, she practised only once with a camera – for one day.

Dee wanted to attend an institution in Dar es Salaam, the Tanzanian School of Journalism. Many prominent East African newspaper editors were among its graduates, as well as South Africans whom Dee thought had considerable talent; the school allocated several spaces to the exiles, which it divided between adherents of the ANC and the Pan Africanist Congress. The programme seemed attractive, especially when compared with living in the Eastern Bloc. But Dee, who possessed a fatalistic streak, was not optimistic about his chances. I'm a Mashinini, he kept telling himself. These guys in the ANC are surely going to pack me off to the other side of the Berlin Wall.

He was stunned when the ANC authorities agreed to give him one of the spots at the journalism school; now they just had to organize a scholarship for him. The ANC usually required students to remain in the Mazimbu camp after passing their examinations to await word of financial aid. Dee had other plans. An acquaintance had offered him an internship at Radio Freedom, the voice of the ANC, in Dar es Salaam. Dee thought it an excellent opportunity: he would learn about broadcast journalism, live in the city and, perhaps most important, escape the camp. He was thoroughly sick of being in the bush. He had spent six years in Mazimbu; another life, his new life, lay tantalizingly near. He could not fathom waiting in the camp while the ANC sorted out his scholarship, which could take as long as a year. When Dee had convinced the necessary officials of the internship's value, he wasted little time in preparing his departure: he packed his belongings, bid farewell to friends and got a ride on the first vehicle he could find leaving for the capital.

Radio Freedom was housed in the same building as Radio Tanzania, down the road from the ANC's offices. The Tanzanian government allowed the exiled South African organizations to transmit programmes for thirty minutes, three days a week, over its external service; the ANC shared the time with the PAC. In addition to Tanzania, Radio Freedom broadcast from numerous other African countries – Angola, Egypt, Ethiopia, Madagascar, Zambia – at different hours to various parts of South Africa. Dee's job was to write a script, culled from ANC propaganda, for a weekly presentation about trade unions that was aimed at workers in South Africa.

The programme lasted for only a few weeks. Dee nonetheless continued his employment at the station, now assisting in all aspects of the broadcasts. He found the work fascinating. The head office in Lusaka would send a taped interview with ANC President Oliver Tambo, for instance, which Dee was required to summarize in a story. If a bomb exploded in South Africa, he monitored the BBC and other international radio services for reactions. He helped to create special presentations that commemorated important political events: the Sharpeville Massacre of 1960; June 16; Women's Day; ANC Formation

Day; etc. He researched topics, wrote scripts, read them on the air. Dee broadcast under the name of David Mokoa, one of his father's uncles. He had chosen it when he first joined the ANC; everyone, he was told, had to have a *nom de guerre*. Dee disliked the notion of taking a pseudonym and thus selected one that at least had some meaning for him. (Years later, he would learn that his family recognized both the name and his voice when they listened clandestinely to the broadcasts.)

Dee derived great satisfaction from his duties at the radio station. He thought it the best job one could have in exile; unlike training people to use AK-47s or being a commissar, Dee worked in what he considered an actual occupation. Broadcasting, even on something so remote as Radio Freedom, was a professional sort of activity. He no longer wanted to drive a tank to South Africa, to kill every Boer he could find; he wanted to be someone. Not that he had relinquished his commitment to destroying the apartheid regime. He simply wished to develop himself at the same time. Of course, he could not imagine fulfilling his desire outside the purview of the ANC; the organization had been his family for almost a decade.

The ANC gave Dee a flat to live in while working at Radio Freedom. It was cramped and in disrepair, but to Dee the place seemed magnificent: its door opened onto a city, not the bush, and he could come and go as he pleased. It also allowed him to provide accommodation for Rocks when he visited. Dee had been communicating with his older brother for years through the ANC's internal mail; Rocks arranged to stop in Dar es Salaam when he returned to the continent after completing his intelligence course in Moscow. The prospect of seeing his brother, after a ten-year hiatus, thrilled Dee. Still, he was not without trepidation. He had encountered several of Rocks' colleagues over the years, all of whom told of his brother's reputation as one of Umkhonto's leading commissars. Stuck in something of a time warp, Dee felt like the unaccomplished younger sibling.

Rocks immediately put Dee's fears to rest. From the moment they met, Rocks treated his brother as an equal. Dee was most struck by the toll Rocks' clandestine life appeared to have taken.

Each time he entered the flat during the three-day visit, Rocks checked every corner, even in the bathroom, for hidden assassins. Once, he and Dee were standing outside on the balcony, smoking cigarettes, when a truck stopped on the street below and disgorged a group of soldiers; Rocks almost leaped over the balustrade in his attempt to flee the apartment. To Dee, Rocks seemed shell shocked. He felt sorry for his brother: having joined the elite of Umkhonto fighters, Rocks could not relax for a moment.

Still, it was a pleasurable reunion. They spent much of the time talking; Rocks recounted tales of his underground work in Swaziland. He spoke of his ambivalence about his Umkhonto existence, of how he felt trapped in the organization. Dee listened, enthralled; the last time he saw Rocks, Dee had been but one of many little brothers. Now his revered older sibling was confiding in him as a man – a transcendent moment for Dee. He told Rocks about his job at Radio Freedom and his plans to study journalism. Rocks nodded approvingly. 'You're doing something with your life,' he said. 'That's good. I wouldn't have wanted you to follow me into Umkhonto.' Rocks paused for a moment. 'You needed an education,' he added, almost wistfully.

Dee worked at Radio Freedom until he got word that the African-American Institute, a non-governmental organization in the US, had awarded him a scholarship to continue his studies. The AAI would pay for fees, books and lodging and provide a monthly stipend of $200. The scholarship came with few requirements. Dee was not obligated to maintain a minimum grade point average; he simply had to obtain a diploma from his institution and write a thesis for the AAI. He could hardly believe his good fortune.

He enrolled in the Tanzanian School of Journalism in 1986. Dee took courses in news writing, mass communications, the history of journalism, English, current affairs, broadcasting, editing. He and the other students produced a mock newspaper; Dee covered the police and the courts, then switched to politics. For part of one term, he worked as a cub reporter at a Tanzanian publication. He was thrilled to see his name in print:

upon awakening every morning, he rushed to fetch a paper and page through it to find his byline. Dee quickly came to love journalism. The work felt vital, relevant, inspiring. He found it an enormous relief to be engaged in subjects that had nothing to do with the ANC. Here was a chance to be something other than an exile sent to Cuba for indoctrination; here was a chance for a career.

Dee's living conditions suited him as well. He stayed in the school's dormitories, which were spacious and uncrowded; for one year, he had a whole room to himself. Several students from Lesotho, with whom he could speak Sotho, attended the institution. His stipend gave Dee more money than he had seen during his entire stay in exile. He could afford to drink at the city's nicer hotels, dance in discos, walk into a shop and purchase clothes. The allowance's dollar denomination allowed Dee to patronise the hard-currency store frequented by diplomats; he purchased large quantities of alcohol each month to break the cheque. The perquisites of his well-funded lifestyle did not go unnoticed. Dee and other South African exiles on similarly generous scholarships were perceived by resentful locals as rich, flashy students; some ANC officials worried that the youngsters' behaviour created a wrong impression of the organization. They also alienated less-fortunate exiles. Dee began to hear envious whispers: How could a Mashinini, of all people, get such a scholarship? Although aspersions on his family name still hurt Dee, he did not worry about their consequences this time; he felt confident that the ANC, which worked so hard to find funding for its students, would not attempt to revoke his scholarship.

Uncertain where his studies would lead, Dee determined that he would enjoy them while they lasted. He had no idea what he would do after that. He could conceivably strike out on his own and work for the Tanzanian press. But Tanzania, he concluded, was too far from South Africa, its culture too foreign. He did not want to spend the rest of his days here. Dee's main objective still was to return home; and the fastest way to achieve his goal was through the ANC. Perhaps he could secure a job with the organization in one of the front-line states like

Botswana, Swaziland or Zimbabwe – places that bordered South Africa and were more similar to it.

An event of great importance occurred during Dee's second year of journalism school: Lindi returned from the Isle of Youth in Cuba. She and Dee had continued to write to one another throughout the years of separation, sending their latest photographs, descriptions of their lives, hopes for the future. Lindi had provided a kind of shelter for Dee. During those interminable stretches of time in the camp, she was someone to whom he could confide his despair. They rekindled their romance upon being reunited in Tanzania. But maintaining a relationship was difficult: Lindi was working as a medical technician – the profession she had studied in Cuba – at the hospital in Mazimbu. Dee could see her only on infrequent weekends. Still, he pursued her; he had fallen in love. All the attributes that had seemed so attractive to him in Cairo – her intelligence, discipline, engagement with the world – were even more pleasing now. Just as he could not fathom remaining in a foreign land, he could not be involved with a foreign woman. He wanted to marry Lindi. She became pregnant in the course of their courtship, which only reinforced their determination to be together.

Not long before his graduation, Dee was informed that he had been selected to go to Lusaka. The ANC's head office lacked people with advanced education and skills; a dozen young men and women, who were studying in various programmes, had been chosen to fill the vacancies. Dee did not know his job description, only that he would be employed in the Department of Information and Publicity. He was ecstatic; he had hoped to do precisely this sort of work. Better yet, he would finally see Head Office, the holy of holies. He would have to leave Lindi behind, despite her pregnant state, but only temporarily; as soon as he was settled in Lusaka, he would arrange for her to follow.

Dee boarded an aeroplane for Zambia a couple of days after finishing his journalism course. He could not even attend his graduation. This omission did not bother Dee; he had had enough of Tanzania. He was happy to be going to the centre of ANC life.

CHAPTER SEVENTEEN

Tsietsi

Tsietsi, bereft of Welma and his two daughters, drifted back to Guinea, then to Nigeria. Without his family and lacking a job, his behaviour became even more erratic. His old comrades from the South African Youth Revolutionary Council were stunned by his deterioration. Comfort Molokoane, who had visited Tsietsi in Liberia, thought his friend was taking drugs. Tsietsi exhibited bizarre personality traits; sometimes he was irritable, mercurial, irrational, at others secretive and withdrawn. He seemed unrecognizable to those who knew him.

He eventually procured a scholarship from the United Nations High Commission for Refugees. It was a special fund for South African exiles that paid for his fees, lodging, books, clothing and incidentals. The UNHCR officials helped Tsietsi to apply to Plateau State Polytechnic in Jos, in the central part of the country, where he was admitted to the department of urban and regional planning. It seemed an unlikely place for Tsietsi. Located several hundred miles from the vitality and political tumult of Lagos, the small campus was little more than a scattering of concrete-block buildings, dirt paths, some desultory trees and shrubs.

Tsietsi found it difficult to concentrate on his studies. His main preoccupation was money: he complained incessantly of being broke, his UNHCR scholarship notwithstanding. His comportment mystified his professors. Here was someone who purportedly would return to his country one day as a political leader; yet all he talked about was money. Often, when his discontentment about his finances seemed to reach a critical level, Tsietsi would disappear from his lectures altogether for a couple of days. Then he would be observed begging for a meal in the nearby village.

He rarely participated in campus activities. Tsietsi kept mostly to himself, avoiding the football matches and parties and political discussions that were the standard fare of student life. He did drink alcohol. 'I have to drink,' he told one of the instructors, who encountered Tsietsi in a local bar with bottles of local and imported beer arrayed before him on the table. 'If not, I won't be happy.' As in Monrovia, his drinking seemed to provoke him to violence. Tsietsi developed an intense dislike of a Liberian student who studied at the polytechnic and would instigate fistfights with the young man when inebriated; the Liberian became convinced that Tsietsi was going to kill him.

Despite his lack of dedication, Tsietsi still managed to do well in his courses. But he no longer had the brilliance, the intellectual flair, that had distinguished him in South Africa. Now he floated through school without any discernible aim or purpose. To his professors, he seemed to have lost his bearings; something had clearly gone wrong with him. Tsietsi periodically became terribly ill, unable even to walk, which required the school authorities to send him to Lagos to be cared for by the UNHCR. The rector thought it might be malaria. Tsietsi was little changed when he returned. Once, an instructor came upon him in the village, scribbling notes madly on scraps of paper. Tsietsi hastily gathered up the writings and left when he saw the professor; he hid the fragments in his clothes so the Nigerian could not see what he had recorded.

Tsietsi sent a letter to Welma describing his feelings about his studies. It was a litany of woe: things were not going well in his life; a fire in his dormitory room had destroyed all his possessions; he was sick of living in Nigeria. Most of all, he missed his daughters and wanted to see them. Tsietsi wrote nothing about Welma or the manner in which they had separated; he spoke only of the children.

The letter frightened Welma. She had returned to her work at the television station and was trying to forge a new life for herself and the children. In her heart and mind, Welma had already divorced Tsietsi by the time she received his letter; she had met someone else. Welma sent Tsietsi a reply saying that he was welcome to come to Liberia, but that he might find her married. Then she began divorce proceedings in earnest. Under Liberian law, Welma had only to publish a notice in the newspapers once a week for a month: Welma Campbell Mashinini is filing for divorce from Tsietsi Mashinini; he or his representative should appear in the appropriate courtroom on the day and hour listed below. She posted the announcement to Tsietsi's address at school and to the UNHCR office in Lagos. When no one showed up in court for him on the appointed day, Welma was granted a divorce from Tsietsi in absentia.

While Tsietsi was studying at the polytechnic, Dee travelled to Nigeria. His trip came about because of a conversation he had had when Rocks visited him in Dar es Salaam. Rocks told him of rumours that Tsietsi might be interested in joining Umkhonto because he believed the guerrilla army was independent of the ANC; if true, it might be a way for them to bring Tsietsi into the care of an exile organization. Dee found it somewhat amazing that stories still circulated throughout the continent about his brother. After leaving Dee, Rocks mentioned the matter to Chris Hani, Umkhonto's Chief-of-Staff and Commissar. Chris thought a visit to Tsietsi a good thing, but objected to Rocks making the journey for fear it might compromise his underground existence. Dee offered himself as an emissary instead. Chris agreed to organize the visit for him; the goal, Chris said, was not to try to bring Tsietsi into the ANC fold, but simply to sound him out about his plans for the future.

Dee had not had contact with Tsietsi since the latter fled South Africa more than a decade earlier. All Dee knew was what he had gleaned from his conversation with Rocks; Victor Matlou, the ANC's chief representative in Lagos, informed him that Tsietsi was studying somewhere in Nigeria, under the care of the UNHCR. Dee flew to Lagos without Tsietsi's knowledge, unsure of what to do. He went first to the UNHCR's office; an official politely informed Dee that he would have to wait several days to meet with his brother. That was when Tsietsi was due to fly down from Jos to obtain his quarterly stipend. (He usually bought a round-trip ticket in Lagos and used the return-half to come back the following quarter.) Although Dee found the delay annoying, it gave the UNHCR authorities time to pass a message to Tsietsi, telling him of Dee's presence in Lagos.

In the meantime, Dee asked the officials about Tsietsi. Oh Tsietsi, one of them said, he spends a lot of time in Lagos, always looking for more money. And did you know that he's been ill several times? Oh yes, he required hospitalization that interrupted his studies for a long time. Mental illness, that's what it was. He had a nervous breakdown and had to be put in a psychiatric institution. We paid for that, you know. But he still finished his studies, and near the top of his class. He's a clever one, your brother.

Dee listened to the bureaucrat's recitation impassively. Among all the other rumours that dogged him across the years and the continent, Dee had heard that Tsietsi suffered a mental break-down. One version put its occurrence in Guinea, another in Liberia. The matter made him terribly nervous about his impending meeting with Tsietsi. He retained the image of his dashing older brother from years ago, the teenage revolutionary whom he had idolized and worshipped. Perhaps more than anything, it was an image he wanted to retain. So much had changed in Dee's life since leaving South Africa; as the years passed, he felt a compulsion to cling to anything that was a bridge, as it were, back to that time of family and home. Yet hearing the official's description of Tsietsi, Dee knew that the heroic youth of his memory had probably ceased to exist. Now he could only imagine in what condition he would find his brother.

On the day that Tsietsi travelled to Lagos, Dee waited for him in Victor Matlou's home. Tsietsi knew the house well, having stayed there on numerous occasions; the ANC representative was a renowned figure in the city whose engaging personality apparently allowed Tsietsi to overlook his political affiliation. Dee spent the morning staring out the living-room window and scrutinzing every passer-by in anticipation of his brother's arrival. Suddenly, there was Tsietsi, sauntering up the path. The sight took Dee's breath away: the man who approached the house was small, shrunken, diminished, a shabby figure clad in a pair of old trousers and a t-shirt. The dandy Dee had known in Soweto, the karate devotee who exuded strength and confidence, was no more. Only the distinctive receding hairline of the Mashinini clan gave Dee any confidence that this was truly his brother.

The two men embraced. For the next few days, the duration of Dee's visit, they played as youngsters. Tsietsi showed Dee around Lagos, took him to his favourite haunts, talked of all that had happened to him. Dee was stunned by the changes in his brother: Tsietsi seemed destroyed, physically and mentally. He had adopted the patois of West Africa, a pidgin English that to Dee's ear made him sound illiterate. Tsietsi had lost his eloquence, the verbal grandeur that had so inspired his comrades in South Africa. His cognitive processes were impaired: Tsietsi started a discourse on one topic, only to jump to another, then another; he could not complete a thought. And he was paranoid. 'Welma is trying to kill me,' he said repeatedly. 'I just know she's trying to kill me.' When Dee asked him what proof he had, Tsietsi pointed to a scar on his forehead. 'Look at this,' he whispered. 'She sent some guys to do this to me with a knife.'

One afternoon, they took a long walk to a lovely, deserted beach. The sea was heavy on that day; Dee decided not to risk swimming. But Tsietsi immediately ran into the water and began bodysurfing the swells. He disappeared into a massive wave and Dee thought he was lost. Then Dee heard his name shouted as Tsietsi appeared at the crest, waved, vanished, then reappeared laughing. For one glorious moment, Tsietsi was his old, devil-may-care self. It saddened Dee to remember the mental and physical powers that Tsietsi once possessed.

The two brothers talked much on that afternoon, stretched out lazily on towels across the dazzling white sand. Dee realized that he would have to relive the events of 1976 – Tsietsi's escapades, comrades, girlfriends – to have a relatively cogent conversation with him. Even that was difficult: Tsietsi believed, for instance, that the South African government had maintained the bounty on his head for all these years. Dee gently tried to disabuse him of the idea, but to no avail. Tsietsi was gone. Dee was powerless to get him back.

Dee returned to Tanzania; and Tsietsi drifted away from school. People lost track of him. In South Africa, Khotso Seatlholo, his old comrade and friend, heard conflicting reports of his whereabouts. Khotso was now in prison; he had been arrested in 1981 trying to sneak back into South Africa after escorting a group of youngsters out of the country for military training in Lebanon. He was taken into custody, tortured (so the authorities could learn about SAYRCO, of which he was still president), and sentenced to fifteen years' imprisonment on Robben Island. Khotso knew that Tsietsi had become somewhat unhinged. Despite their differences, he still cared deeply for his friend. Over the years, rumours of Tsietsi, like whispers carried on the wind, would reach Khotso in his cell: now he was back in school, now he was ill, now he was on his own in Guinea. Khotso tried to obtain more information by writing to friends in Botswana, but the prison authorities censored the letters. Khotso could not discover his friend's fate.

After a long period of silence during which no one heard from Tsietsi or knew of his whereabouts, Nomkhitha received a letter. The handwriting was barely decipherable, the content almost unintelligible. Nomkhitha gathered from the letter that Tsietsi was in a desperate way: he had no means of financial support; he had no friends; he felt terribly alone. He begged his parents to help him. Tsietsi's plea caused Nomkhitha great anguish, particularly as she was unable, quite literally, to assist him: Tsietsi had neglected to include a return address. Nomkhitha had no idea where to find her son.

CHAPTER EIGHTEEN

Rocks

Rocks' return to Swaziland was no less tense than his departure. He was still sought by the authorities in connection with the killing of the Swazi security officer. Despite the ANC supplying him with newly forged identity documents, Rocks had to jump the border fence from the Mozambican side in the dead of night and make his way to Mbabane. He could not risk being recognized by the police.

He was now Umkhonto's deputy chief of intelligence for Swaziland and secretary of the political operations. It was an important job; Rocks knew he should have felt pride in attaining such a position. But he could not rid himself of a certain ambivalence. In his more lucid moments, Rocks acknowledged that it was dangerous to resume working in Swaziland; yet anything worthwhile he had ever done with Umkhonto placed him in danger. He tried not to think of such matters. Besides, with the training he had recently received in the Soviet Union, he could take precautions: Rocks wore a large Afro wig at times, glasses, different styles of clothing when entering areas where he thought he might be known. The various disguises gave him a slightly greater sense of security.

Rocks had to start from scratch with his intelligence work: developing new contacts, resuscitating old ones, finding safe houses, and so forth. Once again Sebenzile, his wife, came to his aid. (She and Rocks had been married with traditional rites before his departure for the Soviet Union; Rocks' criminal status prevented the couple from having a civil ceremony.) As she had done before, Sebenzile arranged meetings with Swazis who were willing to cooperate with Rocks and located houses for him to rent. He and Sebenzile still could not live a conventional life as a family because of Rocks' requirement to remain, for the most part, undercover. Rocks nonetheless managed frequent visits with her and his son Sizwe, who had grown to be a bright and boisterous youngster; the time he spent with them provided a desperately needed respite from the mental strain of his work.

Rocks' job was to infiltrate the South African security forces by enlisting disgruntled black officers. He maintained a band of agents inside the townships, who identified potential candidates and escorted them over the border to Swaziland for vetting. Rocks aimed specifically at compromising the Special Branch of the police; the uprising in the black areas and the government's violent attempts at suppression brought him several recruits. Only one such spy demanded to be paid for his services. The others agreed to work out of sympathy for the anti-apartheid struggle – a lucky thing for Rocks, who found himself, as always, in competition with his military counterparts for funds.

His spies were charged with obtaining information about Special Branch operations: whom the police had under surveillance; any arrests the security men intended to make; what anti-government groups they planned to penetrate. In this way, Rocks and his Umkhonto comrades tried to keep abreast of impending danger to their guerrillas operating in South Africa. The uprising proved a windfall for the organization. Activists, who in earlier times might have left the country for military training, were encouraged to remain in South Africa; they acted as a nexus between the fighters crossing the borders into the country and the leaders in the townships. Now the Umkhonto commanders could realize their dream of creating command structures – called Area Political-Military Councils – throughout South Africa. The policy of waging war from the townships, a 'people's war', as it were, which had been envisioned so many decades ago, finally seemed possible.

Umkhonto thrived as never before in the country's revolutionary atmosphere. The South African government recorded

230 guerrilla attacks in 1986, compared with 50 or so in 1984, at the uprising's inception. Bombs seemed to be exploding every second day. Township youngsters venerated the Umkhonto fighters; some of the revolt's most popular freedom songs celebrated the guerrillas and their triumphs. (Umkhonto's success accounted, in part, for the ANC's emergence during the uprising as the paramount anti-apartheid organization. It transcended all its other competitors: Inkatha, a powerful Zulu-based movement; the Azanian People's Organization, which saw itself as the successor to the Black Consciousness movement; the remnants of the Pan Africanist Congress.)

Umkhonto's glory, as it were, lasted but a brief moment. The South African security forces embarked on a systematic campaign of kidnappings and assassinations to destroy Umkhonto's operations in the surrounding countries; in one particularly gruesome incident, a death squad gunned down seven guerrilla agents in attacks on two houses in neighbouring Lesotho. The uprising by blacks notwithstanding, the Nationalist government demonstrated that its resolve, and its resources, were far from exhausted. Always dangerous, Swaziland became even more perilous a place for Umkhonto fighters.

The heightened tension exacerbated Rocks' already fragile state. His debilitating headaches recurred with ever-greater frequency; his drinking bouts intensified. He felt exhausted all the time. One night, he arrived at a hideout near Manzini more weary than usual. All he wanted to do was rest. Rocks entered the house, removed his shoes and was settling down on the sofa when a group of Swazi security police burst through the door and wrestled him to the ground. They had obviously had the house under surveillance. While a few policemen held Rocks, the others searched his car; there they found ANC leaflets and a cache of AK-47 rifles. The officers were ecstatic as they bundled him off to the police station, convinced they had apprehended an important terrorist.

Rocks, of course, denied any knowledge of the vehicle's contents. 'The car doesn't even belong to me,' he insisted to the commander at the station. 'It's my friend's car. He's the ANC member. I was supposed to meet him at a garage.' Rocks believed

he had a plausible cover story: his papers, which had been manufactured by the ANC and were of convincing quality, identified
him as someone unknown to the Swazi authorities. And the
police had nothing that could link him to the car. But they were
not swayed by his protestations; even though he'd not been
convicted of any crime, the commander wanted to lock him up
in the country's maximum-security prison, outside Manzini.
While the officer tried to get someone to open the facility at
that late hour, Rocks was kept under guard in the Manzini jail.

The arrangements completed, a policeman put Rocks in
shackles and escorted him to a large van. Two security men,
cradling rifles, sat on either side of him in the vehicle. They
drove to the prison in a convoy of police cars, their lights
flashing, sirens wailing. Rocks' appearance in the middle of the
night surprised the warders; they placed him in a brightly lit
room to await the arrival of the interrogators. Rocks mentally
rehearsed his story to keep his fear under control. He tried to
imagine every inconsistency his interrogators might find, every
lapse they would try to exploit. Then the chief security officer
entered the room. 'Ah, Vusi,' he said, with a smirk, 'so nice to
see you again.' Rocks' elaborate preparations were in vain; the
man knew him as an ANC terrorist who was sought for the
killing, at the very least, of a leading Swazi police official.
(Umkhonto's assassination squad had also identified Rocks'
interrogator as a target; Rocks rued that they had not yet done
the job.)

The Swazi authorities charged Rocks with being in the
country illegally and possessing weapons of war. He did not
receive a formal sentence; the ANC, working through such international groups as the Organization of African Unity and the
United Nations, had an agreement with the Swazi government
not to prosecute its guerrillas. Instead, the government would
deport them to Lusaka. But Rocks had to remain in the
maximum-security prison while the ANC organized the proper
documents and a flight.

Rocks found the conditions in the prison repellent. He and
the other ANC prisoners were kept in a filthy, crowded cell
with common criminals; they slept on wafer-like mats on the

concrete floor and performed their ablutions in a lavatory from which emanated an unspeakable stench. As a concession, the warders allowed them to buy their own food. A Swazi lawyer, who had been hired by the ANC, visited occasionally to re-assure the South Africans that they were not going to rot there, that the ANC was working through the UN to get them out of Swaziland. Rocks took comfort from the notion that the Boers, at least, would not be able to kidnap him from a maximum-security facility. Still, he hated being locked up, and he disliked being separated from Sizwe and Sebenzile, who was now preg-nant with their second child. Finally, after two months of waiting, Rocks and six other South Africans were deported to Zambia.

The Umkhonto authorities reassigned Rocks to a job at ANC headquarters in Lusaka. They were not inclined to attempt to send him back to Swaziland; his notoriety there put him at too much risk. Rocks worked in military intelligence, assisting the guerrilla operations in Botswana. His charges' tasks were similar to those Rocks had performed in Swaziland: infiltrating the South African security forces; establishing safe houses; finding good routes in and out of the country for cadres. As always, Rocks had to improvise to compensate for inadequate resources. He lacked even the most basic equipment; he could not provide listening devices, for instance, for his agents. Still they managed to co-opt a number of disaffected South African policemen.

Rocks disliked working in Lusaka. It was an unremarkable city of mostly poured-concrete buildings, dun coloured and chokingly dusty during the winter dry season, verdant when the summer rains fell. The ANC's offices were spread among several cramped buildings in the downtown area. As with its opera-tions everywhere in the world, the organization did not have sufficient space, telephones or vehicles. It did not want for bureaucracy, however. To Rocks, headquarters was a maze of departments, red tape, intrigue, innuendo, gossip. After years of being virtually on his own, with only a few colleagues to notice his comings and goings, Rocks found the presence of so many of his superiors suffocating. He yearned for the simplicity of working in the field.

He also longed to be closer to the action. Lusaka was too far away from South Africa; Rocks thought he might as well be in Tunisia, for all the contact he had with events occurring at home. The long stretches of living in proximity to the South African security forces had turned him into something of a danger addict. Despite the headaches and tremors and excessive drinking it caused, the constant threat of attack had become a kind of narcotic; its sudden absence sent him into a state of withdrawal. Rocks felt depressed, unable to concentrate, without purpose.

Yet there were advantages to being able to live a more normal life. Rocks had a friend who travelled frequently between Zambia and Swaziland and carried letters to Sebenzile. Rocks could telephone her regularly in Mbabane; they spoke with relative openness, taking care only not to talk of 'official' business over what they assumed was a monitored line. He was thus able to learn of the birth of his second son on the day Sebenzile delivered him. She named him Vuyo, happiness in Swati and Xhosa, a name suggested by her mother. Rocks was ecstatic; he made arrangements for Sebenzile, Sizwe and Vuyo to travel to Lusaka when the baby was two weeks old. Their visit was a time of great happiness for Rocks. He spent every free moment with his sons: pushing Vuyo in his little stroller; reading picture books to Sizwe; proudly showing off his family to his friends. Rocks would have liked the idyll to continue indefinitely. But Sebenzile's maternity leave was coming to an end; she could not find work in Zambia and needed to get back to her job in Swaziland. After two months Sebenzile and the boys departed, leaving Rocks to his solitary existence.

His feelings of discontent and aimlessness returned. Only the occasional journey to Botswana, a requirement of his job, broke his sense of unease. On one such trip, Rocks was charged with giving his officers a briefing. Against orders from headquarters, he went to a safe house where one of his closest associates worked. Rocks had trained with the man in the camps of Angola; as a gesture of friendship, he wanted to allow him to view the videocassettes that would be used in the next day's presentation and that contained detailed sensitive information about future operations. It was one of a thousand little infractions that occurred daily in an organization as dispersed as Umkhonto. Most passed unnoticed and with little consequence; that, too, would have been Rocks' fate had misfortune not intervened.

The two friends talked for several hours, catching up on gossip, personal and professional. Someone in the house mentioned that a famous South African singer, Lucky Dube, was performing that night in a nearby venue; Rocks' friend encouraged him to go to the outdoor rock concert. It would do Rocks good to hear some music and relax. Reluctantly, Rocks assented, leaving the cassettes with his friend to watch.

A few hours later, assassins attacked the safe house, killing Rocks' friend, among others, and setting off explosives. Rocks got word of the murders at the concert. Terribly shaken by his friend's death, and the knowledge that his friend had probably saved Rocks' life by insisting he attend the performance, Rocks surreptitiously returned to his hotel. He could not retrieve the videos now. He gathered his belongings and went to the airport to await the next flight to Zambia. Rocks had few concerns about being arrested by the Botswanan authorities; he had entered the country on a Swazi passport and possessed papers identifying him as a lecturer in social sciences at the University of Zambia.

Rocks' superiors in Lusaka were furious when they learned that the videos had, at the very least, been destroyed in the bombing of the safe house; at worst, the enemy assailants appropriated them beforehand. The Umkhonto commanders sent an officer to Gaborone to investigate the incident. The man, who was not on good terms with Rocks, wrote a damning report: Rocks had been drunk, negligent with sensitive material, in dereliction of duty. His superiors were particularly unforgiving of the loss of the videos. Rocks tried to defend his behaviour as foolhardiness, not insubordination, but to no avail; the rift between him and his commanders seemed unbridgeable.

Thus began Rocks' alienation from Umkhonto. His commanders did not know what to do with Rocks; he had been disgraced and could not be given another assignment. So they ostracized him. They allowed Rocks to remain in ANC housing and gave him a small food allowance, but deprived him of participation in Umkhonto and the ANC. The authorities barred Rocks from attending meetings, receiving briefings or engaging in any manner of work. He became a pariah within the community that had, in essence, been his family in exile. Soldiers who were his friends for years now shunned him; officers for whom he had fought refused his entreaties.

Rocks did not endure this enforced purgatory well. His commanders had essentially shut down the sole life he had known as an adult; Rocks battled to think of alternatives. The only people he could confide in were comrades from the 1976 uprising who had joined the ANC and now held senior positions in the organization. Despite Rocks' outcast status, they retained their ties to him; among that generation of exiles, there remained a great bond, a sense of having shared a unique and grand moment of history. Rocks could speak freely to them. They questioned Rocks searchingly about his future. But his comrades had taken a different path: they were educated and thus had seemingly unlimited possibilities; Rocks was a soldier. They found it difficult to formulate a plan.

Rocks became terribly depressed. He drank constantly when he managed to find extra money and dragged himself through the days, bitter beyond words. To be removed from duty in so unceremonious a manner, after all his contributions to the struggle for liberation, was a gross indignity. And what did he have to show for his years of sacrifice? Nothing. He was a broken, dissolute, uneducated ex-guerrilla with few skills to sustain him in civilian life. Rocks' anger eventually gave way to defiance: he would not let them ruin him. He would start again, find a career, strike out on his own. He would fulfil Nomkhitha's hope for her children and study.

CHAPTER NINETEEN

Mpho

The police drove Mpho, China and the others they had taken into custody to the Protea station in Soweto. As Mpho predicted, the officers soon released China; Mpho gave him the names and telephone numbers of people to contact to tell of his arrest. 'Don't let them forget about me in here,' he whispered to his brother. After China departed, a policeman put Mpho in an isolation cell. He began calling out, as soon as the officer left the block, to determine if he knew any of the other prisoners being held. Some of the activists who had travelled to the Eastern Cape for the funeral of a prominent UDF organizer were in nearby cells. They described what had happened to them and the details of their arrest. Hloyi, Mpho's girlfriend who had also made the journey, was not among them; Mpho could not find out what had happened to her.

Mpho spent two weeks in Protea. The security officers did not interrogate him, nor make any other sort of effort to charge him with a crime; the state of emergency allowed them to detain prisoners without cause. Despite being in solitary confinement, Mpho did not feel isolated. Knowing that he was not completely alone, that there were other comrades in the surrounding cells with whom he could communicate, helped to mitigate the hardship of his incarceration. After fourteen days, Mpho and scores of other detainees were transferred to Diepkloof Prison, south of Johannesburg. (Unbeknown to Mpho, Hloyi had been detained there; she was released before his arrival.) The prisoners had a joyful reunion in the yard: having endured a fortnight of shouting blindly from their cells, they could finally hug each other. In their enthusiasm, the comrades began singing anti-apartheid songs and pointing imaginary guns at the police who were guarding them. The officers did not know what to do; they usually had common criminals in their custody and were unaccustomed to such behaviour.

Diepkloof was a new facility that, in comparison with the other prisons he had seen, seemed positively sumptuous to Mpho. It had proper bunk-type beds, with mattresses and pillows and sheets that were changed weekly – a stark contrast with the meagre foam mat that Mpho slept on in Standerton. His fellow comrades were equally impressed: they took to calling the place Sun City, after a luxury resort that had been built in Bophuthatswana, one of the black 'homelands'. The prisoners were placed in large, communal cells, each with about sixty men. Mpho welcomed the change from the isolation of Protea.

Not long after the detainees' arrival, the security officers began their interrogations. The activists under examination called themselves 'horses'; they christened the policemen who did the questioning 'jockeys', because they 'rode' the detainees. Mpho met his jockeys back at the Protea station, where he was taken for the interrogation. The security officer who entered the room, balancing a file of papers about a foot high, greeted him in Afrikaans: '*Ag, Mpho, jy het al die kak gedoen vir tien jare.*' (Oh Mpho, I see you have done this shit for ten years.)

All of the questions he proceeded to ask concerned the Soweto Youth Congress and Mpho's role in it. Although Mpho had been well aware of the security forces' attempts to infiltrate SOYCO, he was stunned by their success; the officer recounted incidents about which very few SOYCO officials had any knowledge. He even recited the details of a meeting that was held among a handful of trusted comrades just before the government imposed the emergency. The activists discussed a plan to unban, as it were, the ANC: they would organize a large gathering in the township where they intended to fly the ANC's flag, read aloud the Freedom Charter and declare the group 'unbanned'. Winnie Mandela enthusiastically supported the idea of the assembly and had promised to attend. Nothing ever came of it: some of the activist leaders had reservations about the wisdom of such an action and wanted to consult with more comrades; then the emergency began, and everyone disappeared or was arrested. 'You think we don't know about you,' the security officer said, peering at Mpho over the top of his glasses, 'but we know a lot. Do you think you can unban the ANC over there in Sun City?'

The confrontation shook Mpho greatly; the government clearly was going to try to put the leaders of the United Democratic Front on trial for treason, using its affiliates such as SOYCO to build the case. The officer's line of questioning seemed to be an attempt to establish a direct link between SOYCO and the ANC. If that were proven, Mpho too could be charged with treason, as the ANC was a banned organization. To keep from panicking, Mpho kept reminding himself of how scrupulous he and the other founding SOYCO members had been to operate legally. Their mentors, the senior comrades who were determined to build a long-lived organization, had helped to restrain their more radical tendencies. (For which Mpho now felt much gratitude.) Besides, Mpho no longer even held a leadership post in SOYCO; he did not stand for re-election at a congress that convened before the emergency's imposition.

As the days passed and his interrogator failed to produce any more damning evidence, Mpho began to relax. What facts the security forces did possess were not enough, in Mpho's estimation, to convict him. And his examiner, who seemed to Mpho inexperienced and not terribly adroit, failed to extract further information from him. Mpho was careful not to say anything that could provide him with new leads. He feigned ignorance to most of the questions, especially those that attempted to draw a connection between SOYCO and the ANC 'communists' in Lusaka. The authorities were obsessed with communism: they saw it and the ANC, which were equivalent in their minds, behind every act of rebellion in the country.

Mpho was called back for further interrogation six times over the next month. The encounters settled into a predictable routine: questioning that lasted for the entire day, punctuated by a few breaks and lunch. One terrifying, but utterly satisfying, moment provided an exception to the customary procedure. A higher-ranking security officer observed the examination on that day; several black and white policemen flanked him. The officer explained that, although he despised Mpho and his sort, there were certain 'types' of blacks whom he could trust. 'Do you trust these men?' Mpho asked, pointing to the black police.

'*Ja*, they are my friends,' said the officer. 'I take risks for them, they would lay down their lives for me. We go into dangerous situations together and fight terrorists.'

Mpho replied, 'I'm sorry, you may think you trust them, but they do what you ask because their jobs depend on it. You are still the boss, and they are still as oppressed as I am. But I want to tell you that none of these men would ever lay down his life for you. And none of them will ever trust you. They'll trust you only when you're a dead white man.'

Suddenly Mpho felt himself knocked to the ground from behind. He turned and saw the white officer who had assaulted him. Mpho stood and lunged for the enraged man's throat; as they fell to the ground, all Mpho could think was how good it felt to hit a white policeman. Another officer threw a blanket over him and pinned him down. The policemen snapped on handcuffs, then dragged Mpho to a cell; after he had cooled down somewhat, they drove him back to Diepkloof. Mpho reflected on how much he had changed over the past ten years. Although he knew that he had courted possible disaster by his actions, that the security men could have beaten him terribly or even resorted to torture, punching the policeman was a kind of revenge for everything the authorities had inflicted on him in 1976. This time, he fought back. That he was not alone gave him courage.

Despite the government's attempt to build a court case against Mpho and the other detainees, they remained in their communal cells. Joseph and Nomkhitha knew of Mpho's whereabouts; although they were forbidden to have contact with their son, the prison officials accepted changes of clothing from them and, depending on the warder, an occasional letter. The warders were still uncertain exactly how to cope with the detainees. Diepkloof had been built to house common criminals; all of its rules were intended to control such offenders. When Mpho and his comrades first arrived, for instance, they were told to squat in the yard so the warders could count them. Most of the activists refused; they found it unseemly. The warders, who had never been disobeyed in this fashion, began beating the young men. A few acquiesced, but the majority still refused. We're not criminals, they told the warders, we're detainees. We want to be treated with dignity.

The hot-tempered young activists were not about to accept this humiliation, nor the other injustices imposed on them. They sent a delegation to the head of the prison; he assigned a subordinate to the detainees, who answered each of their demands by citing a litany of prison rules. The more senior comrades, those who had been incarcerated on Robben Island, watched this little drama with amusement. They offered their youthful cellmates some advice: on the petty issues, deal with the warders who lock you up. They're the ones who can give you ten more minutes in the yard or extra milk rations. The boss man will always go by the book.

Guided by the older activists, Mpho and the other detainees adopted the proffered strategy for improving their lot. The first matter they had to address was self-discipline; the warders could punish the entire cell, all sixty or so detainees, because of one person's transgression. The opportunities for such penalties were numerous. Every morning at six, for instance, a senior prison official inspected the cell. Each detainee had to be dressed and standing at attention next to his bed, which had to be in order. No one must be in the showers. For the first few days of incarceration, the inevitable straggler or two caused all the detainees to miss a meal. Some of the culprits were simply idlers; others committed their infringements in a spirit of defiance. They had to be convinced that random rebelliousness did not help their situation but, in fact, hurt the entire group. Similarly, some detainees refused to observe silence after lights-out at eight o'clock. 'Now look,' a middle-aged Indian comrade lectured his younger cellmates, 'if we don't want to sleep until midnight, let's do it. But do it together.'

The detainees established a disciplinary committee of a

half-dozen or so members and a code of conduct. The committee members were like watchdogs, running around the cell at six o'clock in the morning, ascertaining that everyone was out of the shower and standing by his made-up bed. The code, which was widely discussed in the cell before being adopted, stipulated the times for showering. If a person could not finish by 5.30, he had to wait to bathe until free time after breakfast. The idea was for the detainees themselves to control the cells and deprive their jailers of as much authority as possible. In this manner, a reprimand by a warder for failing the bed inspection represented a code violation. The code forbade fraternizing with common prisoners or smuggling food or drugs into the cell. It also prohibited threatening the guards in any fashion; the detainees needed their cooperation. The punishment for breaking the rules was isolation: a transgressor would be ostracized for the day and prevented from participating in the cell's activities.

Other committees organized those pursuits. There was an education committee, whose members selected topics for discussion and saw to the smuggling of reading material (illegal and highly prized) into the cell. The catering committee undertook to sort out the problems of the dining room. When the detainees first arrived at Diepkloof, the common criminals served them their meals. The convicts had great disdain for the political prisoners. 'You've come here to burn our prison!' one of the servers shouted at the comrades, spitting in their food. The convicts harassed the detainees endlessly: throwing plates at them, kissing the young boys, trying to sell them drugs. Mpho thought them repulsive. The catering committee, of which he was a member, petitioned the prison authorities and received permission to serve their own cells.

It was good work. Mpho, along with the others on the committee, went to the dining room early to prepare the service. There they encountered members of other cells doing a similar job. They could exchange news and gossip; they could also keep an account of how many people were being detained, based on the amount of food the prison allocated, the sugar ration, and so forth. Perhaps most important, their work allowed them access to newcomers as they dished out the food. Mpho and the others could obtain information about what was happening in the townships, whether Soweto was burning, what the government was doing. (The prison officials rarely locked up new arrivals with old-timers.) Mpho would suddenly see, for instance, sixty students in the prison, arrested for throwing stones; he and the other members of the committee could glean news from the outside and explain to the novices how the detainees were organized on the inside.

The catering committee saw to the distribution of other food. The prison authorities confiscated whatever money the comrades had; in return, they received cards that allowed them, once a week, to purchase items from the store. Because only some detainees had money, the committee pooled the cell's funds and bought essentials such as tea, sugar and biscuits to share among everyone. The committee members discouraged hoarding; one comrade, when discovered to be hiding an enormous tin of coffee under his bunk, was roundly and loudly condemned. Although the catering committee bought cigarettes for the cell, the matter of smoking was of sufficient import to warrant a separate group for distribution: gwaico (*gwai* being the Zulu word for cigarette). Gwaico divided a pack of twenty cigarettes among five detainees; each recipient could decide whether to smoke his ration, to barter it for something more prized or to share it with a friend.

In his desire to maintain at least a semblance of activism, Mpho also became a part of the negotiating committee. The members were charged with approaching the prison's liaison officer with grievances. They had a litany of complaints: the warders' heavy-handedness; the poor food; the lack of exercise; the limited access to the shop and the library; the clergyman who treated them as though they were thieves and rapists and thundered against the evils of smoking in his Sunday-morning sermons. (If God wanted us to smoke, the preacher would rant, he'd have put chimneys on top of our heads. To men whose sole pleasure behind bars was to light up a cigarette, those were fighting words.) When the committee failed to obtain results from the liaison officer, the members changed tactics and, in accordance with the advice of the senior comrades, approached the warders who guarded them.

The warders were all black; the detainees undertook to convert them, as it were, to their side. You stay in the townships, they would whisper repeatedly to the warders, you are our brothers. The guards spent most of their waking hours with the detainees, and many succumbed to the relentless pressure. Mpho considered it a victory to overhear a warder quietly humming one of the freedom songs that the comrades sang to keep their spirits high. Some of the guards agreed to buy newspapers for the prisoners with money given to them by the families. Others doubled the time in the exercise yard to forty minutes a day, or even an hour. An elderly warder, whom the comrades called *Ntate* ('Father', in Sotho) would slip a letter in a detainee's pocket every so often and silently walk away; he would not give the recipient a chance to thank him. Mpho understood that he sympathized with their struggle. But *Ntate* was old school; he had been a warder for decades and was about to retire and feared jeopardizing his pension by doing anything overt.

In this way, Mpho settled into a routine. He awoke, made his bed, stood for inspection. In the mornings, he and the other prisoners would be allowed into the yard. Otherwise, they were kept in the locked cell. They sang freedom songs, played cards, invented games. Afternoons were given over to political discussions and workshops: one person would suggest a topic – how the state of emergency affected the struggle, for instance – and certain leaders conducted the debate. Others gave lectures on culture or religion. There were assemblies to discuss the conditions in the prison and meetings of the various committees. Only the weekends brought a change in the schedule. Then the detainees received their supper at two o'clock in the afternoon and were locked down for the night an hour later so that many of the guards could go home. After three o'clock, someone would begin a discourse that usually lasted long into the night; free of supervision, the detainees could ignore the lights-out rule and speak unreservedly.

Mpho generally found the time in Diepkloof more tolerable than his previous incarceration. He was older and stronger; his earlier prison experiences helped him to endure the ordeal. Perhaps the most important difference was that this time he was not facing the enemy alone. But living with fifty-nine or so other people in one room also felt unbearably suffocating to Mpho at times; he longed for solitude and space. There were moments when Mpho thought he might go mad in the presence of all this caged humanity. His fellow detainees clearly harboured similar sentiments. Every so often, the entire cell would suddenly go eerily quiet; the prisoners lay on their bunks, staring at the ceiling or sitting off in a corner alone – as though everyone had disappeared inside himself. Morale slipped precipitously during these spells and stayed that way for a couple of days. Then, inexplicably, the mood would break and spirits rose again.

Several months into his detention, Mpho received an unexpected respite. He had been having constant headaches; a doctor who visited the prison and examined him suggested that he be sent to Johannesburg General Hospital for tests. Mpho managed to smuggle a note out to Nomkhitha and Joseph that told them the day and time of his hospital appointment. They, along with a few of the other Mashinini children, Hloyi and Mpho's friend Mark Swilling, were waiting for him outside the neurologist's office when he arrived. A contingent of mostly white policemen escorted Mpho, who was in handcuffs. 'What is this shit?' an officer demanded when he recognized Hloyi. 'Was this planned?'

'How could I plan it?' replied Mpho. 'I'm in prison.'

The officer dismissed Mpho's answer. 'Any attempts to talk with them and we take you back,' he warned. The policemen led Mpho into the neurologist's rooms; the doctor looked at the gaggle of security officers and asked them to wait outside. The neurologist, who was white, asked Mpho why the policemen were treating him so brutally. Mpho explained that his family was sitting outside in the waiting area. 'Look,' said the doctor, 'I know these fellows and they won't wait an hour. Do you want me to delay your tests so that you can spend some time with your family?' Mpho agreed and the doctor had him stretch out on a bed and attached electrodes to various points on his body. Then he summoned the security men. Pointing to Mpho, he explained that the tests would take a considerable amount of time.

'We can't wait for him to wake up,' an officer said, either out of ignorance or misunderstanding. He conferred with the others, then returned to say they would leave a few black policemen to watch Mpho. After issuing instructions, the white officers left; Mpho and the doctor watched them depart the hospital grounds from a window. The neurologist explained to the remaining black policemen that Mpho had to await the results of his tests and seated him next to his parents.

'You can't stop me from talking to my family,' Mpho said to his guards.

'But we'll get into trouble,' one protested.

'No, no, comrade, there won't be any trouble.'

Irritated by the exchange, a policeman banged on the doctor's office door, demanding to know when Mpho could leave. The neurologist emerged and explained, once again, that he had to stay until all the tests were completed. The policeman returned to his seat. He, the other security officers, the Mashininis, Hloyi and Mark sat in silence. They stared at one another, the floor, the occasional nurse or doctor who passed. A policeman cleared his throat and announced that it was time to buy lunch; did Mpho want anything? Joseph said that he would fetch food for his son. The security officer and Joseph left to purchase the meals for the group. When they returned, everyone ate silently; the slurping of soft drinks accounted for the only noise.

Perhaps the conviviality of sharing a meal influenced the policemen, or simply the discomfiture of maintaining silence; after a while, they relented and allowed Mpho to speak to his family. They even posted a lookout to watch for the return of their white bosses. The afternoon turned into a regular outing for Mpho: a picnic lunch; long discussions of things personal and political; newspapers that Joseph surreptitiously gave him to smuggle back to the cell. It all felt so normal that Mpho could almost forget the handcuffs. After a couple of hours, the doctor came out from his offices. He gave Mpho some tablets and told his guards that he could go. Reluctantly, Mpho bade everyone farewell and returned to his life in prison.

Although the detainees, through petitions and cajoling, managed to change some of their conditions, after several months of such efforts they still had serious grievances. They continued to be denied access to the library, to be locked up for much of the day, to be served meals that were not fit for human consumption. Mpho found the matter of food particularly problematic. The detainees' diet consisted mainly of porridge: watery in the morning, the corn mush would sit on the stove all day so that in the afternoon it had thickened somewhat and by dinner, had reached the proper consistency of mealie *pap*. The porridge was served with tea for breakfast; at lunch, the warders supplemented it with a soup that contained a few errant carrots; dinner included a dish that purported to be meat. (Mpho came to think of it as dirty water with a meat-like taste.)

Some of the more senior comrades in Mpho's cell suggested launching a hunger strike in protest. Among them, Amos Masondo, who had spent six years imprisoned on Robben Island, became a leading advocate of such an action. The concept was widely debated in Mpho's cell; only Amos and the others who had been confined on the Island, as it was known, had experience in this matter. Once everyone in the cell agreed to go forward with the strike, the leaders tried to organize the entire section of detainees. They got themselves locked into the Indian cell – in accordance with apartheid, the Indians had been given a separate cell – after lunch one afternoon to explain the protest. (The warders allowed this sort of fraternizing; they simply kept the prisoners in the cell they were visiting until the final lock-down for the night.) The leaders also passed word of the strike, through the members of the catering committee, to the other cells. Those inmates proved difficult to convince; many of the prisoners were being held for just fourteen or so days. Only the Indian detainees agreed to join in the protest.

The veterans from the Island and a doctor in the Indian cell devised the hunger strike's rules. The participants would be allowed to drink sugared water in small quantities; ingesting too much while fasting could be harmful. The exercise fanatics, who awoke early every morning to do their push-ups, pull-ups and sit-ups, were told to stop. The cell leaders agreed not give any forewarning to the authorities.

On the morning that the strike began, the warders arrived, as usual, to release the members of the catering committee to the kitchen – only to be told that the prisoners refused to go. Moreover, no one in the cell would be eating. The strike leaders read out their list of demands: better food; access to the library; less time spent in the locked cells; the immediate release of all detainees. (The last item was included simply as a kind of political statement; the leaders knew they had no possibility of obtaining their freedom.) At exercise time, the detainees informed the warders they would not go outside. They repeated their refusal to eat at lunch and again at dinner.

The next day, officers from Special Branch appeared at the cell. The policemen escorted some of the hunger strikers to Protea, where they were interrogated: the officers wanted to know the names of the strike's leaders. In exchange for revealing the identities, the prisoners would receive a hot, savoury meal. If any of the detainees succumbed to the temptation, they certainly did not tell their cellmates upon returning to Diepkloof; they joined the others in sipping sugar water at the appointed times.

Mpho found the first several days of fasting almost unbearable. He suffered constant headaches. Despite drinking the sugared water twice a day, he became increasingly weak; his arms and hands shook at times. He was irritable, angry, depressed. Others in the cell vomited and were generally ill. But Amos (who would ultimately be elected the mayor of Johannesburg) thrived on the hardship. He would go from bunk to bunk – where people spent the days, too debilitated to do anything – trying to revive the strikers' flagging spirits. He started a song and sang alone, sometimes for thirty minutes or longer, until the enervated detainees found themselves irresistibly drawn to join him.

The warders tried all manner of ploys to break the strike.

They began appearing at the cell with pots of aromatic, steaming food. For Mpho, the meat pies were the worst torture; he loved meat pies and their smell caused him unspeakable agony when the warders brought them around. The prison authorities tried to frighten the detainees into eating. They made the strikers visit the jail's doctors, who lectured them on the permanent injuries inflicted by long-term fasting: blindness; brain damage; weakened heart. The detainees remained steadfast.

A group of concerned members of Parliament visited the strikers. The legislators were led by the legendary Helen Suzman, the lone member of the liberal Progressive Party and the only true opposition to the Nationalists. They met with a few of the detainees in a kind of holding area. Amos, speaking for the strikers, quickly cut off the visitors before they could begin to talk. We didn't agree to see you, he said, and we consider you as part of the problem of the South African government. We see you as part of the laws that landed us in this place. We won't discuss issues, only the immediate release of all detainees and an end to the state of emergency. We thank you. With that, the strikers turned on their heels and asked the warders to return them to the cell.

A few days later, the prison officials met with the strike leaders. Perhaps they were prompted by the spectre of yet more international condemnation were someone to die from the fast; perhaps the visitors from Parliament had prevailed upon them; perhaps both things influenced the government's decision. In any case, the authorities granted the strikers all of their demands except, of course, their release from prison. The fast had lasted for two weeks. A faint, if widespread, cry went up in the two cells when the leaders announced the victory. Everyone began to eat almost immediately; the veterans warned them to consume small amounts in the beginning. Mpho heeded their advice, chewing slowly and resting often. His stomach hurt after each swallow. Others, unable to exert any manner of self-control, gorged themselves and became ill.

The quality of the detainees' food improved dramatically. Now there was a kind of menu: breakfast consisted of soft porridge and bread. Lunch became the main meal and included tinned tuna or eggs. The detainees were served red meat twice a week; on Fridays, they received pork. The *pap* was interchanged with rice and *samp*, coarse maize meal. Vegetables such as potatoes and cabbage became regular offerings. The prisoners could go to the library and the shop a couple of times during the week. They kept their cell door open during the day, which allowed them to mingle with detainees in other cells or wander outside to the exercise yard; they were locked down only at night. Mpho thought the concessions a real victory. Being imprisoned made him feel powerless, diminished, somehow subhuman; to regain a modicum of control, however small, was to regain a sense of his humanity.

But nothing could compensate for his loss of freedom. Every so often, a prisoner would inexplicably be freed. Mpho and his comrades endlessly debated every release, trying to impart meaning to the departures and how they affected those who remained. Some prisoners took to keeping their few belongings packed in a neat pile, having convinced themselves that their turn was next. Every time a warder clanged open the door to the main part of the jail and shouted for a prisoner from Mpho's cell, the man would spring forward with the utter assurance that this meant his imminent departure. (It usually implied something more prosaic, like a visit to the doctor for an eye test or another interrogation.) Mpho and everyone else clung to the hope that they would be freed when the state of emergency expired at the end of its first six-month period. But they also knew that the government could renew it – and their detention – immediately.

One week before the emergency's end, a warder entered Mpho's cell and announced that some people were going to be released on the following day. The detainees tried, without success, to get him to divulge the names. Mpho could not sleep that night for excitement and anticipation. He tossed in his bunk, wishing the night would finish and peering through the dark for a first glimpse of dawn; surely he would be one of those freed. He could not fathom spending any more time in prison. One moment Mpho was certain his name was on the list; the next, he despaired of ever leaving Diepkloof. He was exhausted by the time the cell took on the greyish tinge of early morning light.

The warders gathered the prisoners in the courtyard, where they read out a list of those who were to be released. Mpho's name was among them. The men returned to the cell to gather up their belongings; the comrades who would remain were singing and dancing around them as they packed. Mpho hugged everyone in farewell. The warders escorted him and the others to reclaim the items that had been taken when they were imprisoned; they opened the doors and told the detainees they could go. Mpho walked from the prison to Baragwanath Hospital, the massive structure that served Soweto, to telephone his parents. Joseph answered the call. 'I'm out,' Mpho said. Then he hailed a taxi and went home.

Mpho returned to find Soweto a different place. For the first few days he drifted around, talking to leaders and observing the changes. He was stunned to see how involved everyone in the township had become in the uprising. Mpho attended a SOYCO branch meeting two days after his release and found the hall packed with about 200 people: students, pensioners, housewives. Six months earlier, the SOYCO officers would have been lucky to have thirty participants. All manner of residents were now members of street or block committees; Mpho even encountered an old drinking friend, a former habitué of the *shebeens*, who had become a local leader. The township positively throbbed with activity: on any given day, there was a demonstration against the state of emergency; a march to protest at the lack of government services; meetings of various groups; the hasty convening of a defence squad to guard against a rumoured attack by vigilantes.

The street and block committees – or civics, as they were called – had, in essence, replaced the local government. With all other official structures having broken down, the street committees organized foot patrols to protect the neighbourhoods against assaults, car thefts, rapes. They saw to the collection of garbage, which otherwise would have rotted on the streets. They acted as a kind of neighbourhood liaison group in arranging the food, transport, speakers, and such that were required for a funeral. Making the townships ungovernable was a political act, but one that still left the residents in need of services. That the civics arose, and could fill the void, became a political gesture unto itself. So too was the militancy that permeated the township. Now activists spoke as though the ANC had already been unbanned; they flew the black, green and gold ANC flag; they recited the Freedom Charter openly.

Mpho could not fathom how all this had occurred under the state of emergency. The restrictions were supposed to have quelled political activities; in fact, they seemed to have had the opposite effect. Mpho conjectured that because of the emergency's reach, the government inadvertently managed to realize the goal that the ANC had pursued for decades: to affect, and thereby mobilize, every level of black society. The curfew provision, in particular, made life in Soweto difficult for virtually everyone. It prevented social activities after dark, which irked young people. Night vigils for funerals had to be abandoned, angering churchgoers. There were rampant curfew violations; people who had never seen the inside of a prison suddenly found themselves spending a weekend or longer in Diepkloof for their infractions. Many of the new 'criminals' returned to the township as committed comrades.

With so many people now involved in the uprising, Mpho did not see a role for himself. The anti-government activities had taken on a momentum of their own during his absence; their continuation did not depend on his participation. Besides, he did not want to go back to Diepkloof. Mpho was afraid of being arrested; he saw informers and traps everywhere. He concluded that he was useless to the struggle in his current state. Better to leave things to those who had yet to be jailed and were willing to take risks. The government's re-imposition of the state of emergency a few months later only strengthened Mpho's resolve. The new decree was even more rigorous; within a few hours of its declaration, more than 2,000 people were arrested. Many of the activists who had been in Diepkloof with Mpho were swept up and imprisoned under the broadened provisions.

The emergency now applied to the entire country, not just to certain districts. It put South Africa under virtual martial law. Organizations and open-air gatherings were banned. The government could prosecute any person who made, printed or recorded a statement that was deemed subversive. The press could not take photographs of a disturbance without permission. The police could search just about any person or building at will. They would arrest nearly 30,000 people under the regulations, including 8,000 children. The new emergency was clearly an attempt to suppress, finally and decisively, the worst uprising in the nation's history. But it did not stop there. It was part of a larger plan, devised by a group of military officers who advised President P.W. Botha, to co-opt South Africa's black population.

The officers had studied classic counter-insurgency strategies in other parts of the world. They concluded that the deplorable conditions in the townships provided fertile ground for the ANC and South African Communist Party to launch their revolts. Remove the activists and begin improving black people's lives, so the thinking went, and the impetus for revolution would wither. And because blacks were more concerned with economic betterment than civil liberties (according to the strategists), they would then be amenable to a limited political dispensation that retained apartheid's basic structure. (This approach the cynics dubbed 'crush, create, negotiate'; the military men called it WHAM: Winning Hearts and Minds.) Unlike the reforms of the early 1980s that attempted, through a new constitution and tri-cameral parliament, to impose change from the top downwards, this plan would begin at the community level. So the civics, the scores of street and block committees, had to be destroyed. In their stead, hundreds of small military-civilian governmental groups were deployed, with little knowledge of the parliament or the public, throughout the country. They coordinated the 'neutralizing' of the activists with the remodelling of squatter camps and townships. The groups would construct roads, lay sewer pipes, build houses. They would create an image of good government among blacks to persuade them to join, not fight, the system.

The repressive measures sent Mpho into a kind of hibernation. He hid in Soweto or in town; he dropped out of sight.

Mpho spent the rest of the year doing odd jobs that kept him away from confrontations with the security forces. He worked at a community newspaper for a while, then at a think-tank that collected data on race relations in South Africa. There he met Ina Perlman, the head of Operation Hunger, a non-governmental organization that provided food to the needy. Mpho and Ina struck up a combative friendship, engaging in lengthy political discussions and disputing various points of the uprising. One day she asked him if he would accompany her to observe a feeding programme she had in a squatter camp in Soweto. Ina was dissatisfied with the project; to Mpho, it seemed that no one was in charge and he offered to help. Mpho found that he had a talent for such work. Ina so liked the way he restructured the Soweto programme that she offered to hire him. Operation Hunger was expanding to rural areas; a job in the northern Transvaal would allow him to escape the perils of the township.

Thus began Mpho's new life. He went to live in an area known as Sekhukhune Land, in the north of the country, among the Pedi people. The language, Sepedi, was similar to Sotho; Mpho communicated with the villagers with relative ease. But theirs was a different world. Mpho had spent little time in the countryside and was stunned to see the extreme poverty and underdevelopment that apartheid mandated. The government had almost totally neglected the black rural areas. Mpho spent his days travelling from one tiny village to another, helping to establish self-help projects among farmers, artisans, women's groups and the like. He also organized food distribution to the poorest people. The local chief and a few old-time comrades befriended him, educating him in the area's history of resistance to the government. For Mpho, steeped in the lore of the urban struggle, it was a revelation.

While his work kept him occupied during the week, Mpho found the weekends boring; there was little diversion. He tried to return to Johannesburg once a month, mostly to see Hloyi. But each visit terrified him. Nonetheless, he and Hloyi decided to get married. Throughout his time in detention, Mpho had longed to wed; he wanted to be settled, to have a sense of normalcy to his life. Slowly, over three months, he paid *lobola* to Hloyi's family, much as Joseph had done before him. Mpho stole back into Soweto for the church ceremony, which took place in the middle of the week. It was a small wedding, with only the families and a few friends in attendance; soldiers had virtually occupied the township, putting a damper on celebrations. Mpho, who was terribly nervous, wished the priest would hurry up with the service. But the clergyman seemed oblivious to Mpho's agitation and plodded on with the ceremony. Mpho fled as soon as the minister finished; he returned to Soweto to be with Hloyi as often as he could at the weekends.

In the meantime, Mpho took on more responsibility at Operation Hunger. He travelled to other areas to work with church and community groups. Ina appointed him as the national coordinator; Mpho opened offices in Durban, Bloemfontein, Port Elizabeth, Cape Town. The aid agencies of Germany and the United States gave funds to the organization, as did big businesses in South Africa – a means of clearing their consciences about apartheid, in Mpho's view. Although he always tried to do a bit of ANC proselytizing when possible, his days of political activism now seemed a distant thing. Still, Mpho derived great satisfaction from his job: this was alternative development, the work the white government refused to do for the majority population. After the years of shouting slogans and engaging in abstract political pursuits, he was doing something concrete. He was helping to empower his people.

CHAPTER TWENTY

Tshepiso

On the aeroplane to Australia, Tshepiso did not stop gripping the armrests of his seat until two hours into the flight. Only then did he relax, convinced that the aircraft would not turn back, that he had truly left South Africa. Still, the journey was not pleasant. Tshepiso was the only black person on the plane; he had been assigned two seats to himself on an otherwise full flight. The airline officials clearly were not going to discomfit a white passenger by seating him next to a black man. This being his first flight, Tshepiso watched with fascination as the attendants moved down the aisles, politely offering a choice of meals and beverages; when they arrived at his seat, a stewardess wordlessly set down a tray of food and a tin of soda, then went on to the next passenger. The obvious discrimination angered Tshepiso at first. But as the novelty of his experience became evident to him – that he was free and hurtling toward an unknown adventure – Tshepiso's anger dissipated: he was not going to allow anything to interfere with the pleasure of the moment.

Twenty or so hours later, Tshepiso landed in Sydney. He disembarked from the aeroplane and could not grasp what he saw. White men pushing luggage trolleys. White men washing floors. White men cleaning toilets. Tshepiso was in something of a daze when David and Jane Mills, the Moral Rearmament couple who would be his hosts, found him. As they drove into the city, Tshepiso saw white men digging ditches. White men doing road repairs. White men engaged in hard labour! In South Africa, blacks did all such work, with a white foreman standing over them, arms usually folded. Tshepiso had never even seen a white person dressed in workmen's overalls. He felt as though the universe had gone awry.

Tshepiso stayed with David and Jane in Sydney for two weeks before continuing to Melbourne for his course. They were wonderfully hospitable, taking him on tours of the city, pointing out the sights of interest, buying him the biggest ice cream cone he had ever eaten. Tshepiso thought Sydney breathtaking: the quaint little streets suddenly opening onto the splendid harbour; the soaring architecture of the Opera House; the boats and ferries charging back and forth across the water; the bustling mood. He had never seen such a beautiful city, everything so new and lovely. Tshepiso found himself drawing in frequent deep breaths. It was as though he could, after years of constriction, finally respire fully. The absence of menacing authority figures, the open atmosphere, the very otherness of the place seized his imagination. Tshepiso felt free for the first time in his life. It occurred to him that he might now be able to be a normal teenager, much like those he had read about for all those years, cocooned in his bed in Soweto to block out the poverty and violence of his existence; he could discover the world.

Such was his state of mind when he visited Bob and Jean Cordiner one day and saw the family's wooden canoe. His hosts, who were friends of the Mills', lived in an elegant district on the banks of the Parramatta River; the back garden meandered down to the water's edge, where the boat was kept. Bob and Jean's grandchildren explained that canoeing across the river was one of their favorite pastimes. Would he like to try it? Tshepiso, who had never been boating before, immediately jumped into the canoe and began paddling. At first, the experience thrilled him; Tshepiso imagined himself a character in a James Fenimore Cooper novel, navigating the waterways of the New World. Then he noticed a small hole and realized that the canoe was taking on water. He paddled faster, hoping he could make it to the other bank without sinking. Jerked from his reverie, Tshepiso also became aware of the traffic around him, of all the larger, faster boats travelling up and down the river – opposite to his course. He managed to make it to the other side without incident; by now, the canoe had taken on a considerable amount of water. He bailed out the boat, turned it around and headed back, much chastened. Life as a normal teenager had its own dangers.

Tshepiso's course in Melbourne was held in a house that Moral Rearmament owned, an enormous structure set in five acres with a swimming pool that easily accommodated fifty people. Entire families, whose parents worked for the organization, lived there, along with the twenty youths participating in the course. They came from an array of countries: America, Australia, Britain, India, Japan, New Zealand, Papua New Guinea, Sweden, Switzerland; Tshepiso was the only African. Tshepiso quickly became friends with an American student, especially when he confided to Tshepiso his reservations about the MRA creed of private morality – a wariness Tshepiso shared.

The morning routine resembled that of the MRA camps he had attended in South Africa. Tshepiso awoke early to engage in 'quiet time', the period of meditation in which God was supposed to tell him what to do and that he would share with his fellow participants. Afterwards, he ate breakfast with the others and listened to the news. Then the first meeting began. Various speakers, who were considered experts in their respective professions, gave talks at the meetings. One such orator was a refugee who had escaped from Communist Poland and moved to Australia; Tshepiso found him the most interesting. The son of an eventual premier of Western Australia addressed the group, as well as other politicians. They all began by talking about social issues, then told stories about themselves and their families, eventually making their way to the topic of private morality. They would recount tales of how they overcame a personal problem or crisis and how their lives had since changed. The epiphanies had a predictable quality about them: the acquisition of personal morality made them better husbands/fathers/businessmen/politicians/professors. That the broad, social themes seemed nothing more than a ruse to discuss issues of private morality greatly disappointed Tshepiso.

When the first meeting ended, there was song learning. The Japanese youth had to teach everyone a Japanese song; the

Swede, a Swedish song; and so on. Tshepiso taught '*Nkosi Sikelel' iAfrika*', the black national anthem; it became one of the most popular songs of the course. The students also went on field trips in Melbourne, which Tshepiso found more sedate and mercantile than Sydney. They met Melbourne's mayor, politicians, journalists, businessmen. After six weeks of these activities, the participants were to be 'deployed' to different parts of Australia for further training. Despite the course's apparently eclectic nature, its objective had become obvious to Tshepiso by the third week of his studies: to transform the young people into full-time advocates for Moral Rearmament. This did not surprise Tshepiso; he had suspected as much when he read the course leaflet in South Africa. But his eagerness to slip the bounds of Soweto's misery was such that, at some level, he had been willing to accept virtually any means of escape. Now faced with the consequences of his decision, that he would have to promote a set of beliefs he found entirely too conservative, Tshepiso rebelled. His visa was valid for a year; he would leave the programme, and devise a way to support himself and remain in Australia.

The opportunity to do so came in the form of an invitation to Adelaide. A branch of the Uniting Church, a major Protestant denomination in Australia, was holding a workshop there about the anti-apartheid movement; its organizer asked Tshepiso to give a lecture. Once he got to Adelaide, he simply decided not to rejoin the MRA course in Melbourne. Some MRA members in Adelaide tried to dissuade him from leaving, but Tshepiso's mind was set. He was not going to waste his time in Australia engaging in what he considered a meaningless pursuit. He wanted to travel the country, see everything, enjoy himself. The sense of liberation from all that he had known – and feared – in South Africa accounted for part of his desire; being twenty years old and footloose was the other part.

Tshepiso found it easier to manage on his own than he had imagined. Adelaide, a lovely city built in sandstone along the lines of a Roman town, struck him as rather progressive. His status as a persecuted South African seemed to carry a certain cachet. The members of the Uniting Church opened a bank account for him, into which they deposited funds on occasion. Local businessmen offered him odd jobs to supplement the allowance. Tshepiso unpacked boxes in a supermarket, worked as a cashier, and so forth. As it was casual employment, he did not have to worry about having the proper visa. Charles Olweny, an expatriate Ugandan oncologist who was active in the local anti-apartheid movement, invited Tshepiso to stay in his home.

The offers of employment and refuge were a pattern that would be repeated throughout his travels. (As was the unsolicited attention from women eager to engage in an affair with an African man.) Tshepiso came to love the Australians for their warmth and generosity. Many of those he encountered were not active members in the anti-apartheid movement, but had, at least, a basic understanding of the black struggle and much sympathy for it. The sanctions against the highly competitive South African cricketers, which prevented them from taking part in international matches, seemed to have made a profound impression on even the most apolitical person in the cricket-mad country. And he never met with racism. Tshepiso knew of the injustices committed against the aboriginal peoples of Australia, but he would not personally experience any form of prejudice.

Now freed from his obligations to MRA, Tshepiso travelled to the north-west to Alice Springs. He wanted to experience the outback; his friends in Adelaide said that Alice was the quintessential frontier town. It did not disappoint him. The place conformed to the image of the American Wild West that Tshepiso had conceived from all the books he read: tough, solitary characters and a plethora of pubs. Tshepiso even managed to find employment. A school that specialized in language studies hired him to do translations. For several days, Tshepiso turned various English expressions into Sotho, Zulu and Xhosa; the queerness of doing such work in such a place only added to Alice's aura. The school paid him handsomely for his labours.

Tshepiso returned to Adelaide; from there, he travelled west to Perth by bus. The trip took two and a half days. At first the road followed the coastline; then it entered the Nullarbor

Plain and came upon an astonishing landscape such as Tshepiso had never seen. For hundreds of miles he found himself staring out the window at nothing. Waves of heat rose from the ground, creating odd, shimmering shapes on the horizon. Hour after hour, Tshepiso watched the same lifeless scene pass by his window; he fell asleep and awoke to find that nothing had changed. The immensity and emptiness of the country felt overwhelming.

It was a great relief to arrive in Perth. Tshepiso stayed with Kim Beazley, whom he had met in South Africa, and his wife Betty. They seemed not to care that he had deserted the MRA course; not once during his two-week stay did they try to convince him to return. Instead, his hosts took him on tours around the city and to the outlying areas. Tshepiso liked everything about Perth; it was so far removed from the other population centres that Tshepiso felt as though he might as well be in another country.

He went back to Adelaide by train, which was faster and more comfortable than the bus. Then he returned to Melbourne; he would use the city, where he had developed the most friends, as a base for his travels. Tshepiso took trips to Sydney, to a fishing village in Queensland province, to various coastal towns. He did not feel guilt at gallivanting about the country; he was also promoting the struggle for liberation. Everywhere he travelled, Tshepiso spoke about conditions in South Africa and worked with local anti-apartheid groups. He made a point of keeping abreast of events at home. Tshepiso relished the Australian news broadcasts about South Africa: its journalists always interviewed blacks, even for the most arcane of economic stories. To see such a thing made him feel proud; his people never received that kind of recognition in South Africa. But it also made him terribly homesick.

In Melbourne, Tshepiso made contact with a white South African emigré who had been Joseph's boss at the construction company. The man and his family welcomed Tshepiso warmly; any child of Joseph would always have a place in their home. Tshepiso became close friends with the teenaged children, going to the cinema with them or to an Asian restaurant for dinner.

The daughter taught Tshepiso how to drive. Through long discussions, they learned of his desire to continue with his studies; one by one, as if by conspiracy, they began talking to him about staying in Australia to study. One afternoon the man presented Tshepiso with a Macquarie dictionary, a huge text used by university students. 'With this,' he said triumphantly, 'you'll be able to go to school in Australia.'

Once the family put the idea into his head, Tshepiso could not forget it. He desperately wanted to go to university; given the situation in South Africa, he had no better chance of achieving his goal there than in Australia. The proposition made sense. Tshepiso ceased his travels and devoted himself to finding out how to apply to Australian institutions. It turned out that the next year's quota for scholarships for South Africans had already been filled but a Member of Parliament, who had befriended Tshepiso, offered to take his case to the proper authorities to determine if an exception could be made. In the meantime, some of Tshepiso's friends from the Uniting Church became aware of his plans. They suggested that he instead consider going to Britain, where they had connections and could help him gain entry to a university. Tshepiso felt positively dizzy with possibilities.

After much reflection, he decided to pursue leads in England. His visa for Australia had already expired; to receive the proper student credentials, he would have to leave the country. Tshepiso feared that if he returned to South Africa to await a new visa, he would never get out again and never go to university – something he was now determined to do. With the decision made, Tshepiso's friends seemed in a competition to surpass one another in helping him. The MRA people, who bore Tshepiso no grudge, obtained a visa for him to Britain. The Uniting Church people gave him money to cover his initial expenses. Everyone provided names and telephone numbers of contacts in England. Tshepiso traded in his return aeroplane ticket to Johannesburg for one to London. He was sad to leave Australia, but it was time to go; his days of revelry were over. It was time to get on with his life.

* * *

Tshepiso arrived in England in the dead of winter. He went directly to Oxford, where a Moral Rearmament family awaited him. When they invited Tshepiso to stay in their home, he readily accepted; he had few qualms about taking advantage of MRA hospitality. His objective was to enter university and he would do anything that might help him to succeed. Tshepiso had already decided on a strategy: he would apply to Oxford Polytechnic (now Oxford Brookes University), which accepted part-time students, as a means of gaining a foothold in an institution. He was required only to take an English test. Tshepiso found the examination absurdly simple, finishing the questions in fifteen minutes – he had been allotted an hour – and passing with ease. He registered for courses in education and history. Tshepiso dreamed of majoring in education, the most respected career for a black person in South Africa. He paid for the courses and the necessary books with some of the money the Australians had given him. He also bought a bicycle for transport around Oxford. Now he had only to wait for the new term to begin.

It was the worst Christmas of Tshepiso's life. He had just come from an Australian summer of brilliant sunshine and heat, a place of noisy, vibrant, frenetic people. By contrast, Tshepiso found Oxford dark and cold. Everything seemed grey to him: the university, the houses, the shops, people, pets. Everybody seemed to move slowly. Tshepiso awoke on Christmas morning to a city that was motionless, the shops closed, the roads empty. He spent the day cooped up in the house with the MRA family, exchanging gifts and watching television. The rituals seemed forced and silly to him. Christmas in Soweto, by comparison, was pulsating: the township resonated with cries of 'Happy!' emanating from just about every home. People sat outside in the hot summer sunshine, drinking beer, listening to music, dancing, sauntering from party to party. There was a warmth and spirit that Tshepiso could not imagine in Oxford.

He remained in his room for much of the holiday season, reading books and waiting for his courses to start. Tshepiso bicycled into town on occasion, each time getting ensnared in the traffic system; he invariably ended up riding in the wrong direction. He walked around the streets, familiarizing himself with the shops and discovering the whereabouts of the library. He practised riding up the hill to his new college. He found a place where he could park his bicycle and lock it. He located his classroom, then timed the journey there from his front door. He tried to contain his excitement about embarking on a much-hoped-for life.

On the first day of term, Tshepiso rose early. There had been a heavy snowfall the night before; he did not want to be late for class. He set out on his bicycle, but the snow made it difficult to manoeuvre. Tshepiso was unused to snow; he had only seen it once at home, when Johannesburg was blanketed by a rare winter storm. That snow had melted quickly. Now, struggling to retain his balance while pedalling, Tshepiso suddenly hit an icy patch on the road; his bicycle flew out from beneath him and he was catapulted into a snowbank. There he sat, immobilized by the shock of the cold and the layers of clothing he was wearing. What am I doing here? he wondered. For the first time since leaving South Africa, Tshepiso doubted the wisdom of his choices. He allowed the feelings to wash over him for a moment. Then he stood, brushed the snow off his clothes and backpack, mounted his bicycle and started up the hill again.

Tshepiso adjusted slowly to the rigours of studying in England. He felt like an outsider; the others in his classes had been students at the polytechnic for a while and were friendly with one another. He led a solitary existence, attending classes in the mornings and spending afternoons in the library. Then he rode to the house, ate dinner and studied in his room for the rest of the evening. He was terribly lonely. The uncertainty he experienced on the first day of term returned to plague him. Tshepiso often wondered whether he had made a mistake in attempting such a difficult task on his own. He questioned whether he would survive England.

Then he met a fellow South African, Carmelo, who had studied in Oxford for several years. Their relationship brightened Tshepiso's existence; now he had a close friend from home. He envied Carmelo living in a student hostel. Carmelo did not

have to telephone his residence each time he stayed late at the
polytechnic or decided to have supper with friends, as Tshepiso
did. Tshepiso chafed under the strictures his hosts placed on
him: accounting for his movements, giving detailed descriptions
of people visited or restaurants frequented. In contrast, Carmelo
could, on a whim, stop at a fish-and-chip shop and have a meal.
Carmelo introduced Tshepiso to an Italian, Julio, who lived in
a house around the corner from the MRA family. The three
young men quickly became an inseparable trio, studying
together in the library, going to pubs, playing tennis or football. The friendships marked a turning point for Tshepiso; he
began to feel less lonely.

Tshepiso excelled at his courses, easily passing them. He
decided to stay at Oxford Polytechnic and apply to be a full-
time student. Although his academic adviser had assured him
he would be accepted at any number of universities in the UK,
Tshepiso could not bear to think of having to start over again
in a strange city. He had already established himself in Oxford.
He knew the courses he wanted to take; he had friends; he had
a life. Tshepiso put in his application and was admitted to the
polytechnic as a full-time student for the start of the next
academic year; he would take courses in education and history.
All he needed now were the funds to pay for his studies.

He had only a bit of money left from the contributions he
received in Australia. Struck by a sudden inspiration, Tshepiso
spent two hours in the library one afternoon compiling a list
of every trust, charity and foundation he could find. He returned
to his room and painstakingly wrote, by hand, 300 letters to
the potential donors: 'Dear Sirs: I'm a South African student in
England trying to study at university. The fees and books and
living costs are all very expensive. I was wondering if you could
see fit to assist me in any way . . .'

The replies were disappointing. Most apologized for not
engaging in this type of assistance or suggested soliciting other
organizations. One respondent wrote that he felt sympathy for
Tshepiso and was including a small contribution of fifty pounds.
A charity in the north of England sent Tshepiso 200 pounds.
Not long after, the movie *Cry Freedom*, chronicling the life of

the Black Consciousness leader Steve Biko, was released; the head of the charity wrote a note to Tshepiso, saying the film had touched him so deeply that he was enclosing another cheque, doubling the charity's original donation. An American member of Moral Rearmament, whom Tshepiso had met in Australia, offered to provide a monthly stipend of $70. He wanted to emulate a kindness bestowed on him as a youth. A philanthropist, who chanced upon the man while he was working as a train steward and took a liking to him, had paid for the man's university education. The man could not muster the largesse of his benefactor, but still wanted to help Tshepiso in a similar fashion.

The donations left Tshepiso hundreds of pounds short of the fees he had to pay as a foreign student. After the term began, he made an appointment to speak with the polytechnic's rector. He entered the rector's office reluctantly; the request for an audience was a desperate act. 'I may have to abandon my courses because I don't have enough money,' he explained. 'I tried to get a scholarship, but failed. And I can't work in Britain because of my visa. I was hoping the university might be able to do something to help.'

'You should have anticipated this before coming to England to study,' the rector replied.

Tshepiso felt his face grow hot with anger. 'If I thought that way, I would never have left Soweto,' he retorted. 'I vowed to myself I would try to do everything I could to get my education. And I will get my education. I will. I'm not going back to South Africa without it.' Trembling, he excused himself and departed; his interlocutor clearly had no notion of the vicissitudes of black South African life. Still, Tshepiso chided himself for having become so emotional. It was not, he knew, the English way.

A week later, he was summoned to the rector's office. The polytechnic had decided 'to mitigate' his fees by fifty per cent; the rector hoped the reduction would allow Tshepiso to remain enrolled. Tshepiso thanked him profusely. Now he might be able to scrape through the year, but only if he could find some sort of employment to supplement his donations. Tshepiso took on a series of jobs (his visa be damned). He did just about anything to survive: served drinks in a pub; took students on tours of Oxford; typed theses; worked as a handyman; wrote articles about Africa for various publications. The number of enterprises that were willing to employ him illegally surprised Tshepiso; they allowed him to finish his first year of studies, albeit barely.

For the next year, Tshepiso received a full scholarship from the Africa Educational Trust, whose founder, Michael Scott, was a strong supporter of black liberation movements throughout Africa. The gift paid for fees and books and provided a monthly living allowance. Tshepiso was ecstatic. Now he could concentrate his energies on studying. He left the house of the MRA people and moved in with a family that was active in the local anti-apartheid movement. They lived in a lovely old part of town; Tshepiso resided in a shed that they had converted to living quarters at the far end of a rambling garden. He could come and go at will. He particularly liked the neighbourhood; his house stood opposite a pub, whose owners befriended Tshepiso. They thought him solid and steady and cajoled him into working on occasion, mostly before and after a football match, when the pub did a brisk business. Tshepiso acted as a bouncer, preventing hooligans from entering and ejecting drinkers who became too disorderly. He enjoyed the gruff swagger he adopted for the role. And the stun gun that he ostentatiously displayed in his pocket made him feel like a character in a crime film.

Tshepiso earned enough money from the pub to visit Rocks in Cologne. Rocks, after waiting for months in Lusaka, had finally received a scholarship from the East German government to study to be a draughtsman. Tshepiso began writing to him when he learned of his proximity; he organized the trip as soon as he could purchase an aeroplane ticket. Tshepiso was shocked to see his revered older brother leading so dissolute an existence. Rocks lived in a shabby flat in a decrepit part of town. He briefly showed Tshepiso the city's sights and introduced him to a few African acquaintances; but most of their ten days together were spent in bars, talking and drinking. Rocks drank incessantly.

Over and over, Rocks told his brother about his falling out with Umkhonto and how he hoped to start life anew by studying. That had not happened. At the age of thirty-four, he was considerably older than the other students and had little in common with them. Most refused to speak to him, let alone befriend him. He attributed this to the differences in age and race. Rocks had encountered much racism in Cologne; on several occasions, his classmates had saluted him with cries of 'Heil Hitler!' Then there was the problem of language. He was too old, his concentration too shattered from living in war zones, to master a new language. He had wanted to study in an English-speaking country, but scholarships to places like Australia or England were highly prized and few in number.

One night, after an especially long bout of drinking, Rocks seemed overcome by despair. 'I've got to get out of Germany,' he said, grasping Tshepiso's hand. 'I hate it here. You've got to help. Help me go to school in England. Promise you'll help me.' Tshepiso nodded, knowing there was little he could do; he just wanted to give Rocks a sense of hope. Rocks relaxed his grip. 'I should never have joined Umkhonto. I should have just gone on with my studies, like you and Dee. After all the years I gave to the struggle and the sacrifices I made, you'd think I'd end up with something better than this,' he said bitterly, gesturing at the dilapidated drinking establishment, the ruined late-night patrons. 'This is my reward for trying to liberate South Africa.'

Tshepiso left East Germany with a profound sense of sadness. He hoped that Rocks would somehow find a way to change his life for the better. Tshepiso felt almost embarrassed that his own life, by comparison, had become so satisfying. The family that provided him with the garden shed embraced him as one of their own. They included Tshepiso in all their anti-apartheid activities, opening up a new world. Now he had friends who were residents of Oxford, not merely transient students; a hatred of the white South African government bound them as partners. Together, they stood outside the local Shell petrol station to promote a boycott of the company's products. They organized protests against other corporations that did business with

South Africa. They worked on various anti-apartheid campaigns in the community.

Tshepiso felt resolved, at one with the decisions he had made; this was the path his life should take. He had his studies, his friends, his political work. But he never lost sight of the fact that he would be going back to South Africa. He kept the rubber bullet that had grazed his head on one turbulent afternoon in Soweto prominently displayed on his bookshelf, a reminder from whence he came. Tshepiso would earn a BA with honours from the polytechnic and move to the University of Warwick, to complete an MA in sociology. Then he would return home. Nomkhitha's dream of education, first envisioned in the Transkei all those years ago, would finally be realized.

CHAPTER TWENTY-ONE

Dee

Dee and his fellow graduates landed at the Lusaka airport, where they expected to be met by representatives from the ANC's Department of Information. Instead, Johnstone (Johnny) Makatini, the Director of International Affairs, greeted them. Dee thought it odd that Johnny, a veteran ANC diplomat, had personally come to meet the dozen or so newcomers – until Johnny announced that they would all be working for him.

Dee decided the change suited him, his degree in journalism notwithstanding. He was designated as the liaison to the ANC's offices in Western Europe – a job that provided considerable intellectual stimulation with no risk of being placed in a dangerous military situation. He served as a conduit for queries coming from the European offices and passed to them relevant policy speeches and other pronouncements from the head office. His companions who had travelled with him from Tanzania were appointed to similar jobs for other parts of the world: Africa, Latin America, Eastern Europe, the Middle East. Dee's section was among the busiest, given the strength of the anti-apartheid movement in England and the Nordic countries. Still, he and the others often found themselves with little to do when their boss travelled abroad; Dee quickly concluded that the ANC's international affairs consisted of little *but* Johnny. He was an indefatigable traveller who, despite a serious diabetic condition, kept up an exhausting pace in promoting the ANC's cause throughout the world.

Dee greatly respected his boss and thus was flattered when Johnny assigned Dee to live in his home. Dee became a personal assistant to the diplomat, helping him to write speeches, scheduling appointments, driving him around Lusaka; Dee suspected he had been singled out because of his journalism skills. Living with such a high-ranking figure afforded certain perquisites. Johnny allowed Lindi, who was well along in the pregnancy, to stay in the house; Dee paid for her ticket from Tanzania with the money that remained from his scholarship. And Johnny gave Dee the use of his car when he travelled.

Otherwise, Dee found life in Lusaka grim. He was used to the anonymity of his Tanzanian exile: if the ANC kept watch over its members there, it did so discreetly. The same did not hold true at head office. The intelligence, or security, department seemed blatantly obtrusive to Dee. He understood the need for its heavy-handed approach; the Boers had been highly successful at infiltrating the exile community. Unlike in Dar es Salaam, the exiles lived under the constant threat of an attack by the South African security forces. Still, the omnipresence of ANC agents made for a tense atmosphere in Lusaka. Dee felt as though he were under constant surveillance. He ceased to believe anything a fellow exile said about the work he did. Everyone Dee met appeared to lead a shadowy existence; everyone appeared to belong to a secret ANC structure. Even social events, parties and such, had a kind of clandestine quality to them.

Early in his stay, Dee tried to escape the tension by going for a drink with a friend at one of Lusaka's better hotels. They had barely settled into their seats when an ANC security officer approached them. 'Hey, you should know very well that you're not allowed to drink in this hotel. You'd better pack it in now and leave.' Dee and his friend ignored the man; why could they not patronize a place of their own choosing? The officer continued to harass them until the two young men became so uncomfortable that they departed. Dee later learned the hotel was a haven for drug dealers, particularly from South Africa; they had managed to recruit several ANC members, which explained the officer's harshness.

Dee also disliked what he perceived as the gossipy, insular nature of the place. Here was where you discovered what people in the organization truly thought of you. Everyone, it seemed, was bent on bettering his image and currying favour with the authorities to gain something: a particular job, a car, a coveted apartment. And if you were simply a young man who had acquired some expertise and wanted to put it to use, you were viewed as pompous or having an attitude. Especially if you were a Mashinini. After all, the disparaging document about Tsietsi that Dee had seen years earlier in Cairo came from Lusaka. It was manufactured here, in the holy of holies. Dee had found it easy to disassociate the ANC from the matter of his brother while living in the East African bush; but not now, not in the organization's nerve centre. The realization disquieted Dee. When people appeared aloof, he felt certain it was because of his surname. He took to searching every face to try to discern who hated Tsietsi and, by extension, him. That the other ANC stalwarts seemed mostly contented only heightened his sense of isolation. Dee resolved to leave Lusaka as soon as possible.

That determination became an imperative when Johnny suddenly died in December 1988. He had developed an abscessed tooth that caused him great pain. Dee, aware of his discomfort, gave Johnny a bottle of Grandpa's, an analgesic that he and Lindi had received in a package from home. The medication worked so well that Johnny began taking it regularly. He did not treat the infected tooth, only the pain; and he continued with his frenetic schedule. Dee could see that Johnny's health was deteriorating. The diplomat's face swelled up, the pain becoming harder to control. By the time Johnny entered a hospital in Lusaka for proper medical care, it was too late: with an immune system weakened by diabetes, he could not fight the infection.

Johnny's death devastated Dee. He had lost a beloved friend and protector. Not long after, the ANC transport committee made Dee return Johnny's car. Dee was fortunate, in the committee's opinion, to have had access to a car at all; cadres spent years in Lusaka without such a luxury. Although Dee and Lindi were allowed to remain in the house, Dee feared that life was about to become more difficult. Several ANC representatives from Europe, who were considerably senior to Dee, had recently returned and were awaiting new assignments at headquarters. Dee believed it only a matter of time before he lost his job. He decided to leave for Harare immediately after Johnny's burial.

First he dispatched Lindi. She had about two months left before the baby was born; Dee told the ANC authorities he wanted her to give birth in Zimbabwe, where the hospitals were better. He would join her for the birth and remain in Harare for a while. His family intended to meet him there: they would see the baby and be reunited with Dee after more than a decade of separation. The ANC officers assented to the plan; this was only a temporary sojourn. And so Dee departed Lusaka.

Dee could organize a visit to Zimbabwe for his family because, despite the continued oppression, the political situation in South Africa was beginning to change. The second state-of-emergency that drove Mpho from Johannesburg had worked only nominally. It essentially crushed the rebellion and restored a modicum of calm to the townships. But the government's more ambitious plan to co-opt the black population did not succeed; it could not entice even those leaders viewed as collaborators by comrades to accept a limited political dispensation that retained apartheid's basic structure. The government renewed the emergency. By 1989, more than 4,000 people had been killed since the uprising's inception; 50,000 had been detained without trial. International sanctions were squeezing the economy. Foreign companies sold their operations and left the country. The value of the rand plummeted. The Nationalists' attempt to preserve apartheid was destroying the country.

Faced with this dire situation, an influential minority of white South Africans began thinking the unthinkable: perhaps someone ought to talk to the ANC to find a solution. The view was shared by the more enlightened members of President P.W. Botha's Nationalist regime, by Afrikaner intellectuals and businessmen. At the ANC's instigation, they started meeting with officials from the organization outside South Africa, sometimes in secret, sometimes in highly publicized gatherings. These occurred while representatives of the Pretoria government were having clandestine discussions with Nelson Mandela in prison. (The encounters had begun in 1986.) Although people in the townships, like the Mashininis, could hardly be privy to the political manoeuvrings, there was a feeling of something astir, the barest flutter of a butterfly's wings. That Nomkhitha and Joseph could now talk freely on the telephone to Dee and plan a trip abroad was evidence enough.

Dee and Lindi settled into the ANC's guesthouse in Harare. As far as the ANC was concerned, they were simply awaiting the delivery of their baby and the visit of Dee's family. Stanley Mabizela, who had been Dee's saviour in Swaziland and was now the ANC's representative in Zimbabwe, welcomed the couple. Lindi gave birth in January 1989 to a daughter. Informed by telephone of the arrival of her new granddaughter, Nomkhitha named the baby Ayanda (to multiply), in the hope that girls would multiply in the family. Dee's greatest wish for his daughter was that she not grow up outside of South Africa. He did not want her to be Zimbabwean; she was South African. He and Lindi decided to raise her speaking only English until they could return to the land of their native tongues.

After Ayanda's birth, Dee became more determined not to return to Lusaka. He found Harare a charming place. Less than a decade had elapsed since independence; Robert Mugabe, the president, had yet to implement the disastrous economic and political policies that would later ruin the country. Harare had a proper business district built around a verdant main square; the roads were planted with jacaranda and flame trees; there were attractive shops, restaurants, hotels. Zimbabwe seemed a world apart to Dee. He could enter a shopping centre (a shopping centre!) and find cheese. It had been years since he had done such a thing: not in the Tanzanian bush, nor in the shortage-plagued cities of Zambia. Harare, Dee decided, was even better than Cairo because everyone spoke English. The city was lovely, there were good clothes to buy and excellent music to enjoy. Dee told Stanley he wanted to stay. He would continue with his studies or take a job. Stanley, a sympathetic man who felt a deep affinity with both Dee and Rocks, accepted his request.

Now Dee needed to find a way to remain in the country. He took a job with a film company that advertised at the offices of the ANC and Pan Africanist Congress for extras. The movie was about South Africa; in one scene, Dee had to coax a herd of cows across a field outside Harare. He repeated the take a few dozen times before mastering the idiosyncrasies of cattle. The company hired Dee to work on a second film, a documentary, in which he played a Namibian guerrilla fighting against South African soldiers. He also worked as a part-time correspondent for an Italian news agency, writing stories about South Africa and dispatching them to the correspondent in Nairobi. The job paid well and in dollars. Dee's work allowed him to move in to Stanley's old, two-bedroom apartment in central Harare when the ANC provided Stanley with a house. Dee considered it a stroke of great fortune: the flat had a good kitchen, a balcony that overlooked the city, and an array of second-hand furniture. Dee and Lindi hired a black-and-white television and set up house.

A couple of months later, Joseph and Nomkhitha drove to Harare for a visit. Mpho and Elvis, the tenth-born Mashinini child, accompanied them. (The government had recently returned Mpho's passport to him.) They left Soweto at four o'clock in the morning to avoid the heaviest traffic at the border post, but got detained there nonetheless; the official questioned the owner-ship of their hired car and the arrangements for insurance. It was evening by the time they arrived at Dee's apartment.

Everyone spent a long time crying at first; they were too over-whelmed to say much. Joseph could not take his eyes off Dee. He no longer looked like the young boy who had gone into exile; he was a man, replete with the receding Mashinini hair-line. When the sobbing stopped, the talking began. Dee did not sleep that night. He stayed up until dawn, trying to compen-sate for a dozen years of separation. Elvis had been a baby when he left; now he was a tall, handsome young man who had inherited Joseph's religious bent and talent for preaching.

It was a splendid, if frenetic, weekend. Dee took his family on a tour of Harare, which delighted Nomkhitha; she marvelled at the novelty of blacks living and working in their own city. An incessant stream of Dee's friends, exiles themselves, popped into the flat to meet the guests and hear news from home. The discussions stretched far into the second night. The morning of the family's departure arrived too soon for Dee and Lindi. They walked the visitors to their car, exchanged kisses and hugs and promised to remain in contact. As they watched the car disappear into the cacophonous Harare traffic, Dee and Lindi burst into tears. To be separated again, to be cut off from the people they loved, felt utterly wrong. Things were changing in South Africa, but it would probably be years before they could end their exile. 'Why can't we just go with them?' Lindi murmured. 'Why can't we just go home?'

In the meantime, Dee struggled with the terms of their exile. He began receiving letters from the ANC's head office ordering him to return to Lusaka: the baby has been born, your family has visited, the reasons for your stay in Harare are finished. The tenor became less polite with each successive missive. Stanley too came under pressure from his superiors to send Dee back to Zambia. He gently, but firmly, told Dee to return to headquarters to sort out his problems.

Unable to resist any longer, Dee decided to drive to Lusaka. He had purchased a 1974 mini-pickup a few months after his arrival in Harare. It was neither the prettiest vehicle nor the shiniest, but it was the first car he had ever owned, and he adored it. Dee loved long-distance driving; and taking the vehicle to Lusaka would make him feel more in control. He could drive to headquarters, have his meeting, drive back to Harare. And if the encounter with his ANC superiors turned sour, he could always make a screeching get-away; he would not be dependent on an airline schedule.

Dee set off for Lusaka early in the morning. The journey took several hours, but he did not mind. He liked the long, lonely stretches of *veldt*, the sensation of speeding along the two-lane, tarmac road. He could think clearly. The ANC had given him his education, his job, his existence; for these, he was deeply grateful. But the time had come to declare his independence. He wanted his own life; of this he was certain. He and Lindi had come to the same conclusion after long, searching discussions.

Dee drove directly to the ANC's head office where he was to report to the assistant secretary-general, Henry Makgothi. A queue of supplicants waited outside Henry's office. Dee grew increasingly nervous sitting in the anteroom, listening to the official deny the requests of his fellow petitioners. (No, you're not going to Botswana to visit your family, it's too far, put it out of your mind!) Dee steeled himself when he was finally called in. He exchanged terse salutations with Henry, then blurted out the speech he had rehearsed on the drive to Lusaka. 'I want to continue studying in Harare. I'm having problems finding a sponsor and am working to finance my studies on my own. So I'm here officially to inform you,' Dee said, taking a deep breath, 'that I'm out of the Foreign Office and I'm going to university.'

Henry stared at him for a long moment. 'You left without permission,' he said slowly. 'You stayed in Harare for too many months. What about your responsibility to your colleagues in the office? What about the work you were supposed to have done? You're just going to walk out of here and go back to Harare without a thought for your comrades?' Henry insisted that Dee remain in Lusaka for a few months to attend to un-finished business. Dee denied that he had anything to complete; the two wrangled over the matter for a while; after what seemed like hours, Henry agreed to release him from Lusaka. He sent Dee to another office to obtain a letter permitting his transfer to Harare. By the time Dee got the document, it was too late to begin the journey home; he had to spend the night in Lusaka. But he did not mind: he had his letter to freedom, which he kept on his person even while he slept. The next day, Dee drove back to Harare.

He had secured a great victory, not only for himself but for his friend Stanley; now the latter would not be seen to be harbouring an ostensible fugitive. Dee could remain within the ANC fold *and* be independent. The arrangement delighted him; it meant that he could keep the job that Stanley's wife found for him before he went to the Lusaka meeting. Dee worked at the Southern African Research and Documentation Centre, an institution that collected information about the politics and economics of the region. The centre chronicled, among other things, the impact of South Africa's destabilization programme on the area; Dee advised the unit that scanned newspapers for relevant articles. That the work was related, if only tangentially, to his profession gave him much satisfaction.

For the first time since leaving South Africa, Dee felt like a normal human being. He had a proper job, a proper salary, a family, a home, friends. Lindi, too, found work, as a laboratory technician at a hospital. Together they earned enough to support themselves, with money left over for recreation. They attended music festivals, especially when performers from home appeared; went to football matches; went for drinks at good hotels with swimming pools; visited the tourist sites; camped out in the countryside. Dee had a sense of tranquillity: neither the South African security forces nor the internal ANC intelligence agents molested him at this remove. It seemed to him, and to Lindi, an auspicious moment at which to marry.

The wedding took place at the end of 1989. Dee paid *lobola* of about five hundred rands to Lindi's family. Joseph, Nomkhitha, and five of the Mashinini children made the trek northward to attend the ceremony. It was to be a 'white wedding', grander than anything Nomkhitha could have imagined. Lindi wore a traditional bridal gown; eight maids of honour formed her retinue. Dee's twin sisters, the eleventh- and twelfth born, were designated as bridesmaids and rented the appropriately frilly dresses in Harare. Dee contributed to the sartorial splendour by purchasing a tuxedo in Botswana when he went to collect his pay from the Italian reporter. He and Lindi invited about 200 guests; they wanted to make it a significant social event in the South African exile community.

The participants went first to the courthouse for the civil formalities, then to a church for a religious ceremony. A minister performed the rites; Joseph and Elvis prayed; Nomkhitha made a speech, giving the young couple her blessings. Their happiness was marred only by the absence of Lindi's family. They had been detained at the border crossing for lack of the proper documentation for their hired car and did not arrive until the following day.

After the church service, the wedding party moved to a reception in a hall that Dee and Lindi had hired and decorated in an elaborate fashion. They were served a formal dinner that included the usual Soweto wedding fare: chicken, beef, vegetables, spicy salads, fancily wrought cake. An abundance of alcohol added to the gaiety. The disc jockey hired for the occasion played only South African music; and the Mashininis and their guests danced far into the night. The exiles wanted to learn all the latest steps from home and insisted that the younger Mashinini siblings, amid much laughter, teach them. It was one of the happiest moments of Dee's life. He celebrated not only his marriage, but the fruits of his struggle. Life was good.

When their families departed for South Africa this time, Dee and Lindi did not cry. The government's discussions with Nelson Mandela were, by now, an open secret. P.W. Botha, the intransigent Nationalist president, had been replaced by F.W. de Klerk, a pragmatist who appeared committed to reforming the political system. The new head-of-state had released several prominent ANC prisoners and begun repealing some apartheid regulations. Dee, Lindi and the others in exile knew they would soon be going home.

CHAPTER TWENTY-TWO

Tsietsi

Dee could not have imagined exactly how soon he might be able to return to South Africa. Two months after the wedding, on 2 February 1990, President F.W. de Klerk made a stunning announcement in Parliament. The ANC, Pan Africanist Congress and South African Communist Party were now legal organizations, as well as dozens of other banned groups. Political prisoners who had been jailed for non-violent activities would be freed. Certain restrictions, imposed by the state of emergency, were being lifted. Negotiations to establish a new political order would begin in earnest.

Eight days later, Nelson Mandela walked through the gates of his prison, a free man after twenty-seven years of incarceration. It was a heady, glorious moment for South Africans, black and white, who for decades had fought against apartheid; the townships erupted in wild celebration. Although incidents of violence continued throughout the country, they were countered by the discussions that ensued between the government and its opponents. The topics included, among others, the terms under which Umkhonto would end the armed struggle and receive indemnity from prosecution for its soldiers and other political exiles. Stories began to circulate about the imminent return of one of the most famous of exiles: Tsietsi Mashinini. That he was living in Conakry, Guinea, as a guest of Miriam Makeba – this much was known. The rumours, much like the myths that arose about Tsietsi during the 1976 rebellion, seemed to take on a life of their own: now he was moving to Zimbabwe to monitor the political situation in South Africa; now he was organizing rallies in Harare; now he was coming home for a celebration of the June 16 uprising.

The day came and went. Tsietsi did not appear.

Welma, Tsietsi's former wife, was at work when she received a telex from Guinea at the end of July: *Tsietsi terminally ill, suggest you come Conakry immediately.* It was signed by Bageot Bah, Miriam's husband. (Miriam and Stokely Carmichael, the black American activist, had divorced.) The message caused Welma much consternation. She was living in Freetown, Sierra Leone, where she had moved with her new husband. Welma now had two young daughters by her second marriage, in addition to Nomkhitha and Thembi, Tsietsi's girls. She had created a life for herself and her children; she was happy, content, wary of stirring up old demons and conflicts. She did not feel prepared emotionally, after all these years, to see Tsietsi.

Welma agonized over the telex. Her boss, observing Welma's obvious distress, called her into his office. (Welma worked as an information officer for the Mano River Union, a customs agreement between Nigeria, Guinea and Sierra Leone.) 'You should go to Conakry,' he said gently. 'There are so many things a person needs to say on his deathbed.' He offered to give Welma an advance on her salary to pay for the aeroplane ticket. His words helped to ease her mind. Welma left soon after; she arrived in Conakry on the night of 25 July and checked into a hotel.

The next morning, she took a taxi into town and went directly to Bageot's office. He worked for a Belgian airline in rooms above the company's ticket agency. To approach the entrance, Welma had to pick her way among the raucous moneychangers, shoe salesmen and brochette vendors lining the street. Bageot wasted little time on niceties: Tsietsi, he announced, died last night. He was equally direct about the cause of death: AIDS. Welma did not know whether to feel relieved or dismayed by the abrupt notice. Bageot suggested they go immediately to the hospital mortuary to view the body.

At Ignace Deen Hospital, an official ushered them into a cool, antiseptic room where Tsietsi lay on a gurney, covered but for his face. It was strange for Welma, seeing him like that. He gave the impression of simply being asleep. He had lost some weight, but did not appear noticeably thinner from his time in Liberia; his hair was sparser on top, the hairline receding. Otherwise, he looked like the Tsietsi she had known. The tableau took her breath away; he seemed so alive. Welma stood in a kind of reverie for several minutes. Here was the man, the father of two of her children, who had caused her so much happiness and so much pain. Bageot, meanwhile, worried out loud about what to do now. He was a Muslim; his burial rites differed radically from those of Christians. Miriam, who was travelling, told him not to do anything when he telephoned her with the news; she would communicate with Tsietsi's family in South Africa to determine what they wanted. Still, he thought it best to make enquiries about embalming.

Welma accompanied Bageot to a few funeral parlours, then went to see Stokely Carmichael. Stokely conveyed his condolences to pass on to the children; he had been fond of Tsietsi and was saddened by his death. Welma and Stokely spoke wistfully of happier days, when Tsietsi was in military training in Guinea and Welma would come from Liberia for long, blissful weekends. As she was leaving, Stokely said: 'You know, Tsietsi still talked about you from time to time.'

Mpho was in a meeting at Operation Hunger in Johannesburg when a secretary interrupted to say that he had an important telephone call from home. Mpho excused himself and went to an outer office. Dichaba, his younger brother, was on the line. 'Tsietsi is dead,' he said.

Mpho grabbed onto a desk to steady himself. 'Who told you?'

'Miriam Makeba,' Dichaba replied. 'We got a call from her.'

Mpho dropped the telephone receiver and left it where it lay. Dazed, he returned to the meeting. After a few minutes, he asked to be excused to go to the lavatory. Mpho splashed water on his face, took several deep breaths and went back to the room. He stood in the doorway, unable to bring himself to rejoin his colleagues. 'What is it, Mpho?' asked the director, noticing his distress. 'What's happened?'

'Tsietsi is dead.' Mpho's co-workers jumped up to console him, stunned. They surrounded him with a barrage of questions: where was he, when did he die, how did it happen? Mpho retreated to an office to telephone Dichaba. Now he was able to hear, in a coherent fashion, that Miriam had contacted the family after receiving the news from Guinea. Mpho furiously scribbled down the telephone numbers in Conakry that Miriam had given them. He called Guinea and was connected almost immediately – no mean feat, given the country's shocking telephone service. An Operation Hunger colleague who spoke French managed to locate Bageot Bah; he told them of Tsietsi's death from AIDS in a rather desultory manner, then rang off. Mpho left for home.

Nomkhitha was already at the house; Dichaba had telephoned her at work. She sat quietly in her bedroom, awaiting the arrival of Joseph and the other children. She had spent years hoping for Tsietsi's return. The police harassment, her imprisonment, the family's vilification, the deprivation – all had been bearable while she could still hope that her children would someday come home, whole and well. Although she had feared most for Tsietsi's well-being, the dream she had had one night, not long after Tsietsi fled the country, fortified her. In it, her deceased father appeared to her to say that Tsietsi would return to rule South Africa. She had held fast to the promise as though it were the word of God; did her father not teach her that the ancestors were divine interlocutors? Did they not intercede on behalf of the living? All the recent talk of indemnity and of Tsietsi's imminent arrival only buoyed her expectation. She had, of late, allowed herself to imagine Tsietsi walking through the front door. And now this. She believed God would never burden her with more than she could endure; but to come so close, only to lose her beloved son, was beyond tolerance. She began to keen.

By the time Mpho arrived home, Nomkhitha was in a state of hysteria, screaming and pulling at her hair. He got her into a car and drove to a nearby doctor's rooms to obtain sedatives. The other members of the family had assembled when they returned; Joseph could barely speak for his grief. They busied themselves with the details of the funeral. Everyone agreed on two things: they had to get Tsietsi's body back to bury him in South Africa. And they must try to get indemnity for Rocks and Dee so they could return home for the funeral. Tshepiso, who had already been informed of his brother's death in England, did not have to worry about such matters; he would simply purchase an aeroplane ticket.

Mpho telephoned Dee in Harare to tell him the terrible news and enlist his help in transporting the body. Dee had difficulty grasping what Mpho said. He understood the words – *Tsietsi is dead* – but they held no meaning for him. It took Mpho several tries until he was certain Dee had absorbed the information. Dee, like his siblings, buried his anguish in activity. He immediately contacted Ghana Airways, which flew from cities in West Africa to Harare. Yes, an agent said, the company could make arrangements to convey Tsietsi's corpse to Zimbabwe, then to South Africa; Dee would just have to organize payment. In the meantime, its Conakry agency would instruct a local mortuary to embalm the body.

The next step was to request indemnity for Dee and Rocks. Mpho applied through the legal department of the ANC, which now had offices in Johannesburg. Dee received his exemption with little fuss; Rocks' was another matter. His name had already appeared on a list of people whose indemnity the police had rejected. Because of the special circumstances, the ANC put in an application asking that Rocks be allowed to return to attend his brother's funeral, after which he would leave the country. Mpho got a reply a few days later: although the police would not prevent Rocks from entering South Africa, they refused to provide assurances they would not arrest him.

The ambiguous response prompted Mpho to solicit the help of the US ambassador, William Swing, who had been friendly with Tsietsi and Welma while posted in Liberia. Mpho had great respect for the ambassador. The two often met to discuss Operation Hunger's programmes, to which the US government contributed funds. Mpho found the encounters enjoyable; the ambassador would speak at length of Tsietsi, whom he held in high esteem. He telephoned Mpho upon hearing of Tsietsi's death to offer his condolences and his assistance. There was nothing he could do, however, about Rocks' dilemma. Mpho then called on Mervyn King, Operation Hunger's first head and a former judge. After making enquiries, Mervyn delivered an ominous warning to Mpho: under no circumstances must Rocks return to South Africa; he will certainly be arrested.

Dee, meanwhile, had devised a plan with Ghana Airways to fly Tsietsi's body to Accra, Ghana, then to Harare. Dee would claim the coffin and accompany it on the final leg of the journey to South Africa. Joseph, Nomkhitha and the children spent days beseeching all manner of sympathizers – chiefs of corporations, church leaders, anti-apartheid activists, diplomats – for contributions to pay for the transport. Although the American ambassador could not help in the matter of Rocks' indemnity, he did find a way to solve the problem of getting Dee the donations. He allowed Mpho to deposit the money at his consulate in Johannesburg, where it was transferred to the US Embassy in Harare. Dee collected the funds, then paid Ghana Airways to begin the task of bringing Tsietsi home.

Rocks was living in Botswana when he learned of Tsietsi's death. He had moved there after spending only one year in East Germany; the utter futility of attempting to study in a foreign tongue prompted him to relinquish his scholarship. Rocks had visions of starting up an electronics firm in Gaborone, the capital. He struggled with that project, too, finding it difficult to accumulate the necessary capital. Worse yet, after becoming aware of his presence, the Botswanan authorities had begun to pursue him. (Rocks had twice been arrested in the country while working for Umkhonto and thus had a police record.) That he was denied permission to return to South Africa for Tsietsi's funeral seemed in keeping with his misfortune-plagued life. He decided to drive to Harare to meet the coffin before Dee took it to Johannesburg. It would be his only chance to bid farewell to his brother.

The coffin arrived at five o'clock in the afternoon on a flight from Accra. Dee and Rocks went to the airport to receive it, along with a large group of South African exiles. The authorities allowed only the two Mashininis into the customs area, where the coffin was to be held overnight. It was a rough wooden box, tightly bolted. Seeing the container that held the remains of their brother made Dee and Rocks begin to weep. They wanted desperately to open the casket, but the airport officials refused; health regulations required the coffin to remain sealed during transit.

Dee and Rocks drove back to Harare to attend a memorial service for Tsietsi. People had already gathered in Trinity Memorial Church when they arrived. Dee ascended the pulpit; he was supposed to talk about having seen the coffin, when it would leave for South Africa, and so on. But he could not speak. The full import of the loss struck him: here was someone who had loomed so large in his life, and in the lives of his comrades, who had left an indelible imprint on the struggle for freedom – and now was no more. Dee broke down sobbing. Suddenly, from the back of the church, someone began to sing a protest song from 1976. It was picked up, pew by pew, by the rest of the mourners, until their lilting voices filled the nave. They sang every song Dee could remember from the uprising. It seemed to him a fitting tribute, as though only through the majesty of music could they fully honour Tsietsi.

The two Mashinini brothers stayed awake for the entire night. Dee was going home: neither he nor Rocks could fathom the notion. This was obviously not the way Dee had envisioned the journey during all the years in exile, but he was going home nonetheless. The South African authorities had granted him an eight-day visa. Dee and Rocks talked endlessly about what he would do in Soweto; Rocks, not knowing when – or if – he would receive indemnity, longed to join him.

At daybreak, he helped Dee to carry his luggage to the car; the two walked slowly back to the flat. Dee suddenly felt he should do something before leaving. In the manner of his father, Dee stood in the kitchen with his wife, daughter and brother, bowed his head and asked God to guide him in his journey, to help him in any way He saw fit. His supplication was reinforced with a resounding 'Amen' by his family; Dee locked the door to the apartment and they departed for the airport. He clung to Rocks until the last moment, crying. Then he boarded the aeroplane for the short journey home.

Epilogue

From the moment the newspapers and other media disseminated the report of Tsietsi's death, people began converging on the Mashinini residence. Tshepiso arrived from England to a house that seemed more like a railway station. Schoolchildren, church groups, all manner of mourners filled the place, singing, shouting political slogans, cooking, preparing endless cups of tea. There was no space for Tshepiso to unpack his bags, no place for him to sleep. It did not matter; the incessant noise precluded resting anyway.

The family could not escape the hordes of well-wishers. On the morning that Dee and the coffin arrived from Harare, Joseph, Nomkhitha and the children set out in vehicles that a local funeral parlour had loaned to them. (The company also contributed a hearse to transport the coffin.) As they left the township, Mpho saw scores of other cars join them; the drive turned into a raucous procession of honking vehicles. At Jan Smuts International Airport hundreds of other people, watched over by policemen and their attack dogs, awaited them. The comrades packed the hangar-sized arrival hall and spilled outside. Tsietsi may have slipped into an ignominious existence in exile, but the youth of Soweto never forgot him. Now, awaiting his return, the next generation of activists chanted his name, sang liberation songs and danced the *toyi-toyi* in his honour; the Zimbabwean war dance was not even known in the townships during Tsietsi's time.

Dee, meanwhile, was depending on the crowd's presence to protect him after his aeroplane landed. He was terribly apprehensive; he did not know if he was heading to a funeral – or a jail cell. Surely there will be a mass of students come to greet

Tsietsi's coffin, Dee thought, and surely the Boers will have to take note of them. He entered the immigration building with trepidation; a knot of Afrikaner immigration officials stood near the entrance, eyeing the arriving passengers. Almost immediately, an older officer stopped Dee. Pulling him out of the queue of people waiting to have their passports stamped, the man told Dee to take a seat. Dee glumly watched all the passengers from his flight pass through the immigration area to collect their bags. He watched another aeroplane arrive and disgorge another set of travellers into the building. He listened to departures being announced to various destinations in Africa. Finally, two young officers approached the man who had detained Dee. After a brief consultation, one of the officers turned to Dee and said, 'Welcome to South Africa. Follow the arrows out.' Dee complied with the instructions. He gathered his luggage, passed through two sets of doors – and was suddenly surrounded by Mashininis who came flying at him, it seemed, from all directions.

Dee and his family went outdoors into the brilliant winter sunshine to await the hearse. The pallbearers from the mortuary emerged from the cargo area carrying Tsietsi's rough, wooden box. A roar went up from the assembled comrades; here were Dee's anticipated protectors. They sang and wept and intoned prayers as the coffin was loaded into the hearse. Mpho got into an argument with the driver, who wanted to return to Soweto by way of the main highways to avoid the traffic and crowds; Mpho envisioned a kind of triumphal entry into the city, which required taking the road that led directly into the heart of downtown Johannesburg. He also wanted to wait just outside the entrance to the airport to give the other well-wishers time to form a convoy with their vehicles. Mpho prevailed; a slow parade of fifty or so cars, filled with singing, chanting comrades, bore Tsietsi's body home.

As the procession made its way into the city, Dee found the vista stunning. Everything seemed so new, tall, gleaming, big. He was even more dumbfounded by the size of Soweto: it had become enormous; Dee barely recognized any familiar landmarks. He would have got lost immediately trying to navigate the streets. Nor could he identify, after a separation of more than thirteen years, any of the uncles, aunts and cousins who streamed out of his parents' home to greet him when they arrived. He felt like a stranger, watching his relatives carry the coffin inside the house. They placed it in the lounge, where the family recited a short prayer; the ceremony affirmed, as it were, the final homecoming of a loved one. Then the pallbearers returned the coffin to the hearse and transported it to the funeral parlour. Dee wished there were a similar rite for him, one that might ease his sense of alienation and thus his return home.

Two days later, Joseph, Nomkhitha and the older boys went to the mortuary to identify Tsietsi's body formally and to choose a casket for the funeral. There was much talk, as they waited in an anteroom, about whether they would be able to recognize Tsietsi; after all, Dee was the only family member who had seen him since 1976. The Mashininis filed into the viewing room to look at the body. Almost immediately they began to murmur, 'No, no, that's not him, that's not him.' Tshepiso was nine years old when he last saw Tsietsi; the man who lay before him did not resemble the teenager he remembered. Besides, one of his eyes had been gouged out of the socket. Nobody in Guinea had said anything about an injury. Joseph turned to Dee. 'Is it Tsietsi?'

'Definitely,' Dee replied. Upon hearing the confirmation, the mortician removed a wad of cotton wool from the base of Tsietsi's skull to reveal a terrible, gaping wound. 'Shit, they killed him!' Tshepiso gasped. Nomkhitha collapsed, weeping; she had to be helped into a chair. It suddenly became clear that something horrible had befallen Tsietsi, the talk of AIDS notwithstanding.

'Do you want to do an autopsy?' the mortician gently asked, 'or should I just clean him up?' The family members, still in shock from seeing the result of what had to have been a brutal assault inflicted on Tsietsi, debated the matter. Joseph and Nomkhitha opposed it; nearly two weeks had passed since Tsietsi's death, and a post-mortem examination would have further delayed the funeral. There was a limit to the amount of tragedy they could stand. Nomkhitha did not want investigations, she wanted to bury her son. She and Joseph decided against having the procedure done – something they would come to regret.

To plan Tsietsi's funeral, the family had to form a committee. It was forced to do so because of all the groups competing to assert control over the memorial ceremony. The representatives of the Azanian People's Organization (Azapo), which saw itself as the successor to the Black Consciousness movement, were particularly aggressive. They felt entitled to play a dominant role, given that Tsietsi had been a Black Consciousness adherent. But the Mashinini family members, all of whom, by now, supported the ANC, demurred; Tsietsi had been a leader of all South Africans. The June 16 uprising was more uniting an event than perhaps any other in the struggle against apartheid. Students joined together to combat a common problem; to allow one faction to claim Tsietsi as its own was to rewrite history. Despite the family's insistence that all organizations be treated equally, arguments erupted daily over the funeral's details: who should speak, in what order, how much time to allot the various orators, and so on. The committee spent hours just working out which group would convey the coffin from one spot to another. On one matter, however, Joseph stood firm: the family alone would plan the church service.

The siblings had to organize food for the hundreds, perhaps thousands, of mourners who would return to the house after the ceremony. They also addressed rallies and attended to visiting journalists. There was little time left to grieve. People made donations to show their sympathy; the Mashininis felt obliged to acknowledge them. Large corporations, small shops, non-governmental organizations, neighbourhoods, old aunties who lived down the road – all wanted to contribute something. A bus company offered vehicles and drivers to transport people to the various venues. The funeral parlour provided its services for free. Local council workers cleaned the open field opposite the Mashinini home, the site of the endless football games when the children were young, and turned it into a car park. Winnie Mandela visited virtually every day. Tshepiso, long removed from township politics, was of two minds about all the outside intervention. The outpouring of well-wishers seemed a fitting recognition for a leader such as Tsietsi; and yet, Tshepiso longed for a bit of privacy, some solitude in which to reclaim the memory of his brother and mourn.

On the day before the funeral, the older siblings had to slaughter a cow to feed all those who would be attending the ceremonies. Before it could meet its end, the animal escaped from the front yard of the house and rampaged across the adjacent gardens. Some people believed that a cow always took on the characteristics of the person for whom it was being sacrificed; for Mpho, Tshepiso and the others giving chase across the township, the cow certainly seemed to reflect the meaning of Tsietsi's name in Sotho: trouble. A few neighbours observing the scene speculated that the animal, inhabited by Tsietsi's spirit, behaved in a contrary fashion to demonstrate its disquiet about the way in which Tsietsi died. Whatever the reason, the brothers did not succeed in catching it and had to scour Soweto to find a replacement.

The night vigil began a few hours later. The family had erected a tent that extended from the rafters of the house, over the garden and onto the street, where the prayer service was held. The atmosphere among the participants was hardly devotional: fistfights erupted regularly between supporters of Azapo and the ANC, with the church people, who came only to pray, caught in the middle. Mpho had to divide the area into two sections. He declared the right side of the house as ANC/United Democratic Front territory; their members controlled the region extending up the road, where they could sing freedom songs and dance the *toyi-toyi* unmolested throughout the night. But they could not pass to the Black Consciousness side, which stretched down the street from the left side of the house. Azapo and the Pan Africanist Congress exercised authority over that domain. All night long buses arrived, some from as far away as Cape Town and Port Elizabeth, disgorging scores of exuberant young mourners – all of whom had to be herded, by the Mashinini brothers, to the correct side. Tshepiso felt as though he were directing an interminable human traffic jam. Insults were hurled from one group to the other that had to be diffused; fights broke out that required mediation.

Mpho tried to enlist Dee to make a speech to calm people. He believed that Dee's status as an ANC exile could influence the highly emotional crowd. Dee refused; he was attempting to have his stay in South Africa extended and did not want to be seen meddling in political matters. The competition among the groups struck him as unseemly. It was one thing for Mpho to become involved in their disputes; he had remained in the country and was familiar with the various sensibilities. Dee, as an outsider, did not feel similarly adept. He was having a difficult enough time just adjusting to being back home. A sense of not-quite-fitting-in plagued him. He had left Soweto as a boy and returned as a man; but people seemed stuck in a kind of time warp. They still thought of him as a child.

Most of the other Mashinini siblings accepted the political nature of the vigil. This could not be a private time of grieving; Tsietsi had been a public figure and thus would be mourned in a public fashion. Still, they tried to shield their parents as much as possible from the chaos. Joseph, surrounded by his fellow church members under the tent, prayed and sang hymns unperturbed. Nomkhitha remained in the bedroom with Tsietsi's body, which had been brought from the mortuary in a sealed casket for the vigil. She sat quietly on a mattress, as was the tradition, accepting the condolences of the women who came to pay their respects. Even in that serene refuge, the singing, chanting and shouting from outside were inescapable. 'This isn't a vigil,' muttered an aunt, who was acting as an attendant to Nomkhitha, 'this is a political rally.'

Mpho and Tshepiso overslept on the morning of the funeral, exhausted by their efforts of the previous night. The Methodist church was jammed with mourners by the time they arrived. A large crowd, the spillover from the nave, blocked the entrance; people recognized the two brothers and stepped aside, creating a path for them. They joined the rest of the family in the front pews. A row of dignitaries – politicians, diplomats, businessmen – sat nearby. To Tshepiso, the setting had a surreal quality to it. Here was the old minister who had baptized him. Here was the choir singing the hymns he had sung when he was a child. Here were the prayers that had inspired him as a youth. It all seemed so familiar and yet so strange: the rites were being invoked to bury one of his brothers. Speaker after speaker arose to praise Tsietsi. Thabo Mbeki, the ANC's representative (and the current South African president), talked of how the country had lost a fine young leader. Dichaba Mashinini began to cry; then the entire family broke down weeping.

If the church service managed to interject, through prayers and hymns, an element of religiosity into the funeral, the ceremony that followed at Jabulani Stadium was purely political. Thousands of people filled the stands by the time the procession bearing the casket arrived. A banner of yellow and gold hung from the seats, emblazoned with the words: *Hamba Kahle Qhawe* – Go Well, Hero. Despite the ostensible solemnity of the occasion, the atmosphere in the stadium resembled that of a football match. On one side sat the Azapo supporters, clad in gold-and-yellow t-shirts that read, 'Azapo Remembers June 16', chanting and stamping with such force that the tiers bounced. The equally vociferous ANC adherents filled the opposite side of the stadium. Their girl scouts, dressed in short yellow-and-green skirts and black shirts adorned with a map of Africa, danced in formation on the ground below the ANC section.

An Azapo colour guard, dressed in black, military-style uniforms trimmed in gold braid, accompanied the coffin as it was brought slowly into the stadium. They marched under the organization's yellow-and-gold flag, singing the haunting lament from the 1950s that had been adopted by the protesters of June 16: *Senzeni na? Senzeni na?* What have we done? Oh, what have we done? (What is our crime?) The pallbearers mounted a dais that stood at one end of the stadium and gingerly laid Tsietsi's casket, draped in the Azapo flag and bedecked with purple and yellow flowers, on a bier. The Mashinini family and invited dignitaries sat behind it in rows of chairs.

Lybon Mabasa, the master of ceremonies, approached the microphone. '*Viva* the spirit of Comrade Tsietsi!' he yelled.

'*Viva!*' the crowd roared.

'I saw some graffiti written on a wall,' Lybon continued, 'near the Mashinini home. It said: He didn't do it for the ANC, he didn't do it for Azapo, he didn't do it for the individual, he did it for our liberation.' The crowd roared again.

A clergyman mounted the platform. 'Through you Lord,' he prayed in Xhosa, 'the Mashininis had a hero. Through the Mashininis, a hero in Soweto was born. And Lord, you allowed his bones to come back to his place of birth. Don't allow any nation to dominate black people. Don't allow one black organization to dominate all others. The day we are asked to vote, let us vote in one voice. Don't let the devil get in between us.'

The Azapo guards sang 'Nkosi Sikelel' iAfrika', their arms upraised, fists clenched. Then it was the ANC's turn. An ANC honour guard replaced the Azapo youths; the ANC flag replaced that of Azapo. A young man, wearing a t-shirt with Nelson Mandela's face on the front, performed a vigorous *toyi-toyi* and sang lustily in Zulu: 'We are going to Pretoria, we are going to take over!' He shouted out the requisite revolutionary exhortations and received the requisite responses. *Viva* the ANC! – *Viva! Amandla!* (Power!) – *Ngawethu!* (It is ours!) A man who identified himself as a representative of the street committees made a short speech about what Tsietsi meant to the youth of the ANC. Then it was Azapo's turn again.

And so it went, back and forth, between the ANC and the Black Consciousness people. Each time the organization being represented was changed, the flag and other symbols had to be changed, too – a cumbersome process. Now the speaker was a teenager with large glasses from the Azanian Students' Movement; now the former principal of Morris Issacson, Tsietsi's high school; now a Black Consciousness poet. Murphy Morobe, a member of Tsietsi's Action Committee at Morris Issacson, addressed the crowd adorned in a shirt of black, green and gold: the colours of the ANC. 'We have every reason to be angry today,' he intoned. 'Because Tsietsi Mashinini lies here with his hands folded on his chest, unable to raise his arm and clench his fist as he always did in 1976.'

The Mashinini family watched from their seats, squinting under the brilliant winter sun and trying to shade their eyes with their hands or the ceremony's printed programme. They could not allow themselves to display emotion for one speech or another; the ceremony had become a kind of political contest to which they were simple bystanders. They listened impassively to the parade of speakers who ascended the dais. Dee dismissed as rubbish their attempts to appropriate Tsietsi; he was an original and belonged to no one. The jostling to lay claim to his memory and his legacy only underscored, in Dee's mind, Tsietsi's importance to the anti-apartheid struggle. Dee felt enormously proud that his brother still figured prominently in the country's political consciousness, more than a dozen years after his history-making exploits.

The orations went on for several hours. It was mid-afternoon by the time the procession lined up outside the stadium to convey the casket to the cemetery for burial. The dozens of cars and buses snaked through Soweto, slowed by the youngsters who jogged alongside them, singing and shouting. People ran from their homes and stood on the curb to catch a glimpse of the coffin as it passed. From the family's limousine, Tshepiso saw three middle-aged women burst into tears as they passed.

Thousands of mourners waited at the cemetery. The place was in chaos, with people singing, shoving, dancing the *toyi-toyi*; the marshals, who were charged with maintaining order, had lost control. The Mashinini family had to push their way to the grave. A preacher uttered a barely audible prayer over the coffin, then left hurriedly to escape the crush. Tshepiso, who had remained stoical throughout most of the proceedings, started crying when the coffin was lowered into the ground. Now it was done, finished; the finality overwhelmed him. All the emotion he had suppressed during the frenetic days preceding the funeral welled up with an intensity that surprised him. Embarrassed, Tshepiso tried to move away from his brothers.

The crowd, meanwhile, had squeezed Dee to the very edge of the grave. A few metres away, a trade unionist was also being buried. Suddenly, everything around Dee seemed to explode: the union members attending their funeral began fighting, with fists and knives, the Black Consciousness supporters who had come for Tsietsi's burial. Dee found himself in the middle of a mêlée. It was his introduction to the violence that so often accompanied political funerals, something Dee had only read about from abroad. He and his younger brother Elvis fought their way out of the mass confusion and, running wildly, skirted the hand-to-hand combat to return to the limousines.

Joseph, Nomkhitha and the other children also managed to retreat to the vehicles. Many of the people who attended the ceremonies accompanied them back to their home, where an enormous spread of food was arrayed on tables that covered the front garden and the grassy area across the street. For the first time that day, Mpho was able to relax. He wandered through the crowd in the half-light of dusk, greeting friends, urging them to eat and drink. There was an ineffable poignancy about the gathering. Mpho imagined Tsietsi's spirit lingering among the little knots of people, taking in their stories and jokes and reminiscences. Some of the guests began to sing; Mpho listened, spellbound, finding solace in the lilting melodies that continued long into the night.

The mourning period began immediately after the funeral. The Mashinini men attached a black armband or strips of black cloth to their shirts; the women wore black headscarves. As tradition dictated, the mourning would continue for three months. During that time, they would lead a sombre, reflective existence with little socializing. On the weekend following the funeral, Joseph, Nomkhitha and the children cleansed the house, the spades used at the cemetery, their funeral attire. Dee, who had been granted a week's extension on his visa, participated in the rituals. Then he returned to Harare, and Tshepiso went back to England.

After bestowing upon Tsietsi his brief moment of glory, South Africa moved on. Over the next few years, the ANC and the Nationalist government thrashed out the details for creating a new democratic system. It was a painful, fitful process, punctuated by much violence in the country. In February 1993, the two sides announced an agreement in principle: elections were to be held to elect a five-year government of national unity, which would include a multi-party cabinet and be charged with writing a new constitution. The protagonists believed such inclusiveness would help to ease the transition to a fully democratic system. After five years, South Africans would vote to elect a government based on proportional representation.

On 27 April 1994, for the first time in the country's history, the black population went to the polls to elect the leaders of their choosing. The world witnessed an astonishing spectacle. Black men and women, dressed in their best church finery, their children in tow, came in droves to vote. They started queuing before dawn, long before the polling stations opened. This being the first such election in the nation, the polling stations were ill-prepared; many did not open on time or possess sufficient ballot papers. In Johannesburg and its township, the lines of voters snaked out the doors of the buildings and down the streets, often for several blocks. People waited patiently, uncomplainingly, for hours in the relentless autumnal sunshine. A neighbour of the Mashinini family said, 'I've waited all my life to vote. What is another hour or two?'

The election was held over a period of four days. The ANC won 63 per cent of the votes, capturing 252 of the 400 seats in the new Parliament. Nelson Mandela was elected president. Two weeks later, in a striking ceremony broadcast around the world, he took the oath of office. Four thousand guests attended the inauguration outside the Union Buildings in Pretoria. Perhaps one of the most affecting moments occurred when the president-elect arrived in his motorcade and was met by the highest-ranking generals from the South African Defence Forces and the police. As Mandela emerged from the car, the officers saluted, then formed a protective cordon to escort him to the dais – the same men who had helped to hunt him down and keep him incarcerated for more than two decades.

The new president spoke of the future on that day: 'Out of the experience of an extraordinary human disaster that lasted too long, must be born a society of which all humanity will be proud . . . Never, never, and never again shall it be that this beautiful land will again experience the oppression of one by another . . . The sun shall never set on so glorious a human achievement.'

Soon after taking power, the ANC-led government designated June 16 as National Youth Day. On that date in 1995, the following year, the Mashinini family unveiled Tsietsi's tombstone. About 500 people attended the event, including the Anglican Archbishop and Nobel laureate Desmond Tutu. Winnie Mandela, now estranged from her husband and a Member of Parliament, told the crowd that Tsietsi, whom she had known well, was a hero. Drake Koka, the 'Godfather' who had been one of Tsietsi's mentors, addressed the assembly. '[Tsietsi] was a spark of political dynamism that opened the world's eye and focused it on the plight of the South African youths in their struggle for their birthright.'

Welma and her daughters by Tsietsi, Nomkhitha and Thembi, also were in attendance. Welma had found it difficult to say anything to the girls about their father over the years. When they were old enough to begin asking questions, she told them only that Tsietsi was South African; they had divorced because of incompatibility. Welma did not maintain contact with the family in Soweto for fear it would incite Tsietsi to communicate with her. Then he died; and so too, her fears. The journey to South Africa for the unveiling was an epiphany for Tsietsi's daughters. They heard the speeches, the tales of bold deeds; they saw the black granite tombstone in Soweto's Avalon Cemetery with the words 'Black Power' chiselled on the sides and the name 'Mashinini' across the top with the date: June 16, 1976. They read the engraving on the white marble base: 'At the height of repression, he gave impetus to the liberation struggle.' They marvelled that this man, who was revered by so many, was their father.

Through the years, the Mashinini family has struggled to have Tsietsi accorded what they believe to be his rightful place in history. The Pan Africanist Congress acknowledged his contribution in a memorial it erected near the entrance to the cemetery to commemorate the twentieth anniversary of the June 16 uprising. The inscription on the stone read: 'Dedicated To All Those Who Lost Their Lives On This Day & There After'; Tsietsi's name was among those listed. But the government has remained aloof, other than to send Jackie Selebi, the national police commissioner and Dee's former history teacher in the Tanzanian camp, to lay a wreath on Tsietsi's grave at a Youth Day ceremony in 2000.

For Joseph and Nomkhitha, this seeming omission was particularly painful. They have watched as the authorities, in constructing a new narrative for the country, heaped honours and official recognition on all manner of freedom fighters – all except their son. And when they learned of Tsietsi's descent into rage and mental illness while in exile, they feared his detractors would seize upon those things to deny him forever what they felt was his due. Apartheid destroyed people in many ways; what befell Tsietsi after he was forced to flee the country, they believed, did not negate the leader he was and the contribution he made.

The family has also struggled with the matter of Tsietsi's death. Nomkhitha regretted her decision not to perform an autopsy; she was haunted by the wounds she saw on Tsietsi's body. Given their severity, she was certain they, and not AIDs, were the cause of his demise – despite the continued insistence to the contrary by Bageot Bah, Tsietsi's former benefactor in Guinea. The family's attempts to determine the truth by other means have proved fruitless. Miriam Makeba refused to discuss the matter with them or anyone else. Tsietsi's death certificate, issued in Guinea, states only that he expired from a *maladie*. Yet papers that Bageot gave Welma indicated Tsietsi was admitted to the neurological unit of Ignace Deen Hospital, not internal medicine or infectious diseases as might have been expected. Oddly, all traces of his records vanished from the hospital within a few years of his death.

Of course, this being Tsietsi, rumours about how he died abound. The newspapers in South Africa reported that he had suffered a nervous breakdown. While in Conakry, Welma was told of a young woman who had been left in charge of Miriam's house and did cooking and cleaning for Tsietsi. One day, she and Tsietsi got into a fight; he went to strike her, but she hit him first, apparently with a heavy object. There were other stories: Tsietsi was involved with West African gangsters; he ran foul of the Guinean government; he was the victim of police brutality. In death, as in life, the mythology about Tsietsi continued.

After his electronics firm in Botswana failed, Rocks decided it was time to go home. He had had his fill of living abroad. He watched the other exiles flocking to South Africa; fearing the Botswanan authorities might decide to act on his previous police record, Rocks asked his family to apply, once again, for indemnity. In the meantime he moved to Lesotho, a tiny, mountainous country surrounded by South Africa, to await a reply.

The government took six months to grant him an exemption from arrest or prosecution. Rocks returned to South Africa in 1991. Even though he had been given indemnity, Rocks was terrified; he entered the country through a remote border post on a Swazi passport. It was difficult for him to believe that he could drive down the road and not be arrested. He had spent his entire adult life trying to evade his pursuers; now here he was, in plain sight, an easy target in what was still, in his mind, enemy territory. Rocks drove directly to Soweto, to the joy of his family and friends.

It was not an easy homecoming. Rocks still suffered from the extreme anxiety he had acquired from living under constant fear of attack in exile. He could not relax; he could not accept that the police were not poised to swoop down upon him. He felt an omnipresent sense of foreboding and unease. The country might be in the throes of change, but Rocks could not assimilate the concept. His hands trembled; the slightest noise made him jump. Only alcohol, in copious quantities, blunted the overwhelming emotions.

Rocks wanted leave his guerrilla existence behind and forge a new life. But he could not find a way. He could not find work as a civilian. He watched with envy as fellow comrades, soldiers who had been in exile with him but somehow managed to finish their education, obtained jobs in government. Rocks regretted ever leaving South Africa and becoming a freedom fighter. It had been good for the country, but not for him personally. He wished he had remained behind and acquired a profession or trade. Oh, he remembered the burning desire to go abroad, to learn to shoot a gun so that he could return and kill every Boer he saw – the impulsiveness of youth. Like so many of his contemporaries, he had thought it would be finished in a year or two. Then one morning he awoke to find himself a middle-aged man in the 'new' South Africa, with no skills to offer, no carefully honed talents to sell. The only place Rocks could find employment was in the recently constituted South African National Defence Force.

He was given the not-insignificant rank of lieutenant colonel, but he did not care. He did not want to be in the army; being there made him despondent. The new army was supposed to blend members of the old armed forces and Umkhonto; about 30,000 former freedom fighters and black 'homeland' soldiers would enter the ranks. Five years after liberation, more than 55 per cent of the 80,000 member Defence Force was black. Rocks found the upper echelons still dominated by Afrikaners. They had a difficult time accepting blacks as equals, let alone ranking officers. For decades, the white soldiers had been taught to think of their ANC counterparts as deadly foes, communists, subhuman. These perceptions were not going to change immediately. Rocks felt ostracized by his fellow commanders; although it was ostensibly illegal to do so, they sometimes conducted meetings in Afrikaans, just so that he would not be able to follow the proceedings.

Over the years, Rocks tried everything he could think of to create a new life. He devised, and ultimately discarded, numerous plans to start up businesses with his brothers or friends. He endeavoured to find a job in a non-governmental agency or at a foreign embassy. He even considered returning to school. In an attempt at domesticity, Rocks bought a tiny matchbox house in Soweto and brought his sons, Sizwe and Vuyo, from Swaziland to live with him after their mother died of tuberculosis. (Sebenzile and Rocks had parted years earlier.) He wanted to ensure that they, at least, received a good education.

Despite his best efforts, Rocks could not adapt to being home. This new South Africa, for which he had sacrificed his youth, his health, his mental well-being, seemed to hold promise for everyone but him. He ceased to try any longer; he was too depressed. Rocks drank steadily. He went to work drunk. His house fell into disrepair; the place became littered with unwashed dishes and rubbish. He neglected his personal appearance. Rocks sometimes did not get out of bed until three or four o'clock in the afternoon. He sent his sons to live with Joseph and Nomkhitha. He stumbled through the days; occasionally, Indres

Naidoo, his old ANC cell-leader, would see him on the streets of Johannesburg, miserable, defeated, despairing. He sought treatment at military hospitals for depression. Each time he was better for a while, displaying flashes of his witty and articulate former self. But the demons invariably returned. Rocks was deteriorating steadily and no one – his parents or siblings or friends – knew quite how to save him.

The new millennium brought little respite. The army transferred Rocks to a different unit; the officers in charge refused to accept him. Nor did his old unit want him. He was shuttled back and forth between the two. He applied for leave at Christmas time; neither of the commanders would approve his request. Rocks took leave nonetheless. In January of the new year, Rocks awoke each morning, dressed, went to work – only to find that he did not have an office anywhere. He stopped going to work.

At about three o'clock in the morning on 12 March 2001, Rocks arose from his bed. Dressed in a gown, he stepped out through his kitchen door into the silence of the night and walked the few paces to the little outhouse in his garden. He seated himself on the toilet. Then, steadying his trembling hand, Rocks put the barrel of a pistol into his mouth and pulled the trigger.

In contrast with his older brother, the transition to the new South Africa for Mpho was an easy, and in some ways, wonderful thing. The transformation seemed miraculous: the relative lack of violence; the replacement of one system with another; the speed with which it occurred. Mpho suddenly found himself a fully-fledged citizen of South Africa. Now citizenship seemed so normal it was hard to imagine that it could have been denied his people for so long. Normal – and yet still so miraculous that he half-expected to hear singing from the heavens every time he contemplated it.

Mpho moved up through the ranks of Operation Hunger. He became the deputy director, then acting director. In early 1995, he was named the organization's director. He and Hloyi bought a house in Bezuidenhout Valley, a formerly all-white suburb of

Johannesburg. It had a small swimming pool and a garden. They furnished it in a manner Mpho could only have imagined as a child. They purchased chairs and a sofa with deep, soft cushions; a sound system and television set that covered one wall of the lounge; a large, formal table with matching chairs and buffet in the dining room and another, smaller table in the kitchen. Mpho viewed liberation as a kind of personal achievement. His generation was lucky enough to have lived through the struggle and seen its fulfilment. He took pride in all the benefits liberation brought: the installation of a water tap in a rural village, the electrification of a township, his ability to lift himself from abject poverty.

And then everything changed. Mpho and three other employees were alleged to have misappropriated hundreds of thousands of rands that belonged to the organization. The board of directors suspended them from their duties. An inquiry ensued. It was a terrible time for Mpho: the police searched his house; the newspapers plastered the story across the front pages for two weeks. Mpho denied any wrongdoing. He decided he would not fight the allegations through the press and refused to talk to journalists. He agreed to cooperate with the investigation.

Mpho, by his account, eventually resigned (although the press reported it as a dismissal). Losing his job in so public a manner was a humiliating experience that left him shaken and embittered. To add to his woes, he was involved in a bad car accident that crushed one of his legs. The long recuperation time, and the terms of his departure from Operation Hunger, made searching for another job difficult. Mpho remained unemployed for almost a year. He and Hloyi had to sell the house.

But he did, ultimately, find employment, and he flourished. The provincial Ministry of Public Transport and Works hired Mpho to help regulate the taxi industry. A kind of mafia had taken control of the various companies, and the ranks were rife with violence. Violent battles erupted daily over routes and territories that resulted in scores of murders. For black people, who relied upon the taxis as their main mode of transport, travelling became an enormous risk. Mpho was charged with trying to sort out the mess. He had to write laws that would give the government power over the industry. He had to mediate among groups pledged to kill one another. It was frightening, dangerous work; Mpho's life, at times, was threatened and he had to move about stealthily at night under the protection of bodyguards. He found he had a talent for such matters. Just as he was able to traverse several political worlds during his years as an activist, Mpho now navigated among the warring sides. He got all manner of people to trust him.

Mpho's success was such that other provinces sought his assistance. He helped to calm the taxi wars, as they were called, in other parts of the country and created a national structure for the industry. By 2003, Mpho was ready to leave the job; it was no longer a challenge. He felt he had made a substantial contribution to the new nation. By his calculations, he had spent much of his life working to make South Africa a better place; now it was time to go into the private sector, to look after himself. He had earned the right to be selfish. Mpho and Hloyi had a daughter, Wendy, who was the joy of Mpho's life. He dreamed of being able to provide her with all the things denied him in his childhood of poverty. He dreamed of being able to take Joseph and Nomkhitha on a trip to America to visit Tsietsi's children, where they now lived after escaping the wars of West Africa. He dreamed the dreams of a free man.

Dee remained in Harare for another year after returning from the funeral. He had a good job there and no similar prospects in South Africa. Dee made another trip to Johannesburg in August 1991 to assess his chances for employment; they still did not seem promising. A year later, he, Lindi and Ayanda returned to South Africa permanently. The ANC had closed its office in Harare by then, and most of the exiles had gone home. Bereft of their community, Dee and Lindi decided it was time for them to leave too.

Dee felt utterly disoriented in Johannesburg. He could not find his way around the city or the township; both, as he surmised in his two previous visits, had grown beyond imagining. He was like a stranger in his own country. He did not know how to board a taxi, how to look for a job, how to accomplish the simplest of tasks. Having to live with his parents only exacerbated Dee's sense of inadequacy. He, his wife and child, of necessity, moved in with Joseph and Nomkhitha, and Dee was suddenly a small boy again, dependent upon his mother and father. He could not help but compare himself with some of his brothers, who possessed their own apartments, cars, credit cards. Dee did not even know how you obtained a credit card.

With her medical technician's degree, Lindi quickly found a job in a Pretoria hospital. She moved to an apartment near to her work with Ayanda; Dee soon joined them. He embarked on what would prove to be, over the years, a struggle to gain a foothold in a business or profession. He became the editor at a tiny publishing firm that produced a newspaper for the taxi industry. The job lasted for two years; the newspaper failed to attract advertisers after the 1994 elections and was forced to close. Next Dee decided to try his hand at running a business. He opened a small pub with the help of an investor, who expected the establishment to be self-sufficient within three months. It was located in an industrial area that had three hostels for migrant labourers nearby. Violent crime prevailed in the neighbourhood. Two months after the pub's opening, gun-men riddled it with bullets, robbed Dee with a pistol pointed at his head, and brutally murdered two people in the shop next door. Dee abandoned the enterprise.

Discouraged by the vicissitudes of business, Dee looked for what he considered a proper job. He prepared a curriculum vitae and found employment with a public relations firm in a suburb of Johannesburg. Dee had the rather weighty title of public affairs manager; he was to act as the liaison person with the government. Dee now spent his days befriending officials: ministers, heads of departments, Members of Parliament and the like. The work required the same skills he had honed as Student Council president in SOMAFCO camp in Tanzania; now, as then, he thrived. His bosses, in recognition of his talent, paid Dee well. The salary allowed him to move into his own apartment (he and Lindi separated in 1995), purchase a car, buy nice clothes. For the first time since returning to South Africa, Dee was optimistic about his possibilities.

He felt confident enough, after working at his job for three years, to strike out on his own. Dee and a friend from the firm started their own public relations company. Once again, Dee specialized in government affairs. In 2000, in a move they thought would greatly benefit the company, Dee and his co-owner took on investors. The deal went badly awry; Dee's firm was liquidated. Dee suddenly had no means of support and numerous bills to pay – school fees, rent, a car loan. Luckily, through Mpho, he was able to find a job at another small publishing house that was launching another magazine for the taxi industry. That publication failed after two years; Dee began to believe he carried some sort of exile's curse. He took a temporary job with a governmental organization that was charged with overseeing the preparations to host an enormous United Nations conference on development. Then Dee went to work as the marketing manager for a large exhibition centre near Soweto.

His social life mirrored the difficulties he encountered in his professional life. He did not seem to fit in with most of his contemporaries. Dee had little in common with friends or schoolmates who had stayed in the country; they had nothing to talk about, no shared experiences to discuss. He felt more comfortable with former exiles. Dee got the idea to start a social club for the returnees, so they could remain in contact and help one another. He invited lecturers to give talks on topics such as how to start up a business or enter a particular profession; inspired by the speeches, the members resolved to establish their own company. To obtain capital, they put on parties and music festivals at which they sold alcohol. They earned a bit of money, which they put in a bank account, but not enough to consider starting a serious enterprise. Still, for Dee, their companionship provided a needed refuge from his frustrations. (As did his new wife, Sizakele, whom he married in 2002; their daughter, Lesedi, was born the following year.)

Daily he battled an enormous sense of disappointment. This was not how Dee had imagined his life, all those years in the East African bush. Going home was supposed to bring tremendous rewards. Upon returning to South Africa, Dee vowed that, having spent the first half of his life in exile, the rest must be perfect. It had not turned out that way. To Dee's mind, the skills he and other exiles acquired were not real skills; industry did not value them. He looked with envy at the youths who had stayed in the country and obtained useful university degrees. They had assimilated a culture of education, constantly taking new courses to expand their expertise; there seemed no limit to what they could achieve. Dee's life, by contrast, had been defined by a culture of politics – a culture that, in its old form, was no longer wanted.

Tshepiso returned to South Africa in 1991, after completing his MA in sociology. Among the Mashinini brothers who left the country, Tshepiso had the easiest time adjusting to the changed conditions. Perhaps it was his relative youth, or the circumstances of his departure and stay abroad; perhaps Tshepiso brought back what Dee felt he lacked: a much-needed proficiency.

He began working in the Johannesburg Metropolitan Chamber on negotiations to unify the white city, as it were, with the black township. He found the matters that had to be considered fascinating. What was to be done with Johannesburg's thirteen racially designated local authorities? How was a single tax base to be created? Where should the boundary lines for a unified city be drawn? How to remedy, in a speedy manner, the decades of gross neglect in the black communities? (An estimated 200,000 people were without running water, and an equal number without housing.) For Tshepiso, they were essential questions. Government affected people's daily lives most at the local level: that was where the promises to redress apartheid's injustices had to be kept, where the real changes in South Africa would be felt, where democracy would succeed or stumble.

As if the issues were not complex enough, the negotiating process to resolve them proved equally complicated. The distrust that existed among the players made it an excruciating exercise. The white bureaucrats, who remained from the old regime, saw the civic activists as communist-inspired anarchists, bent on installing a Stalinist system. And the activists thought of the bureaucrats as extensions of the apartheid apparatus. Amid the hostilities, Tshepiso discovered that he had a talent for diplomacy. He possessed Tsietsi's mix of wit, charm and intelligence, but without the militancy – a product, perhaps, of the times and Tshepiso's education. He won over erstwhile racists who, only a few years earlier, would just have soon seen him behind bars or dead. Many of them became his friends.

Tshepiso came to epitomize the new South Africa. He moved to a flat in Yeoville, a formerly Jewish neighbourhood of Johannesburg now inhabited by young artists and professionals. He frequented good restaurants and clubs. He found a partner, Rhona, a young woman from Swaziland, with whom he had a daughter, Malika. Tshepiso effortlessly traversed the various worlds of the post-apartheid society; he felt at ease in the townships or the still mostly white suburbs. He was endlessly optimistic about the country's future.

As he came into his own, Tshepiso also began to feel more at peace with Tsietsi's legacy. He first noticed the transformation at a rock concert in Johannesburg. Tshepiso was seated next to the premier of Northern Province; the two exchanged desultory pleasantries, until a passing friend yelled out: 'Hey, Mashinini!' The premier turned to Tshepiso. 'Are you Tsietsi's brother?' he asked. His entire demeanour was altered: the premier hugged Tshepiso, said how sorry he was about Tsietsi's death, enquired about Tshepiso's career. For the first time ever, Tshepiso felt no resentment at receiving recognition because of his brother's fame.

In 1996, Tshepiso became the chief of urbanization at what was now the Greater Johannesburg Metropolitan Council. He supervised the drafting of a white paper on local government, a document that would restructure South Africa's cities. The job kept him racing between Johannesburg and Cape Town, and exhausted much of the time. Still, he relished the demands and took great pride in his accomplishments. He liked to bring Joseph and Nomkhitha to the Council's high-rise building, so they could see his office with its polished furniture and thick carpets and revel in his success. Tshepiso bought a shiny, red sports utility vehicle and a house in the suburbs. It was a solidly built structure, so unlike the house of his childhood, with spacious rooms and a swimming pool. When he was not travelling, Tshepiso enjoyed inviting his friends and family for a Sunday *braai*, a barbecue. He would spend hours playing with his daughter, Malika. Rhona became pregnant again; his life seemed to be on an unswerving trajectory.

And then the unthinkable occurred. With no warning, Tshepiso collapsed on the morning of 20 February 1998 and, a few hours later, died of an apparent heart attack. In one of the many eulogies given at the funeral, Mark Swilling, Mpho's old friend who had worked closely with Tshepiso, spoke of him as a new sort of victim of apartheid: one felled by the effort required to right its wrongs. Tshepiso was thirty-one years old.

Ten years after liberation, the Mashininis, like many South Africans, viewed the aftermath of their struggle with mixed feelings. They watched with avid interest the proceedings of the Truth and Reconciliation Commission, the body charged with granting amnesty to those who provided true accounts of politically motivated crimes. The commission's head, Archbishop Desmond Tutu, characterized it as a '. . . compromise between the extreme of Nuremberg trials and blanket amnesty or national amnesia'. The government hoped that such a forum would keep the country from disintegrating into violent acts of revenge.

For several years, the commission moved around the country, taking the testimonies of more than 19,000 victims and their families. (Few of the suspected perpetrators came forward to appear before the inquiry.) They were horrifying stories of torture, mutilation and murder, broadcast day after day on television. The testimonies held Nomkhitha, and much of the black community, riveted to their television screens. (Whites apparently did not view the proceedings with equal interest.) The more Nomkhitha heard, the angrier she became. She had not felt that way when the incidents occurred, when she attended the political funerals and saw the victims, many of them mere children, being put into the ground. But hearing the mothers weep and witnessing their anguish made her want to seek revenge. She could not speak about the matter without becoming emotional, her voice rising almost to a shout. 'You listen to the Truth Commission and you can't sleep!' she said. 'We knew there was torture, but not like this. People really suffered. But even now, the whites don't realize that we bleed just like them. President Mandela wanted peace in the country. And the Bible says we should forgive. So I will have to forgive. But I'm angry.'

Nomkhitha, too, testified about her experiences in solitary confinement in jail and the harassment her family endured at the hands of the security forces. Like the other victims, the Mashininis were to receive compensation of almost £2,600 from the government, a sum that critics derided as insulting. Mpho took a different view of the worth of the commission, which completed its activities in 2003. He believed it provided an alternative model of justice to the world and helped to expose some of the apartheid state's most heinous crimes. But its work did not make him any more conciliatory towards the old regime. He could not forgive, but he would not seek revenge, either; he just wanted the country to move forward.

Liberation freed the Mashininis to concentrate on the more prosaic aspects of their existence. Joseph and Nomkhitha had hoped that democracy would quickly bring economic benefits and lift them from their poverty; but for them, and for most blacks, that expectation was not realized. The government did make significant improvements in some areas. By 2002, 50 per cent of rural households had electricity, compared with 17 per cent in 1994; 76 per cent of all South Africans had plumbed-in water, compared with 68 per cent. But the task the government faced was enormous. Although the percentage of wealthy and middle-class blacks increased, most actually became poorer. In the years between 1995 and 2000, incomes in black households fell by 19 per cent, while white incomes rose by 15 per cent.

Nomkhitha and Joseph found it more difficult than ever to survive. Nomkhitha had never been able to secure a proper job after being released from detention in 1977. She tried to return to her old place of employment, only to find the manager blocking the entrance to the warehouse. 'Virginia,' she said (using Nomkhitha's English name), 'you're a communist. Don't you even try to come in here. We don't want people like you. You stay away from us.' Nomkhitha went for several years without working. Through her church she finally found a job, which paid a pittance, helping to feed senior citizens. Now in her late sixties, her only source of income was the tiny government pension that she collected each month. Joseph had his pension from the construction firm where he had worked as a driver. He scraped together enough money to purchase an old *kombi*, a minivan, in which he transported children to and from school each day. His earnings barely paid for petrol and to keep the *kombi* running. They lived from month to month.

Enough time had passed since the events of 1976 for them to take a philosophical, if resigned, view of their experiences. Their children, and thousands of others, were swept into a political maelstrom from which only a few, the lucky ones, emerged. Nomkhitha regretted that Tsietsi had gone into exile. She wished he had been arrested and sent to Robben Island; many of his friends were incarcerated there and are alive today. But she and Joseph did not feel sorry for themselves. They were not alone in their suffering: every black family was involved, every black family made sacrifices, every black family lost a loved one. Nomkhitha believed there would have been no change in the country without sacrifice. If they had just sat with their arms folded, the Afrikaners would have ruled for ever. To her mind, it was a pity it had to happen that way, because many things went wrong: people died; people became informers; people – like Rocks – turned to drink.

Even now, some have begun to forget the hardships. The son of a friend who had been a comrade plied Mpho with questions one day: What was exile? Why were people arrested? Why did they go to Robben Island? Mpho was stunned; this, from a black boy (who now attended an exclusive private school and had a white girlfriend). Only a decade after liberation, the next generation acted as though the country were Belgium. Mpho worried that normality had overtaken South Africa almost too quickly.

The past would always be with him, however. Mpho was left with only partial hearing in one ear because of the beatings he received in detention. He cannot bear strong light; his warders kept the overhead light glaring in his eyes all night. From his days in solitary confinement, he has a fear of being alone at night. He cannot go to bed if there is no one else in his house; nor can he sleep restfully in a hotel, locked away, as it were, in his rented room.

But daily he has had examples of justice done, of a world made right. Late on one afternoon, Mpho left his office in Government House in Johannesburg for the day. On the ground floor, next to the main entrance, was a notice-board with announcements of openings for various government jobs. As Mpho passed the board, he saw a man who seemed familiar, staring at the lists. Mpho left the building, then returned to take a closer look at the man. After a few moments, he remembered: this was one of the Afrikaner police officers who had interrogated him during his incarceration in Sun City. Mpho watched the man carefully scrutinize each notice, obviously looking for employment, then tapped him on the shoulder. 'Hello,' Mpho said. 'Are you looking for a job? I can help you.' They were among the most satisfying sentences he had ever uttered. The man looked up, startled. A glimmer of recognition passed across his face. Then he turned on his heel and fled from the building, into the lengthening shadows of dusk.

Acknowledgments

This is a book whose writing, for reasons professional and personal, extended over several years and continents. It could not have been realized without the support of many kind and generous people along the way.

First among them were the Mashininis, who sat for more than seventy hours of taped interviews. Tshepiso was an ardent advocate for the project from the start, helping to convince other family members of its worth and encouraging their participation. His intelligence, wit and enthusiasm provided a wellspring of inspiration. I profoundly regret that he did not live to see the book's completion and can only hope that it would have found favour in his eyes.

Nomkhitha and Joseph gave unstintingly of their time. They graciously accompanied me on journeys to their ancestral homes in the Transkei and Vereeniging, and patiently considered my ceaseless stream of questions. Nomkhitha, in particular, became a vociferous proponent, always ready to assist in any way. Joseph's sudden death, on the eve of the book's publication, left an immeasurable void among all who knew him.

I am deeply saddened that Rocks, too, did not live to see the book's finish. He, Mpho and Dee regularly interrupted busy schedules to speak with me and good-naturedly acceded to demands to conjure up often excruciating details from decades earlier. (Rocks, upon meeting my husband on what was obviously one of his better days, quipped, 'So you're married to the woman who asks me questions such as "What colour shoes were you wearing twenty years ago?"') Many thanks, too, to the rest of the Mashinini clan: Cougar, Moeketsi, China, Dichaba, Lindi, Linda and Bandile. Elvis, lamentably, died of leukemia in 1996.

Two people were essential in allowing me to re-create Tsietsi's life. Welma Redd (née Campbell) spoke at length by telephone, first from Sierra Leone, then from Maryland, about her marriage to Tsietsi. Khotso Seatlholo generously set aside time from his job to recount his experiences with Tsietsi in South Africa and in exile. It was with much sorrow that I learned of his death in early 2004.

Gail M. Gerhart provided invaluable assistance in researching this book. She pointed me in the direction of vital texts and sources, shared her voluminous knowledge on the subject and kindly allowed me to peruse the archival collection she and Tom Karis have amassed over the years. She also read the manuscript in its entirety, for which I am most grateful. I am indebted too to Michele Pickover, of the South African History Collection at the Cullen Library of the University of the Witwatersrand in Johannesburg, for helping me to sort through that institution's superb set of documents.

In Johannesburg, my dear friends Sue Albertyn and Dan Rosengarten supplied a lovely refuge, stimulating conversation and much-needed laughter. I am also grateful to Erica Emdon and Jacklyn Cock, for their friendship and advice over the years. Dr Khosi Letlape's trenchant political observations and wry humour were always much appreciated. Thanks, too, to my colleague John Battersby.

In Maputo, Mozambique (where my husband was the US ambassador), Pamela Dos Santos offered memories of the South Africa of her youth. Carlos Cardozo, that country's most courageous journalist, shared his insights and analyses; his brutal murder in 2000, while investigating corruption at the highest reaches of Mozambique's government, is an unfathomable loss.

In Lima, Peru (where we moved after my husband was appointed ambassador there), I am for ever indebted to Isabel Costa, the house manager at the ambassador's residence. Isabel was a formidable lioness at the gate, keeping unwanted visitors at bay, easing my transition to new-motherhood and generally helping to maintain my sanity. Karen and Ben Joubert supplied encouragement, Afrikaans translations and playdates for our respective daughters.

Dr William and Dorothy Ardill, old friends from Liberia, kindly provided photographs and observations from Plateau State Polytechnic in Jos, Nigeria, where they now live. Mary Fitzpatrick, an intrepid colleague and friend, interviewed Bageot Bah, among others, in Guinea. Two other close friends were particularly helpful: Clara Germani, of *The Christian Science Monitor*, offered her knowledge of Russia; Steven Mufson, of *The Washington Post*, was always willing to speak of Nigeria, South Africa and related topics. Andrea Leiman's constant encouragement enabled me to complete the manuscript.

I am grateful to Rebecca M. Hankins, the former chief acquisitions archivist at Tulane University's Amistad Research Center in New Orleans, for her assistance in locating documents pertaining to Tsietsi. Thanks, as well, to Fred Weir in Moscow; David Mills in Sydney; Mike Brown in Adelaide; David Ballard, when he was in Cairo; Rose Smouse, of the School of Languages at the University of Cape Town; Erick de Mul of the United Nations Development Programme.

It was my great fortune to have Dan Franklin, the publisher at Jonathan Cape, as my editor. I thank him for his unwavering enthusiasm and perceptive editing, which only improved the manuscript. I also thank Ellah Allfrey, who shepherded it to publication with intelligence, sensitivity and good humour; and Jonathan Dolger, my literary agent.

I received much encouragement from my parents, Anne Schuster and Monis Schuster, and from the rest of my family. I am particularly indebted to my sister, Beverly Mann, who read a large portion of the manuscript; her keen eye and unflinching honesty made it immeasurably better. But my greatest thanks go to my daughter, Noa, whose joyful presence inspires me daily, and to my husband, Dennis Jett. Dennis was unfailing in his assistance, his wise counsel, his willingness to read and re-read the entire manuscript. For these and other reasons too numerous to mention, this book is dedicated to him.

Gainesville, Florida
January 2004

Sources

Interviews

Bageot Bah (interviewed by Mary Fitzpatrick), Conakry, Guinea, January 1997, May 1998

Willie Bokala, by telephone, Johannesburg, February 1996

Eva Campbell, Silver Springs, Maryland, June 1995

Carlos Cardozo, Maputo, Mozambique, July 1995

Shun Chetty, by telephone from Sydney, May 1996

Tom Crooks, by telephone from Washington, May 2003

Eric Dane, by telephone from Cape Town, October 2003

Clive Emdon, Johannesburg, October 1995

Eddie Funde, by telephone from Johannesburg, March 1996

Gail M. Gerhart, Johannesburg, February 1995

Clara Germani, by telephone from Boston, June 2002

George Houser, by telephone from New York, May 1995

Jennifer Hyman, by telephone from Rochester, New York, May 1995, June 1995

Russell Kaschula, by telephone from the Western Cape, July 1995

Tom Karis, by telephone from New York, May 1995

Drake Koka, Johannesburg, February 1996, March 1996

Paul Langa, by telephone, Johannesburg, March 1996

Tom Lodge, by telephone, Johannesburg, May 1996

Tshepiso Manyelo, by telephone, Johannesburg, March 1996

Dee Mashinini, Johannesburg, September 1995, October 1995, December 1995, February 1996, March 1996, May 1996, June 1996, October 1997; by telephone from Johannesburg, July 2003

Hloyi Mashinini (née Sekgothudi), Johannesburg, October 1995

Joseph Mashinini, Johannesburg, February 1995, April 1995, November 1995, February 1996; by telephone from Johannesburg, July 2003

Lindi Mashinini (née Zikalala), Johannesburg, March 1996

Mpho Mashinini, Johannesburg, September 1995, October 1995, November 1995, December 1995, February 1996, March 1996, May 1996, June 1996; Lima, Peru, February 1999; by telephone from Johannesburg, July 2003

Nomkhitha Mashinini, Johannesburg, February 1995, April 1995, October 1995, November 1995, February 1996, April 1996, May 1996, June 1996, October 1997; by telephone from Johannesburg, July 2003

Rocks Mashinini, Johannesburg, October 1995, November 1995, December 1995, February 1996, October 1997

Tshepiso Mashinini, Johannesburg, September 1995, October 1995, November 1995, December 1995, February 1996, April 1996, May 1996, June 1996; October 1997

Seth Mazibuko, Johannesburg, February 1996

Lekgau Mathabathe, Johannesburg, March 1996

Jelita Mcleod, by telephone from Washington, May 2003

Kate Michaelson, Johannesburg, February 1995

Majakathata Mokoena, Johannesburg, November 1995

Comfort Molokoane, by telephone, Johannesburg, March 1996

Murphy Morobe, Johannesburg, February 1996, April 1996

Glenn Moss, Johannesburg, October 1997

Dr Nthato Motlana, Johannesburg, April 1996

Steven Mufson, by telephone from Washington, June 2002

Indres Naidoo, by telephone from Cape Town, June 1996

Duma Ndlovu, Johannesburg, March 1996

Sam Pono, by telephone from Pretoria, November 1997

Lesiba Pooe, by telephone from Cape Town, March 1996

Welma Redd, by telephone from Freetown, Sierra Leone, April 1996; by telephone from Derwood, Maryland, March 1999, April 1999

Khotso Seatlholo, Johannesburg, February 1996, March 1996, April 1996

Selby Semela, Washington, September 1996

Mark Swilling, Johannesburg, October 1997
Ambassador William Swing, Washington, May 1995
Tsheko Tsehlana, by telephone from Johannesburg, March 2004
Mary and Bernard Whiting, Gainesville, Florida, May 2003

Archives, Collections, Newspapers and Periodicals

The Amistad Research Center, Tulane University
CBS News
Karis-Gerhart Collection
Thames Television: Extract from *This Week – South Africa: There Is No Crisis* transmitted on 2 September 1976. Courtesy FreemantleMedia and John Fielding.
US Department of State, Freedom of Information Office
The University of the Witwatersrand, Cullen Library, Historical Papers
   Press Cuttings: Trials, Student Riots, General
   South African Institute of Race Relations Press Cuttings
   South African Students' Organization Collection
   Soweto Students' Representative Council Collection
   State vs. Vincent Mashinini, Garnet Mahlangeni and Paul Fakudu (Judgement)
   State vs. Twala and Ten Others, Record of Proceedings, 1978–1979

The Atlantic Monthly
Botswana Daily News
Cape Times (Cape Town)
City Press
The Christian Science Monitor
Drum
Financial Mail
Financial Times (Johannesburg)
Harper's
The Intercontinental Press
The Los Angeles Times
The Natal Witness
Newsweek

The New York Review of Books
The New York Times
Pace
Rand Daily Mail
South African Financial Gazette
Sowetan
The Star
Sunday Express
Sunday Times (Johannesburg)
Sunday Tribune
The Wall Street Journal
The Weekend World
The World

Bibliography

Adam, Heribert, and Moodley, Kogila. *South Africa Without Apartheid: Dismantling Racial Discrimination* (University of California Press, Berkeley, 1986)

Beinart, William, Delius, P., and Trapido, S., eds. *Putting a Plough to the Ground: Accumulation and Dispossession in Rural South Africa 1850–1930* (Ravan Press, Johannesburg, 1986)

Benson, Mary. *Nelson Mandela: The Man and the Movement* (W.W. Norton and Co., New York, 1986)

Bernstein, Hilda. *The World That Was Ours: The Story of the Rivonia Trial* (SA Writers, London, 1989)

Boraine, Alex. *A Country Unmasked:* Inside South Africa's Truth and Reconciliation Commission (Oxford University Press, New York, 2001)

Breytenbach, Breyten. *Return to Paradise* (Harvest, New York, 1993)

— *A Season in Paradise* (Harvest, New York, 1980)

— *The True Confessions of an Albino Terrorist* (McGraw-Hill Book Co., New York, 1983)

Brink, Andre, and Coetzee, J.M., eds. *A Land Apart: A Contemporary South African Reader* (Penguin Books, Harmondsworth, 1987)

Brooks, Alan, and Brickhill, Jeremy. *Whirlwind Before the Storm: The Origins and Developments of the Uprising in Soweto and the Rest of South Africa from June–December 1976* (International Defence and Aid Fund for Southern Africa, London, 1980)

Burman, Sandra, and Reynolds, Pamela, eds. *Growing Up in a Divided Society: The Contexts of Childhood in South Africa* (Ravan Press, Johannesburg, 1986)

Butler, Jeffrey, Elphick, R., and Welsh, D., eds. *Democratic Liberalism in South Africa: Its History and Prospect* (Wesleyan University Press, Middletown, CT., 1987)

Cole, Josette. *Crossroads: The Politics of Reform and Repression 1976–1986* (Ravan Press, Johannesburg, 1987)

Commonwealth Report. *Mission to South Africa: The Findings of the Commonwealth Eminent Persons Group on South Africa* (Penguin Books Ltd., Harmondsworth, 1986)

Crapanzano, Vincent. *Waiting: The Whites of South Africa* (Vintage Books, New York, 1986)

Davis, Stephen M. *Apartheid's Rebels: Inside South Africa's Hidden War* (Yale University Press, New Haven, CT., 1987)

De Klerk, F.W. *The Last Trek – A New Beginning* (Macmillan, London, 1998)

Dugard, John. *Human Rights and the South African Legal Order* (Princeton University Press, Princeton, NJ., 1978)

Ellis, Stephen, and Sechaba, Tsepo. *Comrades Against Apartheid: The ANC and the South African Communist Party in Exile* (James Currey Ltd., London, 1992)

Finnegan, William. *Crossing the Line: A Year in the Land of Apartheid* (Perennial Library, New York, 1986)

— *Dateline Soweto: Travels with Black South African Reporters* (Harper & Row, New York, 1988)

Frankel, Glenn. *Rivonia's Children: Three Families and the Cost of Conscience in White South Africa* (Farrar, Straus and Giroux, New York, 1999)

Friedman, Steven. *Building Tomorrow Today: African Workers in Trade Unions, 1970–1984* (Ravan Press, Johannesburg, 1987)

Gerhart, Gail M. *Black Power in South Africa: The Evolution of an Ideology* (University of California Press, Berkeley, 1978)

— and Karis, Thomas. *Political Profiles 1882–1964*, Vol. 4 of *From Protest to Challenge: A Documentary History of African Politics in South Africa 1882–1964*, edited by Thomas Karis and Gwendolen M. Carter (Hoover Institution Press, Stanford, CA., 1977)

Gobodo-Madikizela, Pumla. *A Human Being Died That Night: A South African Story of Forgiveness* (Houghton Mifflin Co., New York, 2003)

Gordimer, Nadine. *A Sport of Nature* (Penguin Books, New York, 1988)

Harrison, David. *The White Tribe of Africa: South Africa in Perspective* (Macmillan South African Ltd., Johannesburg, 1981)

Herbst, Jeffrey. *State and Power in Africa* (Princeton University Press, Princeton, N.J., 2002)

Kane-Berman, John. *Soweto: Black Revolt, White Reaction* (Ravan Press, Johannesburg, 1978)

Kapuscinski, Ryszard. *Author Day of Life* (Picador, London, 1988)

Karis, Thomas, and Gerhart, Gail M. *Challenge and Violence 1953–1964*, Vol. 3 of *From Protest to Challenge: A Documentary History of African Politics in South Africa 1882–1964*, edited by Thomas Karis and Gwendolen M. Carter (Hoover Institution Press, Stanford CA., 1977)

— *Nadir and Resurgence, 1964–1979*, Vol. 5, of *From Protest to Challenge: A Documentary History of African Politics in South Africa, 1882–1990* (Unisa Press, Pretoria, 1997)

Kasrils, Ronnie. *'Armed and Dangerous': My Undercover Struggle Against Apartheid* (Heinemann Publishers Ltd, Oxford, 1993)

Krog, Antjie. *Country of My Skull* (Random House South Africa Ltd., Johannesburg, 1998)

Lelyveld, Joseph. *Move Your Shadow: South Africa, Black and White* (Times Books, New York, 1985)

Libby, Ronald T. *The Politics of Economic Power in Southern Africa* (Princeton University Press, Princeton, NJ, 1987)

Liebenow, J. Gus. *Liberia: The Quest for Democracy* (Indiana University Press, Bloomington, 1987)

Lodge, Tom. *Black Politics in South Africa Since 1945* (Ravan Press, Johannesburg, 1983)

Makeba, Miriam, and Hall, James. *Makeba: My Story* (New American Library, New York, 1987)

Malan, Rian. *My Traitor's Heart: A South African Exile Returns to Face His Country, His Tribe, and His Conscience* (Atlantic Monthly Press, New York, 1990)

McCord, Margaret. *The Calling of Katie Makanya: A Memoir of South Africa* (John Wiley & Sons Inc., New York, 1995)

Mandela, Nelson. *Long Walk to Freedom: The Autobiography of Nelson Mandela* (Little Brown and Co., New York, 1994)

— *The Struggle is My Life* (Pathfinder Press, New York, 1986)

Mandela, Winnie. *Part of My Soul Went with Him* (W.W. Norton and Co., New York, 1984)

Mandy, Nigel. *A City Divided: Johannesburg and Soweto* (Macmillan South Africa Ltd., Johannesburg, 1984)

Mathabane, Mark. *Kaffir Boy: The True Story of a Black Youth's Coming of Age in Apartheid South Africa* (Plume, New York, 1986)

Meredith, Martin. *Coming To Terms: South Africa's Search for Truth* (Public Affairs, New York, 1999)

Mermelstein, David, ed. *The Anti-Apartheid Reader: South Africa and the Struggle Against White Racist Rule* (Grove Press, New York, 1987)

Mufson, Steven. *Fighting Years: Black Resistance and the Struggle for a New South Africa* (Beacon Press, Boston, 1990)

Naidoo, Indres. *Island in Chains: Ten Years on Robben Island* (Penguin Books India, Ltd., New Delhi, 2000)

Pakenham, Thomas. *The Scramble for Africa: The White Man's Conquest of the Dark Continent from 1876 to 1912* (Random House, New York, 1991)

Paton, Alan. *Ah, But Your Land Is Beautiful* (Penguin Books Ltd., Harmondsworth, 1986)

— *Cry, The Beloved Country* (Scribner Paperback Fiction, New York, 1987)

Roberts, Brian. *Cecil Rhodes: Flawed Colossus* (W.W. Norton & Co., New York, 1988)

Roux, Edward. *Time Longer Than Rope: A History of The Black Man's*

Struggle for Freedom in South Africa (University of Wisconsin Press, Madison, 1964)

Samson, Anthony. *Mandela: The Authorized Biography* (Alfred A. Knopf, Inc., New York, 1999)

Schoeman, Karel. *Promised Land* (Jonathan Ball Paperbacks, Johannesburg, 1979)

Slovo, Joe. *Slovo: The Unfinished Autobiography* (Ocean Press, Melbourne, 1997)

Soyinka, Wole. *Collected Plays 2* (Oxford University Press, Oxford, 1974)

Sparks, Allister. *The Mind of South Africa* (Mandarin Paperbacks, London, 1991)

— *Tomorrow Is Another Country: The Inside Story of South Africa's Negotiated Revolution* (Struik Book Distributors, Johannesburg, 1994)

Stengel, Richard. *January Sun: One Day, Three Lives, A South African Town* (Touchstone, New York, 1991)

Straker, Gill. *Faces in the Revolution: The Psychological Effects of Violence on Township Youth in South Africa* (David Philip, Cape Town, 1992)

Suzman, Helen. *In No Uncertain Terms: A South African Memoir* (Alfred A. Knopf, Inc., New York, 1993)

Swilling, Mark, Humphries, R. and Shubane, K., eds. *Apartheid City in Transition* (Oxford University Press, Cape Town, 1991)

Thompson, Leonard. *A History of South Africa* (Yale University Press, New Haven, CT., 1995)

Tutu, Desmond. *No Future Without Forgiveness* (Doubleday, New York, 2000)

Wilson, Charles Morrow. *Liberia: Black Africa in Microcosm* (Harper and Row, New York, 1971)

Winter, Gordon. *Inside Boss: South Africa's Secret Police* (Allen Lane, London, 1981)

Woods, Donald. *Biko: The True Story of the Young South African Martyr and His Struggle to Raise Black Consciousness* (Henry Holt and Co, New York, 1991)

Notes

Prologue

1. *Jan Smuts International Airport* . . . Now called Johannesburg International Airport.
3. *from the exclusionary black-power doctrines of Steve Biko* . . . For more on the black consciousness leader, see Donald Woods, *Biko,* pp. 53–148.
4. *It took apartheid's demise* . . . South Africa held its first-ever democratic elections on 27 April 1994.

Chapter One: Nomkhitha and Joseph

7. *the country's first black university, Fort Hare* . . . Originally called South African Native College, the university was established in 1916.
11. *Many of the guests were 'red people'* . . . Interviews with Nomkhitha Mashinini and Russell Kaschula.
12. *Part socio-political commentator, part oral historian, the imbongi* . . . Interview with Russell Kaschula.
21. *Four years before, the Afrikaner-led National Party had won South Africa's general election* . . . For more on the National Party's legislation, see Robert Rothberg, 'The Ascendancy of Afrikanerdom' in David Mermelstein (ed.) *The Anti-Apartheid Reader,* pp. 78–83.
21. *the Dutch Reformed Church provided its religious justification* . . . Allister Sparks, *The Mind of South Africa,* pp. 32–33.
22. *One thousand blacks were arrested every day for pass law transgressions* . . . Ibid., p. 210.

Chapter Two: Joseph, Nomkhitha and the Children

27. *Being the dutiful daughter-in-law and wife meant subordinating her culture* . . . Interviews with Nomkhitha Mashinini and Russell Kaschula.

28. *The government hoped to engender social stability* . . . For more on the establishment of Soweto and the Nationalist government's policies, see 'The Evolution of Soweto' in Nigel Mandy, *A City Divided*, pp. 173–190.

30. *The African National Congress, the country's oldest black liberation movement* . . . For more on the history of the ANC in the 1950s, see Thomas Karis and Gail M. Gerhart, *Challenge and Violence 1953–1964*, Vol. 3 of Thomas Karis and Gwendolen M. Carter, (eds.), *From Protest To Challenge*, pp. 3–82.

30. Ibid., pp. 205–208, for a complete version of the Freedom Charter.

31. *To purge themselves of these undesirable elements, the dissidents abandoned the ANC in 1959* . . . For a history of the Africanist movement and the creation of the Pan Africanist Congress, see Gail M. Gerhart, *Black Power in South Africa*, pp. 124–211.

31. Ibid., pp. 212–256, for more on the Sharpeville massacre and its aftermath.

37. *in fact, it was about twelve times as much* . . . *Financial Mail*, 25 June 1976.

38. *Umkhonto exploded a series of home-made bombs* . . . For a first-hand account of Umkhonto's creation, see Nelson Mandela in *Long Walk to Freedom*, pp. 231–267.

38. *The officers arrested most of Umkhonto's leaders* . . . Glenn Frankel provides a detailed recounting of the arrests and the subsequent trial in *Rivonia's Children*.

38. *Poqo, or 'pure' in Xhosa, a terrorist group* . . . 'Poqo had no hierarchical structure, no identifiable mass leaders, and no public statement of aims or ideology . . . What was qualitatively new in the attitudes of its members was the intensity of their desperation, their targeting of African collaborators as well as informers for death and their readiness to kill whites indiscriminately. Unlike

Umkhonto, Poqo was genuinely a terrorist organization.' Karis and Gerhart in *Challenge and Violence*, p. 669.

53. *the various denominations discouraged resistance* . . . Sparks, *The Mind of South Africa*, p. 293.

53. *a new ideology began to sprout among university students* . . . For more on Black Consciousness and the various student groups and campaigns it spawned, see Gerhart, *Black Power in South Africa*, pp. 257–299.

54. *the Mozambican flag was raised* . . . Interview with Carlos Cardozo.

55. *Still, Indres organized political classes* . . . Interviews with Rocks Mashinini and Indres Naidoo.

55. *The next lesson analysed the alliance between the ANC and the South African Communist Party* . . . For differing views on the SACP and its relationship to the ANC, see Frankel, *Rivonia's Children*; Karis and Gerhart, *Challenge and Violence*; Stephen Ellis and Tsepo Sechaba, *Comrades Against Apartheid*.

56. *under the patronage of the South African Students' Movement* . . . For more on SASM, see Thomas Karis and Gail M. Gerhart, *Nadir and Resurgence, 1964–1979*, Vol. 5 of *From Protest to Challenge*, pp. 160–163.

Chapter Three: June 16

60. *It was an issue that had been smouldering for months* . . . For more on Bantu education and Afrikaans instruction, see Alan Brooks and Jeremy Brickhill, *Whirlwind Before the Storm*, pp. 44–50; and Thomas Karis and Gail M. Gerhart, *Nadir and Resurgence, 1964–1979*, Vol. 5 of *From Protest to Challenge*, pp. 163–166.

61. *The SASM leaders called a meeting.* . . . The sections about SASM meetings and the preparations of the Action Committee are based on interviews with Seth Mazibuko, Murphy Morobe, and Khotso Seatlholo; and from Brooks and Brickhill, pp. 7–8 and 90–91.

61. *his favourite being Tennyson's poem, 'The Charge of the Light Brigade'.* . . . Tennyson, Alfred, *A Collection of Poems by Alfred Tennyson* (International Collectors

Library, Garden City, New York, 1972), pp.305–307.

64. *And Tsietsi led hundreds of youths.* . . . The sections about Tsietsi leading the demonstrators from school to school through the streets of Soweto are based on interviews with Duma Ndlovu, Dee, Mpho and Tshepiso Mashinini, Mazibuko, Morobe; and from the trial records of *State v. Twala 1978–79* (University of the Witwatersrand Historical Papers), pp. 2013–2015 and 2061–2067.

67. *Tsietsi exhorted them to make way for her* . . . Interview with Morobe.

68. *At that moment, the officers let loose one of the snarling Alsatians* . . . The sections about the confrontation between the youths and the police and the violence that ensued are based on interviews with Dee, Mpho and Tshepiso Mashinini, Mazibuko, Majakathata Mokoena, Morobe and Seatlholo; and from Brooks and Brickhill, pp. 8–10; and Karis and Gerhart, pp. 167–168.

73. *the police had killed at least twenty-five children and injured 200 others* . . . Stephen Ellis and Tsepo Sechaba, *Comrades Against Apartheid,* p. 81.

Chapter Four: The Children

75. *The rioting in Soweto continued for two more days* . . . Alan Brooks and Jeremy Brickhill, *Whirlwind Before the Storm,* pp. 13–19.

76. *Nearly 200 people had died; thousands of others were wounded* . . . Carole A. Douglis and Stephen M. Davis, 'Revolt on the Veldt', in *Harper's,* December 1983, p. 34.

79. *The student leaders were helped by the Black Parents' Association* . . . Brooks and Brickhill, p. 106.

79. *representatives of the exiled liberation organizations in South Africa attempted to recruit Tsietsi* . . . Interview with Khotso Seatlholo.

80. *Drake had the additional allure of having organized an independent black trade union* . . . The Black Allied Workers' Union (BAWU), which was established in 1972.

81. *Tsietsi and his colleagues traversed the township* . . . Interviews with Majakathata Mokoena and Murphy Morobe.

81. *If we take our demonstration into town* . . . Interview with Mpho Mashinini.

82. The section on the 4 August stay-away and march was based on interviews with Morobe and Seatlholo, and from Thomas Karis and Gail Gerhart, *Nadir and Resurgence 1964–1979*, Vol. 5 of *From Protest to Challenge*, p. 172; and Brooks and Brickhill, pp. 100–109.

83. *students plucked it from a banned book* . . . Edward Roux's *Time Longer Than Rope*.

84. *'The students felt they had had enough'* . . . Percy Qoboza, 'Student Leader Speaks to The World'.

85. *'Whites seem to value property more than lives'* . . . Interview with Seatlholo.

86. *the police posted a 500 rand reward* . . . Mervyn Rees, 'R500 Reward for Soweto Student Leader', *Rand Daily Mail*, 21 August 1976.

87. *To a black journalist, Tsietsi said* . . . Interview with Willie Bokala.

90. *Entitled* There Is No Crisis, *it opened with pictures of Soweto in flames* . . . Thames Television, 'South Africa: There Is No Crisis', from *This Week*, 2 September 1976.

93. *as many as 80 per cent of their employees failed to report for work* . . . Karis and Gerhart, p. 172.

96. *as did many Zulu labourers* . . . Ibid., p. 173.

97. *The ANC, like the Pan Africanist Congress, was caught unawares* . . . Ibid., pp. 181, 280. Also, pp. 280–281 for the ANC's attempts at recruitment.

97. *About 4,000 youths would leave the country* . . . Stephen Ellis and Tsepo Sechaba, *Comrades Against Apartheid*, p. 84.

97. *Indres sought out Reinhard Brueckner, a Lutheran minister* . . . Brueckner, who worked with the Christian Institute, an anti-apartheid group. Naidoo says that Brueckner funnelled substantial sums to underground activities.

97. *the organization known as the Suicide Squad* . . . For more on the group, see Karis and Gerhart, pp. 182, 281.

98. *recounted the story of Simon and Jane* . . . Interview with Morobe.

98. *Paul Langa, the Suicide Squad's leader* . . . Interviews with Langa and Morobe. Langa was ultimately arrested and, a year after the uprising, tried and sentenced to twenty-five years' imprisonment for acts of sabotage. (Brooks and Brickhill, p. 160.)

98. *Rocks pointed a gun at the doctor's head* . . . Interviews with Langa and Rocks Mashinini.

100. *Indres delivered Rocks to the small, unremarkable house* . . . The section on Rocks' stay in the northern suburbs was based on interviews with him, Jennifer Hyman, Clive Emdon and Indres Naidoo.

105. *the police intensified their raids* . . . Karis and Gerhart, p. 175.

107. *An interview that Tsietsi gave in exile* . . . Published in the *Intercontinental Press* in London on 9 October 1976.

Chapter Five: Tsietsi

113. *The boys were adamant about not wanting to join* . . . Interviews with Selby Semela and Tshepiso Manyelo.

116. *The articles angered activists* . . . Interview with Khotso Seatlholo.

116. *The ANC members did, in fact, try to convert Tsietsi* . . . The sections on the ANC and Tsietsi's reaction to the organization were based on interviews with Drake Koka, Manyelo and Semela.

118. *'Tsietsi Trained at Vanessa's Red School'* . . . David Beresford, *Sunday Times* (Johannesburg), 30 January 1977.

119. *It sent a cable to its embassy in London* . . . Department of State cable no. State 283417, 18 November 1976.

119. *that was organized by a group of university students* . . . National Student Coalition Against Racism.

119. *he told a reporter for the* New York Times . . . Kathleen Teltsch, 'Soweto Student, in City, Predicts Race War', *New York Times*, 8 December 1976.

119. *For that reason, he decided against sponsoring Tsietsi* . . . Interview with George Houser.
119. *in letters to donors, George felt compelled to explain* . . . The American Committee on Africa collection at the Amistad Research Center.
120. *A picture of the two appeared in the South African papers* . . . Duma Ndlovu, *The World*, 21 January 1977.
120. *'It is the White man who has the problem'* . . . Mateu Nonyane, 'Mashinini Tells "Why I'm Here"', *Rand Daily Mail*, 18 January 1977.
121. *'Is Rebel Mashinini Losing Some Glitter?'* . . . Langa Skosana, *The Star*, 25 January 1977.
122. *The embassies of various African nations* . . . Cameroon, Guinea, Kenya, Nigeria, Tanzania, Uganda, Zimbabwe. From interviews with Manyelo and Semela.
123. *Oliver Tambo, the ANC's president, had spent years toiling* . . . Lee Lescaze, 'ANC: Apartheid's Foes – The Long Struggle: Foes of Apartheid, Beset But Undefeated, Grow Stronger In Exile,' *Wall Street Journal*, 18 April 1988.
125. *'I will use it,' he cried, 'to call for IBM'* . . . Interview with Tom Karis.
125. *Instead, he accused the press* . . . John Kane-Berman, *Soweto*, p. 146.
125. *In a cable to the State Department* . . . Department of State cable no. Gaborone 0340, 7 February 1977.
126. *Tsietsi negotiated with two advisers* . . . Interview with Seatlholo.
126. *'Mashinini to Head New Force'* . . . David Beresford, *Sunday Times* (Johannesburg), 28 August 1977.

Chapter Six: Mpho and Nomkhitha

129. *nearly 700 activists had died* . . . Stephen Ellis and Tsepo Sechaba, *Comrades Against Apartheid*, p. 82.
130. *The house was a kind of reception site* . . . The sections on the PAC house and its routines were based on interviews with Dee and Mpho Mashinini and Lesiba Pooe (Tiger).
134. *Special Branch formed the elite corps* . . . Interview with Glenn Moss.

136. *he was being arrested under Section 6 of the Terrorism Act* . . . 'The principal laws allowing indefinite detention without trial are the Terrorism Act and the General Laws Amendment Act . . . Under these laws detainees have no legal rights or access to the courts and are denied the right to see any visitors, family or lawyers. These harsh laws are used principally for investigation, interrogation and torture purposes.' Alan Brooks and Jeremy Brickhill, *Whirlwind Before the Storm*, p. 261.

139. *'Security Cops Detain Tsietsi's Mum'* . . . *The World*, 14 February 1977.

141. *Interrogative detention, as conducted by the security police* . . . Interview with Moss.

142. *the South African government was bizarrely legalistic* . . . Ibid.

143. *this was known as 'the helicopter'* . . . The sections on torture were based on interviews with Mpho Mashinini and Moss.

145. *In one of the more fantastic twists of the country's legalism* . . . Interview with Moss.

151. *whose fees were being paid by the South African Council of Churches* . . . The SACC was a national, ecumenical organization that vigorously opposed apartheid.

154. *The Rand Daily Mail reported on the dramatic scene* . . . Wally Karbe, 'SP Drag Man From Court', *Rand Daily Mail*, 23 August 1977.

159. *'reminiscent of Alice in Wonderland'* . . . 'Evidence Likened to a Fairy Tale', *The Star*, 31 August 1977.

Chapter Seven: Rocks

163. *The sanctuary functioned like a military camp* . . . The sections on the Matola safe house were based on interviews with Dee and Rocks Mashinini.

166. *Angola was a complicated patchwork of Cold War hostilities* . . . The sections on Angola were based on interviews with Rocks Mashinini; and from Stephen Ellis and Tsepo Sechaba, *Comrades Against Apartheid*, pp. 74–77.

167. *This was how the Portuguese left the country* . . . The sections on Luanda and the city's past are from James Brooke 'On an Angolan Street, Traces of a Richer Past,' *New York Times*, 2 March 1986; and Ryszard Kapuscinski, *Another Day of Life,* pp. 3–41.

167. *to send him and his cadres to Novo Catengue* . . . The camp's name also appears in some documents as Nova Katenga.

167. *The soldiers were designated as the June 16 Detachment* . . . The sections on Novo Catengue camp were based on interviews with Rocks Mashinini; and from Ellis and Sechaba, pp. 87–88; Ronnie Kasrils, *'Armed and Dangerous'*, pp. 149, 171–173; Jack Simons, *Angolan Diaries of Prof. Jack Simons, 1977–1979*, Karis–Gerhart Collection.

169. *Each Umkhonto unit and training facility thus assumed a Soviet-style structure* . . . Ellis and Sechaba, p. 88.

170. *Rocks wrote out careful notes of Jack's talks* . . . From interviews with Mashinini; and Simons, Chapter 5 'Lectures on Marxism–Leninism in Novo Catengue Military Academy 1977–1979', p. 27.

170. *The examinations covered a wide spectrum of material* . . . From interviews with Mashinini; and Simons, Chapter 4, pp. 7–12.

171. *The Cuban instructors conducted the military training* . . . The sections on military training were based on interviews with Mashinini; and from Kasrils, p. 149; and Simons, Chapter 2 'Novo Catengue: Military Academy of Umkhonto Recruits', p. 1.

173. *One of Rocks' comrades wrote a letter* . . . Interview with Mashinini.

173. *In punishment for their insubordination* . . . Interview with Mashinini; Ellis and Sechaba, pp. 128–129, 133–136.

178. *One of Jack's lectures was on How to Combat Enemy Propaganda* . . . Interview with Mashinini; and from Simons, Chapter 3, 'Comrade Jack's Diary – Life in a MK camp and Political Instruction in MK in 1978–1979', p. 18.

179. *about half the camp's residents contracted the disease . . .*
Interview with Mashinini; and from Simons, Chapter 3,
p. 16.

179. *The attack came one cloudy morning . . .* The description of the destruction of Novo Catengue was based on
interviews with Mashinini; and from Kasrils, pp.
186–187; and Simons, Chapter 3, pp. 15–29.

Chapter Eight: Dee

184. *It had not weathered its years in exile well . . .* Stephen Ellis
and Tsepo Sechaba, *Comrades Against Apartheid*, p. 85.

184. *'You sold us out!' . . .* Interviews with Dee Mashinini and
Lesiba Pooe.

189. *The ANC generally tried to discourage the youngest . . .*
Interview with Eddie Funde.

192. *It was the site of a conference in 1969 . . .* Ellis and
Sechaba, pp. 54–58.

194. *the representative slowly explained to him the process
. . .* From interviews with Funde and Dee Mashinini.

Chapter Nine: Tsietsi

205. *The meeting was held in General Obasanjo's office . . .*
Interview with Khotso Seatlholo.

206. *Tsietsi's successful wooing of General Obasanjo . . .*
Interview with Tom Lodge.

206. *Now he would show those flabby, emasculated . . .*
Interview with Seatlholo.

206. *His comrades believed that although Tsietsi . . .* Interviews
with Comfort Molokoane and Seatlholo.

207. *the guesthouse felt like a prison to Tsietsi . . .* Interview
with Molokoane.

209. *'I can't rest until I've achieved justice' . . .* Interview with
Welma Redd.

210. *After declaring independence in 1847 . . .* For more on
Liberian history and politics, see J. Gus Liebenow,
Liberia; Charles Morrow Wilson, *Liberia*; Lynda
Schuster, 'The Final Days of Dr Doe,' in *Granta*, No. 48,
'Africa'.

213. *It was the start of a passionate, all-consuming love affair* . . . The sections on Tsietsi's relationship with Welma were based on interviews with Redd, Molokoane, Eva Campbell and Tshepiso Manyelo.

216. *'This is an embarrassment'* . . . Interview with Redd.

216. *Some Nigerian officials and colleagues* . . . Interviews with Manyelo and Molokoane.

217. *A film crew from the U.S. news programme* . . . CBS News, 'Native Sons', from *60 Minutes*, 6 January 1980.

217. *Tsietsi's colleagues learned of the wedding* . . . The reactions to Tsietsi's marriage were based on interviews with Manyelo, Molokoane and Seatlholo.

218. *'My personal life is no one else's business!'* . . . Interview with Molokoane.

219. *The man curtly informed Tsietsi* . . . Interview with Manyelo.

219. *the appearance of an article about Tsietsi in a black magazine* . . . *Pace*, January 1979. Other periodicals linked the magazine to a scandal in the country's Department of Information, which '. . . had spent huge sums on secret projects to improve South Africa's image after the Soweto uprising . . .' Thomas Karis and Gail M. Gerhart, *Nadir and Resurgence, 1964–1979* in Vol. 5 of *From Protest to Challenge*, p. 86.

Chapter Ten: Mpho

221. *Founded in the 1930s by an American academic* . . . Interview with Sam Pono.

224. *Mpho came to think of MRA as a kind of glorified tea party* . . . Interview with Mpho Mashinini.

224. *Mark, too, had conflicting feelings* . . . Interview with Mark Swilling.

226. *The two worked to create SUCA cells* . . . Interviews with Mashinini and Swilling.

226. *The police now monitored every SUCA meeting* . . . Ibid.

227. *Rhodesia, as it was formerly called* . . . For more on newly independent Zimbabwe, see Allister Sparks, *The Mind of South Africa*, p. 249.

227. *The white students who intended to make the journey*

suddenly found themselves ... Interviews with Mashinini and Swilling.
228. *They found it difficult to concentrate* ... Ibid.
228. *Joe said he felt he could trust Mpho* ... Interview with Mashinini.

Chapter Eleven: Dee
235. *Fewer than one-quarter of the teachers were certified* ... Stephen M. Davis, *Apartheid's Rebels*, p. 63.
240. *They punished the young men by expelling them* ... Interview with Dee Mashinini.
241. *But Dee decided that Tambo's zeal* ... Ibid.

Chapter Twelve: Tsietsi
246. *a long-reigning dictator of unspeakable ruthlessness* ... For more on Guinean history and politics, see Jeffrey Herbst, *State and Power in Africa*.
247. *He was fixated by what he perceived as the* ... Interview with Welma Redd.
249. *The interviewer wrote that* ... *Drum*, April 1979.
252. *Tsietsi seemed withdrawn and isolated* ... Interview with Khotso Seatlholo.
252. *Tsietsi hoped that he might find meaningful work* ... For more on the April 1980 coup d'état and its aftermath, see J. Gus Liebenow, *Liberia*.
255. *what he saw in Liberia discouraged and depressed him* ... Interview with Redd.
255. *Tsietsi never lost an opportunity at the US cocktail parties* ... Interview with Ambassador William Swing.
256. *Philemon would brook no nonsense* ... Interview with Redd.
257. *His mental health seemed to deteriorate further* ... The sections on Tsietsi's deterioration were based on interviews with Eva Campbell, Comfort Molokoane and Redd.

Chapter Thirteen: Rocks
261. *He often clashed with his counterpart* ... Interview with Rocks Mashinini.

262. *born of a trip that ANC and Umkhonto leaders took* . . . Stephen Ellis and Tsepo Sechaba, *Comrades Against Apartheid*, p. 100.

262. *that bore the unlikely name of Senior Organ* . . . For more on the command, see Ronnie Kasrils, '*Armed and Dangerous*', pp. 193–194.

263. *He felt like a man led to a cool stream* . . . Interview with Mashinini.

263. *Privately, the Mozambicans complained* . . . Interview with Carlos Cardozo.

264. *There he joined the Umkhonto structure known as Transvaal Urban Political Machinery* . . . For more on this structure, see Ellis and Sechaba, p. 154.

265. *The guerrillas launched rockets against police stations* . . . Ibid., p. 101.

265. *Swazi police hunted down ANC members* . . . Kasrils, p. 200.

267. *An absolute monarch ruled the nation* . . . Suzanne Daley, 'Tradition-Bound Swazis Chafing Under Old Ties', *New York Times*, 16 December 1995.

271. *Such invasions increased in frequency* . . . Kasrils, p. 224.

271. *More than 100 of Rocks' colleagues were deported* . . . Ibid., p. 226.

Chapter Fourteen: Mpho

273. *The most visible among them was COSAS* . . . For more on the student movement, see Steven Mufson, *Fighting Years*.

274. *The launch of the Soweto Youth Congress* . . . The sections on SOYCO were based on interviews with Mpho Mashinini, Hloyi Mashinini, Tsheko Tsehlana and Steven Mufson.

275. *Mpho and his friends often consulted with Winnie Mandela in the tiny dorp* . . . For more on Winnie Mandela's banishment to Brandfort, see Winnie Mandela, *Part of My Soul Went with Him*.

276. *his genius lay in his ability to traverse several worlds* . . . Interview with Mufson.

277. *Mpho and his friends often clashed* . . . Interviews with Mashinini and Tsehlana.

282. *The place had become a kind of finishing school* . . . For more on Robben Island and what came to be called the 'University', see Nelson Mandela, *Long Walk to Freedom*, pp. 406–408; and Steven Mufson, *Fighting Years*, pp. 65–68.

283. *In August 1983 they formed a coalition* . . . Allister Sparks, *The Mind of South Africa*, pp. 332–333.

284. *Some dissidents, such as those who still subscribed* . . . For more on the divisions within the UDF, see Mufson, pp. 58–59.

284. *And then the townships exploded* . . . For an overview of the insurrection, see Ibid., pp. 333–341.

285. *Now the focus of the UDF shifted* . . . Ibid., p. 337.

285. *Mpho and the others resolved the problem by starting their own movement* . . . Interviews with Mashinini and Tsehlana.

288. *The full extent of their concealed activities would later come to light* . . . For descriptions of the death squads' activities, see the proceedings of the Truth and Reconciliation Commission, South African Government Website, Internet.

288. *when the government declared a state of emergency* . . . Sparks, p. 349.

Chapter Fifteen: Tshepiso

293. *to detain, by its own count, almost 8,000 people* . . . Steven Mufson, *Fighting Years*, p. 113.

298. *a scheme designed by Nelson Mandela in the 1950s known as the Mandela, or M-, plan* . . . Nelson Mandela, *Long Walk to Freedom*, pp. 126–128.

301. *would cause more than 300 businesses to go bankrupt* . . . Allister Sparks, *The Mind of South Africa*, p. 339.

301. *Others were made to drink the bottles of cooking oil they had bought* . . . Ibid., p. 340.

304. *'Necklacing' represented the worst of the excesses* . . . For more on the reaction of the UDF to necklacing, see Mufson, pp. 96–100.

Chapter Seventeen: Tsietsi

317. *His comportment mystified his professors* . . . The sections on Tsietsi's life in Jos were based on conversations that Dr William Ardill had, at the author's request, with people at Plateau State Polytechnic, all of whom requested anonymity.

319. *the goal, Chris said, was not to try to bring Tsietsi into the ANC fold* . . . Interview with Rocks Mashinini.

Chapter Eighteen: Rocks

324. *The uprising proved a windfall* . . . Stephen Ellis and Tsepo Sechaba, *Comrades Against Apartheid*, p. 145.

324. *The South African government recorded 230 guerilla attacks* . . . Ibid., p. 171.

325. *Umkhonto's success accounted, in part, for the ANC's emergence* . . . Ibid., p. 157.

325. *in one particularly gruesome incident* . . . For an account of the Maseru murders, see Ronnie Kasrils, '*Armed and Dangerous*', p. 242.

327. *As with its operations everywhere in the world* . . . Lee Lescaze, 'ANC: Apartheid's Foes – The Long Struggle: Foes of Apartheid Beset but Undefeated, Grow Stronger in Exile', *Wall Street Journal*, 18 April 1988.

329. *assassins attacked the safe house* . . . Kasrils, p. 282.

329. *The man, who was not on good terms with Rocks, wrote a damning report* . . . Interview with Mashinini.

Chapter Nineteen: Mpho

345. *or civics, as they were called* . . . For more on the civics, see M. Swilling, R. Humphries and K. Shubane (eds.), *Apartheid City in Transition*.

346. *they seemed to have had the opposite effect* . . . Steven Mufson, *Fighting Years*, pp. 114–117.

347. *They would arrest nearly 30,000 people* . . . Allister Sparks, *The Mind of South Africa*, p. 356.

347. *the military men called it WHAM* . . . For more on the government's counter-insurgency strategy, see Ibid., pp. 273–285; and Lynda Schuster, 'Pretoria's Bid for

"Hearts and Minds"', *The Christian Science Monitor*, 11 May 1988.

Chapter Twenty-One: Dee

368. *By 1989, more than 4,000 people had been killed* . . . Allister Sparks, *Tomorrow is Another Country*, p. 48.
368. *perhaps someone ought to talk to the ANC to find a solution* . . . For more on the meetings, see Ibid.
369. *clandestine discussions with Nelson Mandela in prison* . . . For a personal account, see Nelson Mandela, *Long Walk to Freedom*, pp. 447–486.
374. *had released several prominent ANC prisoners and begun repealing some apartheid regulations* . . . Ibid., pp. 480–482.

Chapter Twenty-Two: Tsietsi

375. *President F.W. de Klerk made a stunning announcement* . . . For more on the dismantling of apartheid and the release of Nelson Mandela, see Nelson Mandela, *Long Walk to Freedom*, pp. 484–494.
376. *He was equally direct about the cause of death* . . . Interview with Welma Redd.

Epilogue

386. *which saw itself as the successor* . . . Steven Mufson, *Fighting Years*, p. 69.
392. *the ANC and the Nationalist government thrashed out* . . . For a detailed account of the negotiations, see Allister Sparks, *Tomorrow is Another Country*.
393. *the black population went to the polls* . . . Ibid., pp. 226–229.
393. *The new president spoke of the future on that day* . . . Nelson Mandela, *Long Walk to Freedom*, pp. 540–541.
394. *told the crowd that Tsietsi, whom she had known well, was a hero* . . . ANC website, Internet.
395. *despite the continued insistence to the contrary* . . . Interviews with Bageot Bah in Conakry by Mary Fitzpatrick.
395. *Miriam Makeba refused to discuss the matter* . . .

Interview with Nomkhitha Mashinini. Numerous attempts by the author to contact Makeba directly and through her publicity agent in Johannesburg were rebuffed.

395. *all traces of his records vanished* . . . Search done by Mary Fitzpatrick at Ignace Deen Hospital.

397. *more than 55 per cent of the eighty-thousand-member* . . . Rachel L. Swarns, 'South Africa Army's Enemy Within: Old Hatreds', *The New York Times*, 26 September 1999.

398. *his old ANC cell-leader, would see him on the streets* . . . Interview with Indres Naidoo.

398. *The army transferred Rocks to a different unit* . . . Interview with Dee Mashinini.

399. *(although the press reported it as a dismissal)* . . . ANC website, 2 September 1995, Internet.

403. *An estimated 200,000 people were without running water* . . . Lynda Schuster, 'The Struggle to Govern Johannesburg', *The Atlantic Monthly*, September 1995, p. 32.

405. *Archbishop Desmond Tutu, characterized it as* . . . Desmond Tutu, No *Future Without Forgiveness*, p. 30.

405. *They were horrifying stories of torture, mutilation* . . . See Ibid.; Alex Boraine, *A Country Unmasked;* and South African Government Website, Internet.

406. *a sum that critics derided as insulting* . . . Ginger Thompson, 'South Africa to Pay $3,900 to Each Family of Apartheid Victims', *The New York Times*, 16 April 2003.

406. *By 2002, 50 per cent of rural households had electricity* . . . Rachel Swarns, 'In South Africa, Leaders Face Blacks' Ire', *The New York Times*, 2 October 2002.

406. *incomes in black households fell by 19 per cent* . . . BBC website, 13 May 2003, Internet.

Index